WHAT WOULD WALLY DO?

Other DILBERT® books from Andrews McMeel Publishing

Thriving on Vague Objectives
ISBN: 0-7407-5533-1

The Fluorescent Light Glistens Off Your Head
ISBN: 0-7407-5113-1

It's Not Funny If I Have to Explain It
ISBN: 0-7407-4658-8

Don't Stand Where the Comet Is Assumed to Strike Oil
ISBN: 0-7407-4539-5

Words You Don't Want to Hear During Your Annual Performance Review
ISBN: 0-7407-3805-4

When Body Language Goes Bad
ISBN: 0-7407-3298-6

What Do You Call a Sociopath in a Cubicle? Answer: A Coworker
ISBN: 0-7407-2663-3

Another Day in Cubicle Paradise
ISBN: 0-7407-2194-1

When Did Ignorance Become a Point of View?
ISBN: 0-7407-1839-8

Excuse Me While I Wag
ISBN: 0-7407-1390-6

Dilbert—A Treasury of Sunday Strips: Version 00
ISBN: 0-7407-0531-8

Random Acts of Management
ISBN: 0-7407-0453-2

Dilbert Gives You the Business
ISBN: 0-7407-0338-2 hardcover
ISBN: 0-7407-0003-0 paperback

Don't Step in the Leadership
ISBN: 0-8362-7844-5

Journey to Cubeville
ISBN: 0-8362-7175-0 hardcover
ISBN: 0-8362-6745-1 paperback

I'm Not Anti-Business, I'm Anti-Idiot
ISBN: 0-8362-5182-2

Seven Years of Highly Defective People
ISBN: 0-8362-5129-6 hardcover
ISBN: 0-8362-3668-8 paperback

Casual Day Has Gone Too Far
ISBN: 0-8362-2899-5

Fugitive from the Cubicle Police
ISBN: 0-8362-2119-2

Bring Me the Head of Willy the Mailboy!
ISBN: 0-8362-1779-9

Always Postpone Meetings with Time-Wasting Morons
ISBN: 0-8362-1758-6

Build a Better Life by Stealing Office Supplies
ISBN: 0-8362-1757-8

Shave the Whales
ISBN: 0-8362-1740-3

Dogbert's Clues for the Clueless
ISBN: 0-8362-1737-3

Still Pumped from Using the Mouse
ISBN: 0-8362-1026-3

It's Obvious You Won't Survive by Your Wits Alone
ISBN: 0-8362-0415-8

For ordering information, call 1-800-223-2336.

06 07 08 09 10 BAM 10 9 8 7 6 5 4 3 2 1

ISBN-13: 978-0-7407-5769-3
ISBN-10: 0-7407-5769-5

Library of Congress Control Number: 2005935608

www.dilbert.com
www.andrewsmcmeel.com

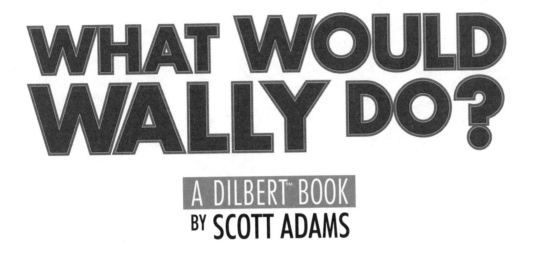

WHAT WOULD WALLY DO?

A DILBERT™ BOOK
BY SCOTT ADAMS

Andrews McMeel
Publishing, LLC

Kansas City

Introduction

You might be aware that Dilbert's coworker Wally was inspired by a real person. Let's call him Wally Version 1.0. He has a fascinating backstory.

One day in the mid '90s, at my old employer Pacific Bell, Wally Version 1.0 made a judgment call that went bad, i.e., he trusted some weasels. Management didn't want to fire him because he had been an excellent employee up to that point. However, they told him that he could never again be promoted, nor would he ever get a raise. It was their subtle way of encouraging him to seek other opportunities.

As fate would have it, somewhere in the bowels of Human Resources, a downsizing scheme was being hatched. The idea was to identify the worst 10 percent of employees and offer them a sizable pot of money to leave peacefully.

Wally Version 1.0 was a brilliant MIT graduate and recognized an opportunity when he saw it. Since he knew he had to leave, he figured it was better to do so with a pot of money than with none. All he had to do was become one of the worst 10 percent of employees.

Now, I don't like to talk smack about my old employer, but I have to tell you that making it into the lowest 10 percent of performers wasn't easy. There was fierce competition for those spots. Luckily, Version 1.0 was up to the challenge.

During the several months it took Version 1.0 to realize his career aspiration of getting laid off with money, he was the most amusing coworker you would ever hope to have. He made his transition gradually so it wouldn't be too obvious. Each day he wore increasingly casual clothes. Toward the end he looked like a blind hobo on laundry day. And it was during this period when he started openly running his side business from his cubicle.

My favorite Wally Version 1.0 experience happened on the day we met our new gaggle of consultants. They were freshly minted MBAs with no experience in the telecommunications field. The idea was that they would learn our entire industry in a few days and then tell us how to do our jobs.

This was no more absurd than anything else the company was doing, so the rest of us accepted it for its entertainment value and went with the flow. Wally Version 1.0 saw more humor potential in the situation and couldn't leave it alone. He stopped the meeting five minutes in and pointedly asked the consultants to defend their qualifications for even being in the room, much less telling us how to do our jobs. The consultant newbies tried their best, but Wally Version 1.0 was on them like a Labrador on a pork chop. He would listen to their explanations about the power of their "process" and then he'd scrunch up his face and ask, "How does that make you qualified to be here?" That question, repeated relentlessly and paired with some head shaking and grimacing, created a humor event that threatened the pants of everyone in the room, excluding the consultants.

Well, maybe you had to be there. Luckily, I was. Soon after, *Dilbert*'s Wally took on this same sociopath personality. The culmination is this book.

Speaking of sociopath culminations, you can join Dogbert's New Ruling Class and be by his side when he conquers the world. All you need to do is sign up for the free *Dilbert Newsletter* that is published approximately whenever I feel like it. To sign up, go to www.dilbert.com and follow the subscription instructions. If that doesn't work for some reason, send e-mail to newsletter@unitedmedia.com.

S. Adams

Scott Adams

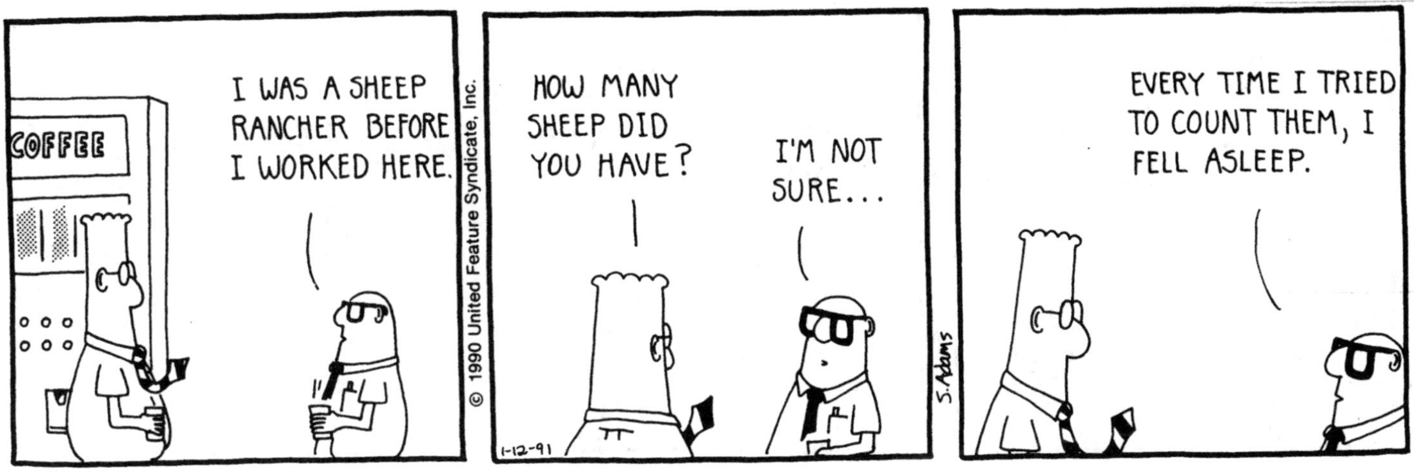
COFFEE
I WAS A SHEEP RANCHER BEFORE I WORKED HERE.
© 1990 United Feature Syndicate, Inc.
HOW MANY SHEEP DID YOU HAVE?
I'M NOT SURE...
1-12-91
S. Adams
EVERY TIME I TRIED TO COUNT THEM, I FELL ASLEEP.

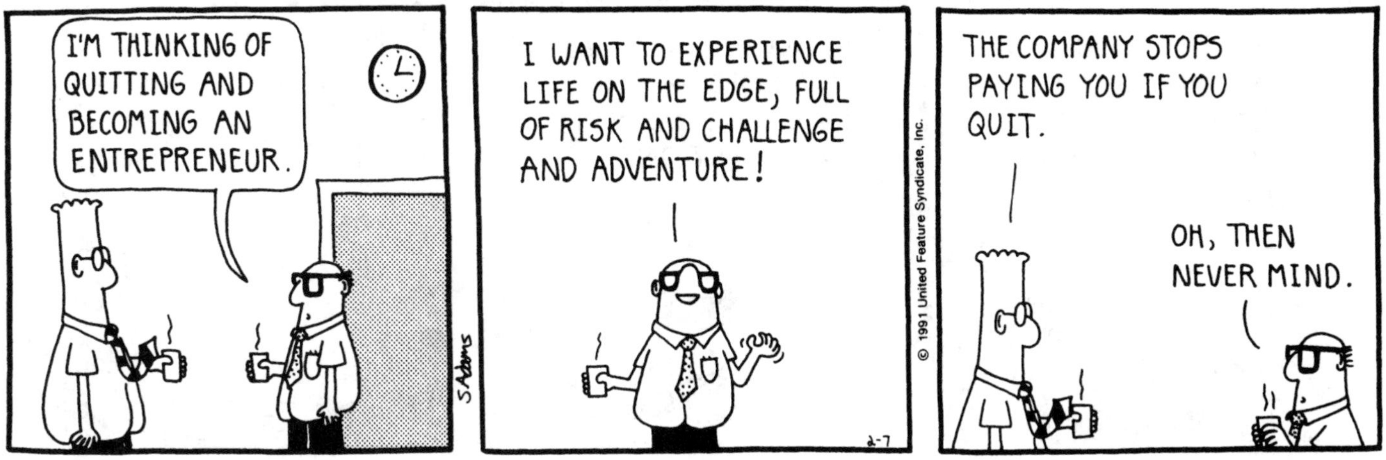
I'M THINKING OF QUITTING AND BECOMING AN ENTREPRENEUR.
S. Adams
I WANT TO EXPERIENCE LIFE ON THE EDGE, FULL OF RISK AND CHALLENGE AND ADVENTURE!
2-7
© 1991 United Feature Syndicate, Inc.
THE COMPANY STOPS PAYING YOU IF YOU QUIT.
OH, THEN NEVER MIND.

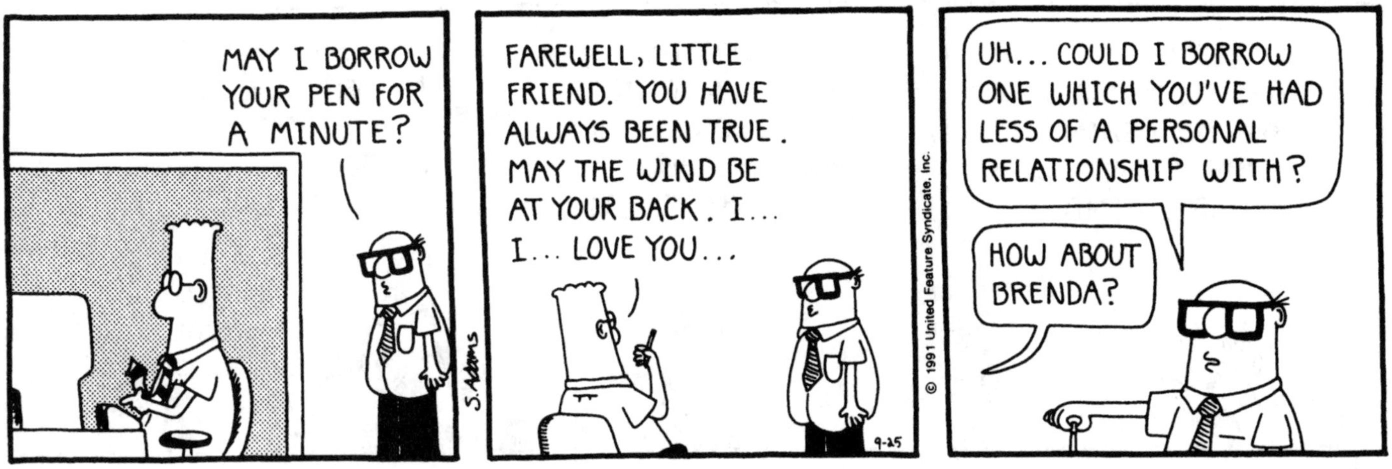
MAY I BORROW YOUR PEN FOR A MINUTE?
S. Adams
FAREWELL, LITTLE FRIEND. YOU HAVE ALWAYS BEEN TRUE. MAY THE WIND BE AT YOUR BACK. I... I... LOVE YOU...
9-25
© 1991 United Feature Syndicate, Inc.
UH... COULD I BORROW ONE WHICH YOU'VE HAD LESS OF A PERSONAL RELATIONSHIP WITH?
HOW ABOUT BRENDA?

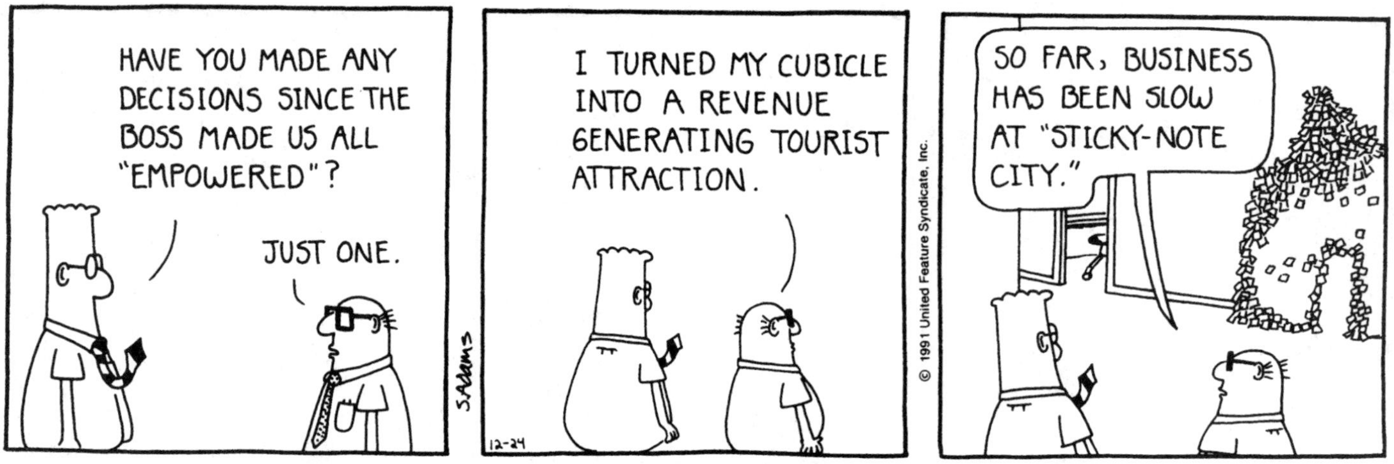
HAVE YOU MADE ANY DECISIONS SINCE THE BOSS MADE US ALL "EMPOWERED"?
JUST ONE.
I TURNED MY CUBICLE INTO A REVENUE GENERATING TOURIST ATTRACTION.
SO FAR, BUSINESS HAS BEEN SLOW AT "STICKY-NOTE CITY."
© 1991 United Feature Syndicate, Inc.

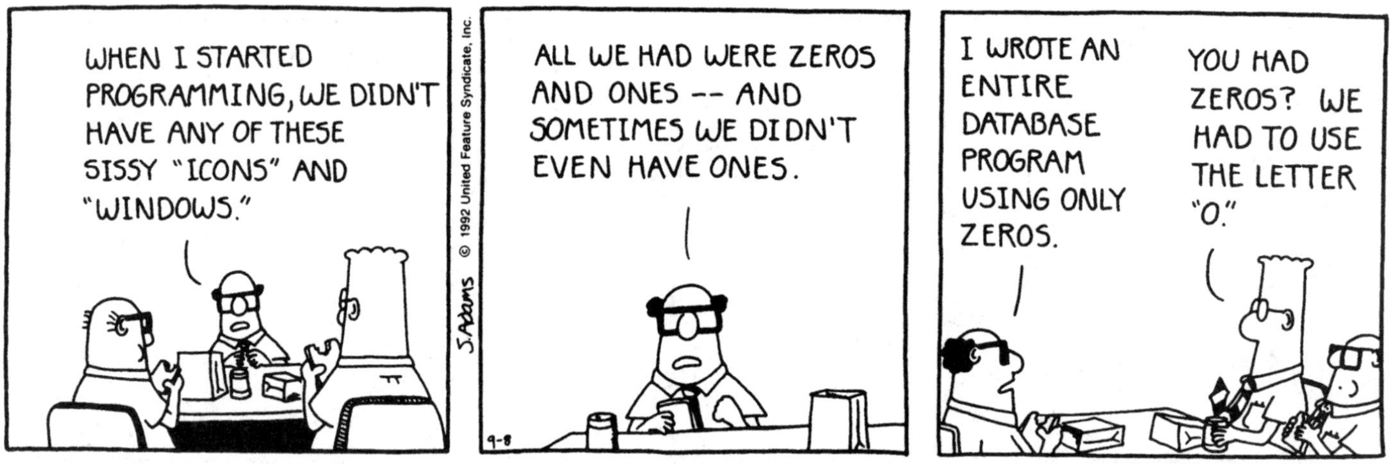
WHEN I STARTED PROGRAMMING, WE DIDN'T HAVE ANY OF THESE SISSY "ICONS" AND "WINDOWS."
© 1992 United Feature Syndicate, Inc.
ALL WE HAD WERE ZEROS AND ONES -- AND SOMETIMES WE DIDN'T EVEN HAVE ONES.
I WROTE AN ENTIRE DATABASE PROGRAM USING ONLY ZEROS.
YOU HAD ZEROS? WE HAD TO USE THE LETTER "O."

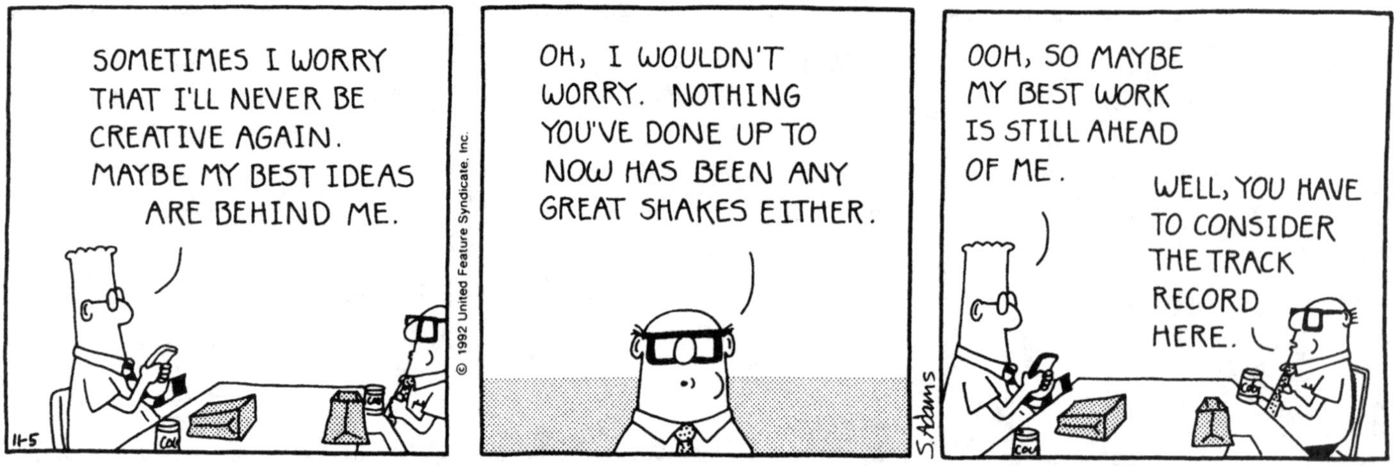
SOMETIMES I WORRY THAT I'LL NEVER BE CREATIVE AGAIN. MAYBE MY BEST IDEAS ARE BEHIND ME.
© 1992 United Feature Syndicate, Inc.
OH, I WOULDN'T WORRY. NOTHING YOU'VE DONE UP TO NOW HAS BEEN ANY GREAT SHAKES EITHER.
OOH, SO MAYBE MY BEST WORK IS STILL AHEAD OF ME.
WELL, YOU HAVE TO CONSIDER THE TRACK RECORD HERE.

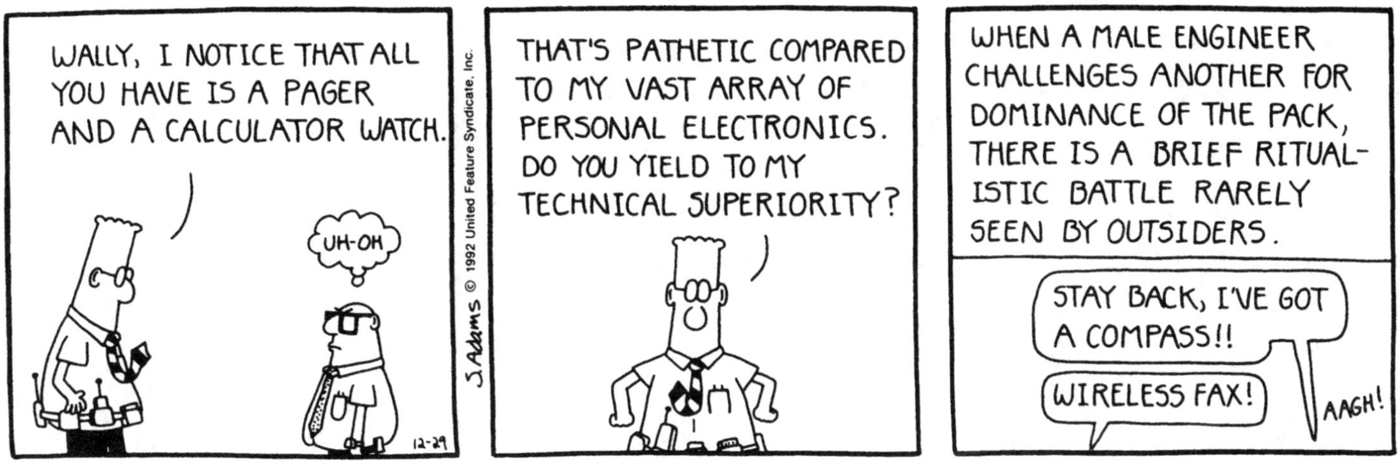
WALLY, I NOTICE THAT ALL YOU HAVE IS A PAGER AND A CALCULATOR WATCH.
UH-OH
S. Adams © 1992 United Feature Syndicate, Inc.
12-29
THAT'S PATHETIC COMPARED TO MY VAST ARRAY OF PERSONAL ELECTRONICS. DO YOU YIELD TO MY TECHNICAL SUPERIORITY?
WHEN A MALE ENGINEER CHALLENGES ANOTHER FOR DOMINANCE OF THE PACK, THERE IS A BRIEF RITUALISTIC BATTLE RARELY SEEN BY OUTSIDERS.
STAY BACK, I'VE GOT A COMPASS!!
WIRELESS FAX!
AAGH!

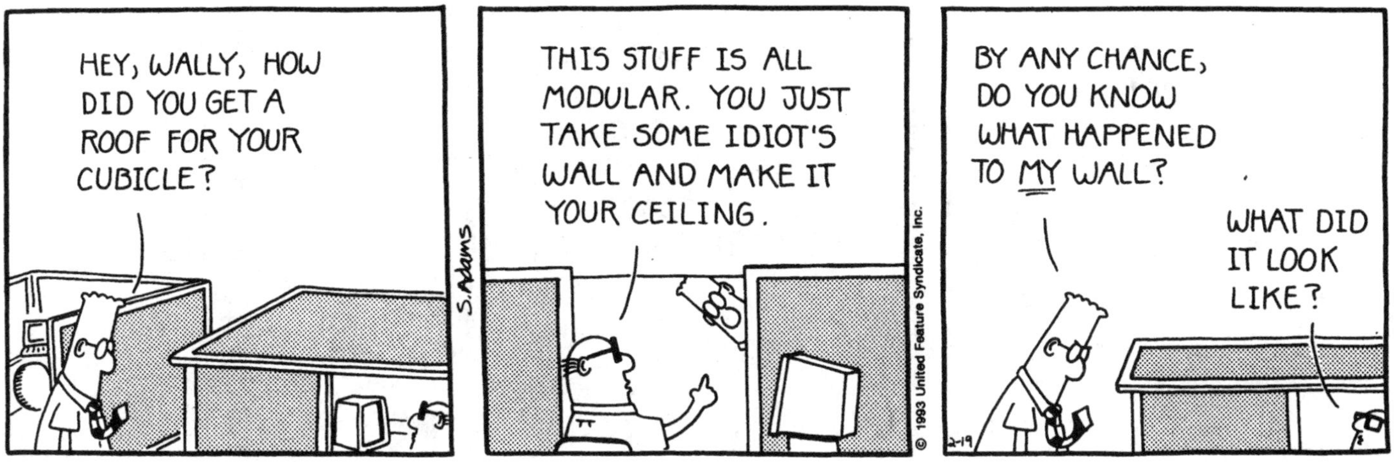
HEY, WALLY, HOW DID YOU GET A ROOF FOR YOUR CUBICLE?
S. Adams
THIS STUFF IS ALL MODULAR. YOU JUST TAKE SOME IDIOT'S WALL AND MAKE IT YOUR CEILING.
© 1993 United Feature Syndicate, Inc.
BY ANY CHANCE, DO YOU KNOW WHAT HAPPENED TO MY WALL?
WHAT DID IT LOOK LIKE?
2-19

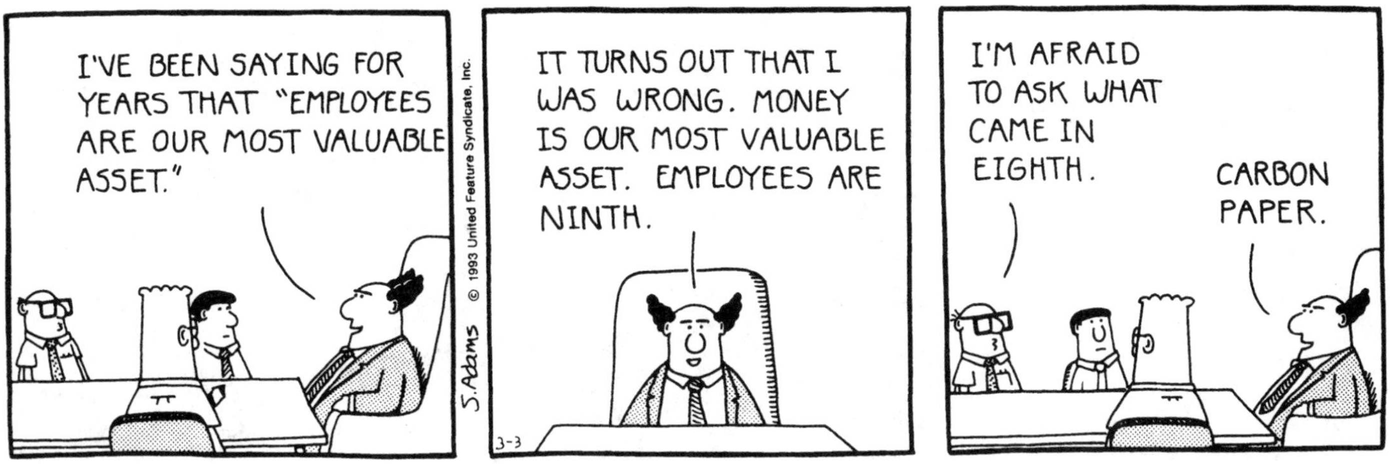
I'VE BEEN SAYING FOR YEARS THAT "EMPLOYEES ARE OUR MOST VALUABLE ASSET."
S. Adams © 1993 United Feature Syndicate, Inc.
IT TURNS OUT THAT I WAS WRONG. MONEY IS OUR MOST VALUABLE ASSET. EMPLOYEES ARE NINTH.
3-3
I'M AFRAID TO ASK WHAT CAME IN EIGHTH.
CARBON PAPER.

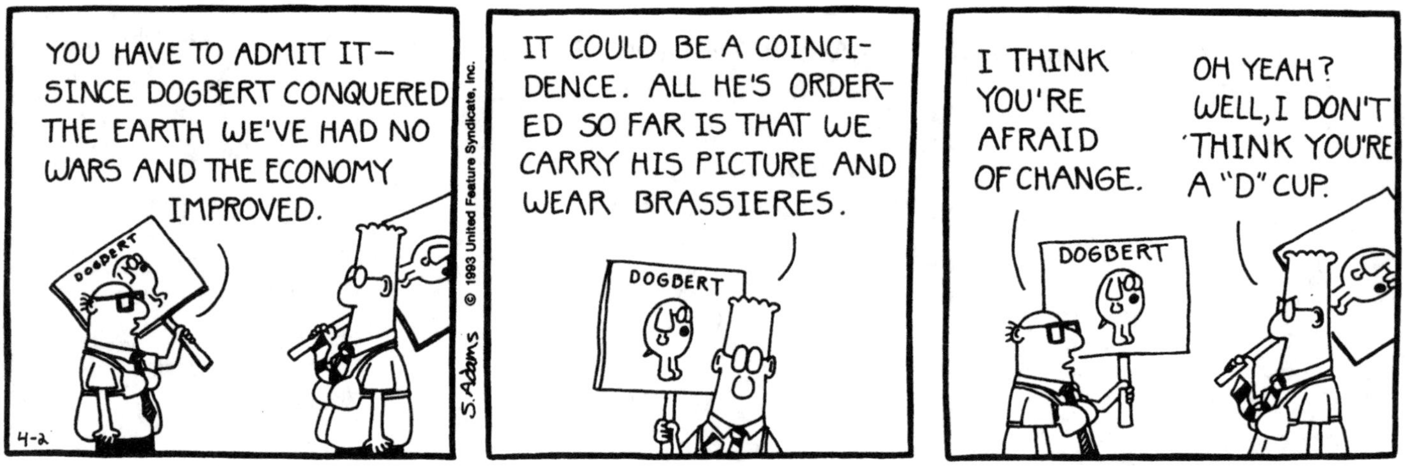
YOU HAVE TO ADMIT IT—SINCE DOGBERT CONQUERED THE EARTH WE'VE HAD NO WARS AND THE ECONOMY IMPROVED.
DOGBERT
© 1993 United Feature Syndicate, Inc.
S. Adams
4-2
IT COULD BE A COINCIDENCE. ALL HE'S ORDERED SO FAR IS THAT WE CARRY HIS PICTURE AND WEAR BRASSIERES.
DOGBERT
I THINK YOU'RE AFRAID OF CHANGE.
OH YEAH? WELL, I DON'T THINK YOU'RE A "D" CUP.
DOGBERT

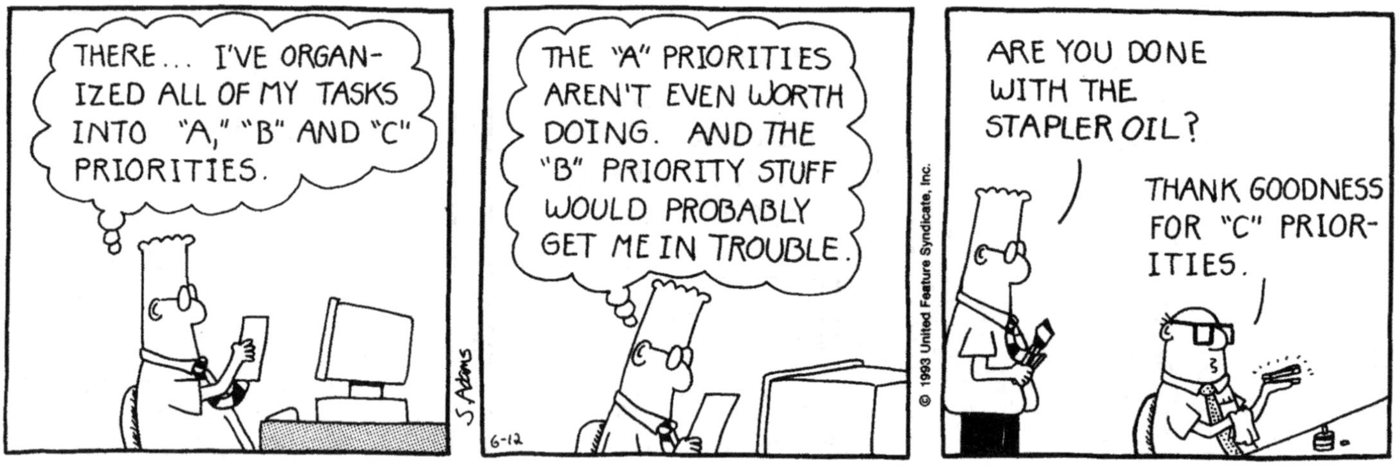
THERE... I'VE ORGANIZED ALL OF MY TASKS INTO "A," "B" AND "C" PRIORITIES.
S. Adams
6-12
THE "A" PRIORITIES AREN'T EVEN WORTH DOING. AND THE "B" PRIORITY STUFF WOULD PROBABLY GET ME IN TROUBLE.
© 1993 United Feature Syndicate, Inc.
ARE YOU DONE WITH THE STAPLER OIL?
THANK GOODNESS FOR "C" PRIORITIES.

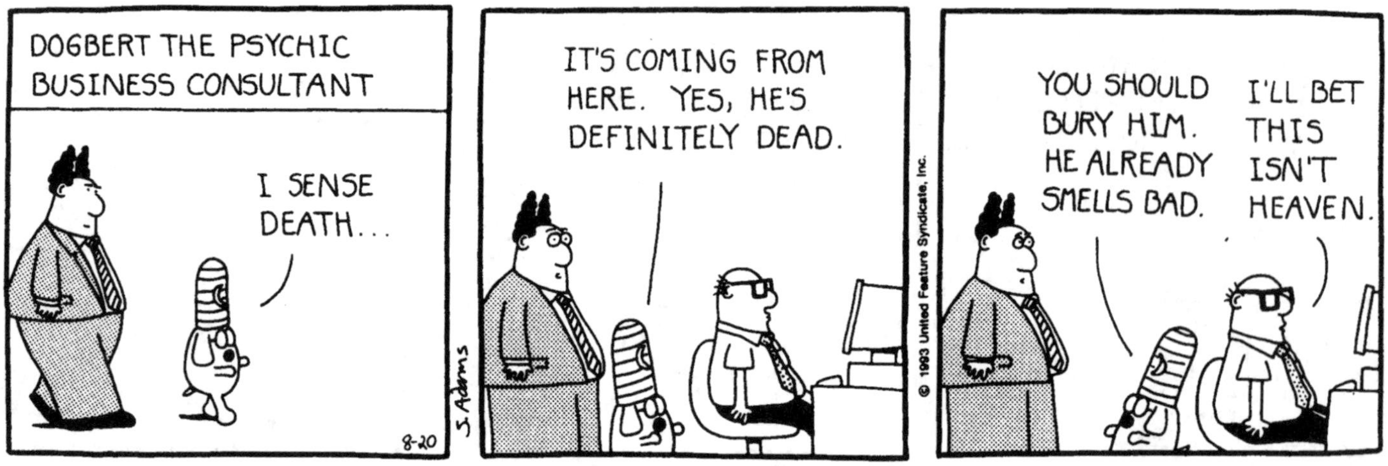
DOGBERT THE PSYCHIC BUSINESS CONSULTANT
I SENSE DEATH...
S. Adams
8-20
IT'S COMING FROM HERE. YES, HE'S DEFINITELY DEAD.
© 1993 United Feature Syndicate, Inc.
YOU SHOULD BURY HIM. HE ALREADY SMELLS BAD.
I'LL BET THIS ISN'T HEAVEN.

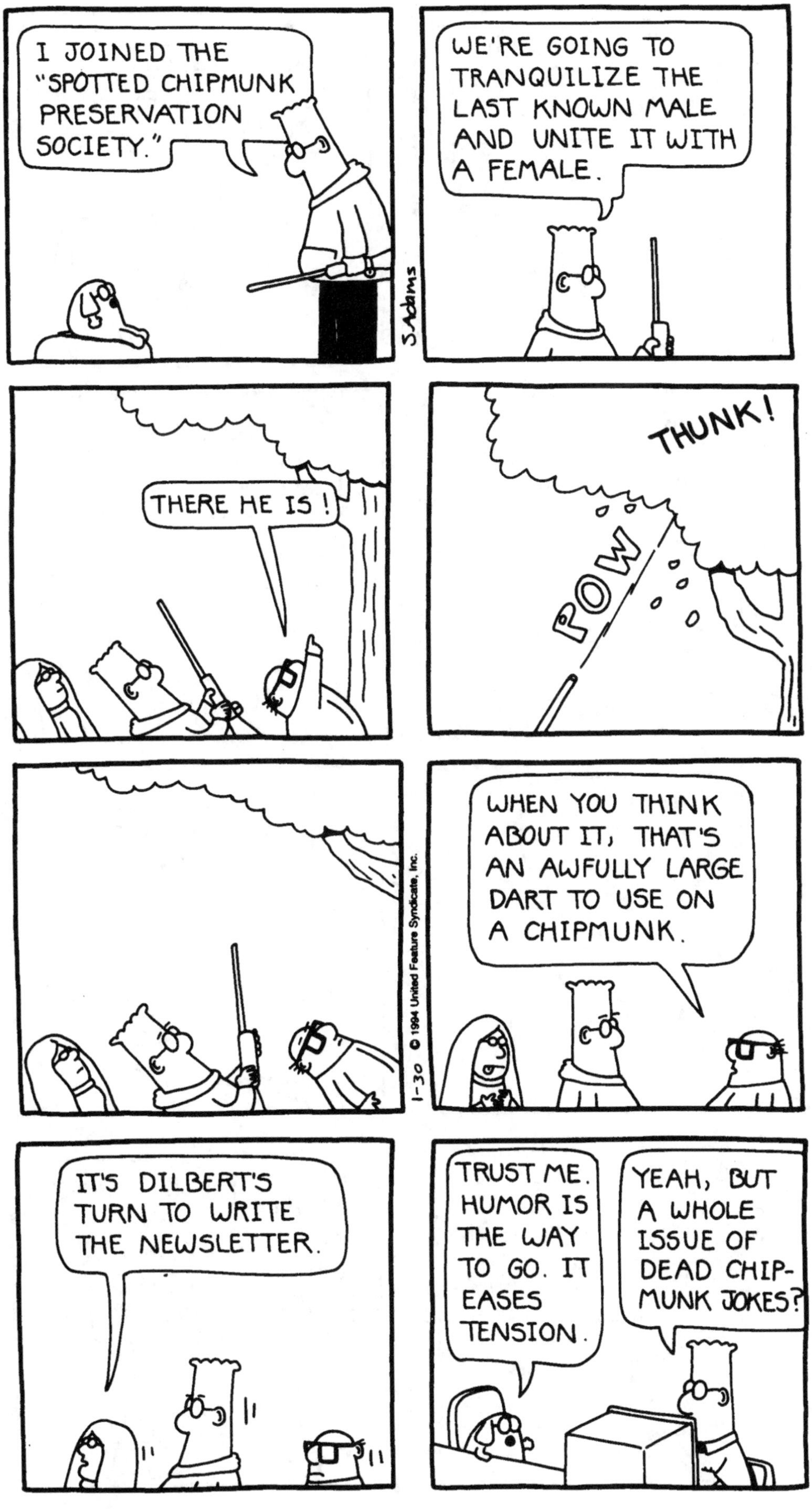
I JOINED THE "SPOTTED CHIPMUNK PRESERVATION SOCIETY."
S. Adams
WE'RE GOING TO TRANQUILIZE THE LAST KNOWN MALE AND UNITE IT WITH A FEMALE.
THERE HE IS!
THUNK!
POW
© 1994 United Feature Syndicate, Inc.
1-30
WHEN YOU THINK ABOUT IT, THAT'S AN AWFULLY LARGE DART TO USE ON A CHIPMUNK.
IT'S DILBERT'S TURN TO WRITE THE NEWSLETTER.
TRUST ME. HUMOR IS THE WAY TO GO. IT EASES TENSION.
YEAH, BUT A WHOLE ISSUE OF DEAD CHIP-MUNK JOKES?

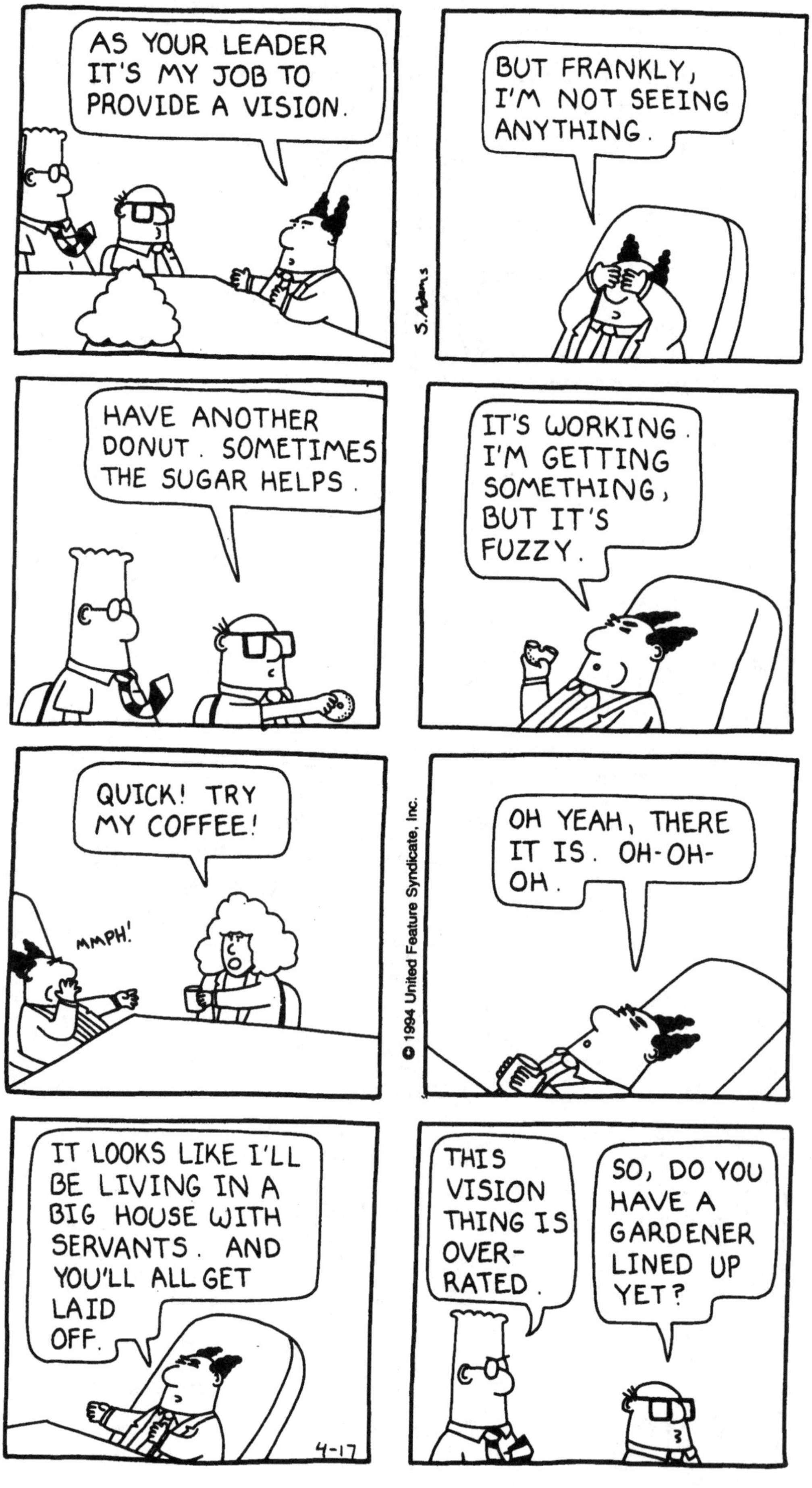
AS YOUR LEADER IT'S MY JOB TO PROVIDE A VISION.
S. Adams
BUT FRANKLY, I'M NOT SEEING ANYTHING.
HAVE ANOTHER DONUT. SOMETIMES THE SUGAR HELPS.
IT'S WORKING. I'M GETTING SOMETHING, BUT IT'S FUZZY.
QUICK! TRY MY COFFEE!
MMPH!
© 1994 United Feature Syndicate, Inc.
OH YEAH, THERE IT IS. OH-OH-OH.
IT LOOKS LIKE I'LL BE LIVING IN A BIG HOUSE WITH SERVANTS. AND YOU'LL ALL GET LAID OFF.
4-17
THIS VISION THING IS OVER-RATED.
SO, DO YOU HAVE A GARDENER LINED UP YET?

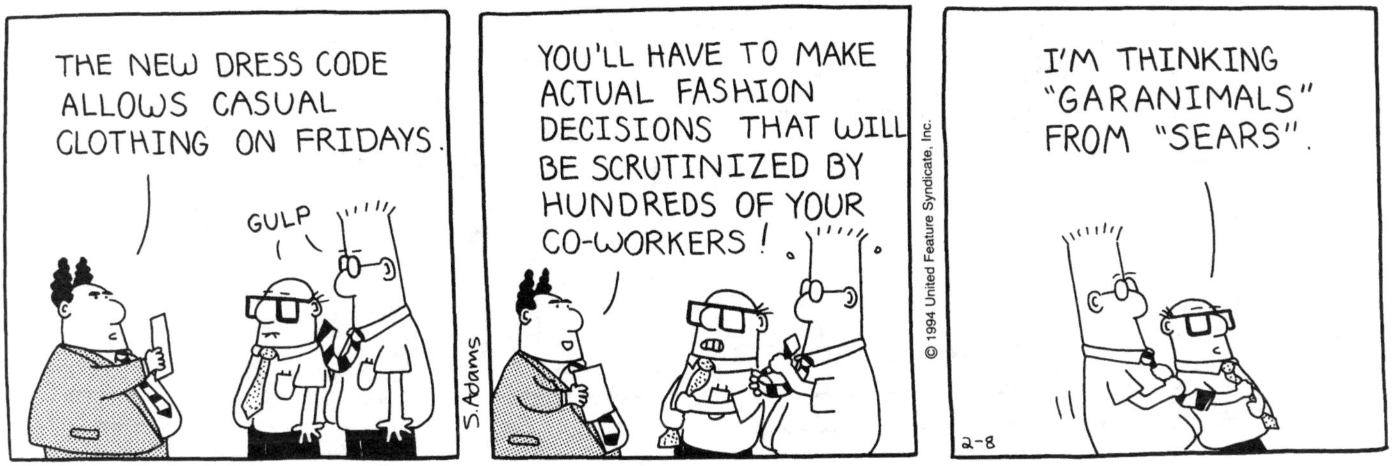
THE NEW DRESS CODE ALLOWS CASUAL CLOTHING ON FRIDAYS.
GULP
YOU'LL HAVE TO MAKE ACTUAL FASHION DECISIONS THAT WILL BE SCRUTINIZED BY HUNDREDS OF YOUR CO-WORKERS!
I'M THINKING "GARANIMALS" FROM "SEARS".
S. Adams
© 1994 United Feature Syndicate, Inc.
2-8

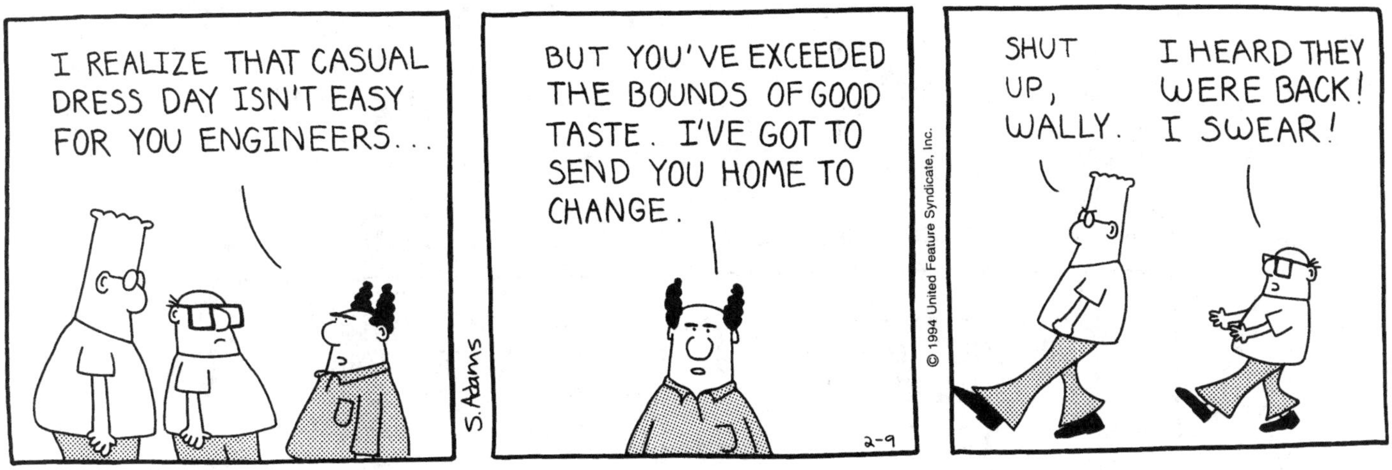
I REALIZE THAT CASUAL DRESS DAY ISN'T EASY FOR YOU ENGINEERS...
BUT YOU'VE EXCEEDED THE BOUNDS OF GOOD TASTE. I'VE GOT TO SEND YOU HOME TO CHANGE.
SHUT UP, WALLY.
I HEARD THEY WERE BACK! I SWEAR!
S. Adams
© 1994 United Feature Syndicate, Inc.
2-9

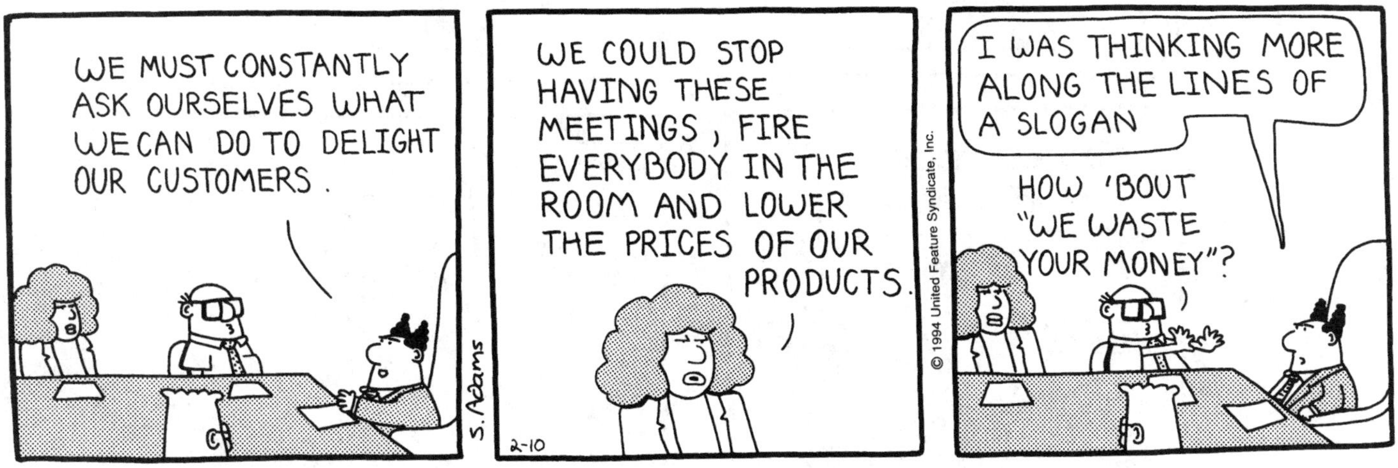
WE MUST CONSTANTLY ASK OURSELVES WHAT WE CAN DO TO DELIGHT OUR CUSTOMERS.
WE COULD STOP HAVING THESE MEETINGS, FIRE EVERYBODY IN THE ROOM AND LOWER THE PRICES OF OUR PRODUCTS.
HOW 'BOUT "WE WASTE YOUR MONEY"?
I WAS THINKING MORE ALONG THE LINES OF A SLOGAN
S. Adams
© 1994 United Feature Syndicate, Inc.
2-10

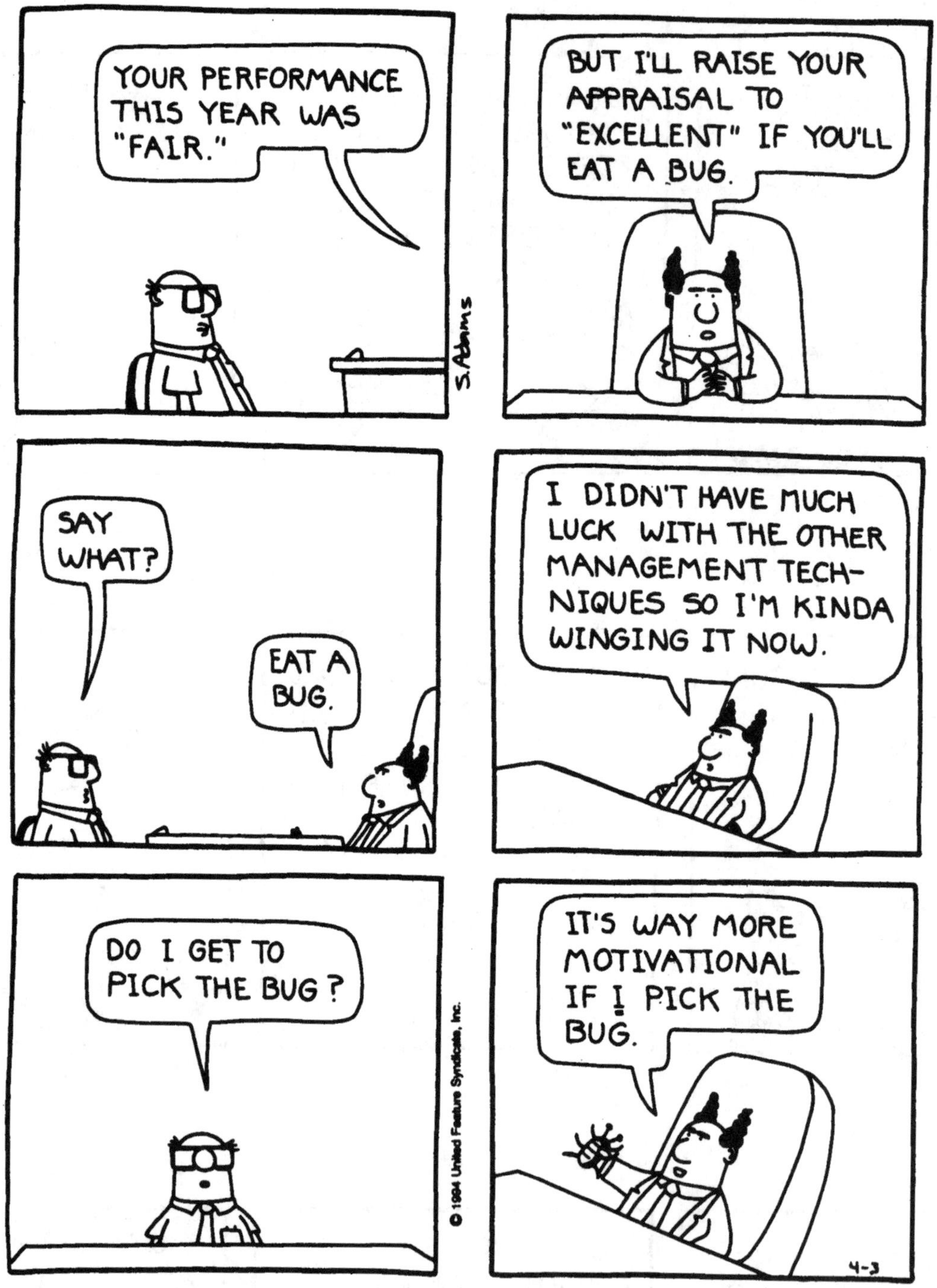
YOUR PERFORMANCE THIS YEAR WAS "FAIR."
S. Adams
BUT I'LL RAISE YOUR APPRAISAL TO "EXCELLENT" IF YOU'LL EAT A BUG.
SAY WHAT?
EAT A BUG.
I DIDN'T HAVE MUCH LUCK WITH THE OTHER MANAGEMENT TECHNIQUES SO I'M KINDA WINGING IT NOW.
DO I GET TO PICK THE BUG?
IT'S WAY MORE MOTIVATIONAL IF I PICK THE BUG.
4-3

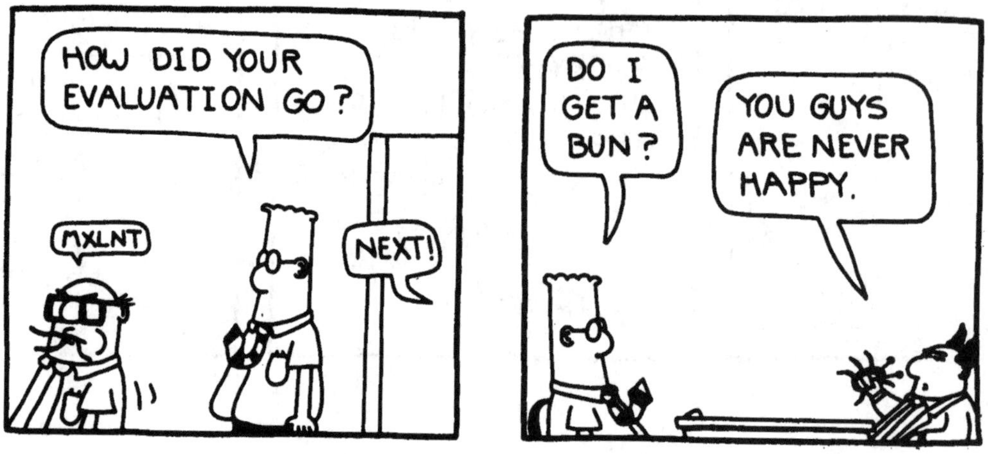
HOW DID YOUR EVALUATION GO?
MXLNT
NEXT!
DO I GET A BUN?
YOU GUYS ARE NEVER HAPPY.

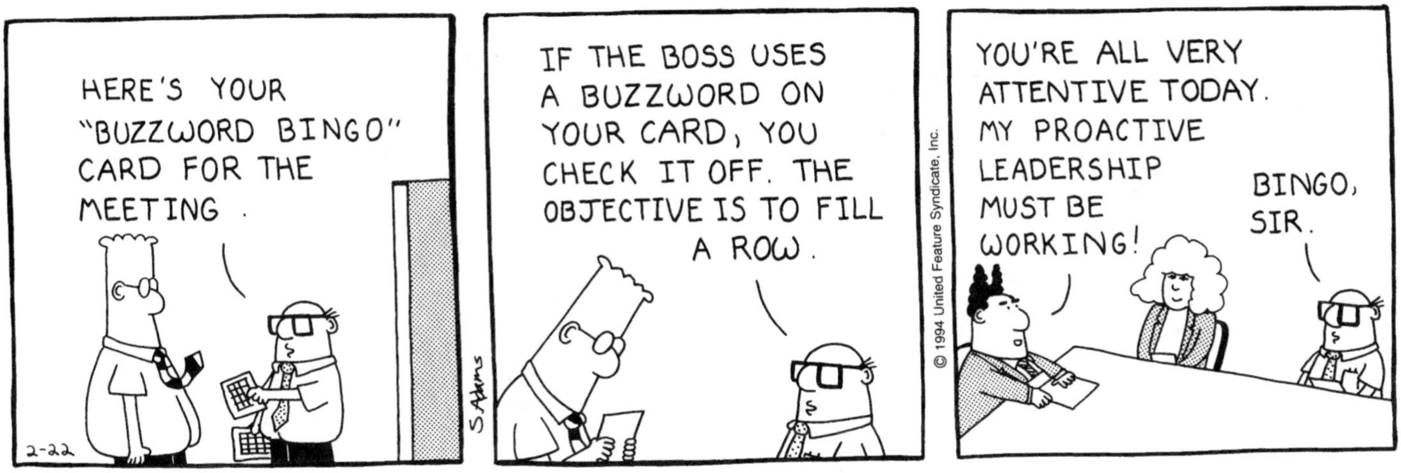
HERE'S YOUR "BUZZWORD BINGO" CARD FOR THE MEETING.
IF THE BOSS USES A BUZZWORD ON YOUR CARD, YOU CHECK IT OFF. THE OBJECTIVE IS TO FILL A ROW.
YOU'RE ALL VERY ATTENTIVE TODAY. MY PROACTIVE LEADERSHIP MUST BE WORKING!
BINGO, SIR.
© 1994 United Feature Syndicate, Inc.

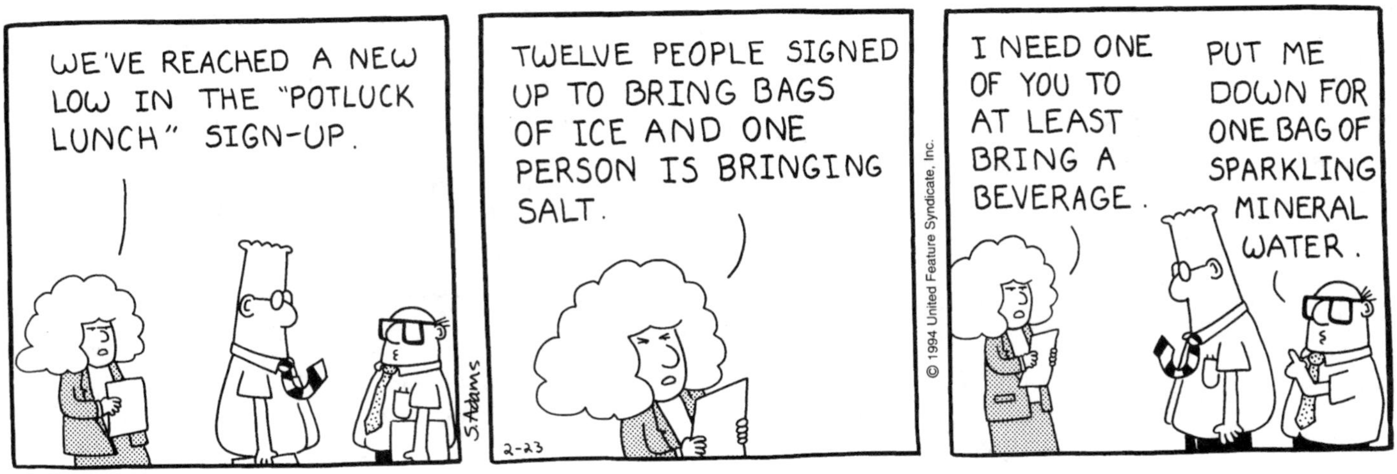
WE'VE REACHED A NEW LOW IN THE "POTLUCK LUNCH" SIGN-UP.
TWELVE PEOPLE SIGNED UP TO BRING BAGS OF ICE AND ONE PERSON IS BRINGING SALT.
I NEED ONE OF YOU TO AT LEAST BRING A BEVERAGE.
PUT ME DOWN FOR ONE BAG OF SPARKLING MINERAL WATER.
© 1994 United Feature Syndicate, Inc.

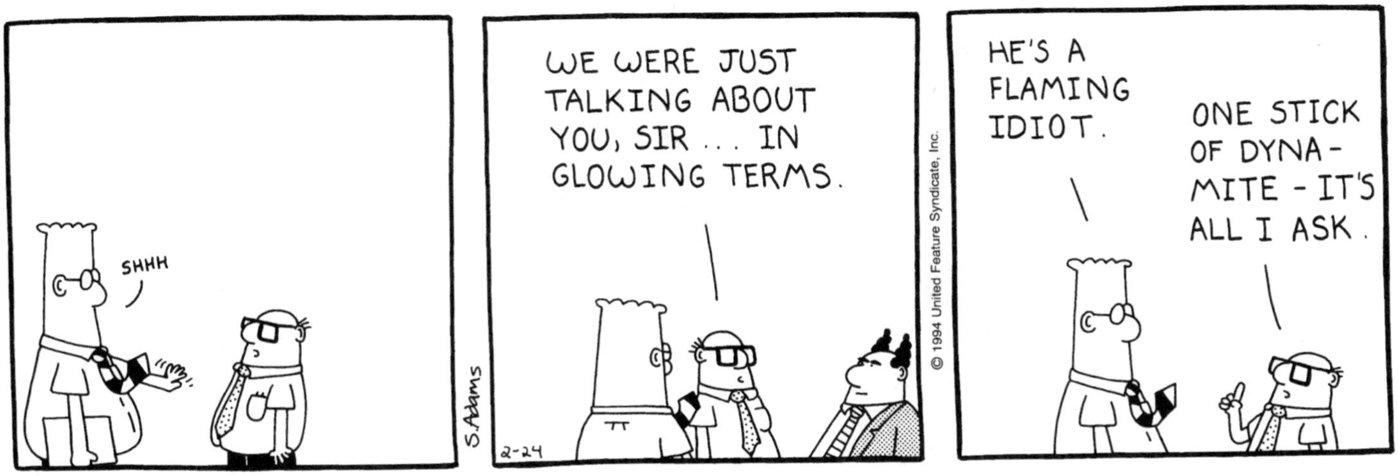
SHHH
WE WERE JUST TALKING ABOUT YOU, SIR... IN GLOWING TERMS.
HE'S A FLAMING IDIOT.
ONE STICK OF DYNA-MITE - IT'S ALL I ASK.
© 1994 United Feature Syndicate, Inc.

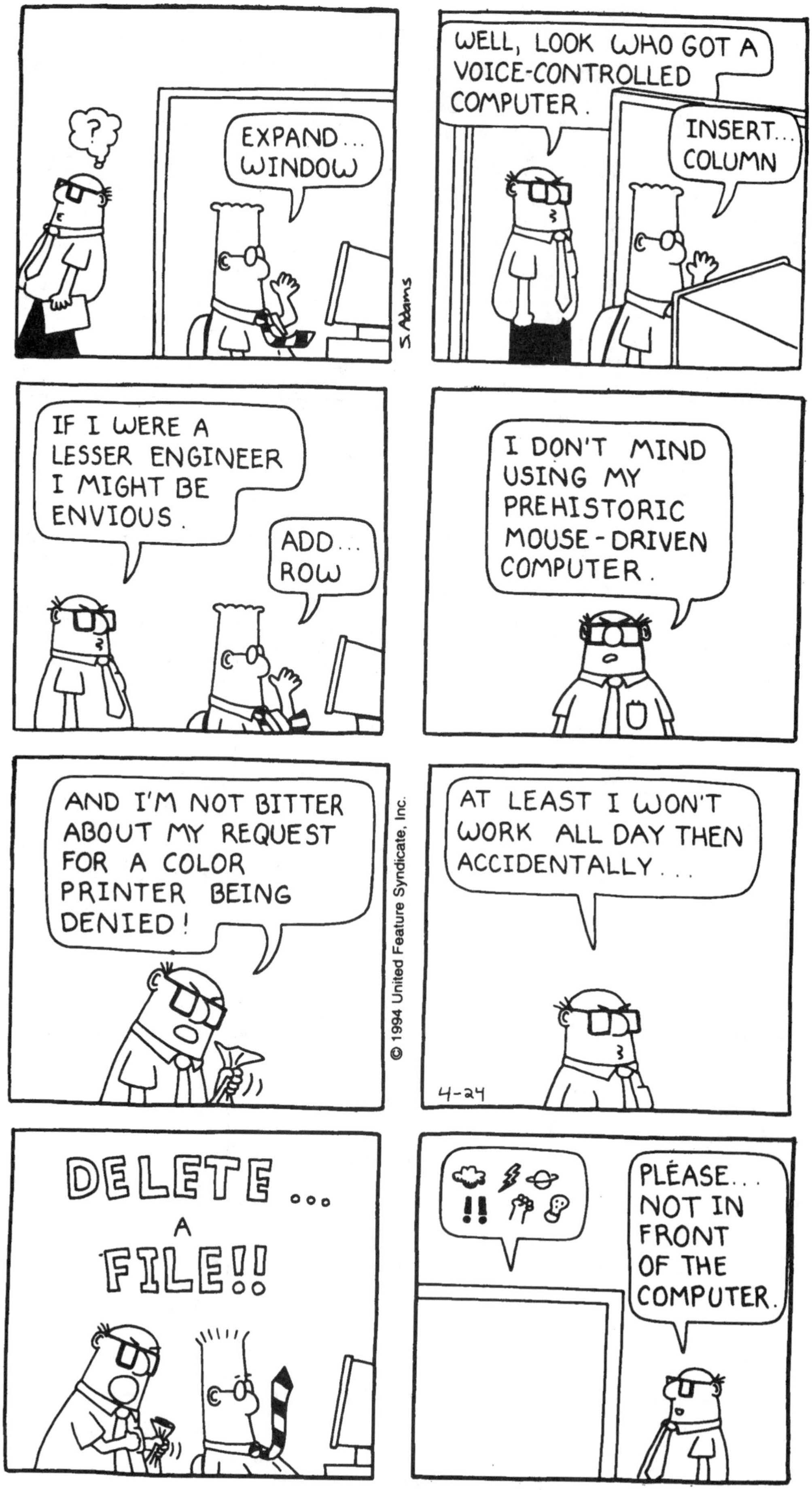
?
EXPAND... WINDOW
S. Adams
WELL, LOOK WHO GOT A VOICE-CONTROLLED COMPUTER.
INSERT... COLUMN
IF I WERE A LESSER ENGINEER I MIGHT BE ENVIOUS.
ADD... ROW
I DON'T MIND USING MY PREHISTORIC MOUSE-DRIVEN COMPUTER.
AND I'M NOT BITTER ABOUT MY REQUEST FOR A COLOR PRINTER BEING DENIED!
© 1994 United Feature Syndicate, Inc.
AT LEAST I WON'T WORK ALL DAY THEN ACCIDENTALLY...
4-24
DELETE... A FILE!!
PLEASE... NOT IN FRONT OF THE COMPUTER.

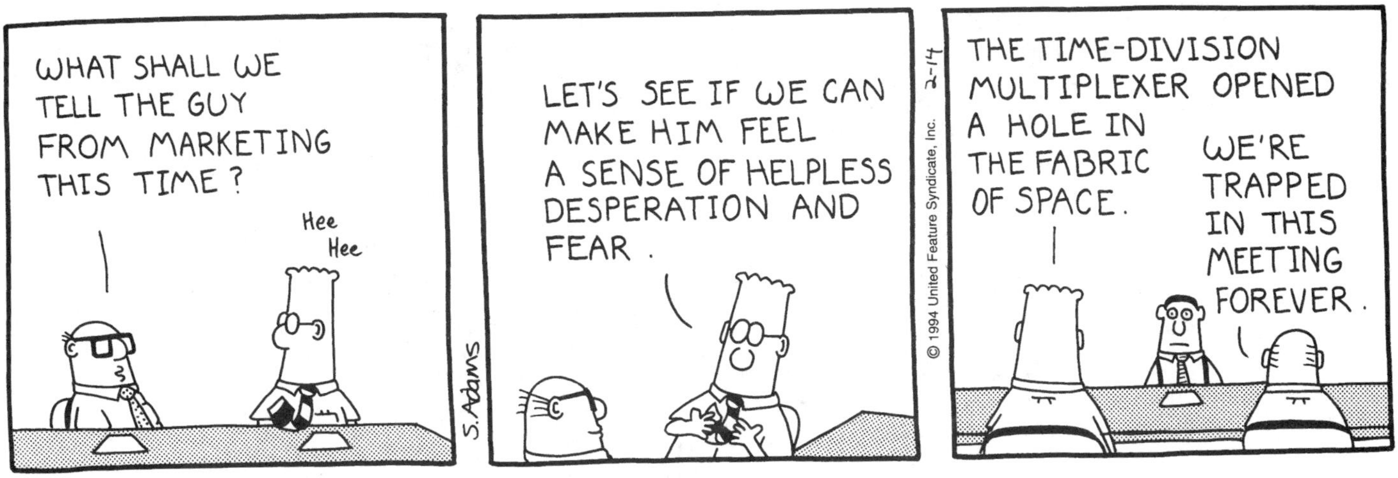
WHAT SHALL WE TELL THE GUY FROM MARKETING THIS TIME?
Hee Hee
S. Adams
LET'S SEE IF WE CAN MAKE HIM FEEL A SENSE OF HELPLESS DESPERATION AND FEAR.
2-14
© 1994 United Feature Syndicate, Inc.
THE TIME-DIVISION MULTIPLEXER OPENED A HOLE IN THE FABRIC OF SPACE.
WE'RE TRAPPED IN THIS MEETING FOREVER.

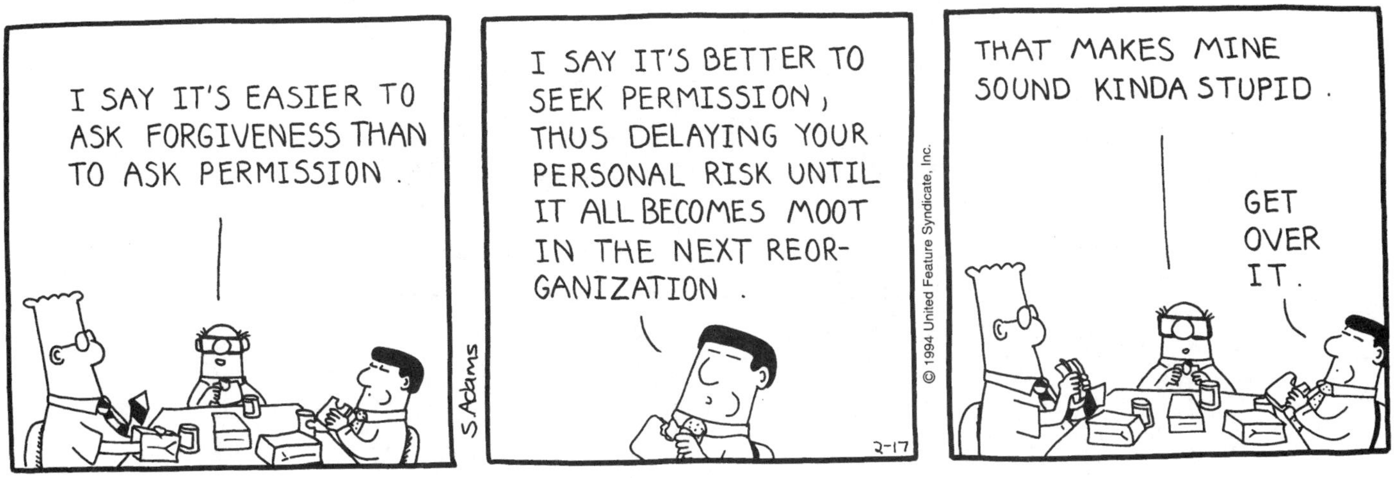
I SAY IT'S EASIER TO ASK FORGIVENESS THAN TO ASK PERMISSION.
S. Adams
I SAY IT'S BETTER TO SEEK PERMISSION, THUS DELAYING YOUR PERSONAL RISK UNTIL IT ALL BECOMES MOOT IN THE NEXT REORGANIZATION.
2-17
© 1994 United Feature Syndicate, Inc.
THAT MAKES MINE SOUND KINDA STUPID.
GET OVER IT.

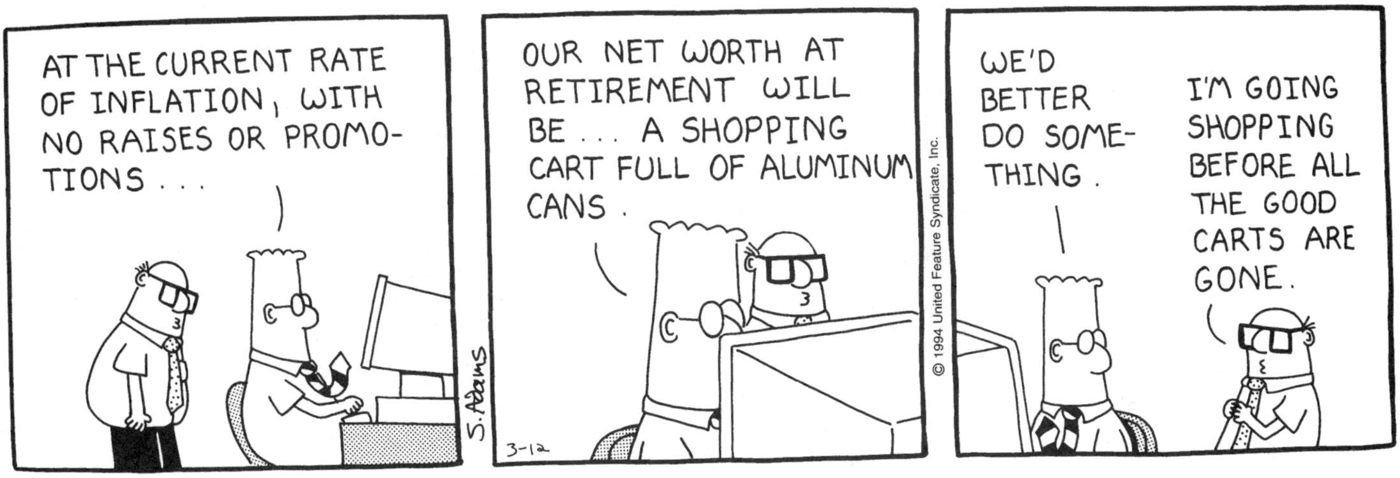
AT THE CURRENT RATE OF INFLATION, WITH NO RAISES OR PROMOTIONS...
S. Adams
3-12
OUR NET WORTH AT RETIREMENT WILL BE... A SHOPPING CART FULL OF ALUMINUM CANS.
© 1994 United Feature Syndicate, Inc.
WE'D BETTER DO SOMETHING.
I'M GOING SHOPPING BEFORE ALL THE GOOD CARTS ARE GONE.

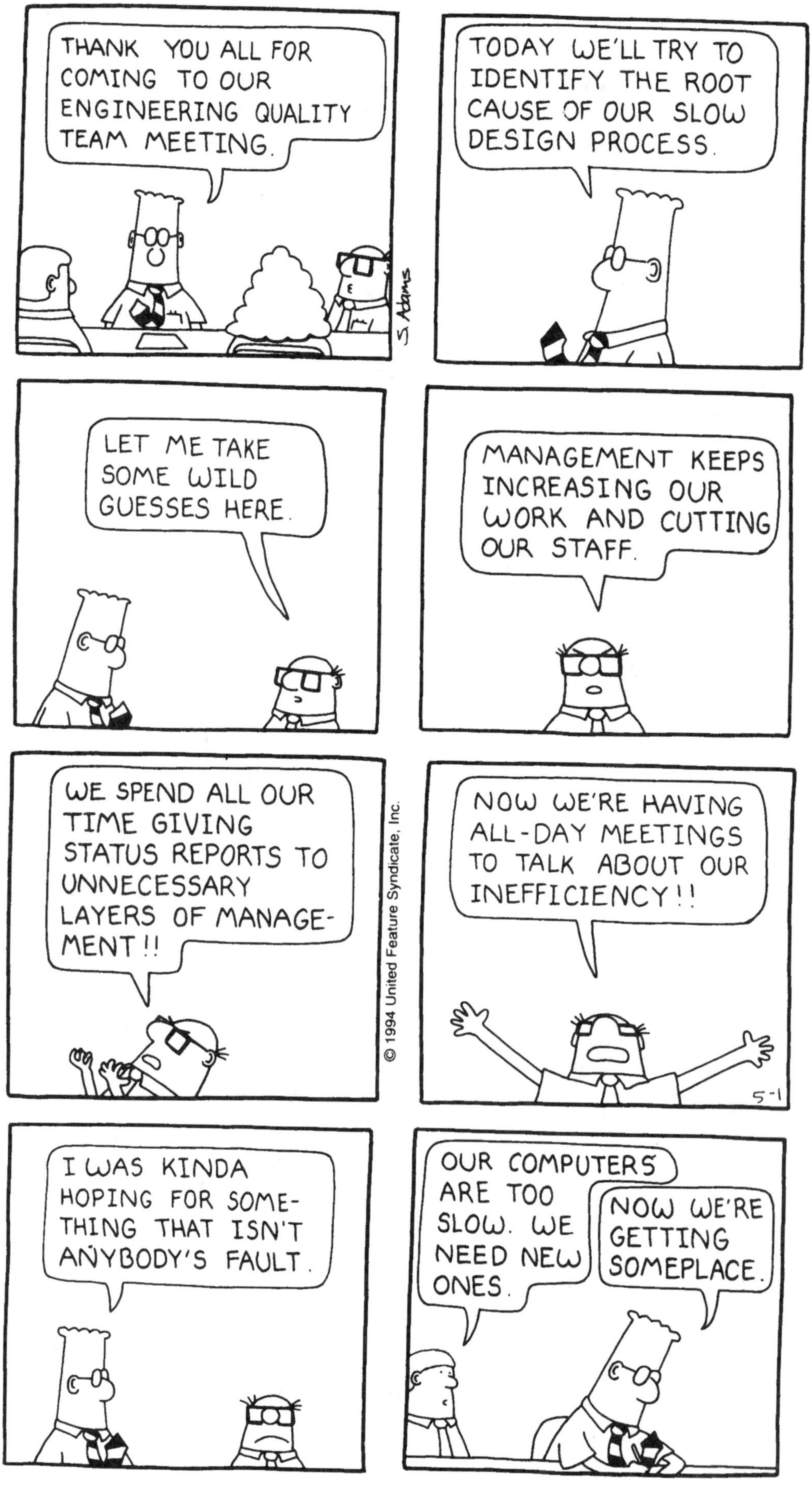
THANK YOU ALL FOR COMING TO OUR ENGINEERING QUALITY TEAM MEETING.
S. Adams
TODAY WE'LL TRY TO IDENTIFY THE ROOT CAUSE OF OUR SLOW DESIGN PROCESS.
LET ME TAKE SOME WILD GUESSES HERE.
MANAGEMENT KEEPS INCREASING OUR WORK AND CUTTING OUR STAFF.
WE SPEND ALL OUR TIME GIVING STATUS REPORTS TO UNNECESSARY LAYERS OF MANAGEMENT!!
© 1994 United Feature Syndicate, Inc.
NOW WE'RE HAVING ALL-DAY MEETINGS TO TALK ABOUT OUR INEFFICIENCY!!
5-1
I WAS KINDA HOPING FOR SOMETHING THAT ISN'T ANYBODY'S FAULT.
OUR COMPUTERS ARE TOO SLOW. WE NEED NEW ONES.
NOW WE'RE GETTING SOMEPLACE.

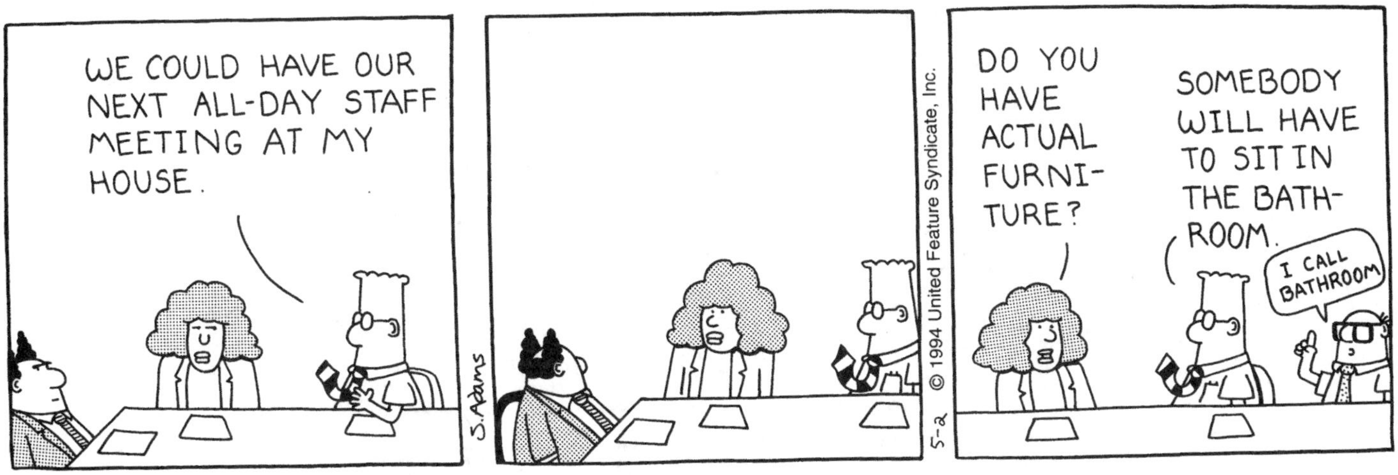
WE COULD HAVE OUR NEXT ALL-DAY STAFF MEETING AT MY HOUSE.
S. Adams
5-2
© 1994 United Feature Syndicate, Inc.
DO YOU HAVE ACTUAL FURNI-TURE?
SOMEBODY WILL HAVE TO SIT IN THE BATH-ROOM.
I CALL BATHROOM

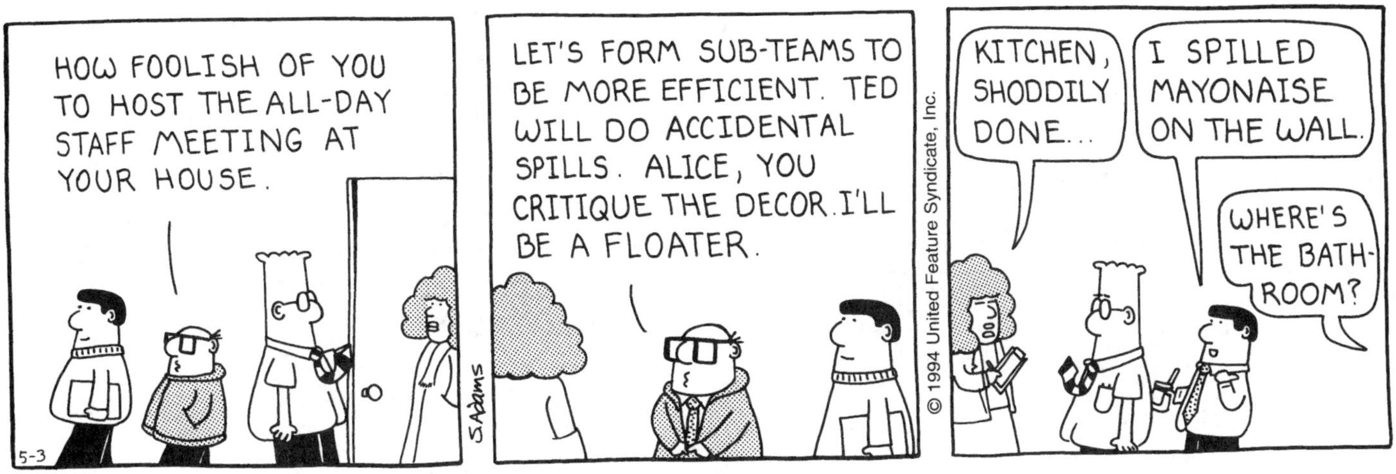
HOW FOOLISH OF YOU TO HOST THE ALL-DAY STAFF MEETING AT YOUR HOUSE.
5-3
S. Adams
LET'S FORM SUB-TEAMS TO BE MORE EFFICIENT. TED WILL DO ACCIDENTAL SPILLS. ALICE, YOU CRITIQUE THE DECOR. I'LL BE A FLOATER.
© 1994 United Feature Syndicate, Inc.
KITCHEN, SHODDILY DONE...
I SPILLED MAYONAISE ON THE WALL.
WHERE'S THE BATH-ROOM?

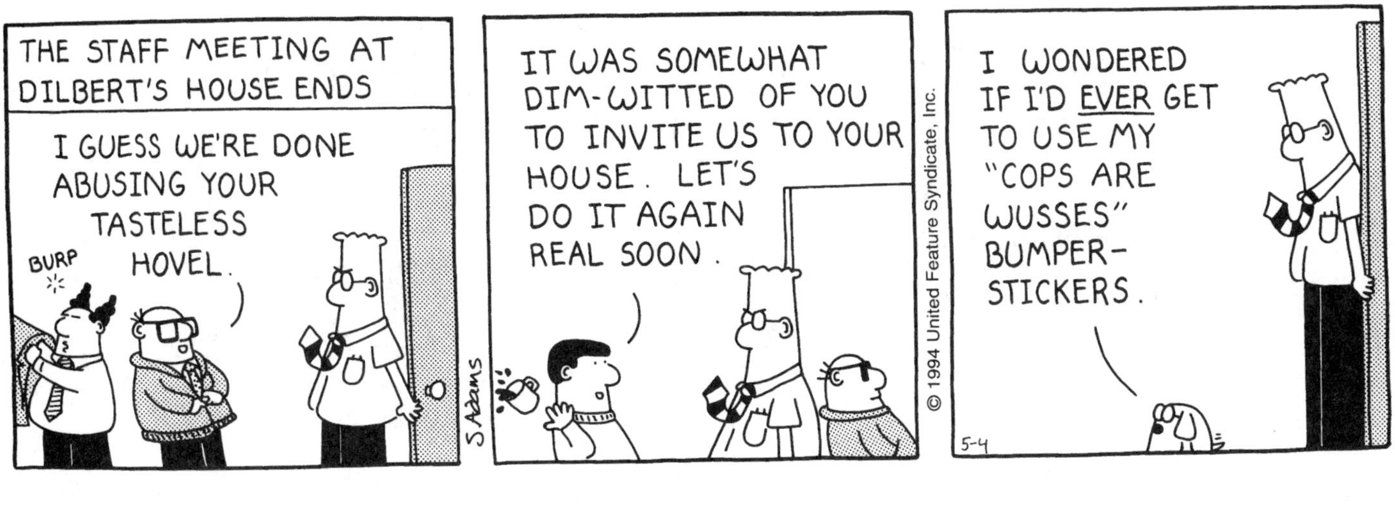
THE STAFF MEETING AT DILBERT'S HOUSE ENDS
I GUESS WE'RE DONE ABUSING YOUR TASTELESS HOVEL.
BURP
S. Adams
IT WAS SOMEWHAT DIM-WITTED OF YOU TO INVITE US TO YOUR HOUSE. LET'S DO IT AGAIN REAL SOON.
© 1994 United Feature Syndicate, Inc.
I WONDERED IF I'D EVER GET TO USE MY "COPS ARE WUSSES" BUMPER-STICKERS.
5-4

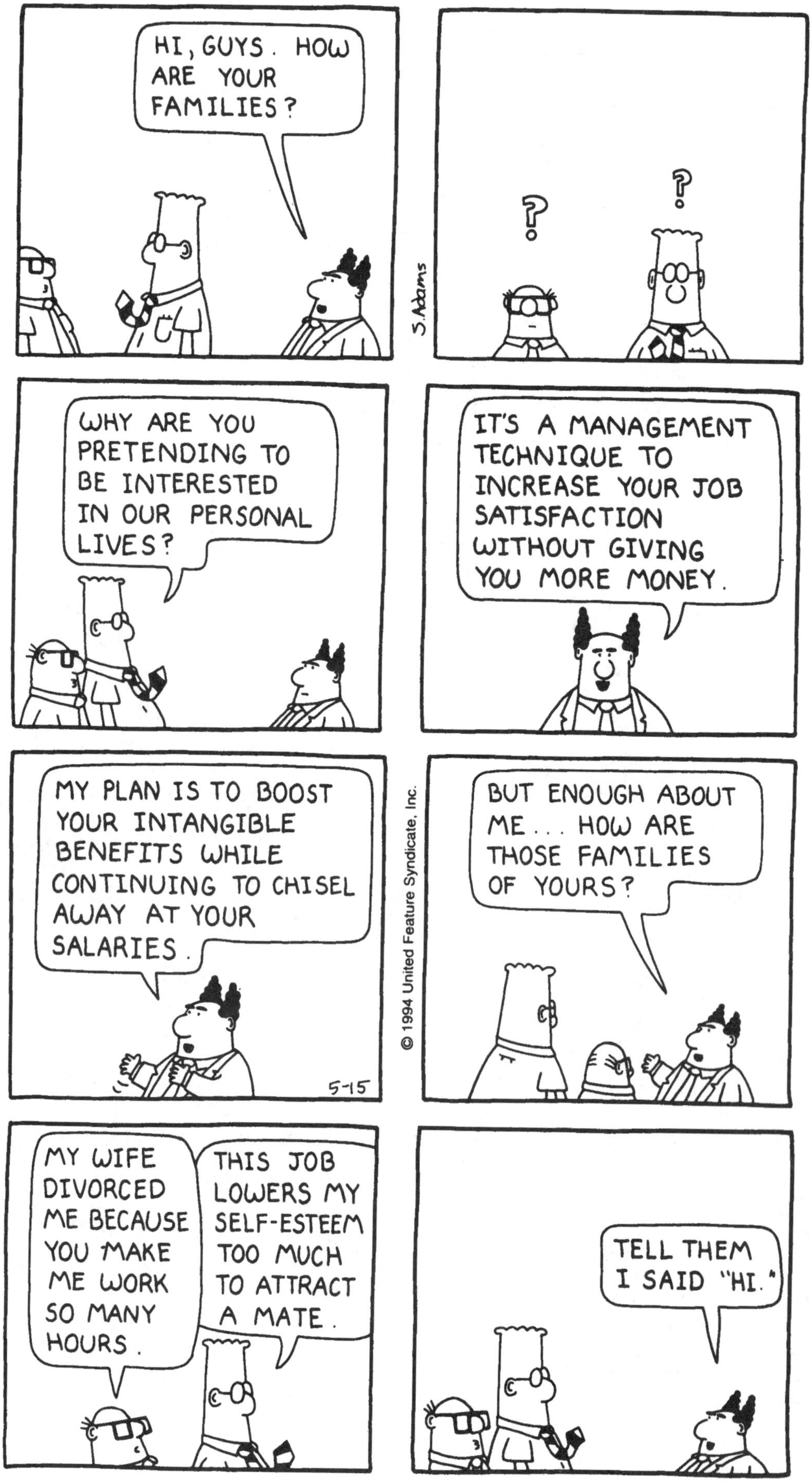
HI, GUYS. HOW ARE YOUR FAMILIES?
S. Adams
WHY ARE YOU PRETENDING TO BE INTERESTED IN OUR PERSONAL LIVES?
IT'S A MANAGEMENT TECHNIQUE TO INCREASE YOUR JOB SATISFACTION WITHOUT GIVING YOU MORE MONEY.
MY PLAN IS TO BOOST YOUR INTANGIBLE BENEFITS WHILE CONTINUING TO CHISEL AWAY AT YOUR SALARIES.
5-15
© 1994 United Feature Syndicate, Inc.
BUT ENOUGH ABOUT ME... HOW ARE THOSE FAMILIES OF YOURS?
MY WIFE DIVORCED ME BECAUSE YOU MAKE ME WORK SO MANY HOURS.
THIS JOB LOWERS MY SELF-ESTEEM TOO MUCH TO ATTRACT A MATE.
TELL THEM I SAID "HI."

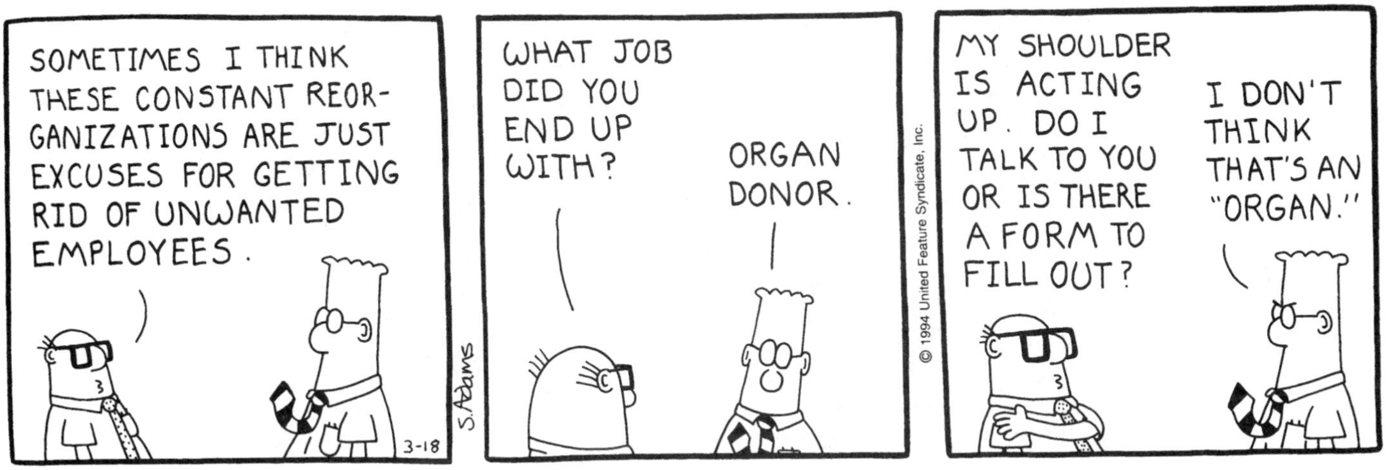
SOMETIMES I THINK THESE CONSTANT REORGANIZATIONS ARE JUST EXCUSES FOR GETTING RID OF UNWANTED EMPLOYEES.
3-18
S. Adams
WHAT JOB DID YOU END UP WITH?
ORGAN DONOR.
© 1994 United Feature Syndicate, Inc.
MY SHOULDER IS ACTING UP. DO I TALK TO YOU OR IS THERE A FORM TO FILL OUT?
I DON'T THINK THAT'S AN "ORGAN."

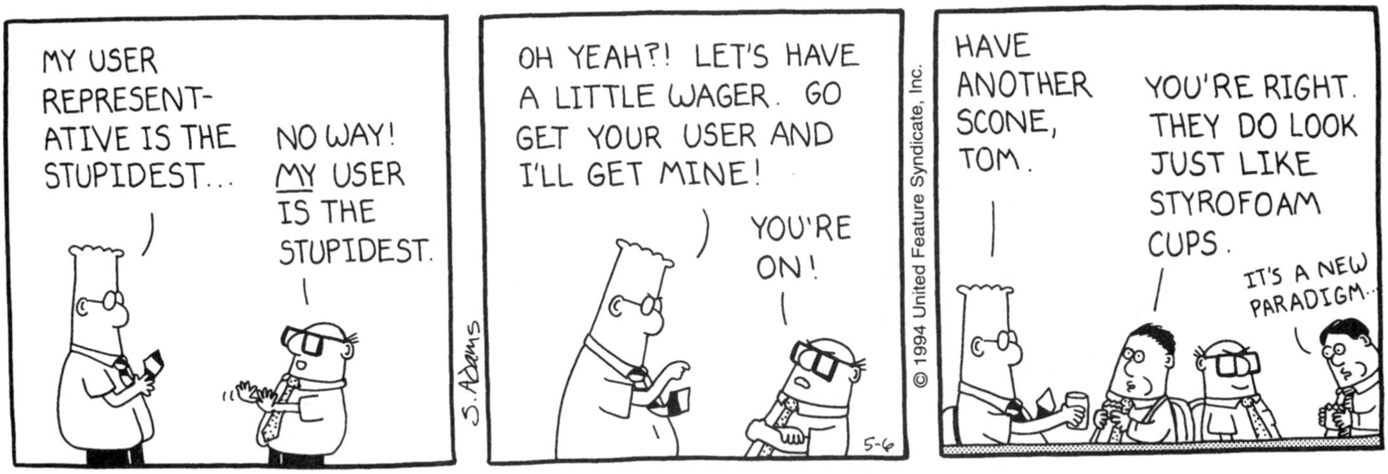
MY USER REPRESENTATIVE IS THE STUPIDEST...
NO WAY! MY USER IS THE STUPIDEST.
S. Adams
OH YEAH?! LET'S HAVE A LITTLE WAGER. GO GET YOUR USER AND I'LL GET MINE!
YOU'RE ON!
5-6
© 1994 United Feature Syndicate, Inc.
HAVE ANOTHER SCONE, TOM.
YOU'RE RIGHT. THEY DO LOOK JUST LIKE STYROFOAM CUPS.
IT'S A NEW PARADIGM...

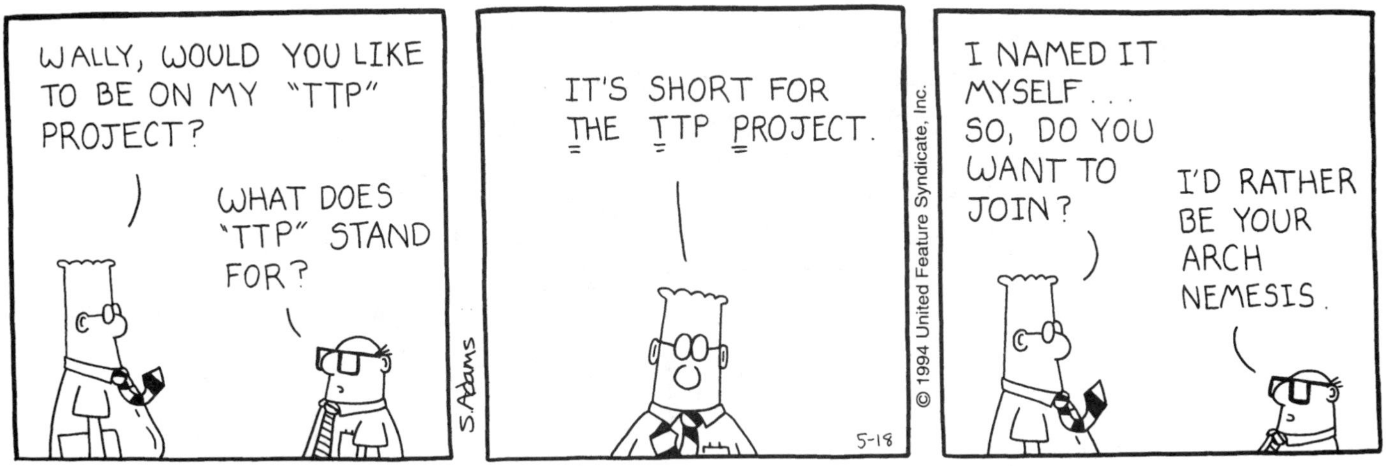
WALLY, WOULD YOU LIKE TO BE ON MY "TTP" PROJECT?
WHAT DOES "TTP" STAND FOR?
S. Adams
IT'S SHORT FOR THE TTP PROJECT.
5-18
© 1994 United Feature Syndicate, Inc.
I NAMED IT MYSELF... SO, DO YOU WANT TO JOIN?
I'D RATHER BE YOUR ARCH NEMESIS.

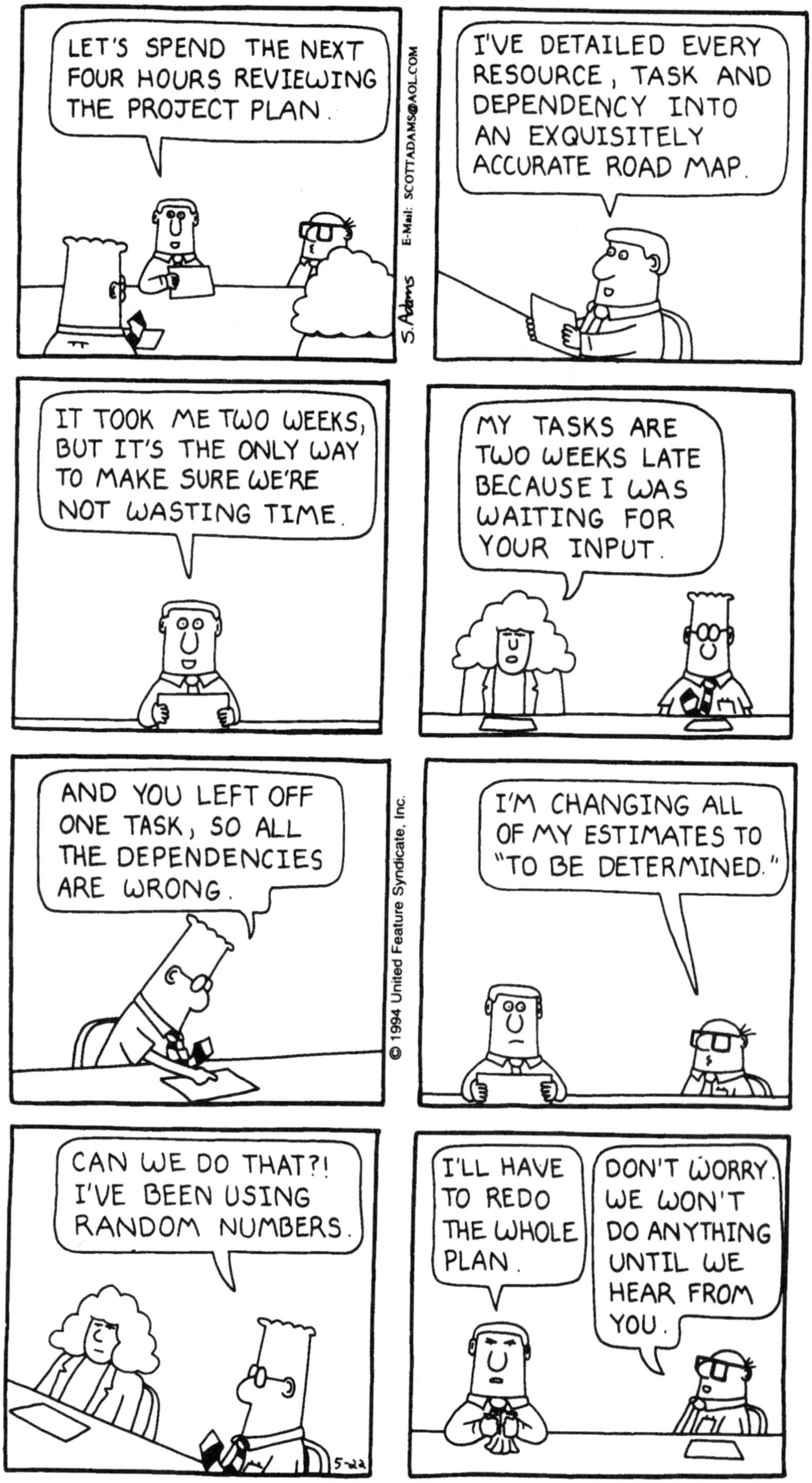
LET'S SPEND THE NEXT FOUR HOURS REVIEWING THE PROJECT PLAN.
E-Mail: SCOTTADAMS@AOL.COM
S. Adams
I'VE DETAILED EVERY RESOURCE, TASK AND DEPENDENCY INTO AN EXQUISITELY ACCURATE ROAD MAP.
IT TOOK ME TWO WEEKS, BUT IT'S THE ONLY WAY TO MAKE SURE WE'RE NOT WASTING TIME.
MY TASKS ARE TWO WEEKS LATE BECAUSE I WAS WAITING FOR YOUR INPUT.
AND YOU LEFT OFF ONE TASK, SO ALL THE DEPENDENCIES ARE WRONG.
© 1994 United Feature Syndicate, Inc.
I'M CHANGING ALL OF MY ESTIMATES TO "TO BE DETERMINED."
CAN WE DO THAT?! I'VE BEEN USING RANDOM NUMBERS.
5-22
I'LL HAVE TO REDO THE WHOLE PLAN.
DON'T WORRY. WE WON'T DO ANYTHING UNTIL WE HEAR FROM YOU.

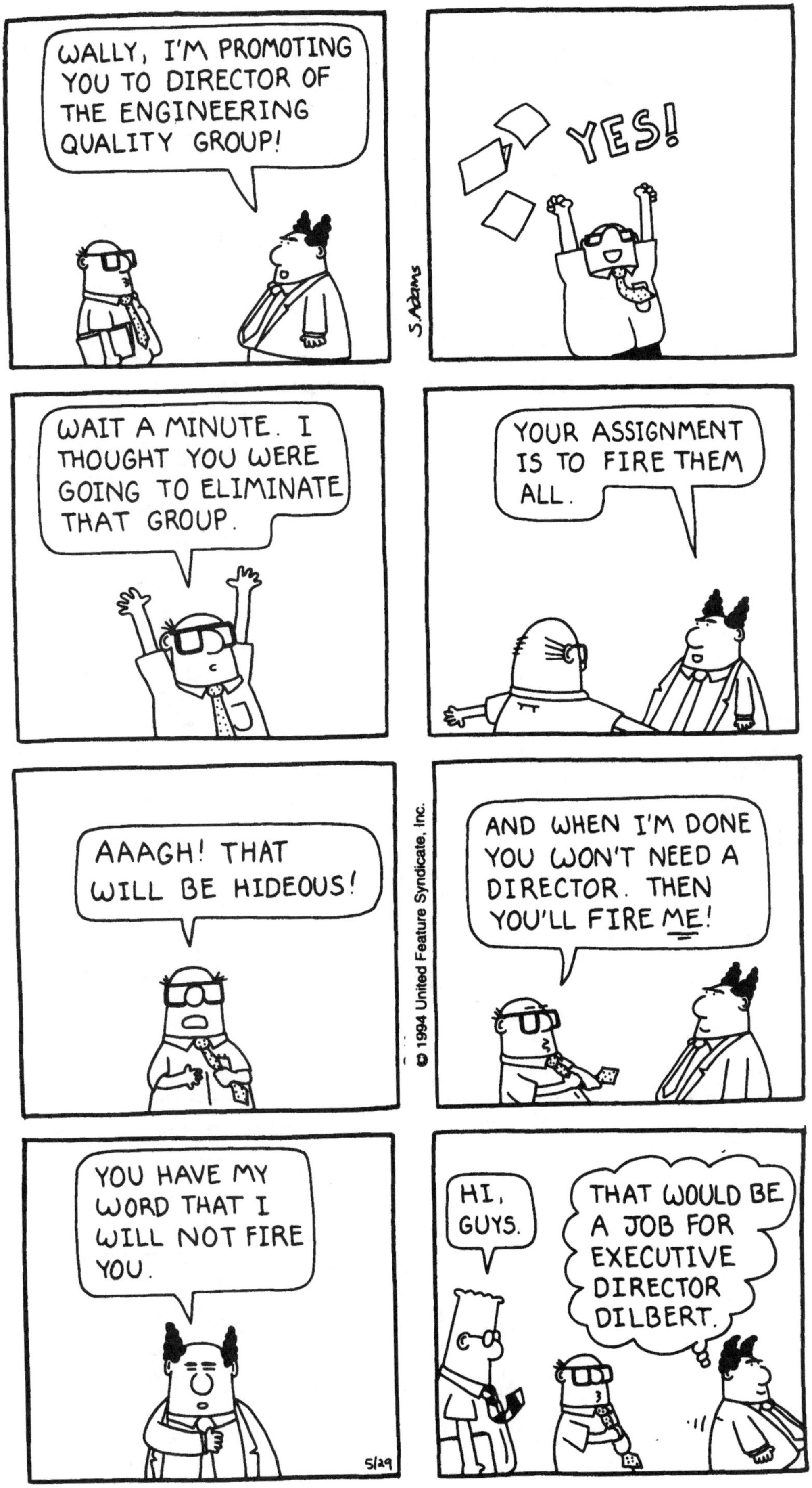
WALLY, I'M PROMOTING YOU TO DIRECTOR OF THE ENGINEERING QUALITY GROUP!
YES!
S. Adams
WAIT A MINUTE. I THOUGHT YOU WERE GOING TO ELIMINATE THAT GROUP.
YOUR ASSIGNMENT IS TO FIRE THEM ALL.
AAAGH! THAT WILL BE HIDEOUS!
© 1994 United Feature Syndicate, Inc.
AND WHEN I'M DONE YOU WON'T NEED A DIRECTOR. THEN YOU'LL FIRE ME!
YOU HAVE MY WORD THAT I WILL NOT FIRE YOU.
5/29
HI, GUYS.
THAT WOULD BE A JOB FOR EXECUTIVE DIRECTOR DILBERT.

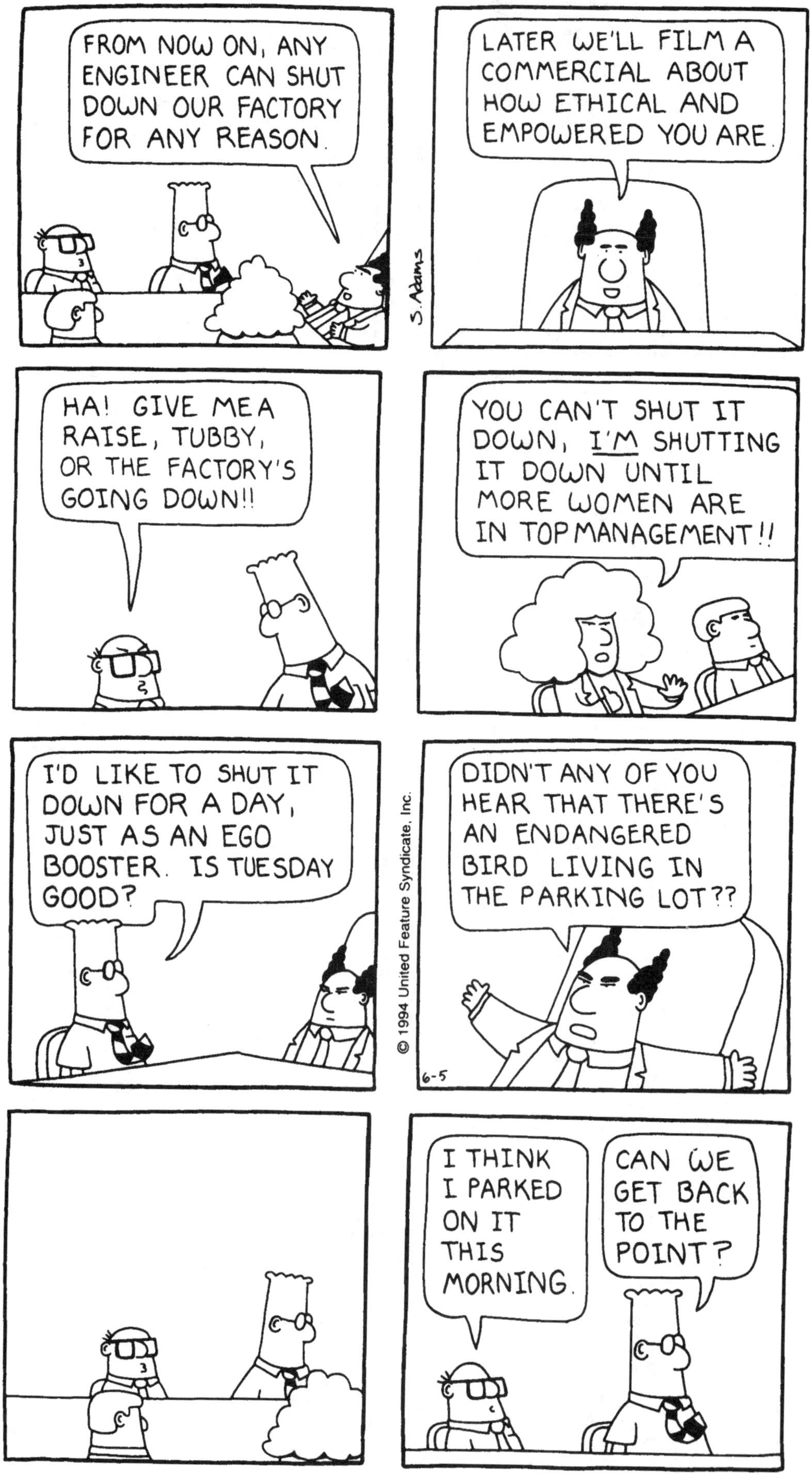
FROM NOW ON, ANY ENGINEER CAN SHUT DOWN OUR FACTORY FOR ANY REASON.
LATER WE'LL FILM A COMMERCIAL ABOUT HOW ETHICAL AND EMPOWERED YOU ARE.
S. Adams
HA! GIVE ME A RAISE, TUBBY, OR THE FACTORY'S GOING DOWN!!
YOU CAN'T SHUT IT DOWN, I'M SHUTTING IT DOWN UNTIL MORE WOMEN ARE IN TOP MANAGEMENT!!
I'D LIKE TO SHUT IT DOWN FOR A DAY, JUST AS AN EGO BOOSTER. IS TUESDAY GOOD?
© 1994 United Feature Syndicate, Inc.
DIDN'T ANY OF YOU HEAR THAT THERE'S AN ENDANGERED BIRD LIVING IN THE PARKING LOT??
6-5
I THINK I PARKED ON IT THIS MORNING.
CAN WE GET BACK TO THE POINT?

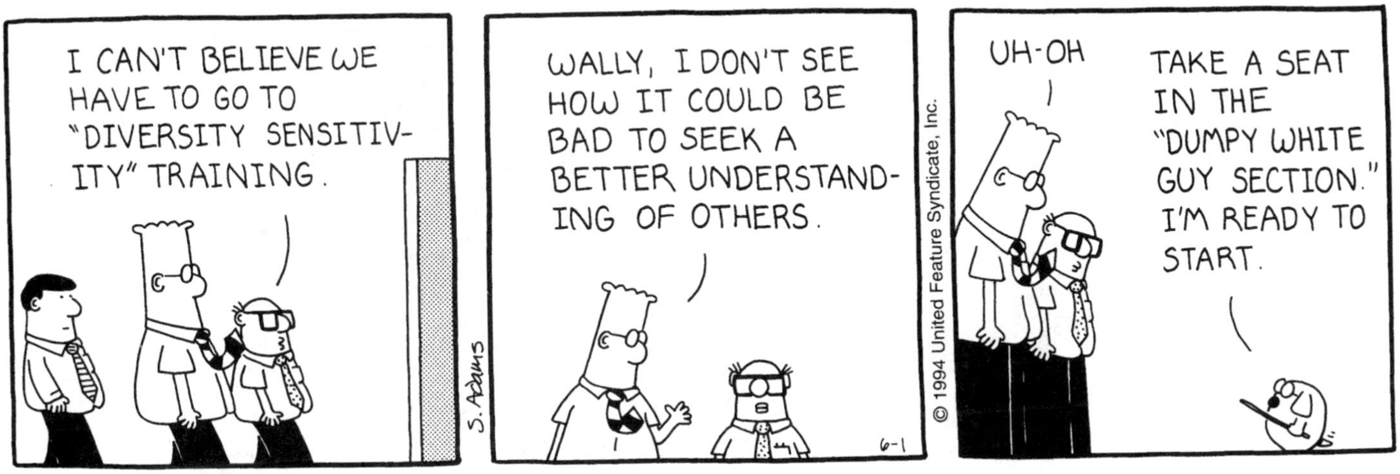
I CAN'T BELIEVE WE HAVE TO GO TO "DIVERSITY SENSITIVITY" TRAINING.
S. Adams
WALLY, I DON'T SEE HOW IT COULD BE BAD TO SEEK A BETTER UNDERSTANDING OF OTHERS.
6-1
© 1994 United Feature Syndicate, Inc.
UH-OH
TAKE A SEAT IN THE "DUMPY WHITE GUY SECTION." I'M READY TO START.

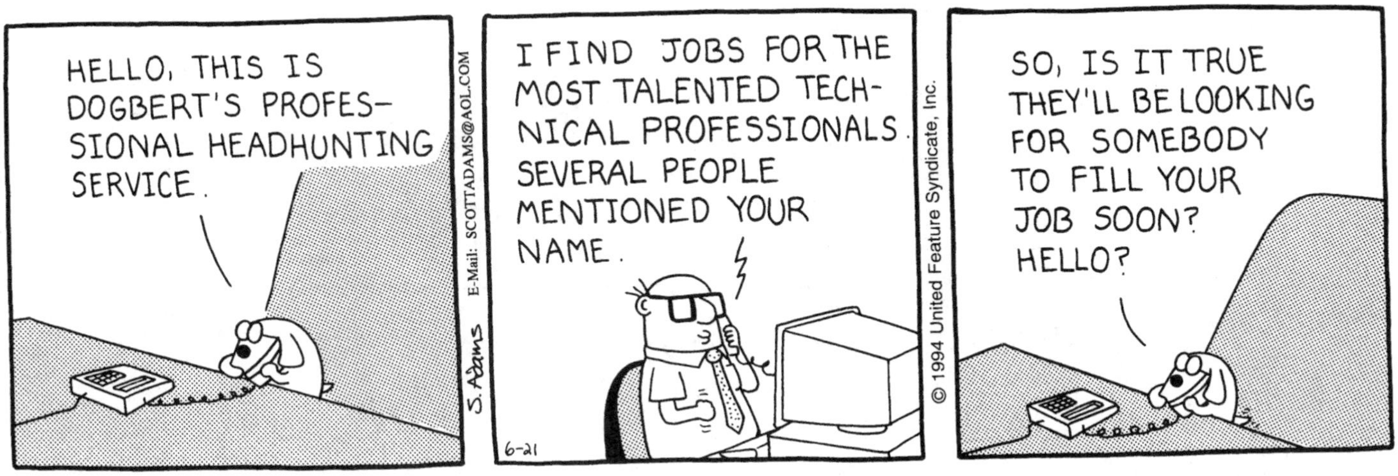
HELLO, THIS IS DOGBERT'S PROFESSIONAL HEADHUNTING SERVICE.
S. Adams
E-Mail: SCOTTADAMS@AOL.COM
I FIND JOBS FOR THE MOST TALENTED TECHNICAL PROFESSIONALS. SEVERAL PEOPLE MENTIONED YOUR NAME.
6-21
© 1994 United Feature Syndicate, Inc.
SO, IS IT TRUE THEY'LL BE LOOKING FOR SOMEBODY TO FILL YOUR JOB SOON? HELLO?

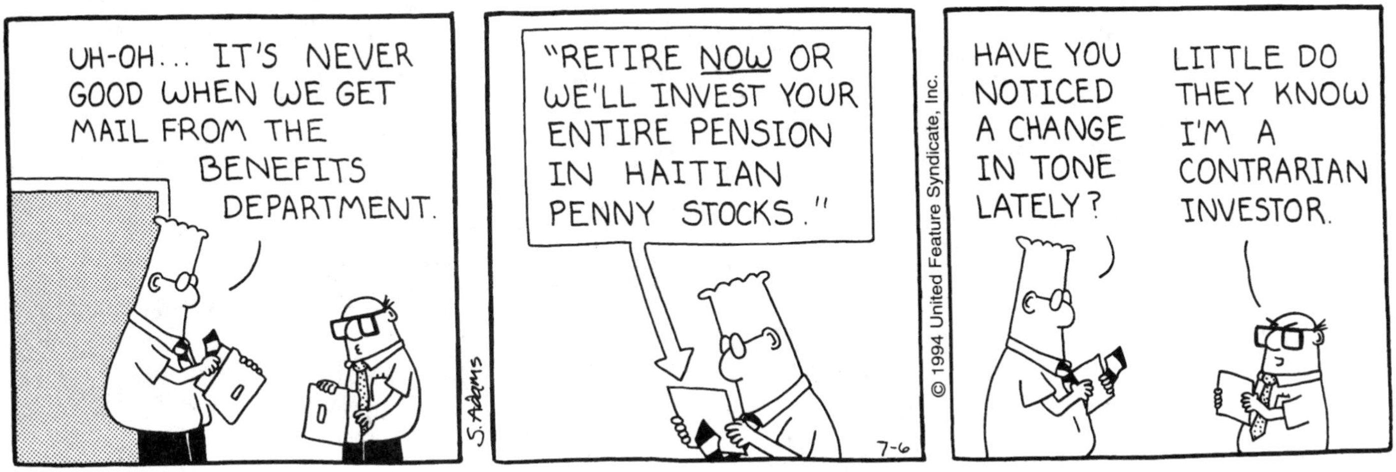
UH-OH... IT'S NEVER GOOD WHEN WE GET MAIL FROM THE BENEFITS DEPARTMENT.
S. Adams
"RETIRE NOW OR WE'LL INVEST YOUR ENTIRE PENSION IN HAITIAN PENNY STOCKS."
7-6
© 1994 United Feature Syndicate, Inc.
HAVE YOU NOTICED A CHANGE IN TONE LATELY?
LITTLE DO THEY KNOW I'M A CONTRARIAN INVESTOR.

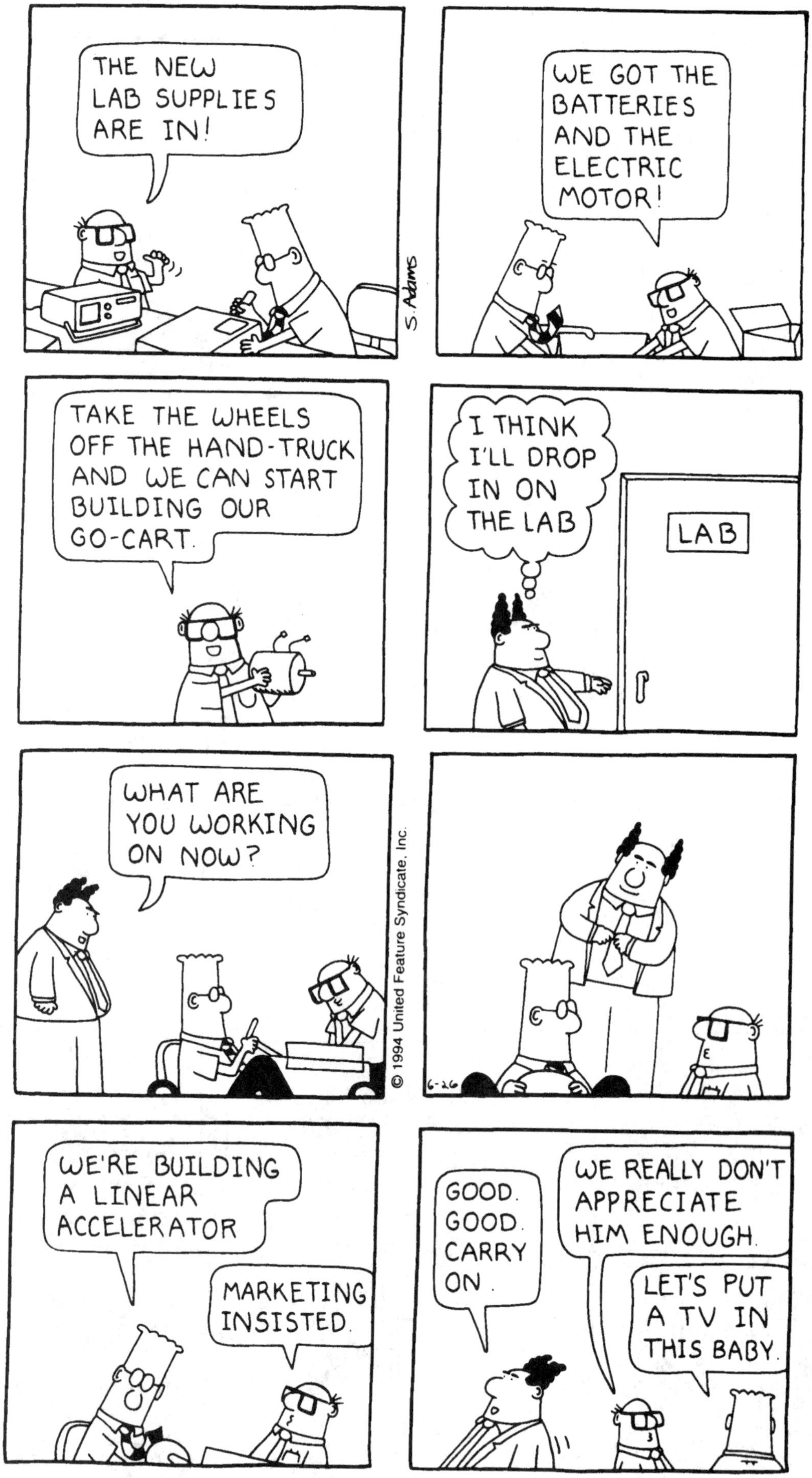
THE NEW LAB SUPPLIES ARE IN!
S. Adams
WE GOT THE BATTERIES AND THE ELECTRIC MOTOR!
TAKE THE WHEELS OFF THE HAND-TRUCK AND WE CAN START BUILDING OUR GO-CART.
I THINK I'LL DROP IN ON THE LAB
LAB
WHAT ARE YOU WORKING ON NOW?
© 1994 United Feature Syndicate, Inc.
6-26
WE'RE BUILDING A LINEAR ACCELERATOR
MARKETING INSISTED.
GOOD. GOOD. CARRY ON.
WE REALLY DON'T APPRECIATE HIM ENOUGH.
LET'S PUT A TV IN THIS BABY.

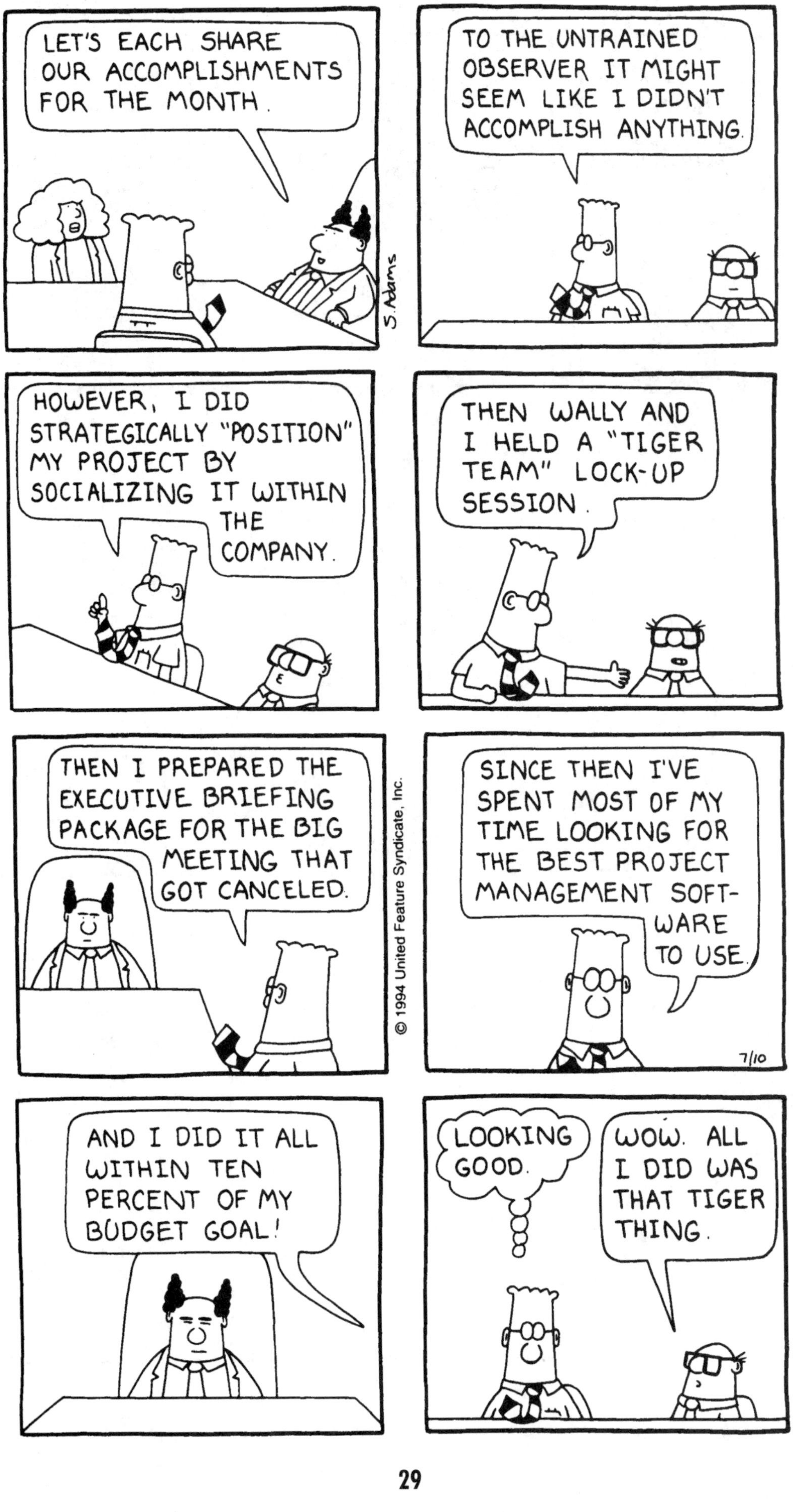
LET'S EACH SHARE OUR ACCOMPLISHMENTS FOR THE MONTH.
S. Adams
TO THE UNTRAINED OBSERVER IT MIGHT SEEM LIKE I DIDN'T ACCOMPLISH ANYTHING.
HOWEVER, I DID STRATEGICALLY "POSITION" MY PROJECT BY SOCIALIZING IT WITHIN THE COMPANY.
THEN WALLY AND I HELD A "TIGER TEAM" LOCK-UP SESSION.
THEN I PREPARED THE EXECUTIVE BRIEFING PACKAGE FOR THE BIG MEETING THAT GOT CANCELED.
© 1994 United Feature Syndicate, Inc.
SINCE THEN I'VE SPENT MOST OF MY TIME LOOKING FOR THE BEST PROJECT MANAGEMENT SOFT-WARE TO USE.
7/10
AND I DID IT ALL WITHIN TEN PERCENT OF MY BUDGET GOAL!
LOOKING GOOD.
WOW. ALL I DID WAS THAT TIGER THING.

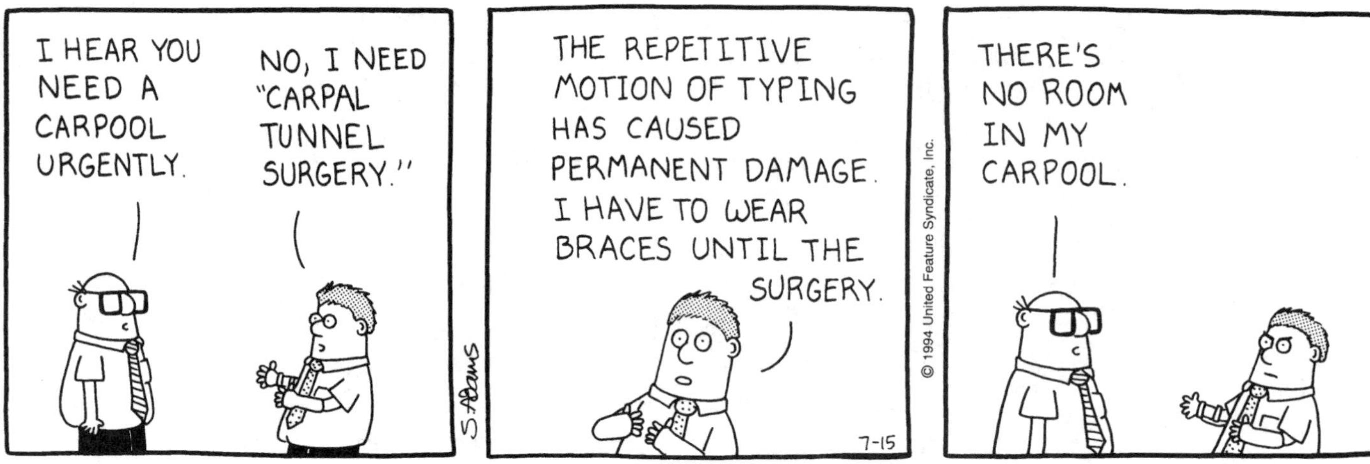
I HEAR YOU NEED A CARPOOL URGENTLY.
NO, I NEED "CARPAL TUNNEL SURGERY."
S. Adams
THE REPETITIVE MOTION OF TYPING HAS CAUSED PERMANENT DAMAGE. I HAVE TO WEAR BRACES UNTIL THE SURGERY.
7-15
© 1994 United Feature Syndicate, Inc.
THERE'S NO ROOM IN MY CARPOOL.

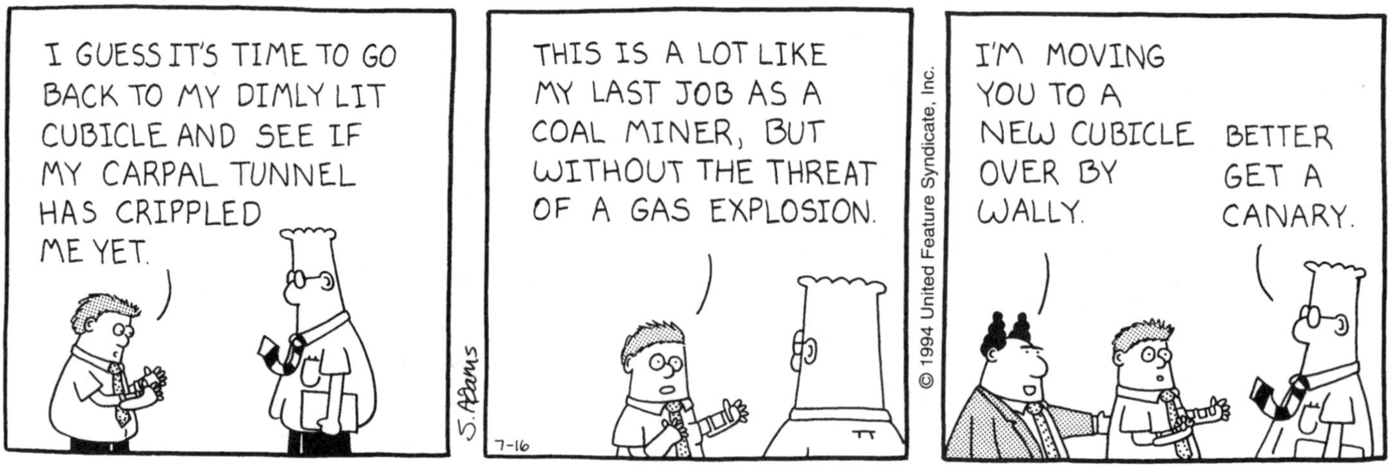
I GUESS IT'S TIME TO GO BACK TO MY DIMLY LIT CUBICLE AND SEE IF MY CARPAL TUNNEL HAS CRIPPLED ME YET.
S. Adams
7-16
THIS IS A LOT LIKE MY LAST JOB AS A COAL MINER, BUT WITHOUT THE THREAT OF A GAS EXPLOSION.
© 1994 United Feature Syndicate, Inc.
I'M MOVING YOU TO A NEW CUBICLE OVER BY WALLY.
BETTER GET A CANARY.

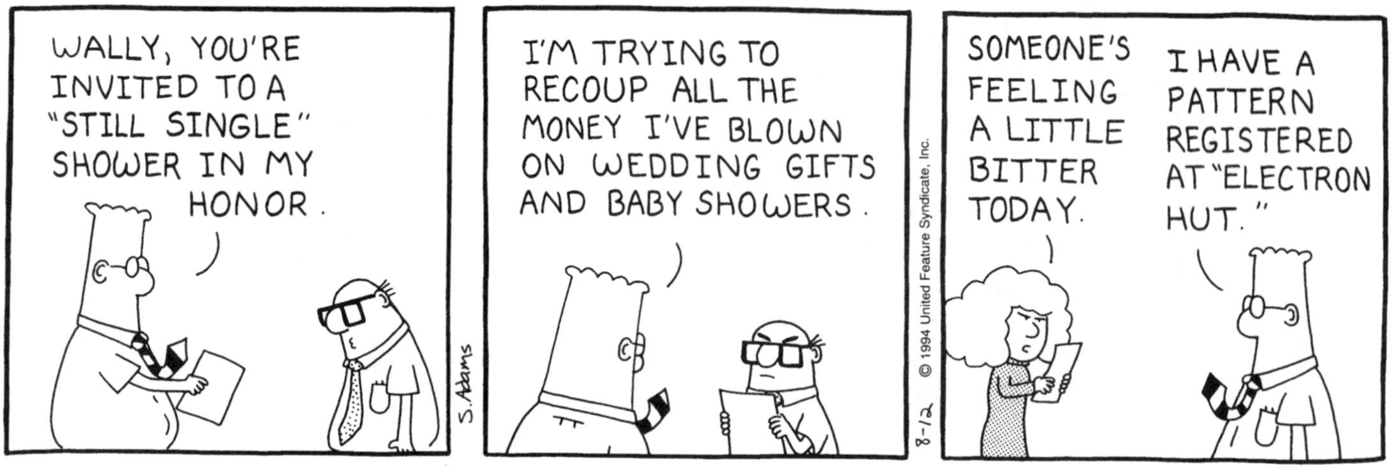
WALLY, YOU'RE INVITED TO A "STILL SINGLE" SHOWER IN MY HONOR.
S. Adams
I'M TRYING TO RECOUP ALL THE MONEY I'VE BLOWN ON WEDDING GIFTS AND BABY SHOWERS.
© 1994 United Feature Syndicate, Inc.
8-12
SOMEONE'S FEELING A LITTLE BITTER TODAY.
I HAVE A PATTERN REGISTERED AT "ELECTRON HUT."

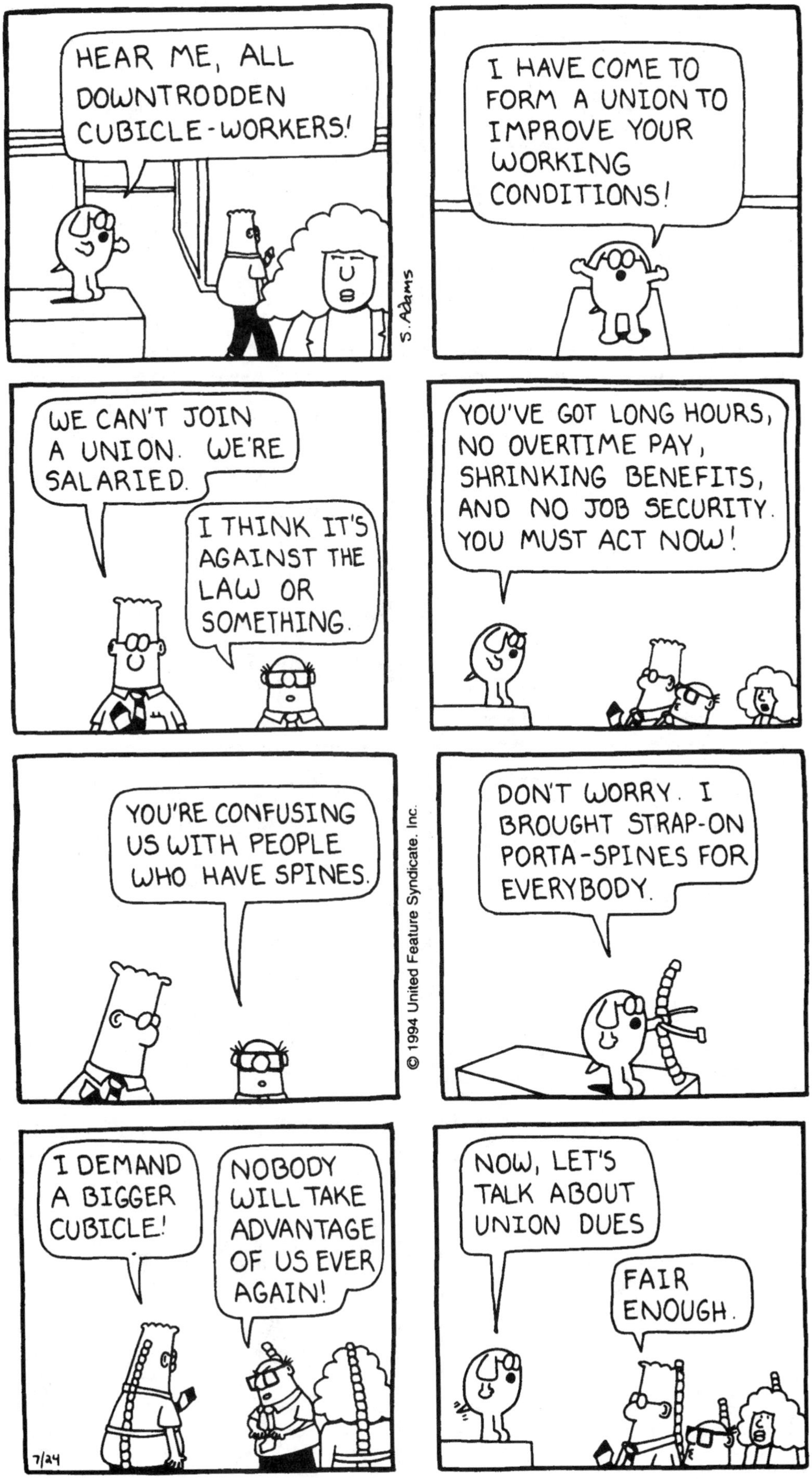
HEAR ME, ALL DOWNTRODDEN CUBICLE-WORKERS!
S. Adams
I HAVE COME TO FORM A UNION TO IMPROVE YOUR WORKING CONDITIONS!
WE CAN'T JOIN A UNION. WE'RE SALARIED.
I THINK IT'S AGAINST THE LAW OR SOMETHING.
YOU'VE GOT LONG HOURS, NO OVERTIME PAY, SHRINKING BENEFITS, AND NO JOB SECURITY. YOU MUST ACT NOW!
YOU'RE CONFUSING US WITH PEOPLE WHO HAVE SPINES.
© 1994 United Feature Syndicate, Inc.
DON'T WORRY. I BROUGHT STRAP-ON PORTA-SPINES FOR EVERYBODY.
I DEMAND A BIGGER CUBICLE!
NOBODY WILL TAKE ADVANTAGE OF US EVER AGAIN!
7/24
NOW, LET'S TALK ABOUT UNION DUES
FAIR ENOUGH.

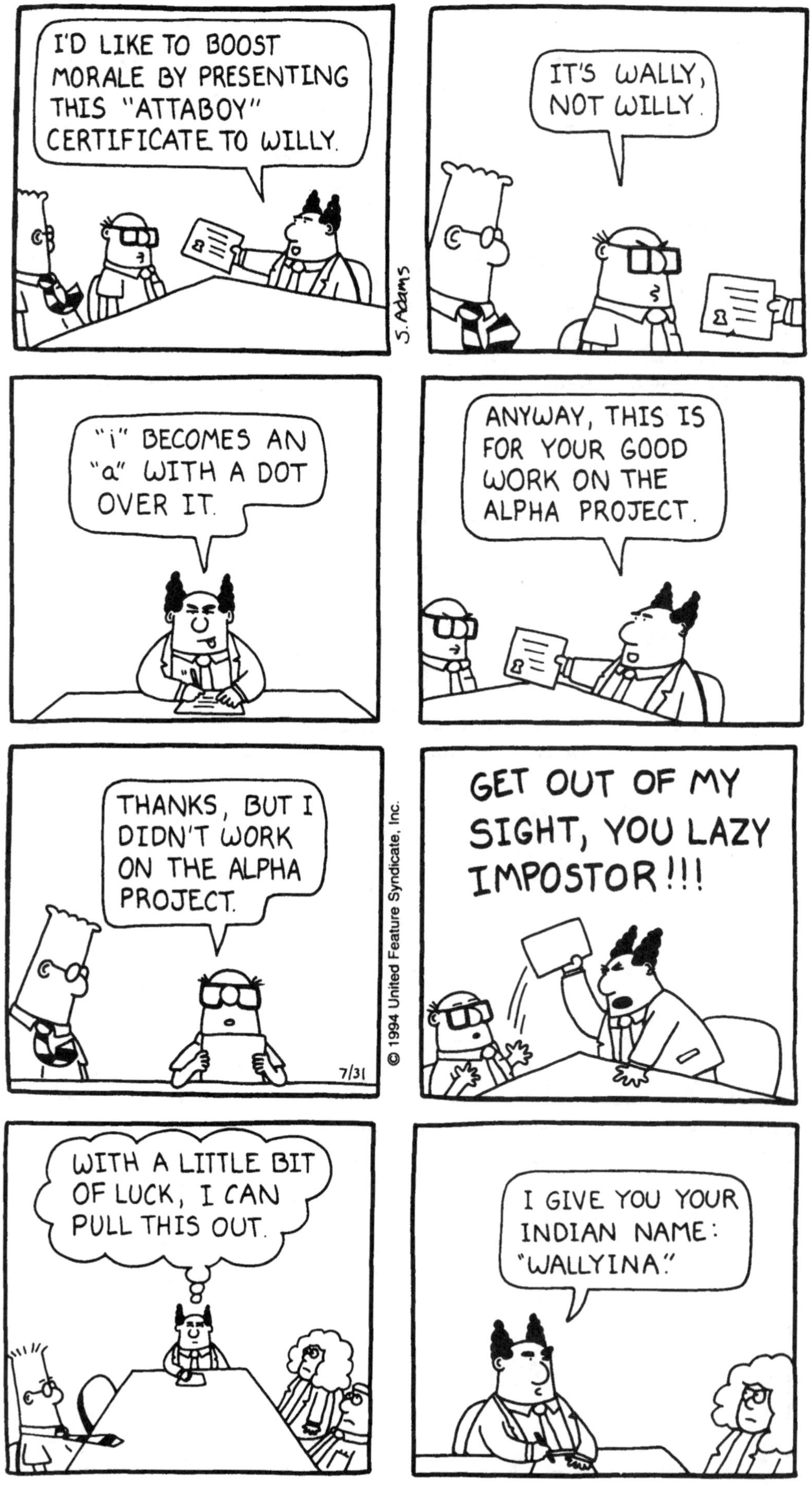
I'D LIKE TO BOOST MORALE BY PRESENTING THIS "ATTABOY" CERTIFICATE TO WILLY.
S. Adams
IT'S WALLY, NOT WILLY.
"i" BECOMES AN "a" WITH A DOT OVER IT.
ANYWAY, THIS IS FOR YOUR GOOD WORK ON THE ALPHA PROJECT.
THANKS, BUT I DIDN'T WORK ON THE ALPHA PROJECT.
7/31
GET OUT OF MY SIGHT, YOU LAZY IMPOSTOR!!!
WITH A LITTLE BIT OF LUCK, I CAN PULL THIS OUT.
I GIVE YOU YOUR INDIAN NAME: "WALLYINA."

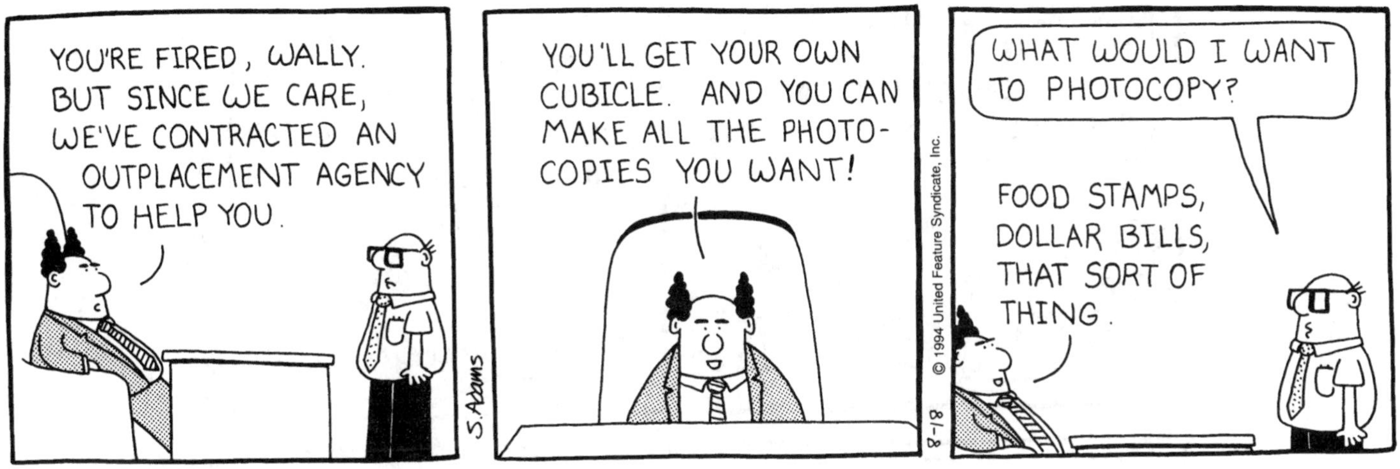

YOU'RE FIRED, WALLY. BUT SINCE WE CARE, WE'VE CONTRACTED AN OUTPLACEMENT AGENCY TO HELP YOU.
S. Adams
YOU'LL GET YOUR OWN CUBICLE. AND YOU CAN MAKE ALL THE PHOTOCOPIES YOU WANT!
8-18
© 1994 United Feature Syndicate, Inc.
WHAT WOULD I WANT TO PHOTOCOPY?
FOOD STAMPS, DOLLAR BILLS, THAT SORT OF THING.

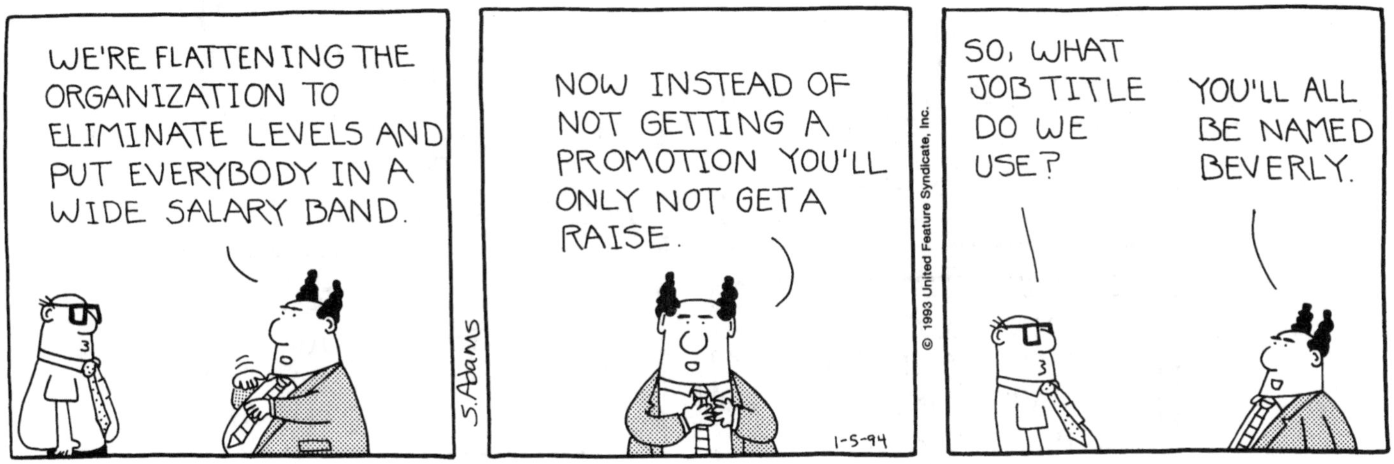

WE'RE FLATTENING THE ORGANIZATION TO ELIMINATE LEVELS AND PUT EVERYBODY IN A WIDE SALARY BAND.
S. Adams
NOW INSTEAD OF NOT GETTING A PROMOTION YOU'LL ONLY NOT GET A RAISE.
1-5-94
© 1993 United Feature Syndicate, Inc.
SO, WHAT JOB TITLE DO WE USE?
YOU'LL ALL BE NAMED BEVERLY.

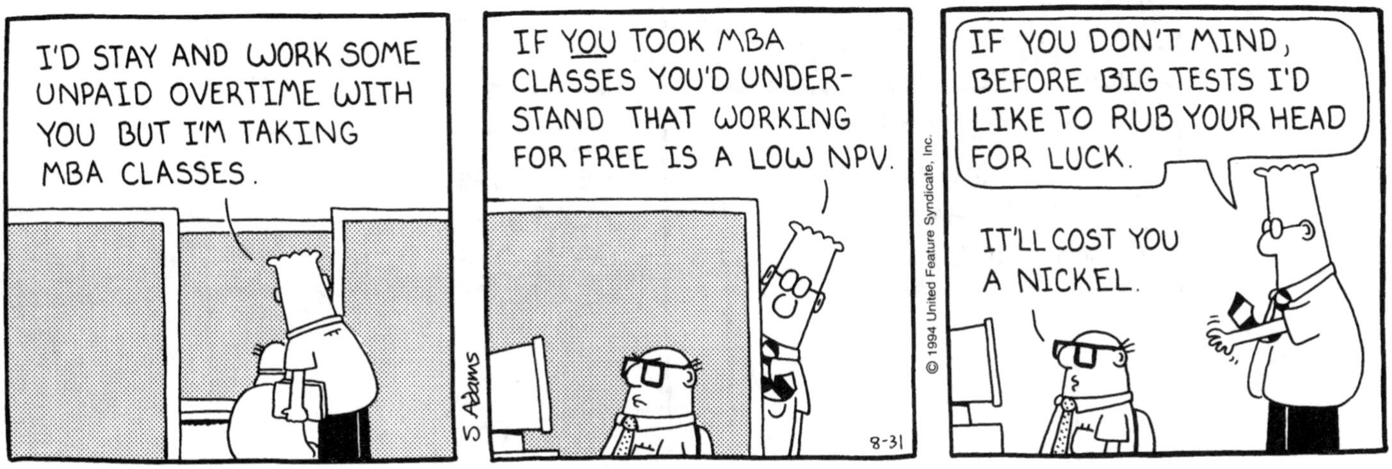

I'D STAY AND WORK SOME UNPAID OVERTIME WITH YOU BUT I'M TAKING MBA CLASSES.
S. Adams
IF YOU TOOK MBA CLASSES YOU'D UNDERSTAND THAT WORKING FOR FREE IS A LOW NPV.
8-31
© 1994 United Feature Syndicate, Inc.
IF YOU DON'T MIND, BEFORE BIG TESTS I'D LIKE TO RUB YOUR HEAD FOR LUCK.
IT'LL COST YOU A NICKEL.

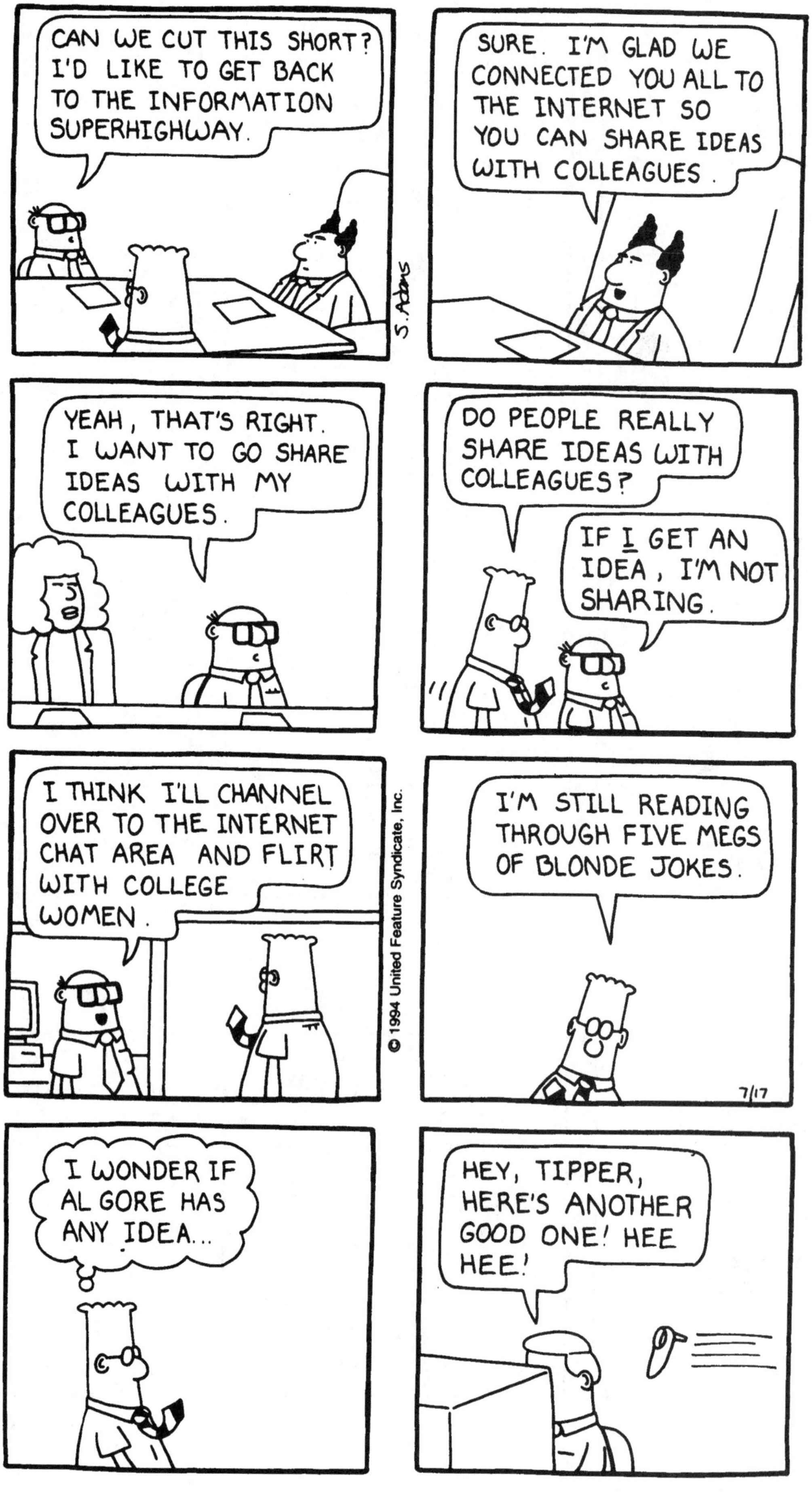
CAN WE CUT THIS SHORT? I'D LIKE TO GET BACK TO THE INFORMATION SUPERHIGHWAY.
SURE. I'M GLAD WE CONNECTED YOU ALL TO THE INTERNET SO YOU CAN SHARE IDEAS WITH COLLEAGUES.
S. Adams
YEAH, THAT'S RIGHT. I WANT TO GO SHARE IDEAS WITH MY COLLEAGUES.
DO PEOPLE REALLY SHARE IDEAS WITH COLLEAGUES?
IF I GET AN IDEA, I'M NOT SHARING.
I THINK I'LL CHANNEL OVER TO THE INTERNET CHAT AREA AND FLIRT WITH COLLEGE WOMEN.
© 1994 United Feature Syndicate, Inc.
I'M STILL READING THROUGH FIVE MEGS OF BLONDE JOKES.
7/17
I WONDER IF AL GORE HAS ANY IDEA...
HEY, TIPPER, HERE'S ANOTHER GOOD ONE! HEE HEE!

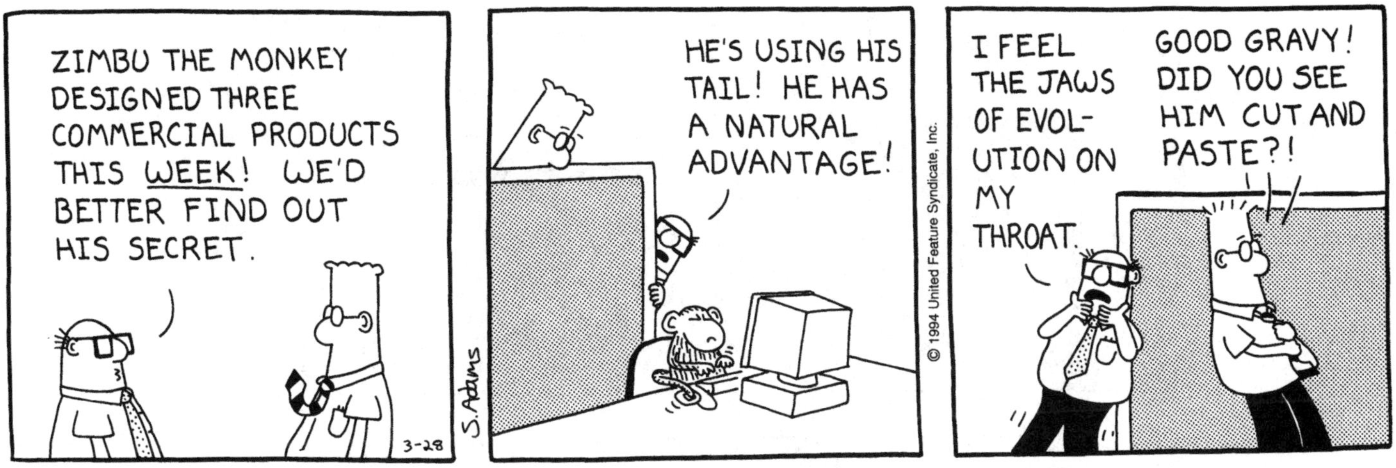
ZIMBU THE MONKEY DESIGNED THREE COMMERCIAL PRODUCTS THIS WEEK! WE'D BETTER FIND OUT HIS SECRET.
3-28
S. Adams
HE'S USING HIS TAIL! HE HAS A NATURAL ADVANTAGE!
© 1994 United Feature Syndicate, Inc.
I FEEL THE JAWS OF EVOLUTION ON MY THROAT.
GOOD GRAVY! DID YOU SEE HIM CUT AND PASTE?!

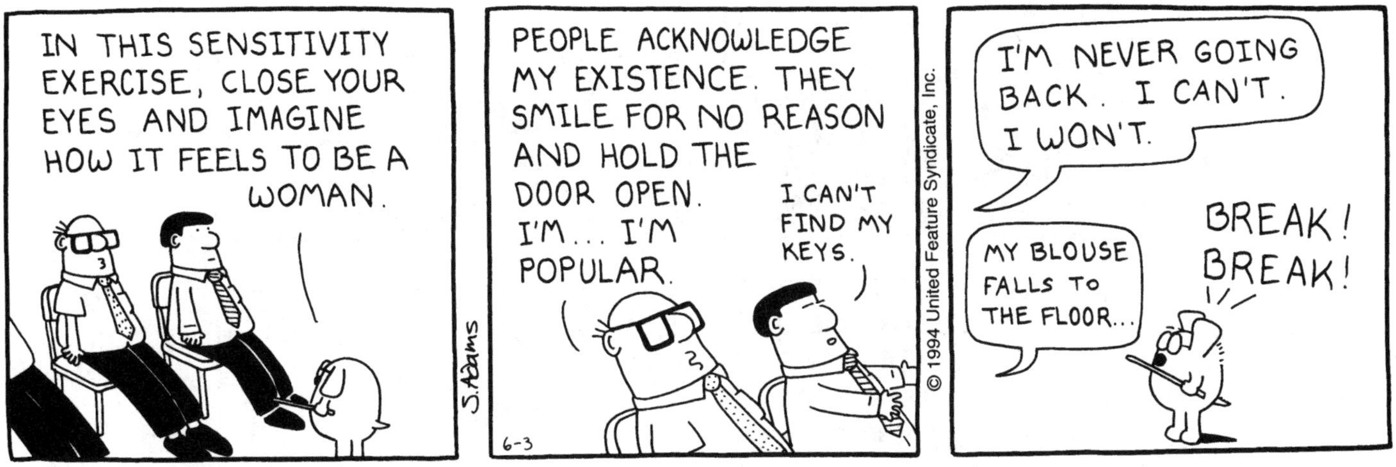
IN THIS SENSITIVITY EXERCISE, CLOSE YOUR EYES AND IMAGINE HOW IT FEELS TO BE A WOMAN.
S. Adams
PEOPLE ACKNOWLEDGE MY EXISTENCE. THEY SMILE FOR NO REASON AND HOLD THE DOOR OPEN. I'M... I'M POPULAR.
I CAN'T FIND MY KEYS.
6-3
© 1994 United Feature Syndicate, Inc.
I'M NEVER GOING BACK. I CAN'T. I WON'T.
MY BLOUSE FALLS TO THE FLOOR...
BREAK! BREAK!

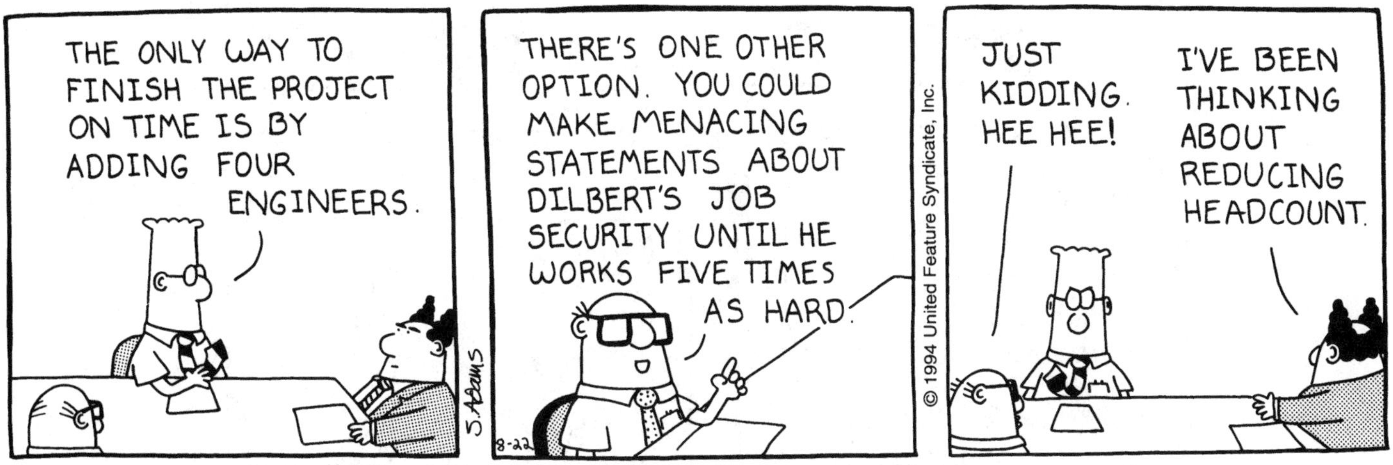
THE ONLY WAY TO FINISH THE PROJECT ON TIME IS BY ADDING FOUR ENGINEERS.
S. Adams
THERE'S ONE OTHER OPTION. YOU COULD MAKE MENACING STATEMENTS ABOUT DILBERT'S JOB SECURITY UNTIL HE WORKS FIVE TIMES AS HARD.
8-22
© 1994 United Feature Syndicate, Inc.
JUST KIDDING. HEE HEE!
I'VE BEEN THINKING ABOUT REDUCING HEADCOUNT.

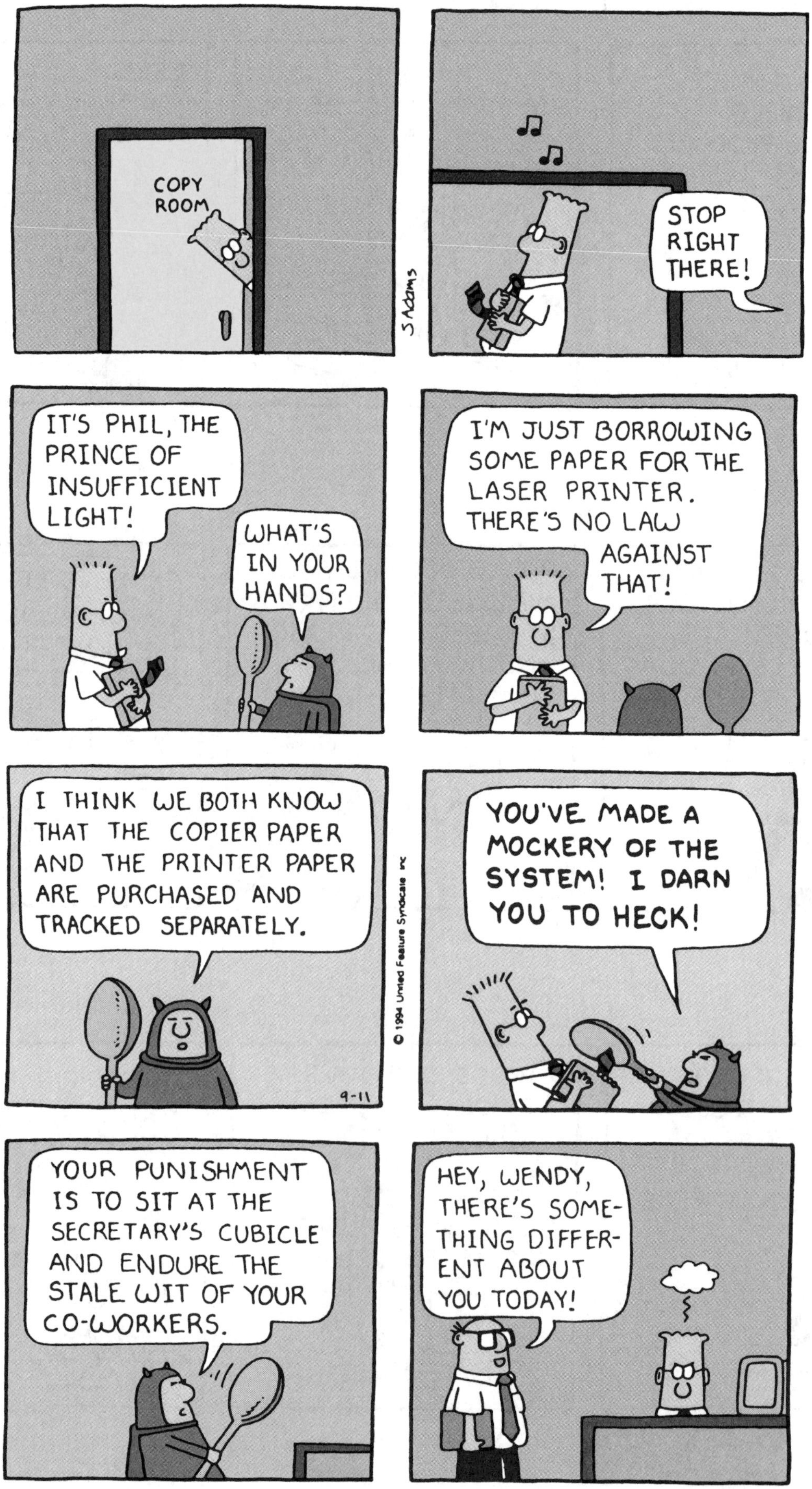
COPY ROOM
S Adams
STOP RIGHT THERE!
IT'S PHIL, THE PRINCE OF INSUFFICIENT LIGHT!
WHAT'S IN YOUR HANDS?
I'M JUST BORROWING SOME PAPER FOR THE LASER PRINTER. THERE'S NO LAW AGAINST THAT!
I THINK WE BOTH KNOW THAT THE COPIER PAPER AND THE PRINTER PAPER ARE PURCHASED AND TRACKED SEPARATELY.
© 1994 United Feature Syndicate Inc
9-11
YOU'VE MADE A MOCKERY OF THE SYSTEM! I DARN YOU TO HECK!
YOUR PUNISHMENT IS TO SIT AT THE SECRETARY'S CUBICLE AND ENDURE THE STALE WIT OF YOUR CO-WORKERS.
HEY, WENDY, THERE'S SOMETHING DIFFERENT ABOUT YOU TODAY!

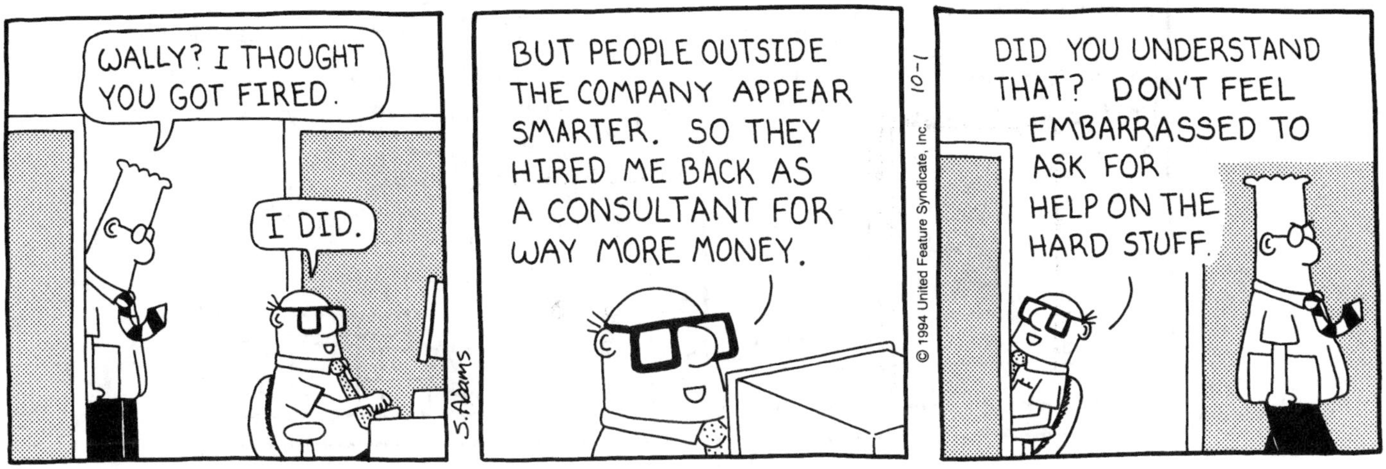
WALLY? I THOUGHT YOU GOT FIRED.
I DID.
S. Adams
BUT PEOPLE OUTSIDE THE COMPANY APPEAR SMARTER. SO THEY HIRED ME BACK AS A CONSULTANT FOR WAY MORE MONEY.
10-1
© 1994 United Feature Syndicate, Inc.
DID YOU UNDERSTAND THAT? DON'T FEEL EMBARRASSED TO ASK FOR HELP ON THE HARD STUFF.

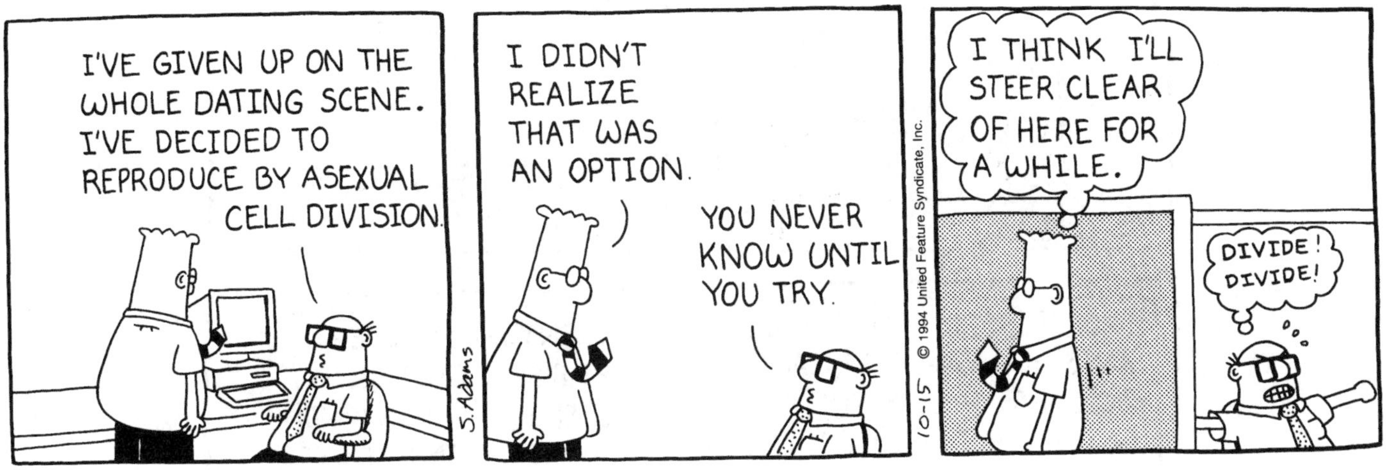
I'VE GIVEN UP ON THE WHOLE DATING SCENE. I'VE DECIDED TO REPRODUCE BY ASEXUAL CELL DIVISION.
S. Adams
I DIDN'T REALIZE THAT WAS AN OPTION.
YOU NEVER KNOW UNTIL YOU TRY.
10-15
© 1994 United Feature Syndicate, Inc.
I THINK I'LL STEER CLEAR OF HERE FOR A WHILE.
DIVIDE! DIVIDE!

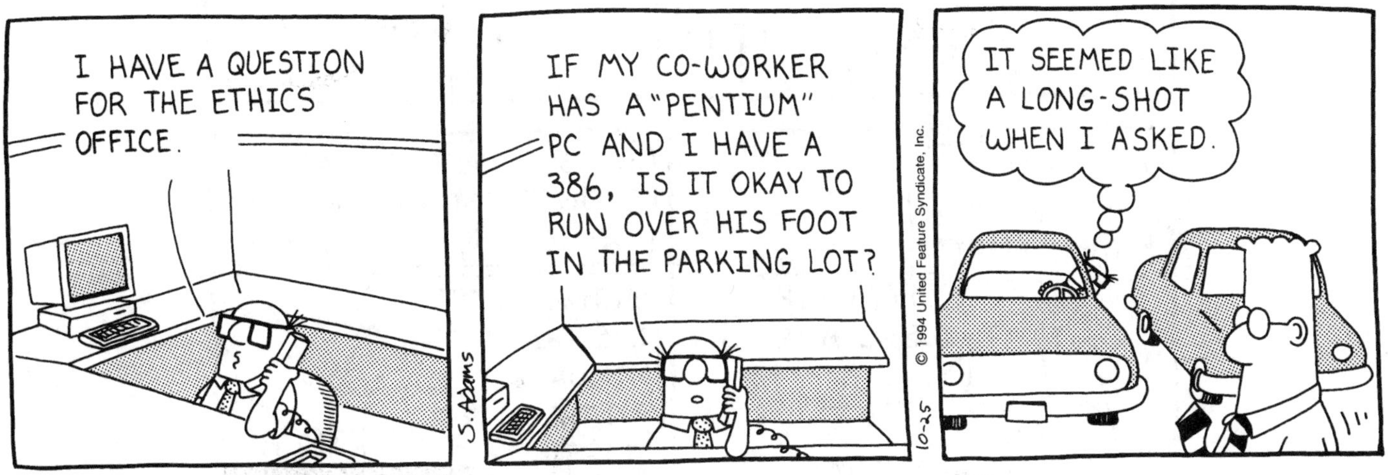
I HAVE A QUESTION FOR THE ETHICS OFFICE.
S. Adams
IF MY CO-WORKER HAS A "PENTIUM" PC AND I HAVE A 386, IS IT OKAY TO RUN OVER HIS FOOT IN THE PARKING LOT?
10-25
© 1994 United Feature Syndicate, Inc.
IT SEEMED LIKE A LONG-SHOT WHEN I ASKED.

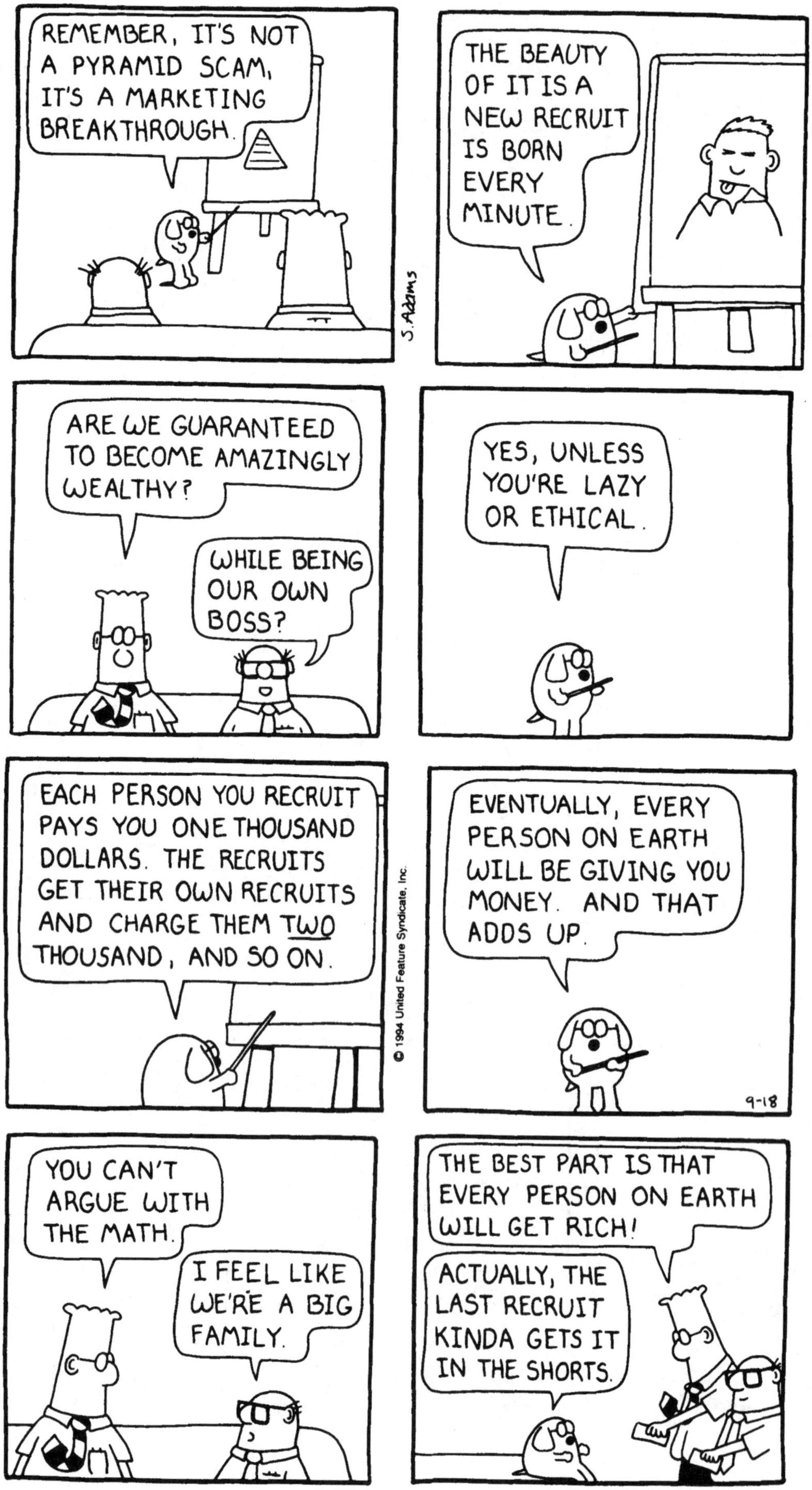
REMEMBER, IT'S NOT A PYRAMID SCAM, IT'S A MARKETING BREAKTHROUGH.
S. Adams
THE BEAUTY OF IT IS A NEW RECRUIT IS BORN EVERY MINUTE.
ARE WE GUARANTEED TO BECOME AMAZINGLY WEALTHY?
WHILE BEING OUR OWN BOSS?
YES, UNLESS YOU'RE LAZY OR ETHICAL.
EACH PERSON YOU RECRUIT PAYS YOU ONE THOUSAND DOLLARS. THE RECRUITS GET THEIR OWN RECRUITS AND CHARGE THEM TWO THOUSAND, AND SO ON.
© 1994 United Feature Syndicate, Inc.
EVENTUALLY, EVERY PERSON ON EARTH WILL BE GIVING YOU MONEY. AND THAT ADDS UP.
9-18
YOU CAN'T ARGUE WITH THE MATH.
I FEEL LIKE WE'RE A BIG FAMILY.
THE BEST PART IS THAT EVERY PERSON ON EARTH WILL GET RICH!
ACTUALLY, THE LAST RECRUIT KINDA GETS IT IN THE SHORTS.

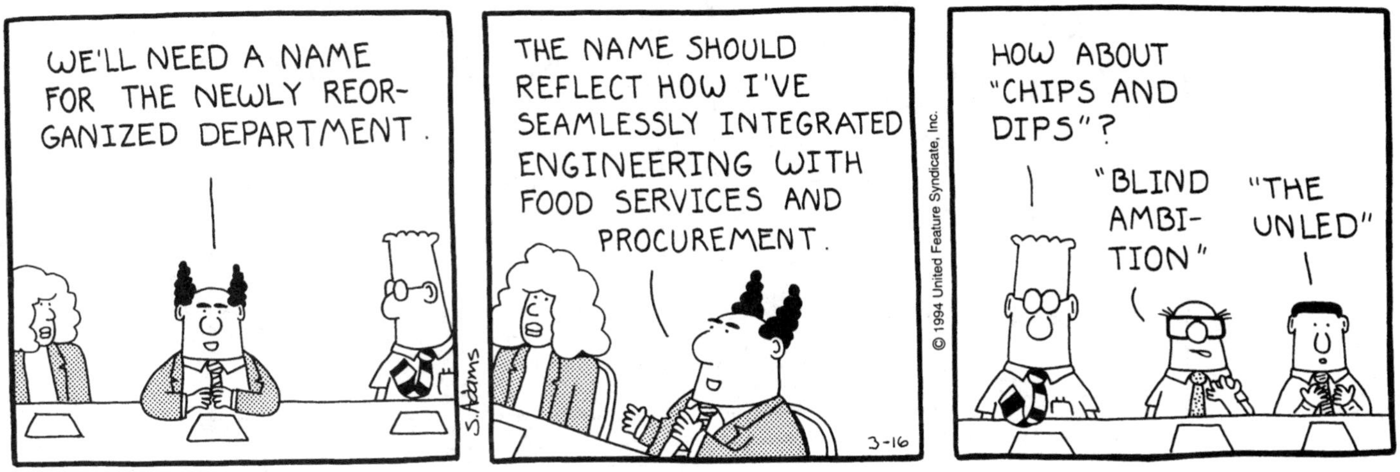
WE'LL NEED A NAME FOR THE NEWLY REORGANIZED DEPARTMENT.
THE NAME SHOULD REFLECT HOW I'VE SEAMLESSLY INTEGRATED ENGINEERING WITH FOOD SERVICES AND PROCUREMENT.
HOW ABOUT "CHIPS AND DIPS"?
"BLIND AMBITION"
"THE UNLED"
S. Adams
3-16
© 1994 United Feature Syndicate, Inc.

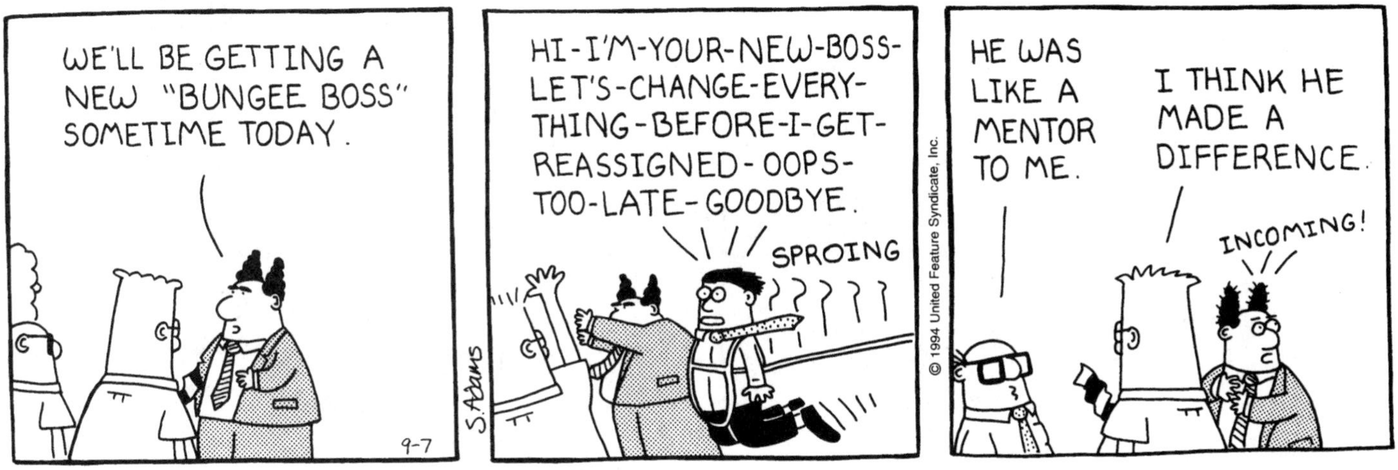
WE'LL BE GETTING A NEW "BUNGEE BOSS" SOMETIME TODAY.
9-7
HI-I'M-YOUR-NEW-BOSS-LET'S-CHANGE-EVERYTHING-BEFORE-I-GET-REASSIGNED-OOPS-TOO-LATE-GOODBYE.
SPROING
S. Adams
HE WAS LIKE A MENTOR TO ME.
I THINK HE MADE A DIFFERENCE.
INCOMING!
© 1994 United Feature Syndicate, Inc.

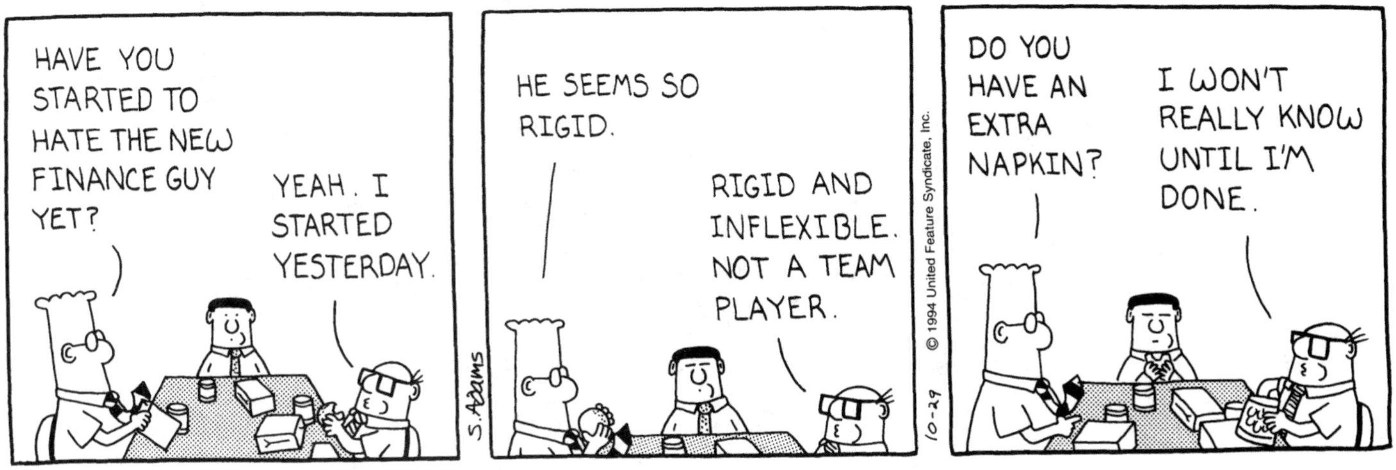
HAVE YOU STARTED TO HATE THE NEW FINANCE GUY YET?
YEAH. I STARTED YESTERDAY.
S. Adams
HE SEEMS SO RIGID.
RIGID AND INFLEXIBLE. NOT A TEAM PLAYER.
10-29
© 1994 United Feature Syndicate, Inc.
DO YOU HAVE AN EXTRA NAPKIN?
I WON'T REALLY KNOW UNTIL I'M DONE.

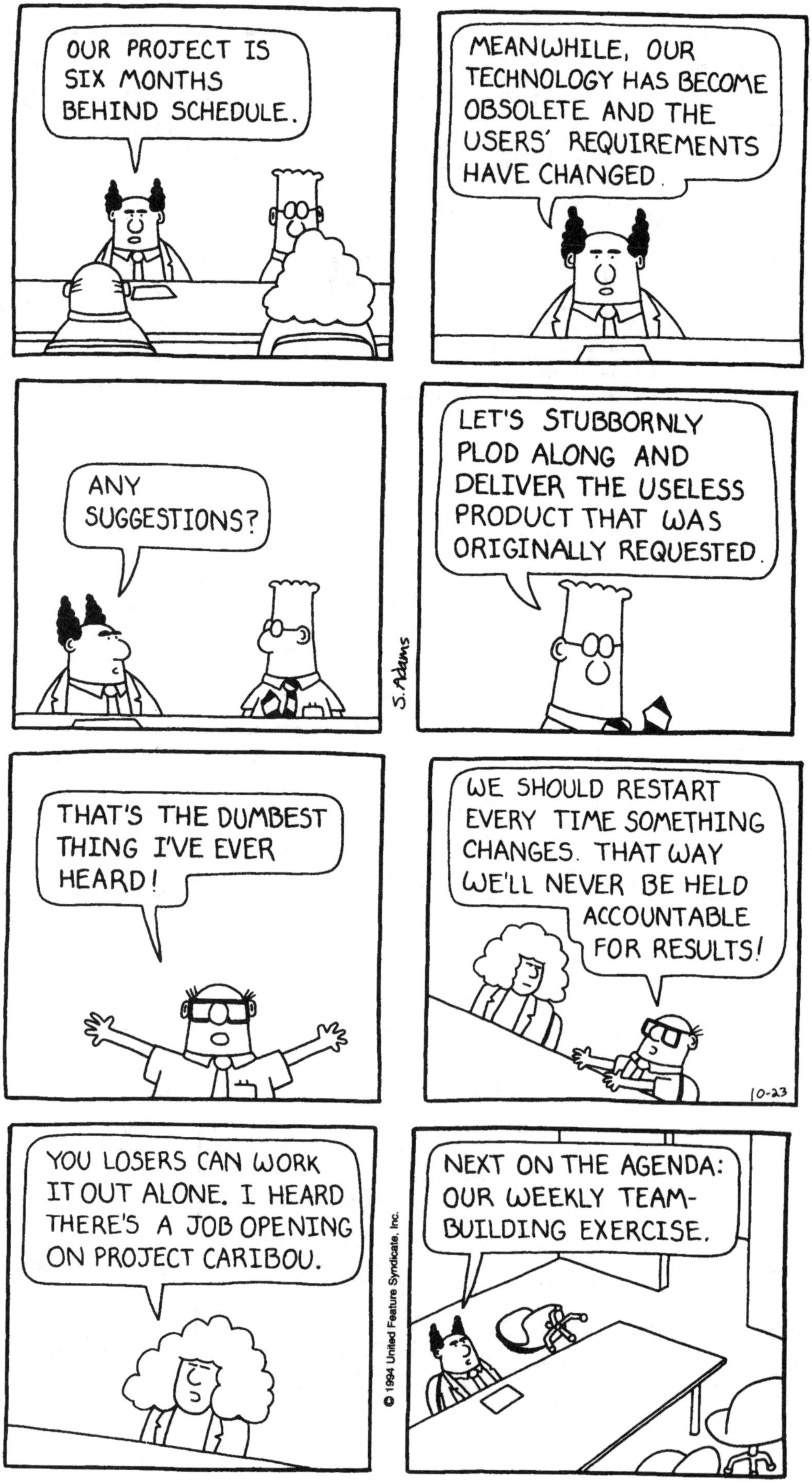
OUR PROJECT IS SIX MONTHS BEHIND SCHEDULE.
MEANWHILE, OUR TECHNOLOGY HAS BECOME OBSOLETE AND THE USERS' REQUIREMENTS HAVE CHANGED.
ANY SUGGESTIONS?
LET'S STUBBORNLY PLOD ALONG AND DELIVER THE USELESS PRODUCT THAT WAS ORIGINALLY REQUESTED.
S. Adams
THAT'S THE DUMBEST THING I'VE EVER HEARD!
WE SHOULD RESTART EVERY TIME SOMETHING CHANGES. THAT WAY WE'LL NEVER BE HELD ACCOUNTABLE FOR RESULTS!
10-23
YOU LOSERS CAN WORK IT OUT ALONE. I HEARD THERE'S A JOB OPENING ON PROJECT CARIBOU.
© 1994 United Feature Syndicate, Inc.
NEXT ON THE AGENDA: OUR WEEKLY TEAM-BUILDING EXERCISE.

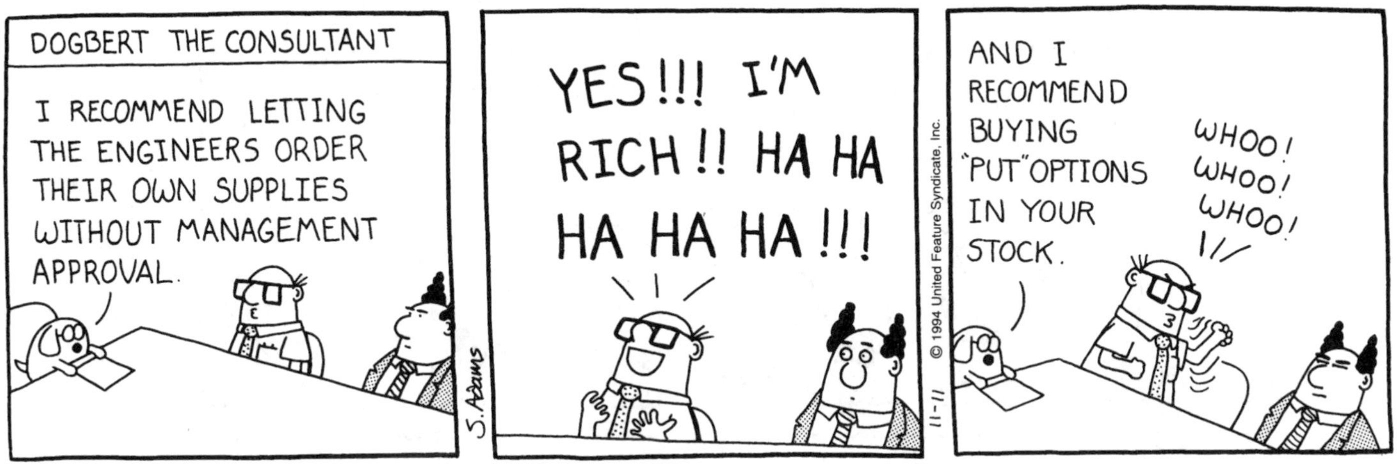
DOGBERT THE CONSULTANT
I RECOMMEND LETTING THE ENGINEERS ORDER THEIR OWN SUPPLIES WITHOUT MANAGEMENT APPROVAL.
S. ADAMS
YES!!! I'M RICH!! HA HA HA HA HA!!!
11-11 © 1994 United Feature Syndicate, Inc.
AND I RECOMMEND BUYING "PUT" OPTIONS IN YOUR STOCK.
WHOO! WHOO! WHOO!

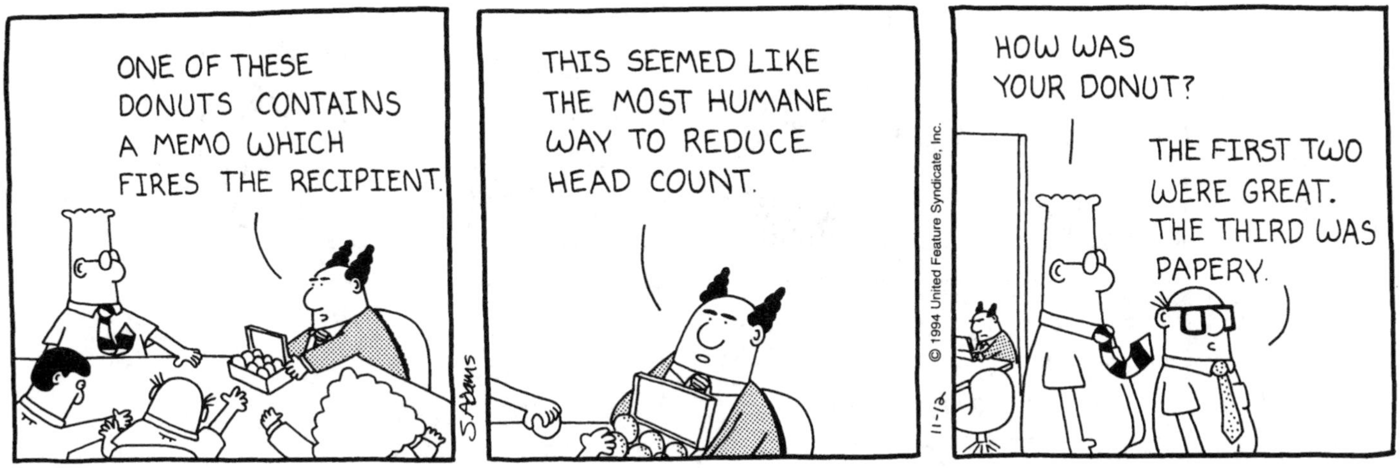
ONE OF THESE DONUTS CONTAINS A MEMO WHICH FIRES THE RECIPIENT.
S. ADAMS
THIS SEEMED LIKE THE MOST HUMANE WAY TO REDUCE HEAD COUNT.
11-12 © 1994 United Feature Syndicate, Inc.
HOW WAS YOUR DONUT?
THE FIRST TWO WERE GREAT. THE THIRD WAS PAPERY.

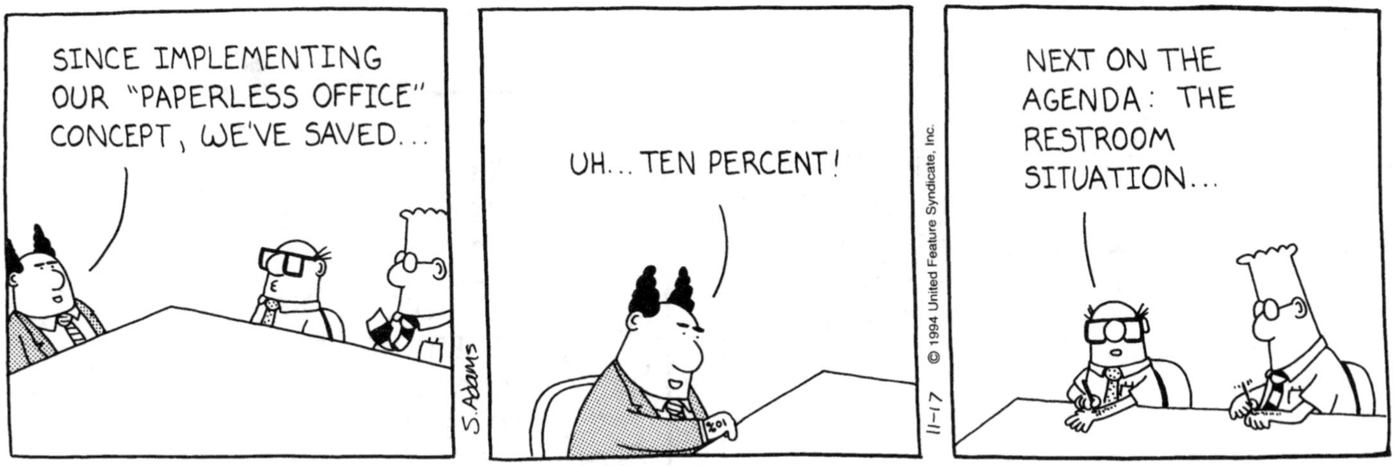
SINCE IMPLEMENTING OUR "PAPERLESS OFFICE" CONCEPT, WE'VE SAVED...
S. ADAMS
UH... TEN PERCENT!
11-17 © 1994 United Feature Syndicate, Inc.
NEXT ON THE AGENDA: THE RESTROOM SITUATION...

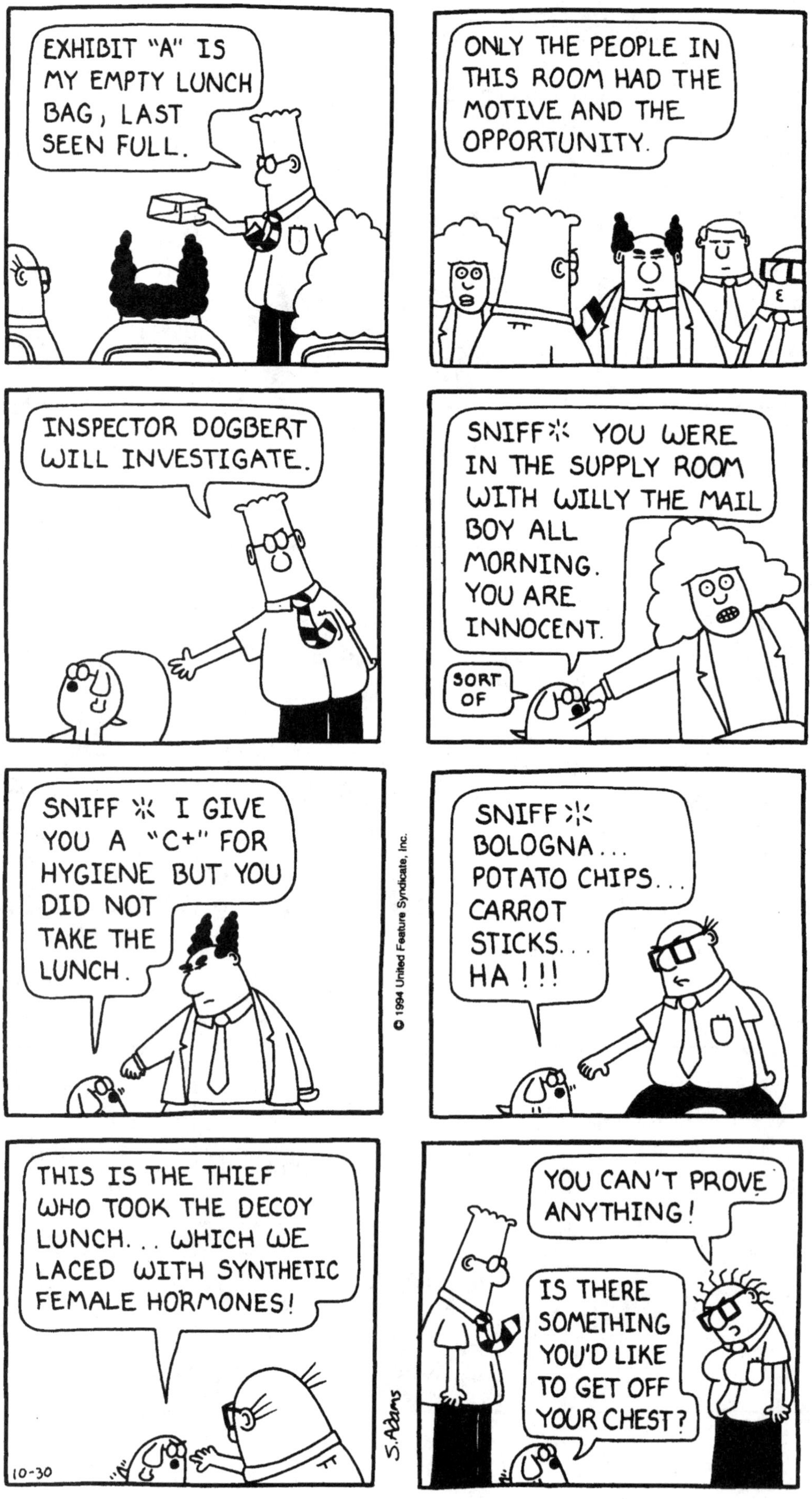
EXHIBIT "A" IS MY EMPTY LUNCH BAG, LAST SEEN FULL.
ONLY THE PEOPLE IN THIS ROOM HAD THE MOTIVE AND THE OPPORTUNITY.
INSPECTOR DOGBERT WILL INVESTIGATE.
SNIFF ⁘ YOU WERE IN THE SUPPLY ROOM WITH WILLY THE MAIL BOY ALL MORNING. YOU ARE INNOCENT.
SORT OF
SNIFF ⁘ I GIVE YOU A "C+" FOR HYGIENE BUT YOU DID NOT TAKE THE LUNCH.
© 1994 United Feature Syndicate, Inc.
SNIFF ⁘ BOLOGNA... POTATO CHIPS... CARROT STICKS... HA!!!
THIS IS THE THIEF WHO TOOK THE DECOY LUNCH... WHICH WE LACED WITH SYNTHETIC FEMALE HORMONES!
10-30
S. Adams
YOU CAN'T PROVE ANYTHING!
IS THERE SOMETHING YOU'D LIKE TO GET OFF YOUR CHEST?

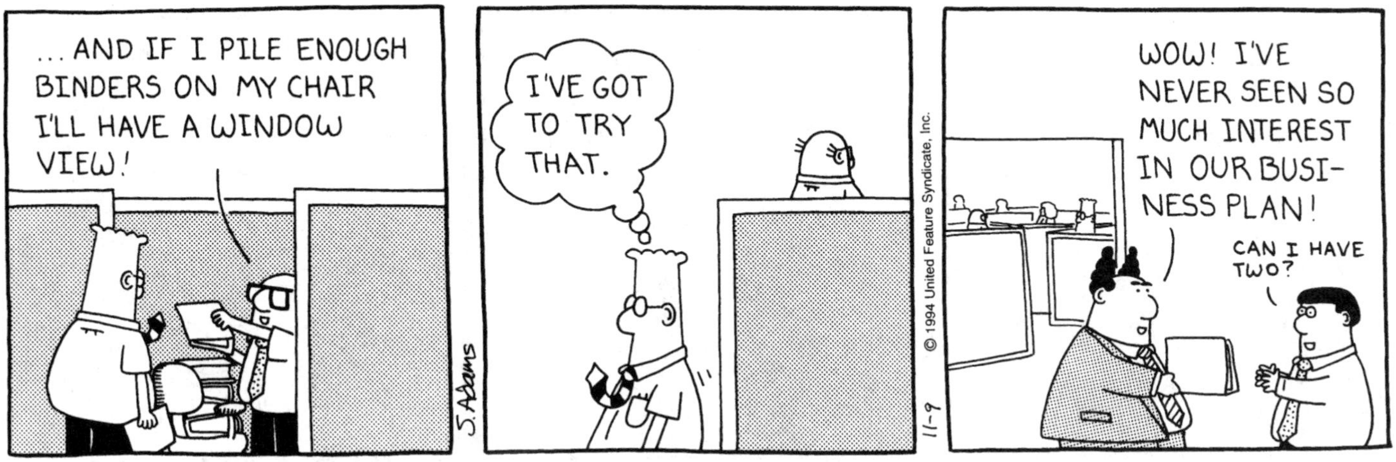
... AND IF I PILE ENOUGH BINDERS ON MY CHAIR I'LL HAVE A WINDOW VIEW!
I'VE GOT TO TRY THAT.
S. Adams
11-9
© 1994 United Feature Syndicate, Inc.
WOW! I'VE NEVER SEEN SO MUCH INTEREST IN OUR BUSINESS PLAN!
CAN I HAVE TWO?

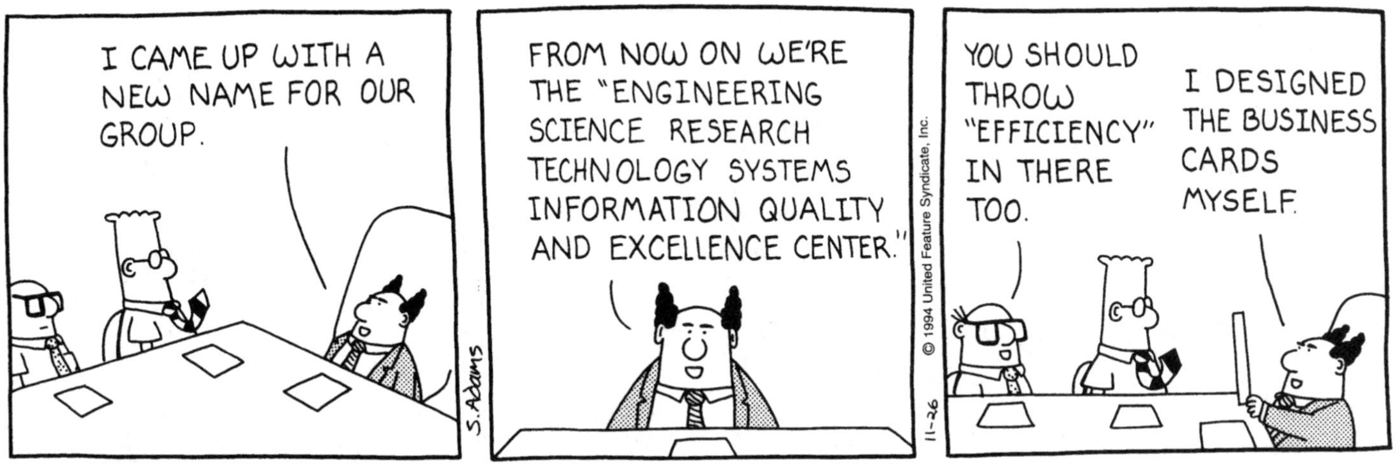
I CAME UP WITH A NEW NAME FOR OUR GROUP.
S. Adams
FROM NOW ON WE'RE THE "ENGINEERING SCIENCE RESEARCH TECHNOLOGY SYSTEMS INFORMATION QUALITY AND EXCELLENCE CENTER."
11-26
© 1994 United Feature Syndicate, Inc.
YOU SHOULD THROW "EFFICIENCY" IN THERE TOO.
I DESIGNED THE BUSINESS CARDS MYSELF.

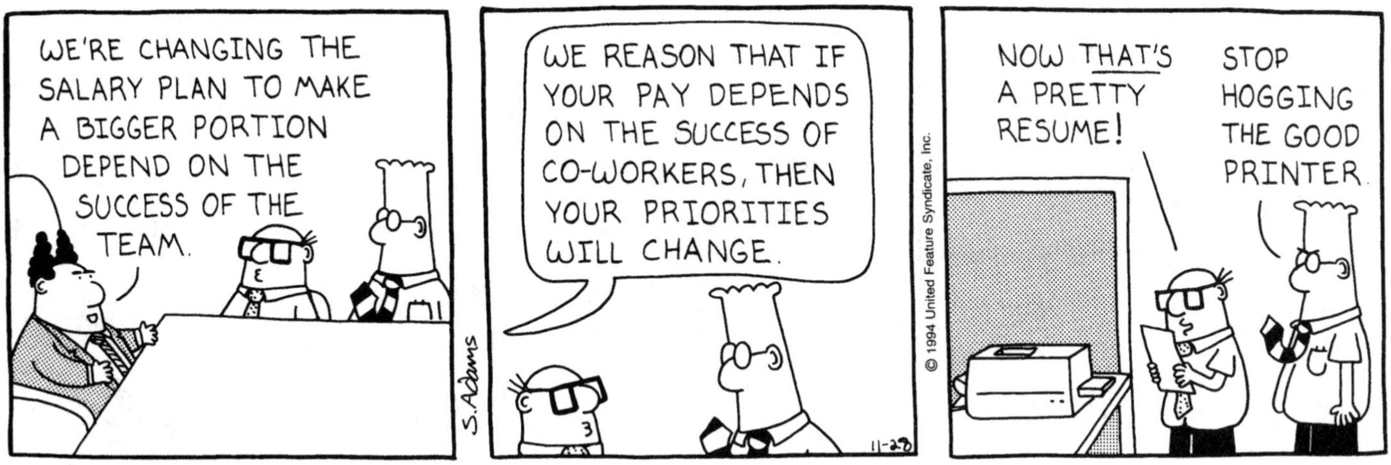
WE'RE CHANGING THE SALARY PLAN TO MAKE A BIGGER PORTION DEPEND ON THE SUCCESS OF THE TEAM.
S. Adams
WE REASON THAT IF YOUR PAY DEPENDS ON THE SUCCESS OF CO-WORKERS, THEN YOUR PRIORITIES WILL CHANGE.
11-28
© 1994 United Feature Syndicate, Inc.
NOW THAT'S A PRETTY RESUME!
STOP HOGGING THE GOOD PRINTER.

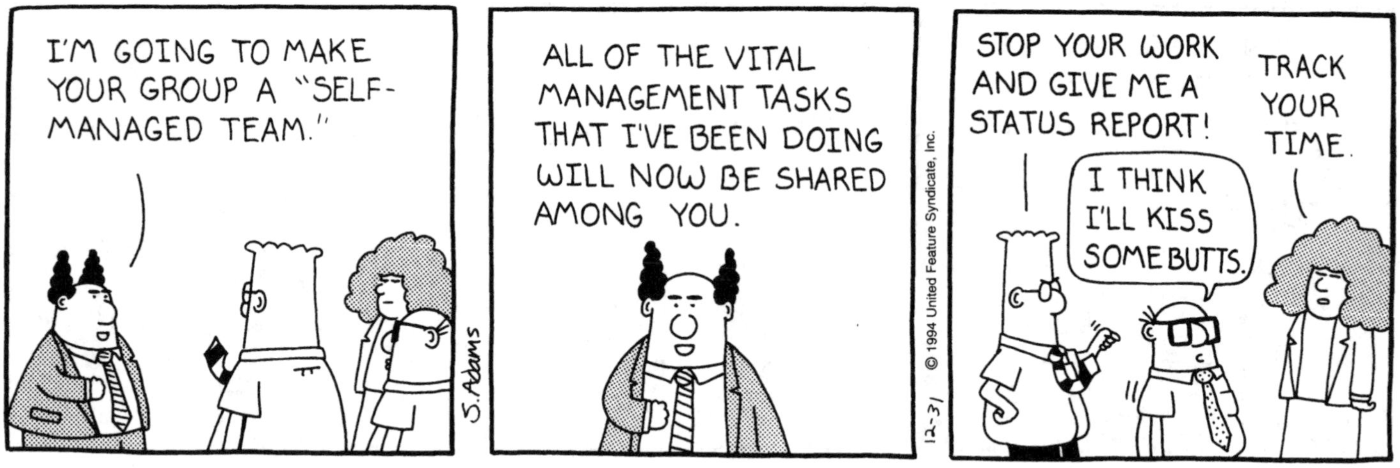
I'M GOING TO MAKE YOUR GROUP A "SELF-MANAGED TEAM."
S. Adams
ALL OF THE VITAL MANAGEMENT TASKS THAT I'VE BEEN DOING WILL NOW BE SHARED AMONG YOU.
© 1994 United Feature Syndicate, Inc.
12-31
STOP YOUR WORK AND GIVE ME A STATUS REPORT!
I THINK I'LL KISS SOME BUTTS.
TRACK YOUR TIME.

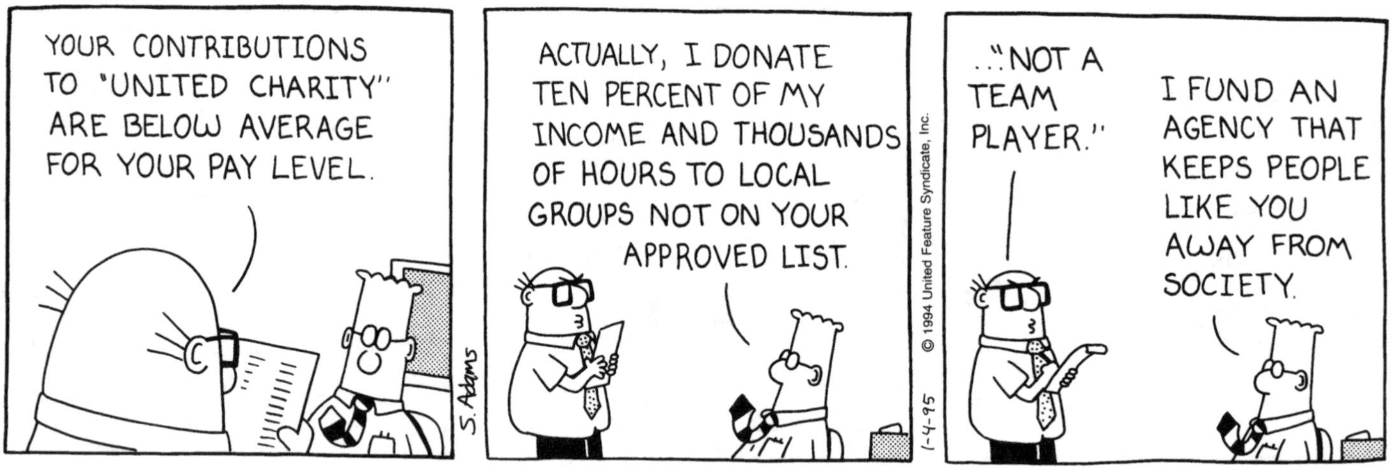
YOUR CONTRIBUTIONS TO "UNITED CHARITY" ARE BELOW AVERAGE FOR YOUR PAY LEVEL.
S. Adams
ACTUALLY, I DONATE TEN PERCENT OF MY INCOME AND THOUSANDS OF HOURS TO LOCAL GROUPS NOT ON YOUR APPROVED LIST.
© 1994 United Feature Syndicate, Inc.
1-4-95
..."NOT A TEAM PLAYER."
I FUND AN AGENCY THAT KEEPS PEOPLE LIKE YOU AWAY FROM SOCIETY.

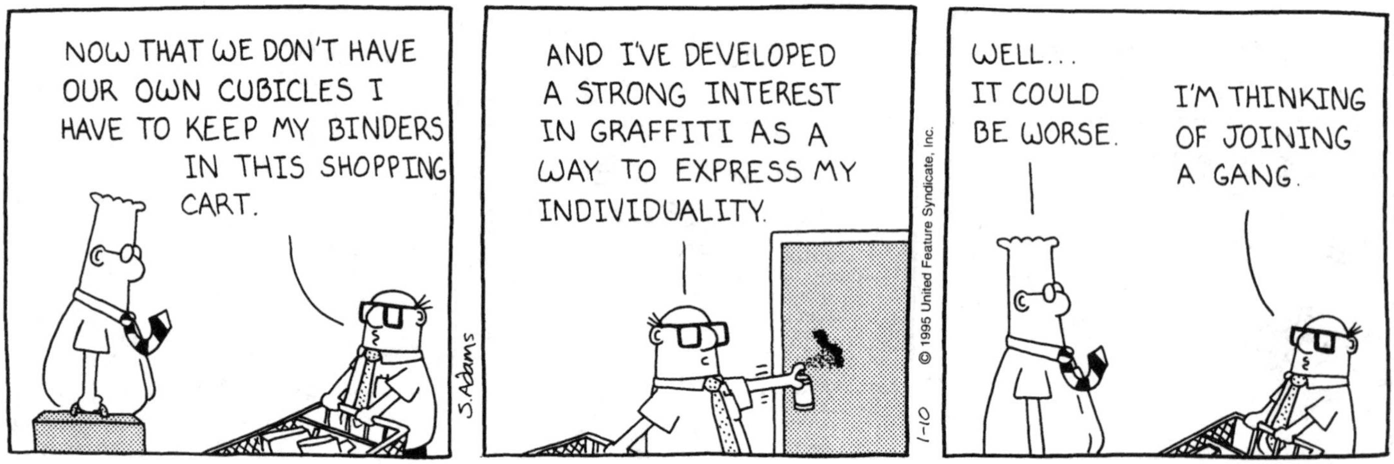
NOW THAT WE DON'T HAVE OUR OWN CUBICLES I HAVE TO KEEP MY BINDERS IN THIS SHOPPING CART.
S. Adams
AND I'VE DEVELOPED A STRONG INTEREST IN GRAFFITI AS A WAY TO EXPRESS MY INDIVIDUALITY.
© 1995 United Feature Syndicate, Inc.
1-10
WELL... IT COULD BE WORSE.
I'M THINKING OF JOINING A GANG.

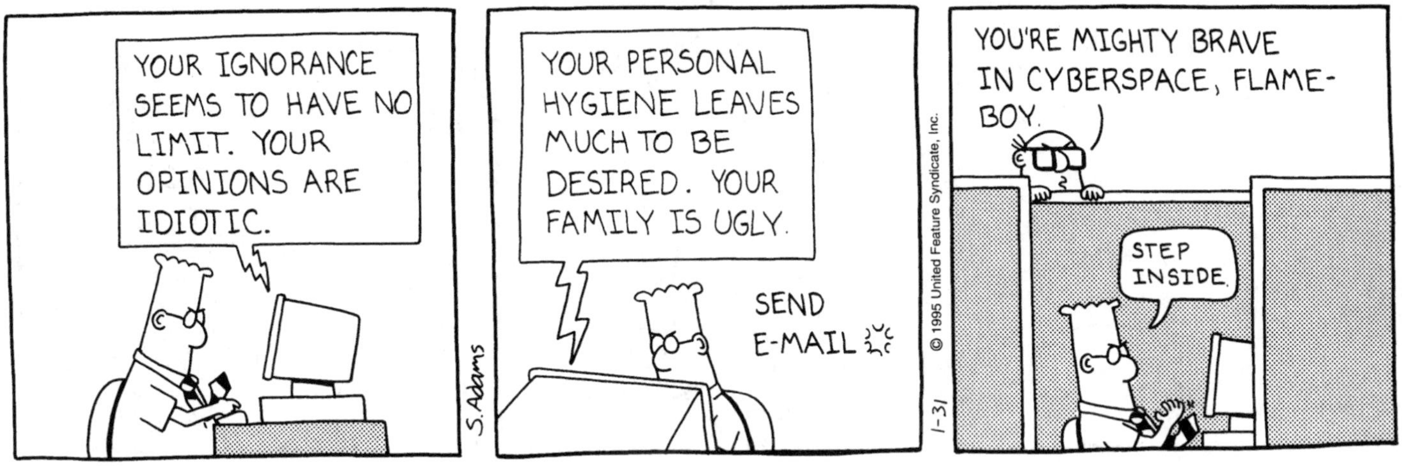
YOUR IGNORANCE SEEMS TO HAVE NO LIMIT. YOUR OPINIONS ARE IDIOTIC.
S. Adams
YOUR PERSONAL HYGIENE LEAVES MUCH TO BE DESIRED. YOUR FAMILY IS UGLY.
SEND E-MAIL
1-31 © 1995 United Feature Syndicate, Inc.
YOU'RE MIGHTY BRAVE IN CYBERSPACE, FLAME-BOY.
STEP INSIDE.

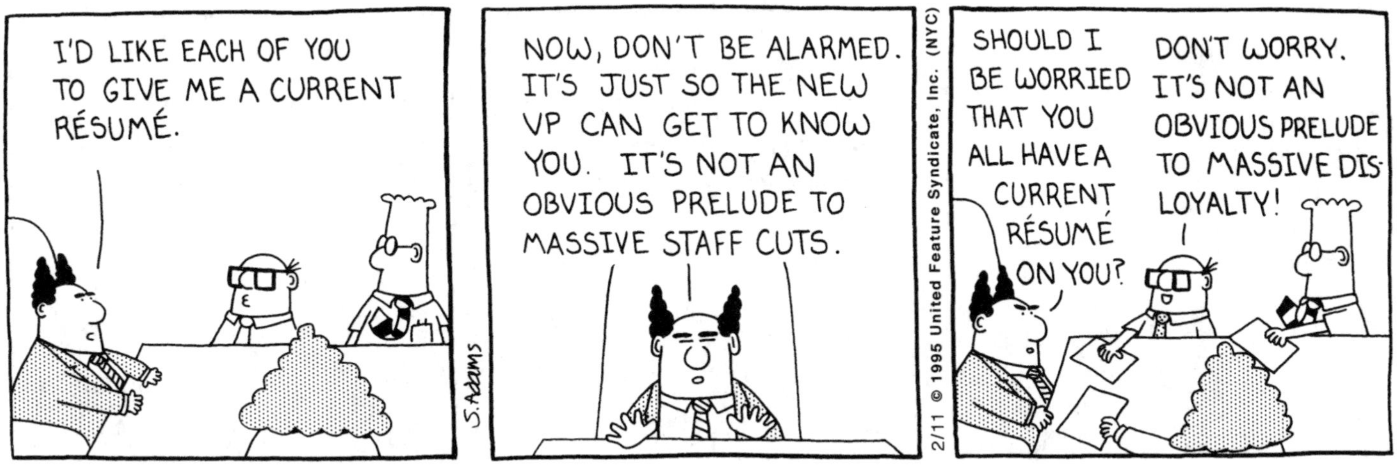
I'D LIKE EACH OF YOU TO GIVE ME A CURRENT RÉSUMÉ.
S. Adams
NOW, DON'T BE ALARMED. IT'S JUST SO THE NEW VP CAN GET TO KNOW YOU. IT'S NOT AN OBVIOUS PRELUDE TO MASSIVE STAFF CUTS.
2/11 © 1995 United Feature Syndicate, Inc. (NYC)
SHOULD I BE WORRIED THAT YOU ALL HAVE A CURRENT RÉSUMÉ ON YOU?
DON'T WORRY. IT'S NOT AN OBVIOUS PRELUDE TO MASSIVE DIS-LOYALTY!

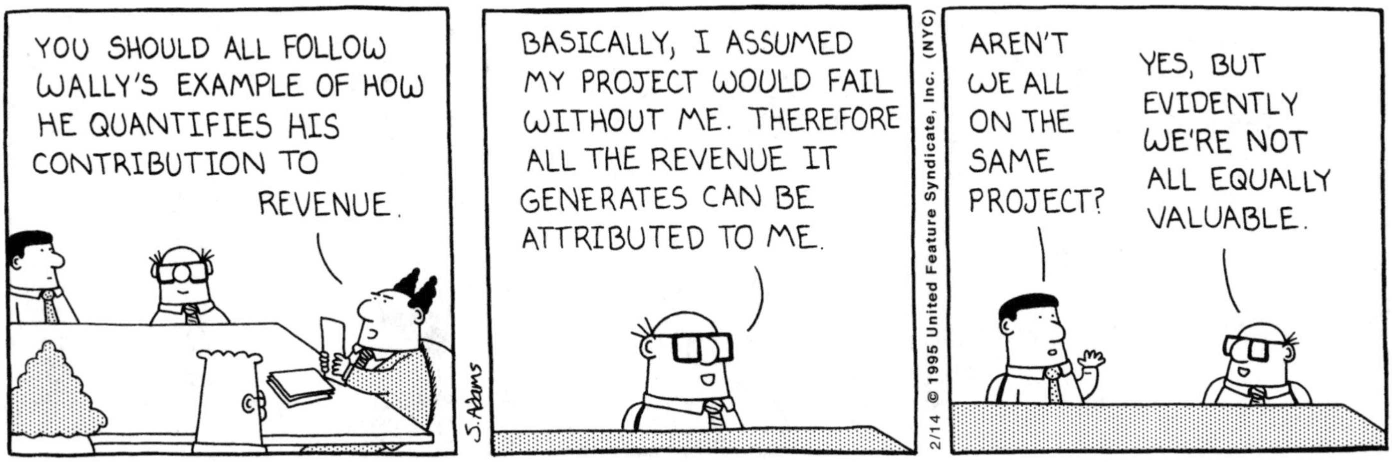
YOU SHOULD ALL FOLLOW WALLY'S EXAMPLE OF HOW HE QUANTIFIES HIS CONTRIBUTION TO REVENUE.
S. Adams
BASICALLY, I ASSUMED MY PROJECT WOULD FAIL WITHOUT ME. THEREFORE ALL THE REVENUE IT GENERATES CAN BE ATTRIBUTED TO ME.
2/14 © 1995 United Feature Syndicate, Inc. (NYC)
AREN'T WE ALL ON THE SAME PROJECT?
YES, BUT EVIDENTLY WE'RE NOT ALL EQUALLY VALUABLE.

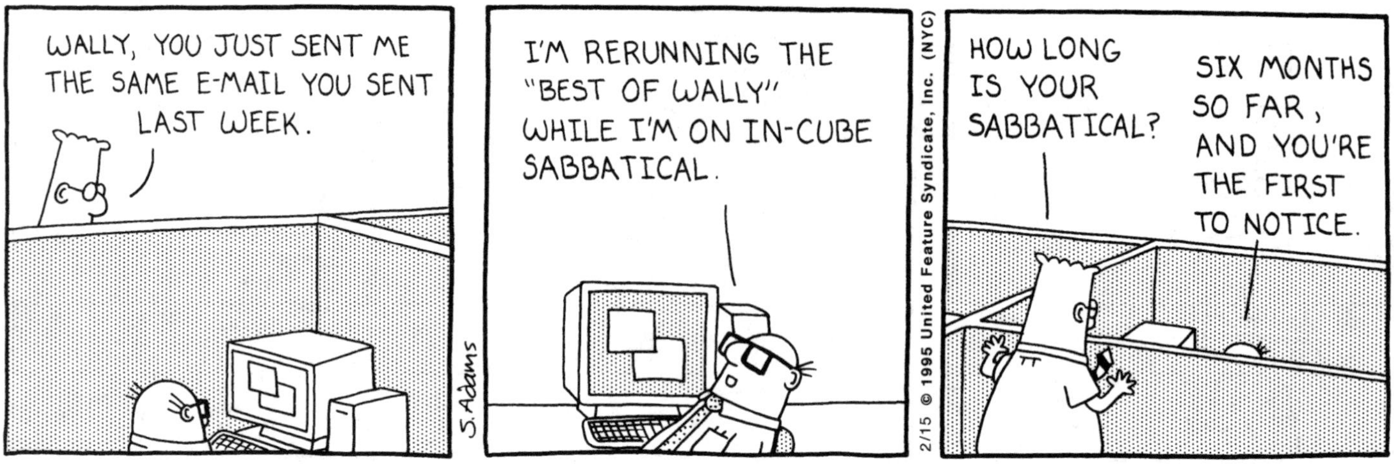
WALLY, YOU JUST SENT ME THE SAME E-MAIL YOU SENT LAST WEEK.
I'M RERUNNING THE "BEST OF WALLY" WHILE I'M ON IN-CUBE SABBATICAL.
HOW LONG IS YOUR SABBATICAL?
SIX MONTHS SO FAR, AND YOU'RE THE FIRST TO NOTICE.
S. Adams
2/15 © 1995 United Feature Syndicate, Inc. (NYC)

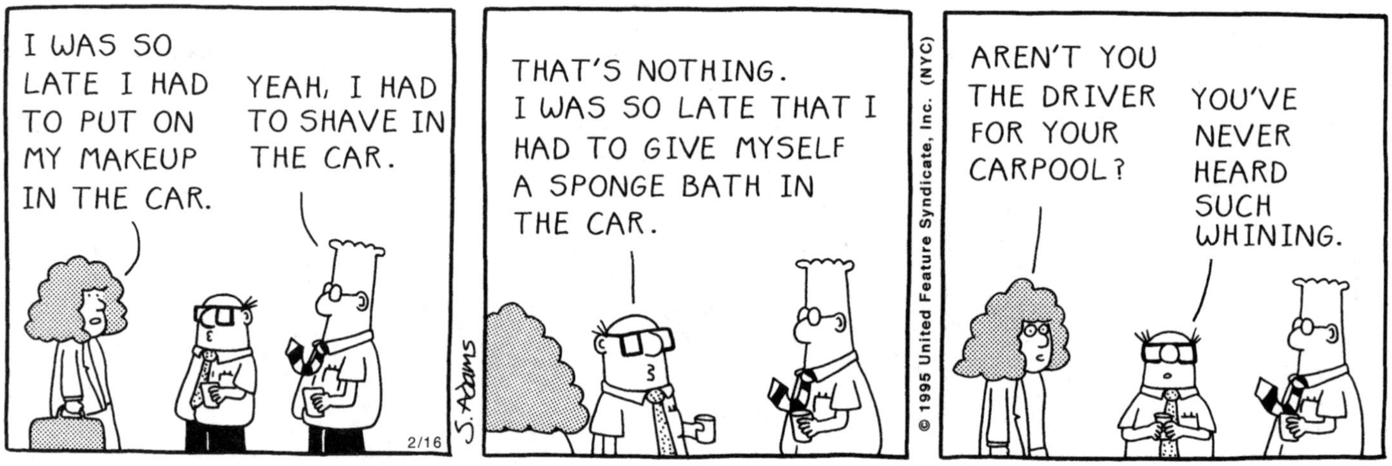
I WAS SO LATE I HAD TO PUT ON MY MAKEUP IN THE CAR.
YEAH, I HAD TO SHAVE IN THE CAR.
2/16
S. Adams
THAT'S NOTHING. I WAS SO LATE THAT I HAD TO GIVE MYSELF A SPONGE BATH IN THE CAR.
© 1995 United Feature Syndicate, Inc. (NYC)
AREN'T YOU THE DRIVER FOR YOUR CARPOOL?
YOU'VE NEVER HEARD SUCH WHINING.

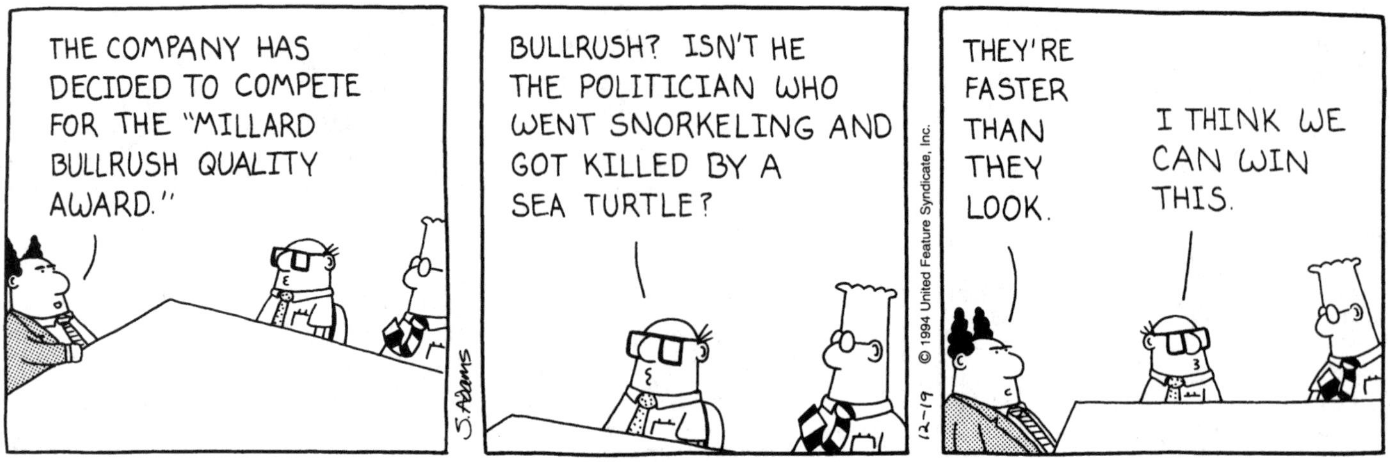
THE COMPANY HAS DECIDED TO COMPETE FOR THE "MILLARD BULLRUSH QUALITY AWARD."
S. Adams
BULLRUSH? ISN'T HE THE POLITICIAN WHO WENT SNORKELING AND GOT KILLED BY A SEA TURTLE?
12-19 © 1994 United Feature Syndicate, Inc.
THEY'RE FASTER THAN THEY LOOK.
I THINK WE CAN WIN THIS.

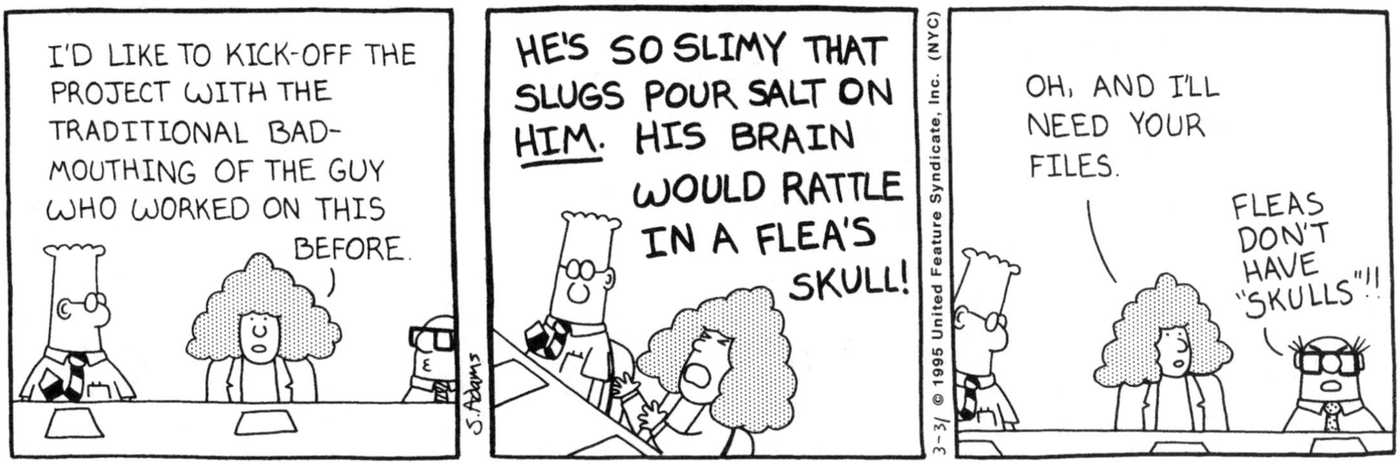
I'D LIKE TO KICK-OFF THE PROJECT WITH THE TRADITIONAL BAD-MOUTHING OF THE GUY WHO WORKED ON THIS BEFORE.
HE'S SO SLIMY THAT SLUGS POUR SALT ON HIM. HIS BRAIN WOULD RATTLE IN A FLEA'S SKULL!
OH, AND I'LL NEED YOUR FILES.
FLEAS DON'T HAVE "SKULLS"!!
S. Adams
3-31 © 1995 United Feature Syndicate, Inc. (NYC)

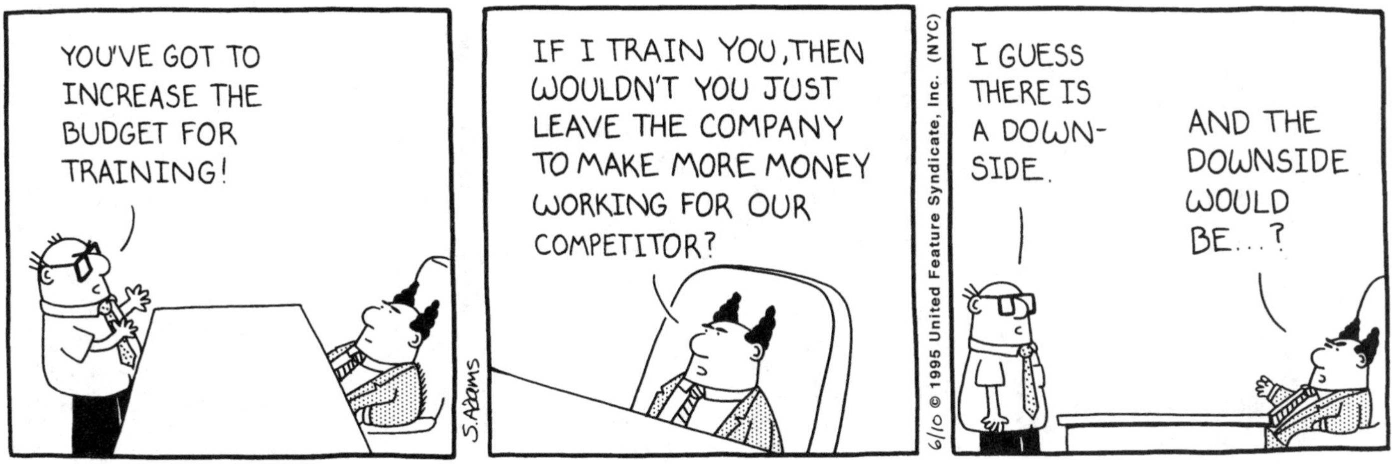
YOU'VE GOT TO INCREASE THE BUDGET FOR TRAINING!
IF I TRAIN YOU, THEN WOULDN'T YOU JUST LEAVE THE COMPANY TO MAKE MORE MONEY WORKING FOR OUR COMPETITOR?
I GUESS THERE IS A DOWN-SIDE.
AND THE DOWNSIDE WOULD BE...?
S. Adams
6/10 © 1995 United Feature Syndicate, Inc. (NYC)

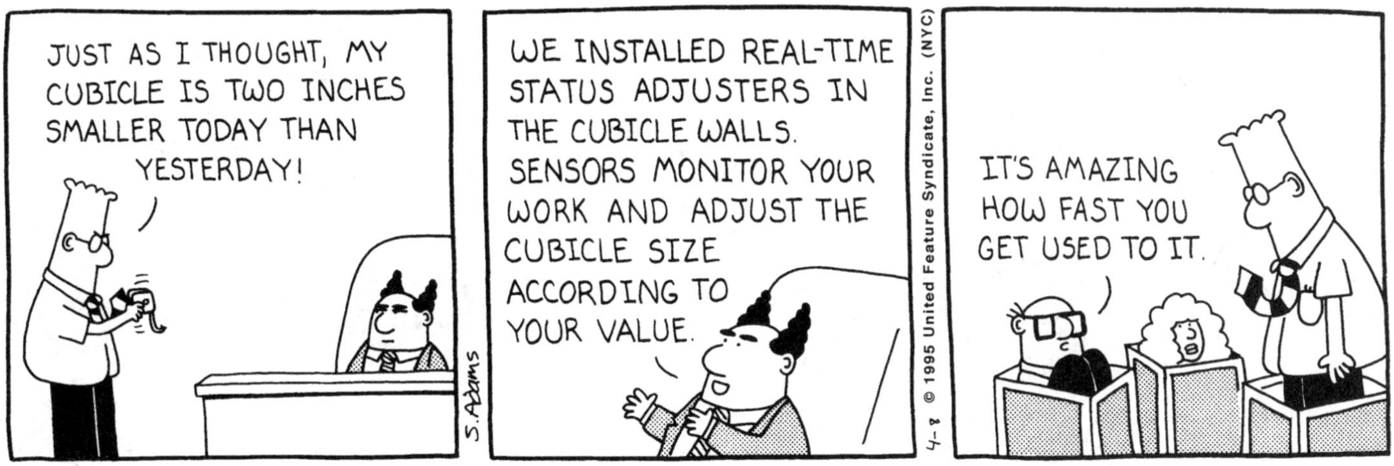
JUST AS I THOUGHT, MY CUBICLE IS TWO INCHES SMALLER TODAY THAN YESTERDAY!
WE INSTALLED REAL-TIME STATUS ADJUSTERS IN THE CUBICLE WALLS. SENSORS MONITOR YOUR WORK AND ADJUST THE CUBICLE SIZE ACCORDING TO YOUR VALUE.
IT'S AMAZING HOW FAST YOU GET USED TO IT.
S. Adams
4-8 © 1995 United Feature Syndicate, Inc. (NYC)

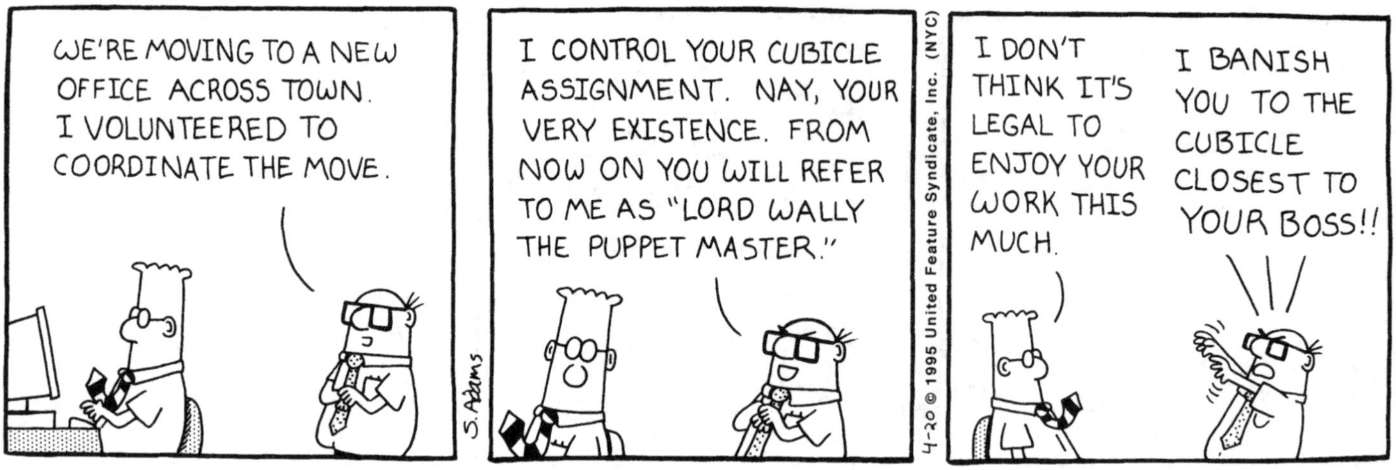
WE'RE MOVING TO A NEW OFFICE ACROSS TOWN. I VOLUNTEERED TO COORDINATE THE MOVE.
S. Adams
I CONTROL YOUR CUBICLE ASSIGNMENT. NAY, YOUR VERY EXISTENCE. FROM NOW ON YOU WILL REFER TO ME AS "LORD WALLY THE PUPPET MASTER."
4-20 © 1995 United Feature Syndicate, Inc. (NYC)
I DON'T THINK IT'S LEGAL TO ENJOY YOUR WORK THIS MUCH.
I BANISH YOU TO THE CUBICLE CLOSEST TO YOUR BOSS!!

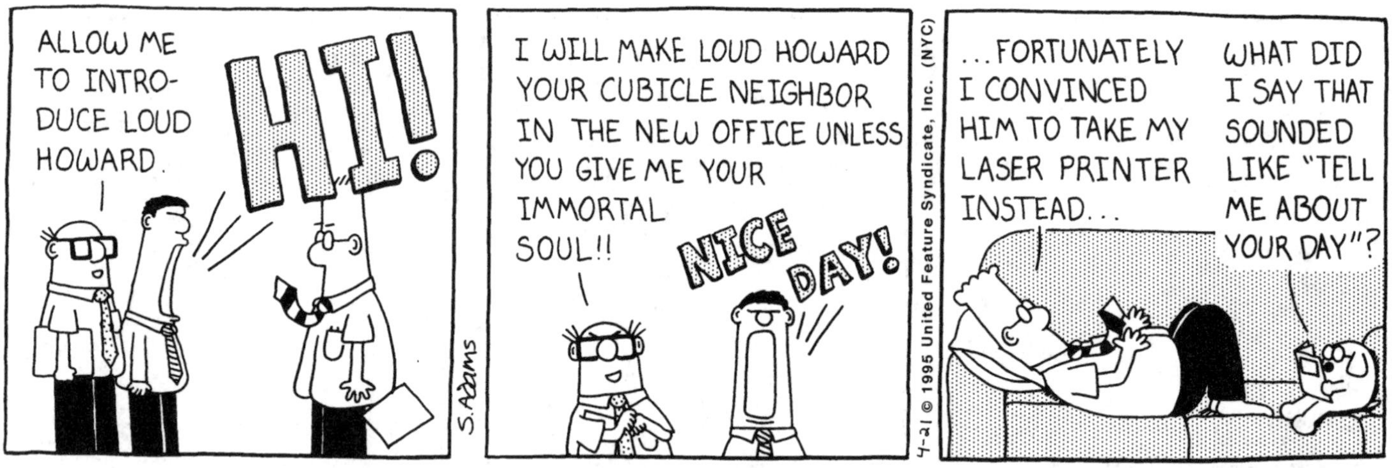
ALLOW ME TO INTRO-DUCE LOUD HOWARD.
HI!
S. Adams
I WILL MAKE LOUD HOWARD YOUR CUBICLE NEIGHBOR IN THE NEW OFFICE UNLESS YOU GIVE ME YOUR IMMORTAL SOUL!!
NICE DAY!
4-21 © 1995 United Feature Syndicate, Inc. (NYC)
...FORTUNATELY I CONVINCED HIM TO TAKE MY LASER PRINTER INSTEAD...
WHAT DID I SAY THAT SOUNDED LIKE "TELL ME ABOUT YOUR DAY"?

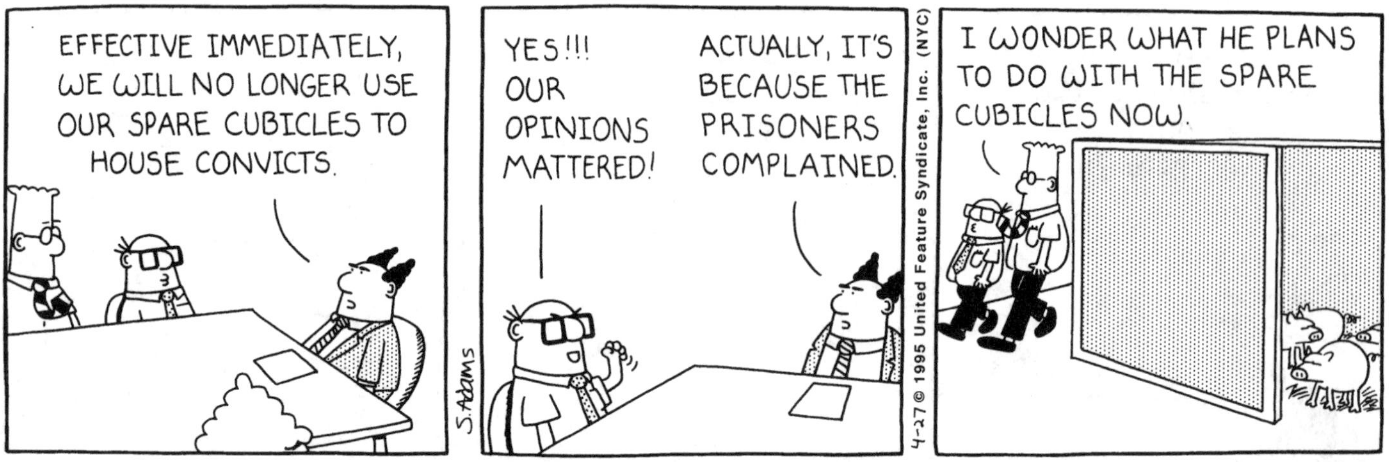
EFFECTIVE IMMEDIATELY, WE WILL NO LONGER USE OUR SPARE CUBICLES TO HOUSE CONVICTS.
S. Adams
YES!!! OUR OPINIONS MATTERED!
ACTUALLY, IT'S BECAUSE THE PRISONERS COMPLAINED.
4-27 © 1995 United Feature Syndicate, Inc. (NYC)
I WONDER WHAT HE PLANS TO DO WITH THE SPARE CUBICLES NOW.

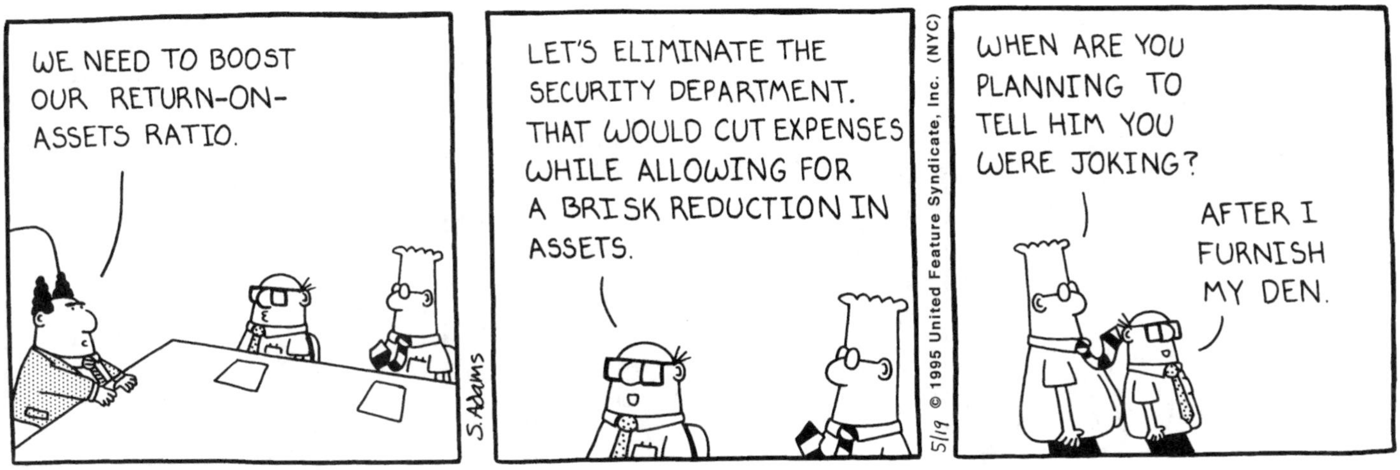
WE NEED TO BOOST OUR RETURN-ON-ASSETS RATIO.
S. Adams
LET'S ELIMINATE THE SECURITY DEPARTMENT. THAT WOULD CUT EXPENSES WHILE ALLOWING FOR A BRISK REDUCTION IN ASSETS.
5/19 © 1995 United Feature Syndicate, Inc. (NYC)
WHEN ARE YOU PLANNING TO TELL HIM YOU WERE JOKING?
AFTER I FURNISH MY DEN.

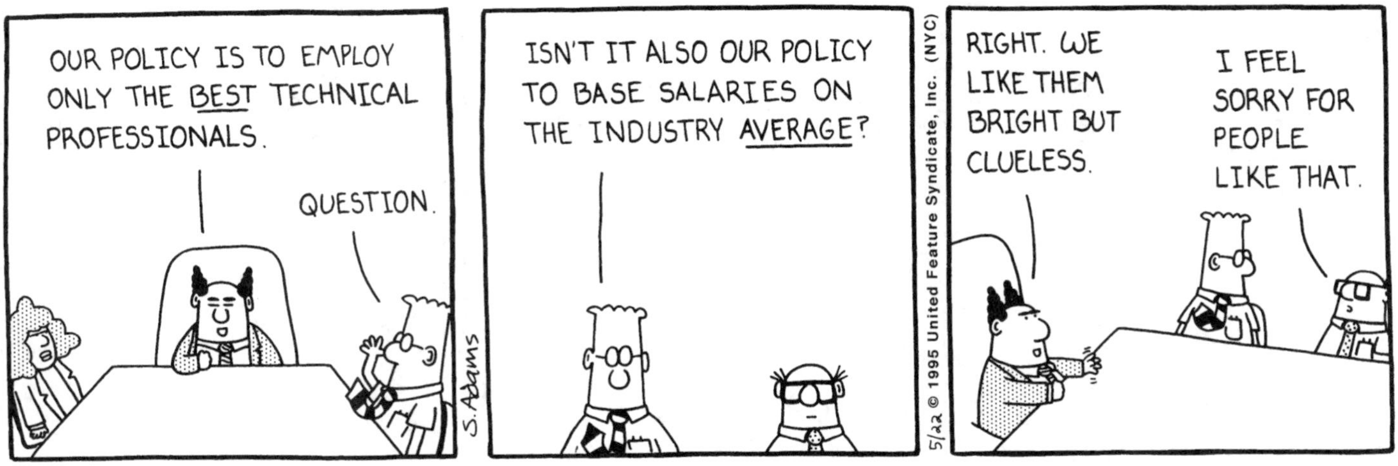
OUR POLICY IS TO EMPLOY ONLY THE BEST TECHNICAL PROFESSIONALS.
QUESTION.
S. Adams
ISN'T IT ALSO OUR POLICY TO BASE SALARIES ON THE INDUSTRY AVERAGE?
5/22 © 1995 United Feature Syndicate, Inc. (NYC)
RIGHT. WE LIKE THEM BRIGHT BUT CLUELESS.
I FEEL SORRY FOR PEOPLE LIKE THAT.

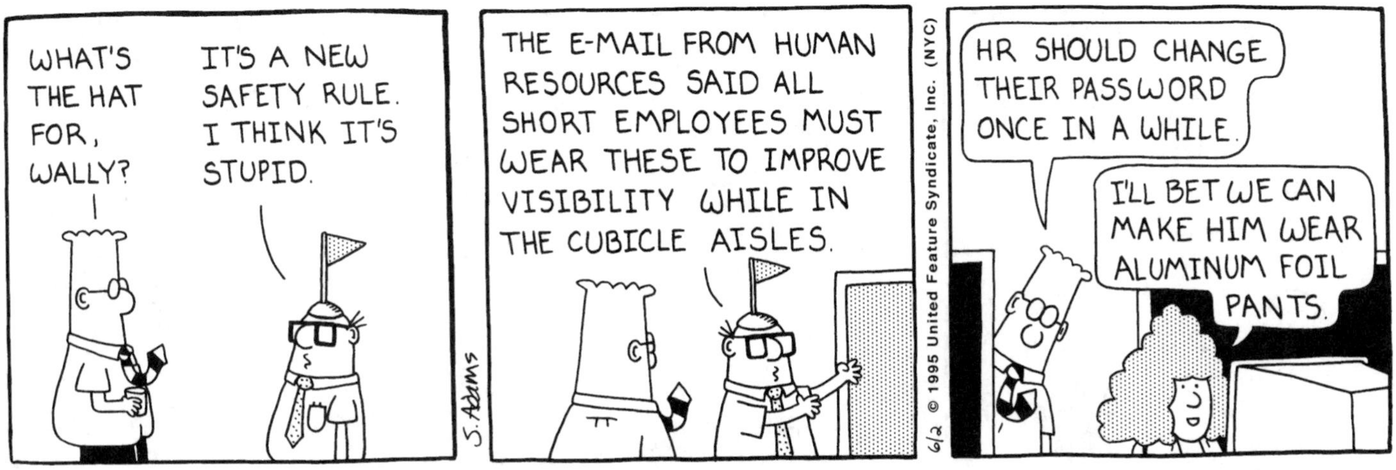
WHAT'S THE HAT FOR, WALLY?
IT'S A NEW SAFETY RULE. I THINK IT'S STUPID.
S. Adams
THE E-MAIL FROM HUMAN RESOURCES SAID ALL SHORT EMPLOYEES MUST WEAR THESE TO IMPROVE VISIBILITY WHILE IN THE CUBICLE AISLES.
6/2 © 1995 United Feature Syndicate, Inc. (NYC)
HR SHOULD CHANGE THEIR PASSWORD ONCE IN A WHILE.
I'LL BET WE CAN MAKE HIM WEAR ALUMINUM FOIL PANTS.

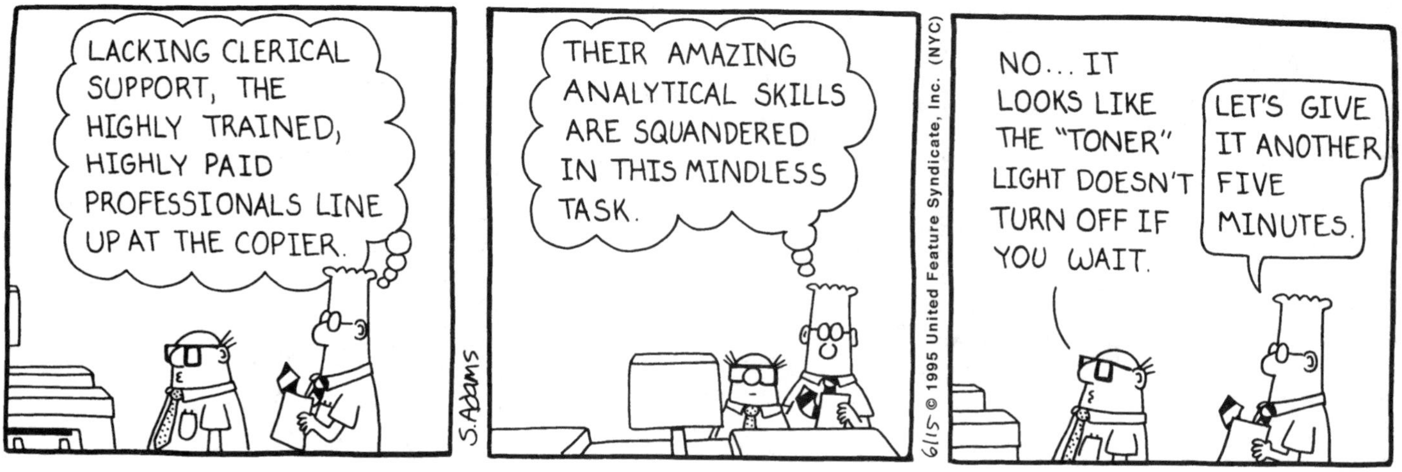
LACKING CLERICAL SUPPORT, THE HIGHLY TRAINED, HIGHLY PAID PROFESSIONALS LINE UP AT THE COPIER.
S. Adams
THEIR AMAZING ANALYTICAL SKILLS ARE SQUANDERED IN THIS MINDLESS TASK.
6/15 © 1995 United Feature Syndicate, Inc. (NYC)
NO... IT LOOKS LIKE THE "TONER" LIGHT DOESN'T TURN OFF IF YOU WAIT.
LET'S GIVE IT ANOTHER FIVE MINUTES.

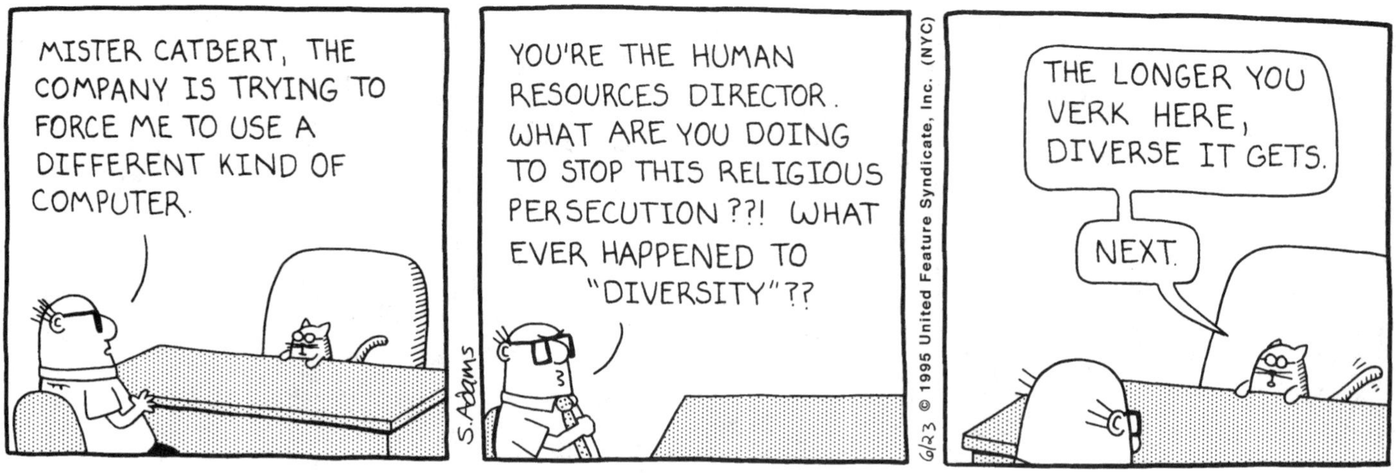
MISTER CATBERT, THE COMPANY IS TRYING TO FORCE ME TO USE A DIFFERENT KIND OF COMPUTER.
S. Adams
YOU'RE THE HUMAN RESOURCES DIRECTOR. WHAT ARE YOU DOING TO STOP THIS RELIGIOUS PERSECUTION??! WHAT EVER HAPPENED TO "DIVERSITY"??
6/23 © 1995 United Feature Syndicate, Inc. (NYC)
THE LONGER YOU VERK HERE, DIVERSE IT GETS.
NEXT.

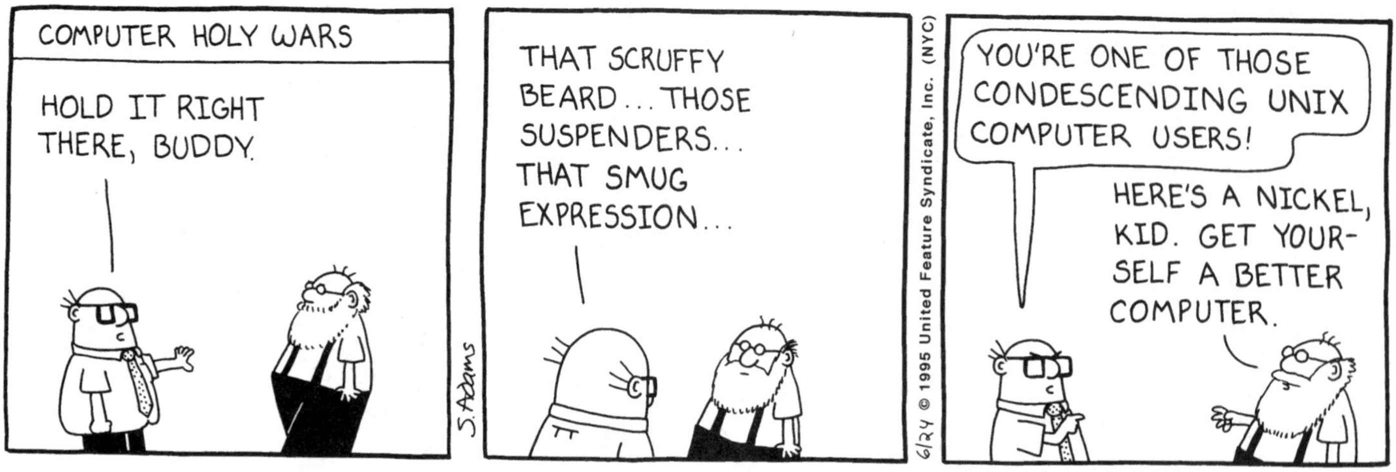
COMPUTER HOLY WARS
HOLD IT RIGHT THERE, BUDDY.
S. Adams
THAT SCRUFFY BEARD... THOSE SUSPENDERS... THAT SMUG EXPRESSION...
6/24 © 1995 United Feature Syndicate, Inc. (NYC)
YOU'RE ONE OF THOSE CONDESCENDING UNIX COMPUTER USERS!
HERE'S A NICKEL, KID. GET YOURSELF A BETTER COMPUTER.

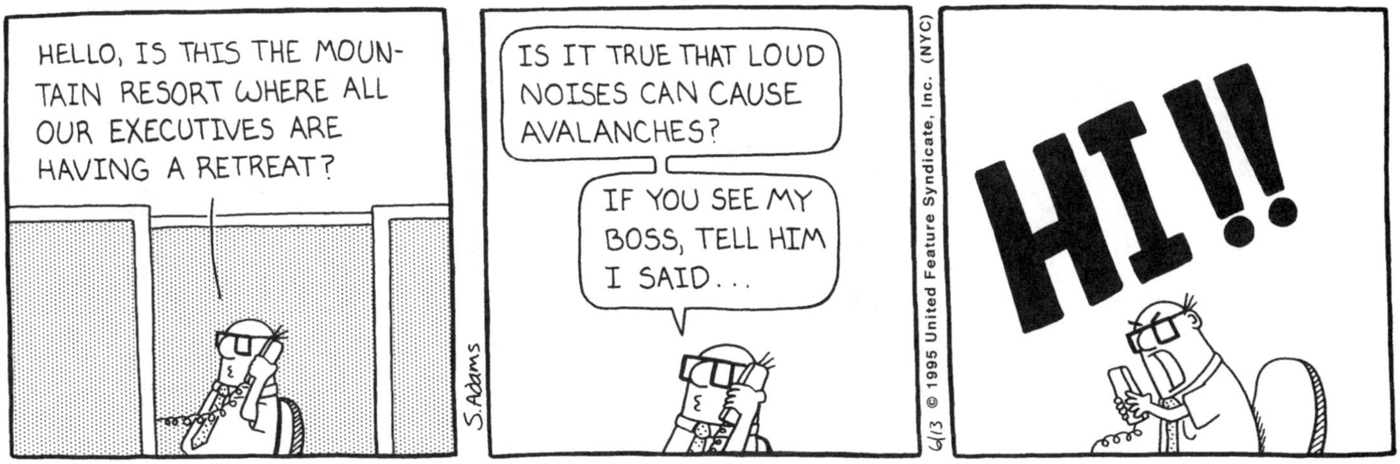
HELLO, IS THIS THE MOUNTAIN RESORT WHERE ALL OUR EXECUTIVES ARE HAVING A RETREAT?
S.Adams
IS IT TRUE THAT LOUD NOISES CAN CAUSE AVALANCHES?
IF YOU SEE MY BOSS, TELL HIM I SAID...
6/13 © 1995 United Feature Syndicate, Inc. (NYC)
HI!!

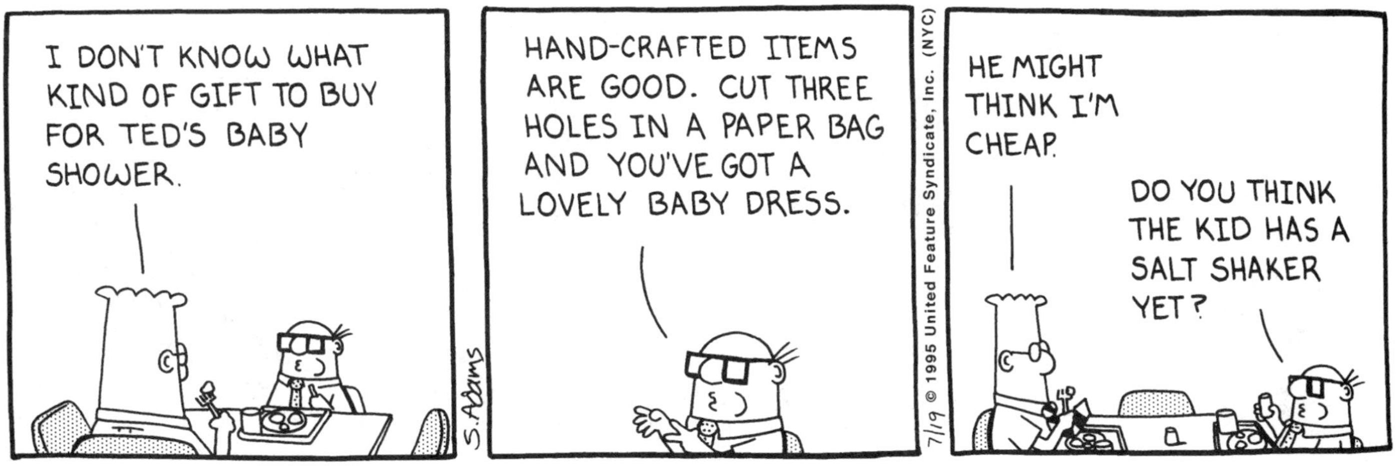
I DON'T KNOW WHAT KIND OF GIFT TO BUY FOR TED'S BABY SHOWER.
S.Adams
HAND-CRAFTED ITEMS ARE GOOD. CUT THREE HOLES IN A PAPER BAG AND YOU'VE GOT A LOVELY BABY DRESS.
7/19 © 1995 United Feature Syndicate, Inc. (NYC)
HE MIGHT THINK I'M CHEAP.
DO YOU THINK THE KID HAS A SALT SHAKER YET?

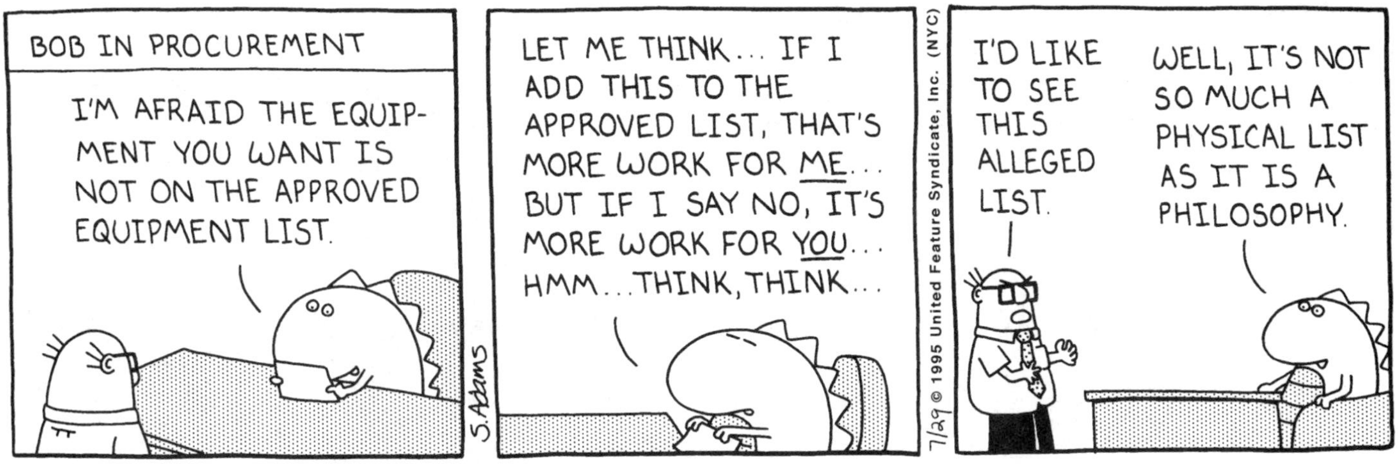
BOB IN PROCUREMENT
I'M AFRAID THE EQUIPMENT YOU WANT IS NOT ON THE APPROVED EQUIPMENT LIST.
S.Adams
LET ME THINK... IF I ADD THIS TO THE APPROVED LIST, THAT'S MORE WORK FOR ME... BUT IF I SAY NO, IT'S MORE WORK FOR YOU... HMM...THINK, THINK...
7/29 © 1995 United Feature Syndicate, Inc. (NYC)
I'D LIKE TO SEE THIS ALLEGED LIST.
WELL, IT'S NOT SO MUCH A PHYSICAL LIST AS IT IS A PHILOSOPHY.

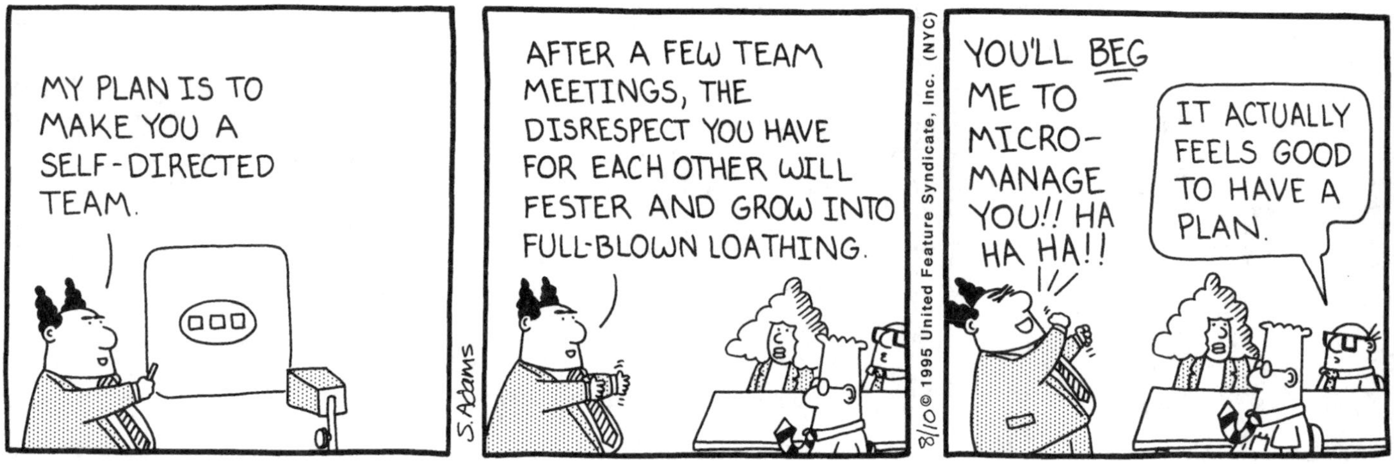
MY PLAN IS TO MAKE YOU A SELF-DIRECTED TEAM.
AFTER A FEW TEAM MEETINGS, THE DISRESPECT YOU HAVE FOR EACH OTHER WILL FESTER AND GROW INTO FULL-BLOWN LOATHING.
YOU'LL BEG ME TO MICRO-MANAGE YOU!! HA HA HA!!
IT ACTUALLY FEELS GOOD TO HAVE A PLAN.
S. Adams
8/10 © 1995 United Feature Syndicate, Inc. (NYC)

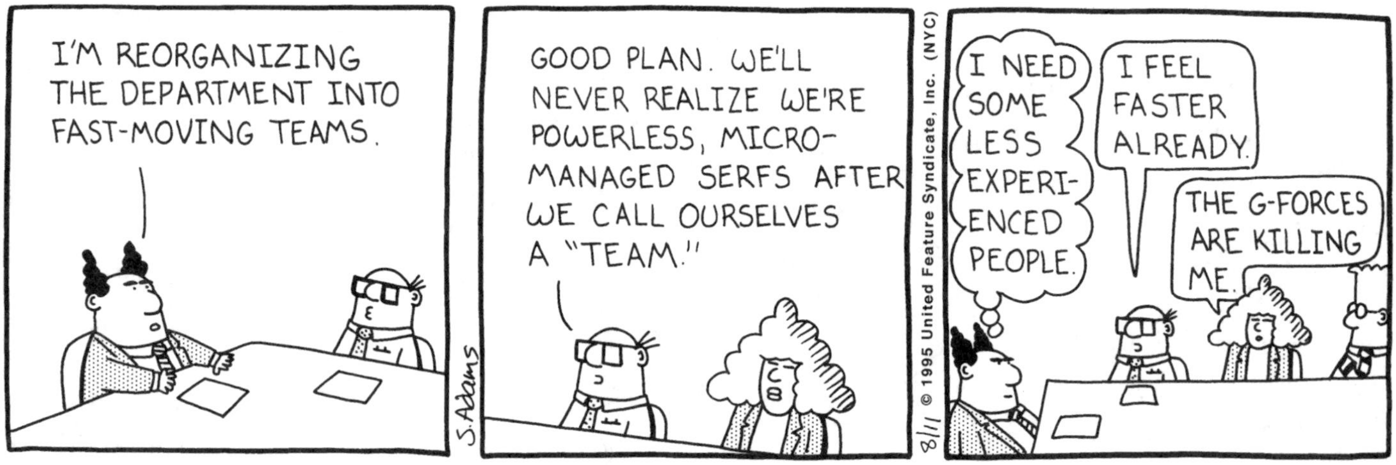
I'M REORGANIZING THE DEPARTMENT INTO FAST-MOVING TEAMS.
GOOD PLAN. WE'LL NEVER REALIZE WE'RE POWERLESS, MICRO-MANAGED SERFS AFTER WE CALL OURSELVES A "TEAM."
I NEED SOME LESS EXPERI-ENCED PEOPLE.
I FEEL FASTER ALREADY.
THE G-FORCES ARE KILLING ME.
S. Adams
8/11 © 1995 United Feature Syndicate, Inc. (NYC)

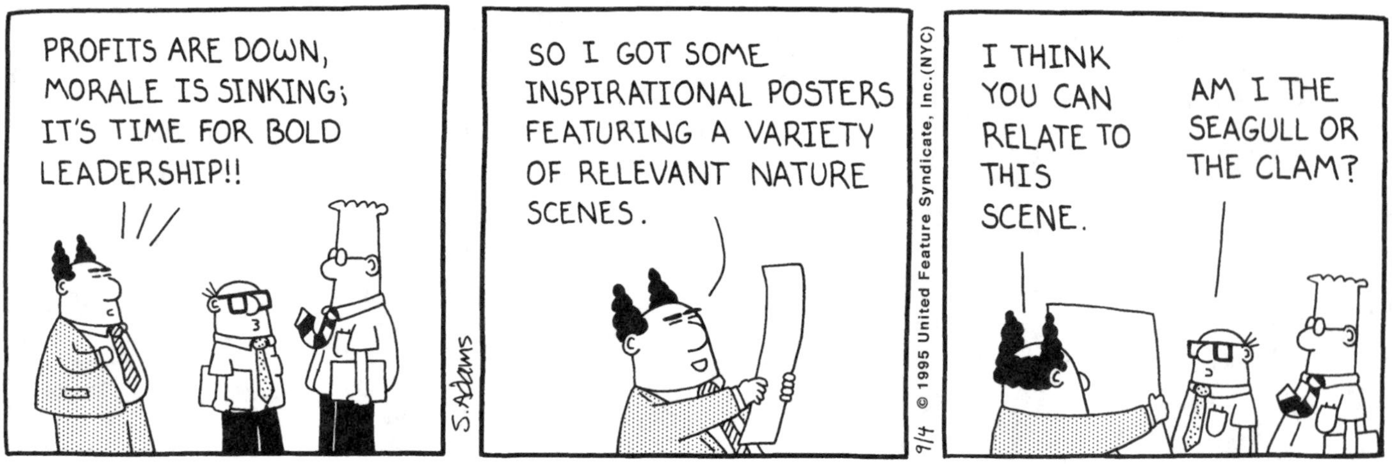
PROFITS ARE DOWN, MORALE IS SINKING; IT'S TIME FOR BOLD LEADERSHIP!!
SO I GOT SOME INSPIRATIONAL POSTERS FEATURING A VARIETY OF RELEVANT NATURE SCENES.
I THINK YOU CAN RELATE TO THIS SCENE.
AM I THE SEAGULL OR THE CLAM?
S. Adams
9/4 © 1995 United Feature Syndicate, Inc. (NYC)

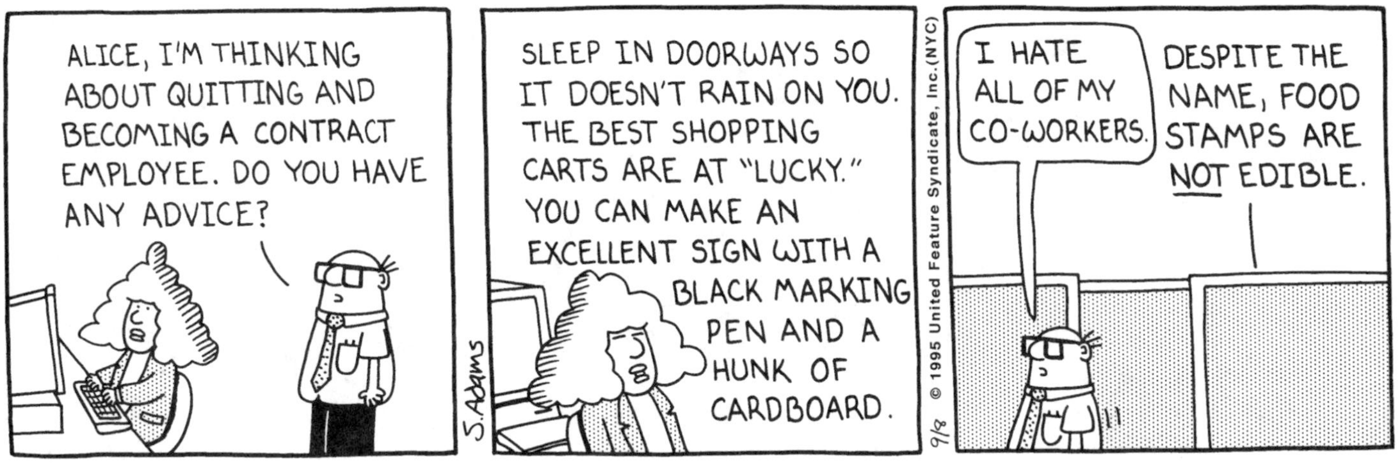
ALICE, I'M THINKING ABOUT QUITTING AND BECOMING A CONTRACT EMPLOYEE. DO YOU HAVE ANY ADVICE?
SLEEP IN DOORWAYS SO IT DOESN'T RAIN ON YOU. THE BEST SHOPPING CARTS ARE AT "LUCKY." YOU CAN MAKE AN EXCELLENT SIGN WITH A BLACK MARKING PEN AND A HUNK OF CARDBOARD.
I HATE ALL OF MY CO-WORKERS.
DESPITE THE NAME, FOOD STAMPS ARE NOT EDIBLE.
S. Adams
9/8 © 1995 United Feature Syndicate, Inc.(NYC)

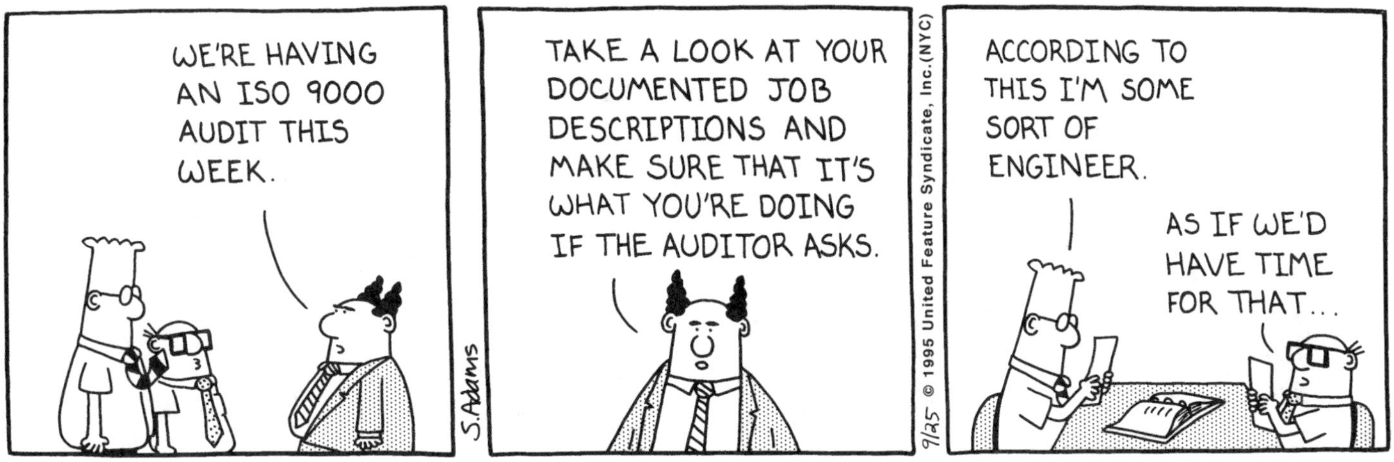
WE'RE HAVING AN ISO 9000 AUDIT THIS WEEK.
TAKE A LOOK AT YOUR DOCUMENTED JOB DESCRIPTIONS AND MAKE SURE THAT IT'S WHAT YOU'RE DOING IF THE AUDITOR ASKS.
ACCORDING TO THIS I'M SOME SORT OF ENGINEER.
AS IF WE'D HAVE TIME FOR THAT...
S. Adams
9/25 © 1995 United Feature Syndicate, Inc.(NYC)

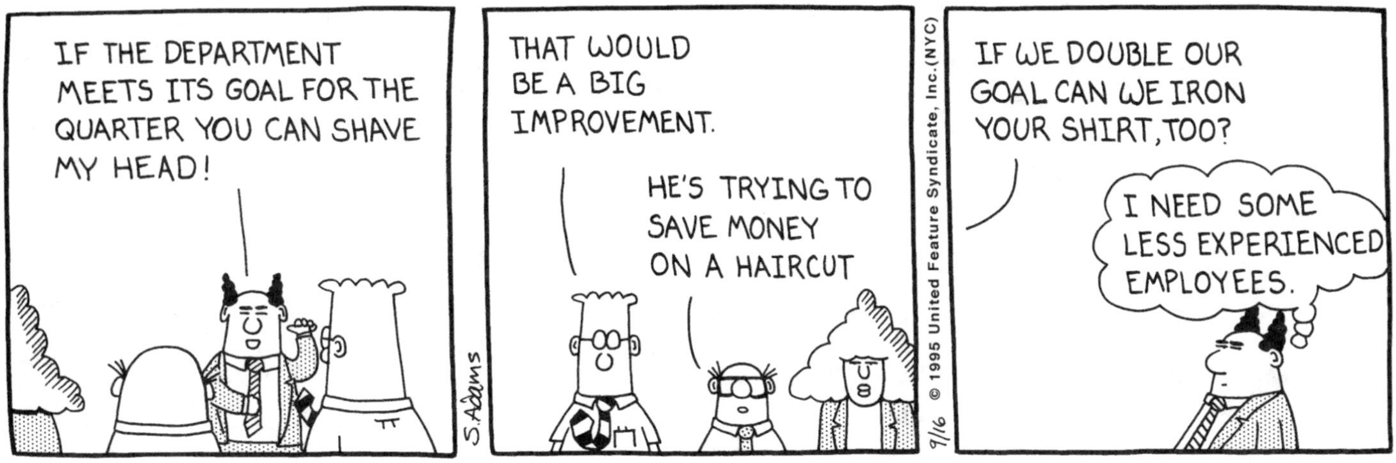
IF THE DEPARTMENT MEETS ITS GOAL FOR THE QUARTER YOU CAN SHAVE MY HEAD!
THAT WOULD BE A BIG IMPROVEMENT.
HE'S TRYING TO SAVE MONEY ON A HAIRCUT
IF WE DOUBLE OUR GOAL CAN WE IRON YOUR SHIRT, TOO?
I NEED SOME LESS EXPERIENCED EMPLOYEES.
S. Adams
9/16 © 1995 United Feature Syndicate, Inc.(NYC)

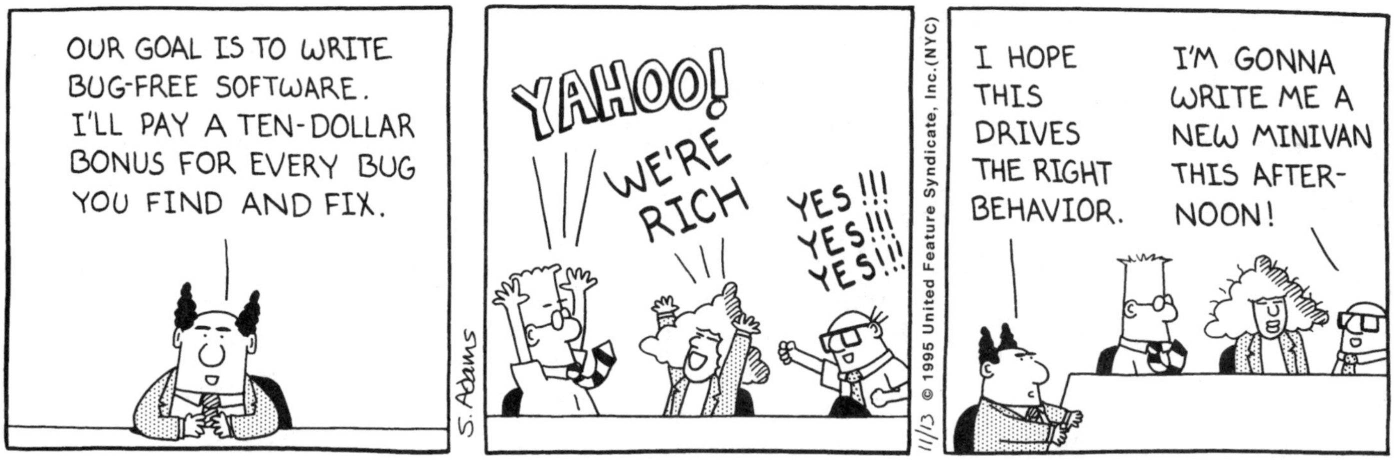
OUR GOAL IS TO WRITE BUG-FREE SOFTWARE. I'LL PAY A TEN-DOLLAR BONUS FOR EVERY BUG YOU FIND AND FIX.
YAHOO!
WE'RE RICH
YES!!! YES!!! YES!!!
S. Adams
11/13 © 1995 United Feature Syndicate, Inc.(NYC)
I HOPE THIS DRIVES THE RIGHT BEHAVIOR.
I'M GONNA WRITE ME A NEW MINIVAN THIS AFTER-NOON!

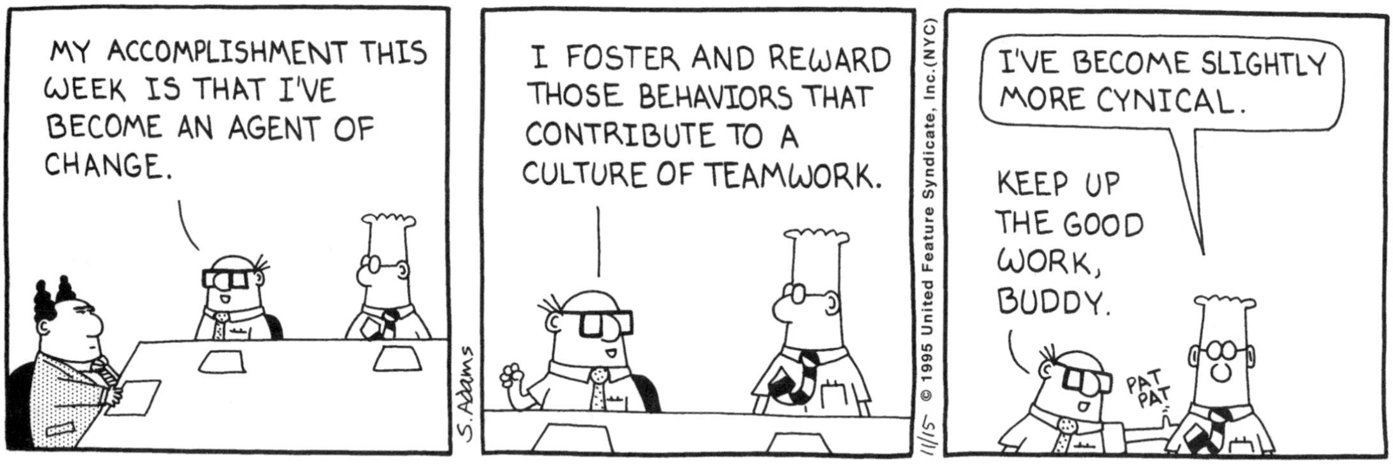
MY ACCOMPLISHMENT THIS WEEK IS THAT I'VE BECOME AN AGENT OF CHANGE.
S. Adams
I FOSTER AND REWARD THOSE BEHAVIORS THAT CONTRIBUTE TO A CULTURE OF TEAMWORK.
11/15 © 1995 United Feature Syndicate, Inc.(NYC)
I'VE BECOME SLIGHTLY MORE CYNICAL.
KEEP UP THE GOOD WORK, BUDDY.
PAT PAT

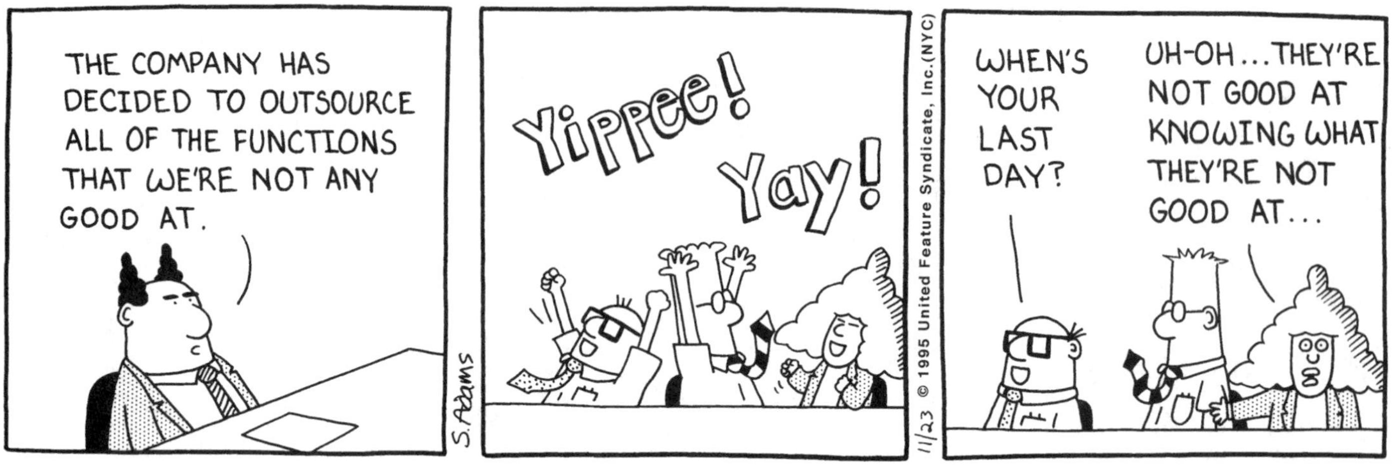
THE COMPANY HAS DECIDED TO OUTSOURCE ALL OF THE FUNCTIONS THAT WE'RE NOT ANY GOOD AT.
S. Adams
Yippee!
Yay!
11/23 © 1995 United Feature Syndicate, Inc.(NYC)
WHEN'S YOUR LAST DAY?
UH-OH... THEY'RE NOT GOOD AT KNOWING WHAT THEY'RE NOT GOOD AT...

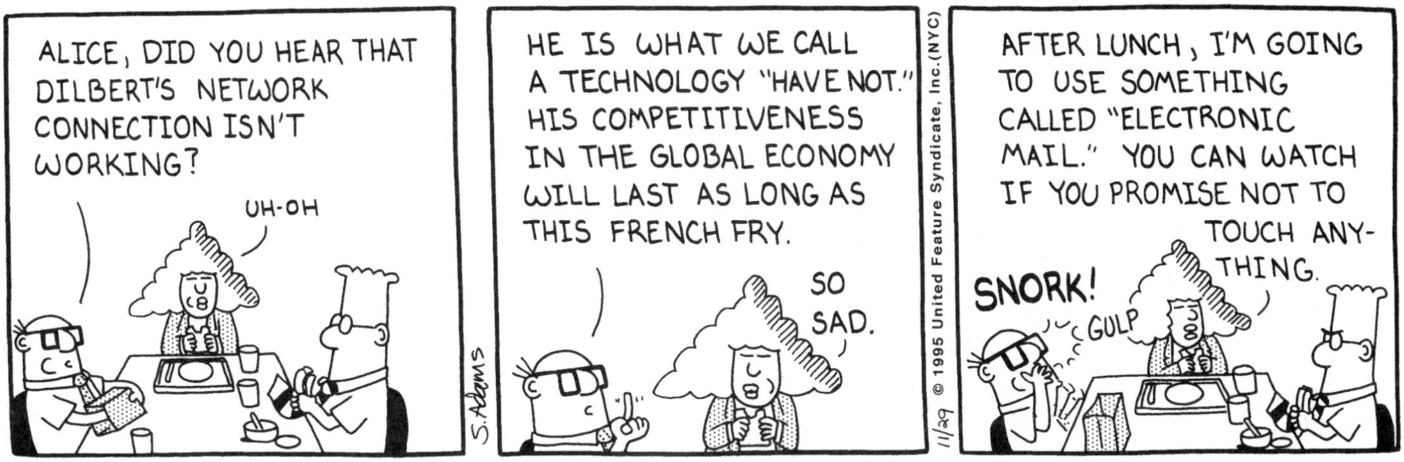
ALICE, DID YOU HEAR THAT DILBERT'S NETWORK CONNECTION ISN'T WORKING?
UH-OH
S. Adams
HE IS WHAT WE CALL A TECHNOLOGY "HAVE NOT." HIS COMPETITIVENESS IN THE GLOBAL ECONOMY WILL LAST AS LONG AS THIS FRENCH FRY.
SO SAD.
11/29 © 1995 United Feature Syndicate, Inc.(NYC)
AFTER LUNCH, I'M GOING TO USE SOMETHING CALLED "ELECTRONIC MAIL." YOU CAN WATCH IF YOU PROMISE NOT TO TOUCH ANY-THING.
SNORK!
GULP

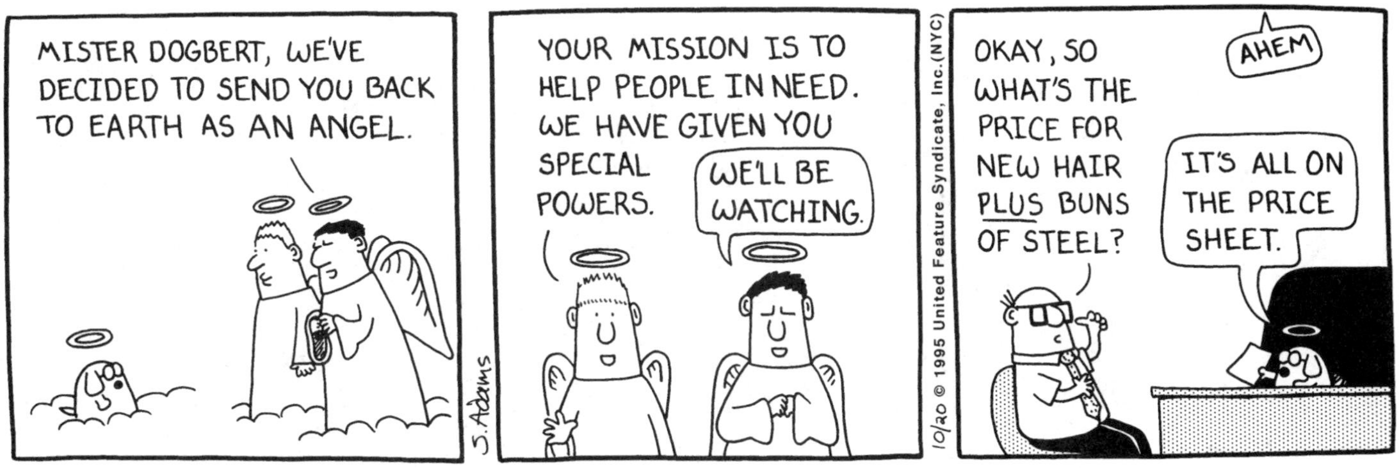
MISTER DOGBERT, WE'VE DECIDED TO SEND YOU BACK TO EARTH AS AN ANGEL.
S. Adams
YOUR MISSION IS TO HELP PEOPLE IN NEED. WE HAVE GIVEN YOU SPECIAL POWERS.
WE'LL BE WATCHING.
10/20 © 1995 United Feature Syndicate, Inc.(NYC)
OKAY, SO WHAT'S THE PRICE FOR NEW HAIR PLUS BUNS OF STEEL?
AHEM
IT'S ALL ON THE PRICE SHEET.

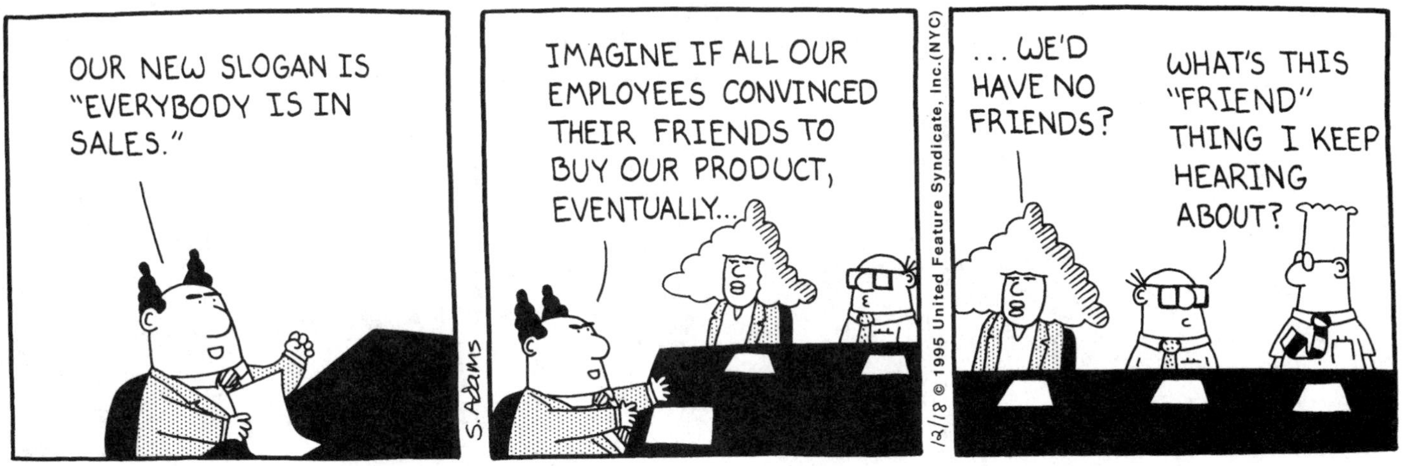
OUR NEW SLOGAN IS "EVERYBODY IS IN SALES."
S. Adams
IMAGINE IF ALL OUR EMPLOYEES CONVINCED THEIR FRIENDS TO BUY OUR PRODUCT, EVENTUALLY...
12/18 © 1995 United Feature Syndicate, Inc.(NYC)
...WE'D HAVE NO FRIENDS?
WHAT'S THIS "FRIEND" THING I KEEP HEARING ABOUT?

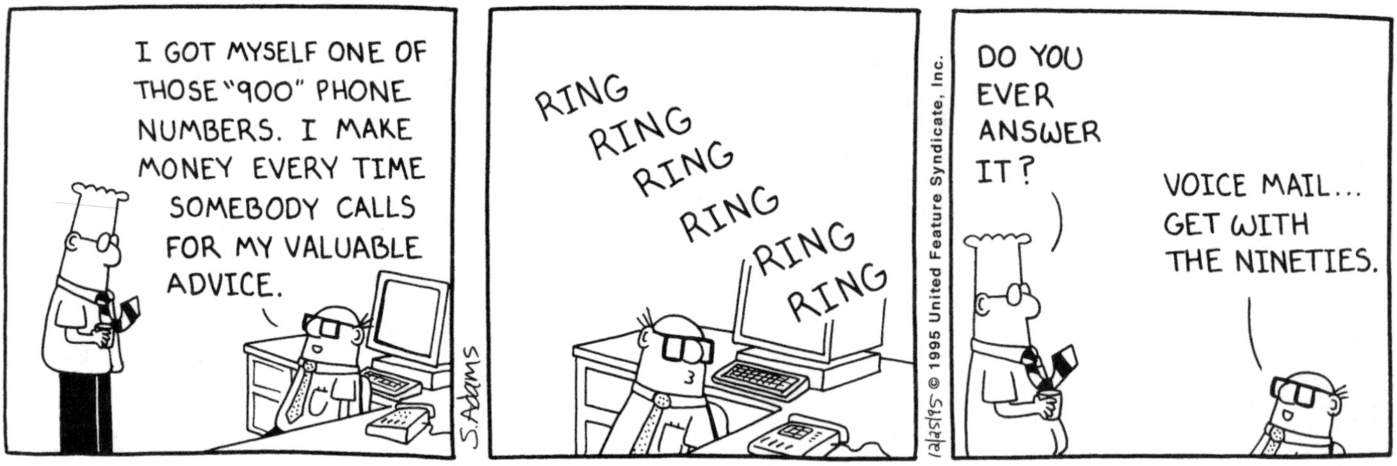
I GOT MYSELF ONE OF THOSE "900" PHONE NUMBERS. I MAKE MONEY EVERY TIME SOMEBODY CALLS FOR MY VALUABLE ADVICE.
S. Adams
RING
RING
RING
RING
RING
RING
12/25/95 © 1995 United Feature Syndicate, Inc.
DO YOU EVER ANSWER IT?
VOICE MAIL... GET WITH THE NINETIES.

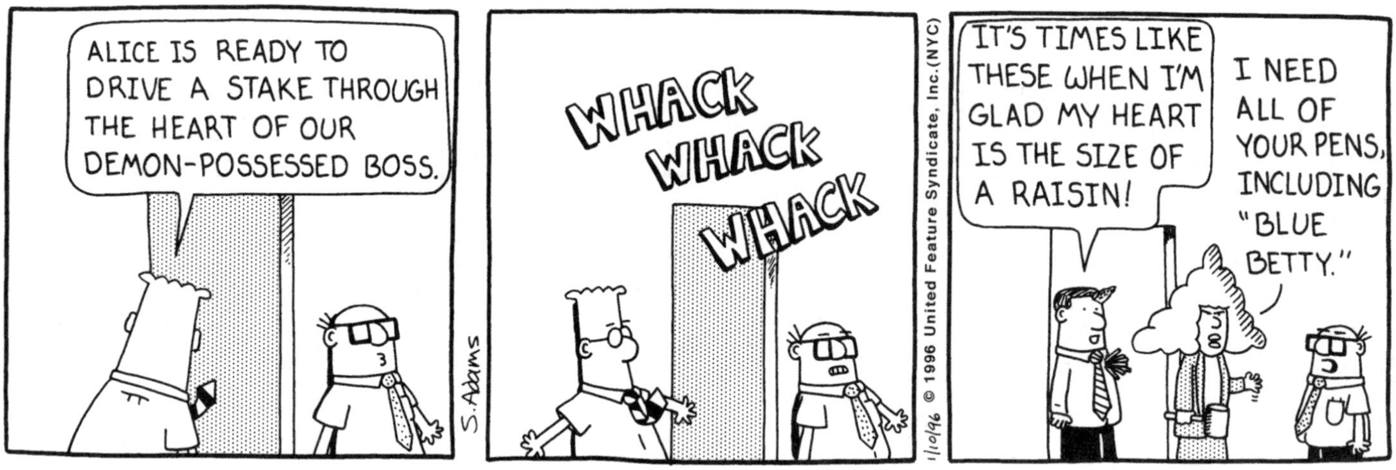
ALICE IS READY TO DRIVE A STAKE THROUGH THE HEART OF OUR DEMON-POSSESSED BOSS.
S. Adams
WHACK
WHACK
WHACK
1/10/96 © 1996 United Feature Syndicate, Inc.(NYC)
IT'S TIMES LIKE THESE WHEN I'M GLAD MY HEART IS THE SIZE OF A RAISIN!
I NEED ALL OF YOUR PENS, INCLUDING "BLUE BETTY."

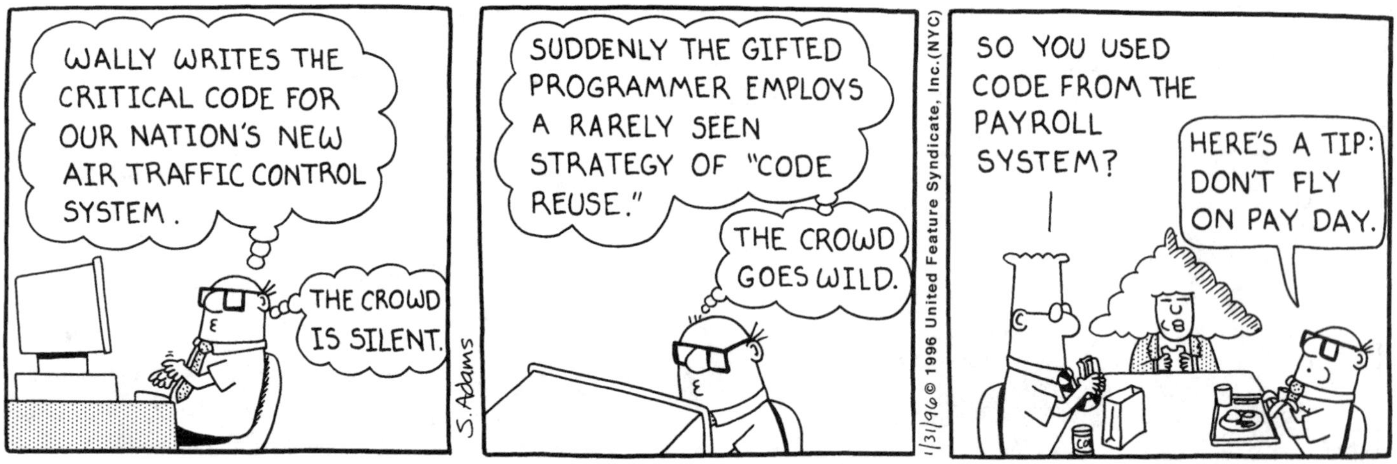
WALLY WRITES THE CRITICAL CODE FOR OUR NATION'S NEW AIR TRAFFIC CONTROL SYSTEM.
THE CROWD IS SILENT.
S. Adams
SUDDENLY THE GIFTED PROGRAMMER EMPLOYS A RARELY SEEN STRATEGY OF "CODE REUSE."
THE CROWD GOES WILD.
1/31/96 © 1996 United Feature Syndicate, Inc.(NYC)
SO YOU USED CODE FROM THE PAYROLL SYSTEM?
HERE'S A TIP: DON'T FLY ON PAY DAY.

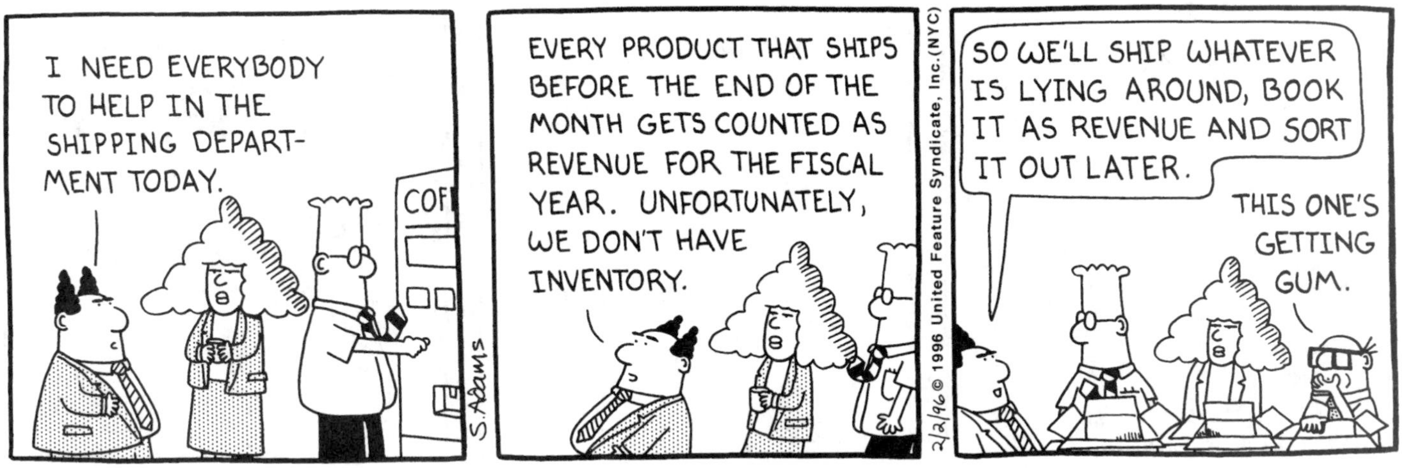
I NEED EVERYBODY TO HELP IN THE SHIPPING DEPARTMENT TODAY.
EVERY PRODUCT THAT SHIPS BEFORE THE END OF THE MONTH GETS COUNTED AS REVENUE FOR THE FISCAL YEAR. UNFORTUNATELY, WE DON'T HAVE INVENTORY.
SO WE'LL SHIP WHATEVER IS LYING AROUND, BOOK IT AS REVENUE AND SORT IT OUT LATER.
THIS ONE'S GETTING GUM.
S.Adams
2/2/96 © 1996 United Feature Syndicate, Inc.(NYC)

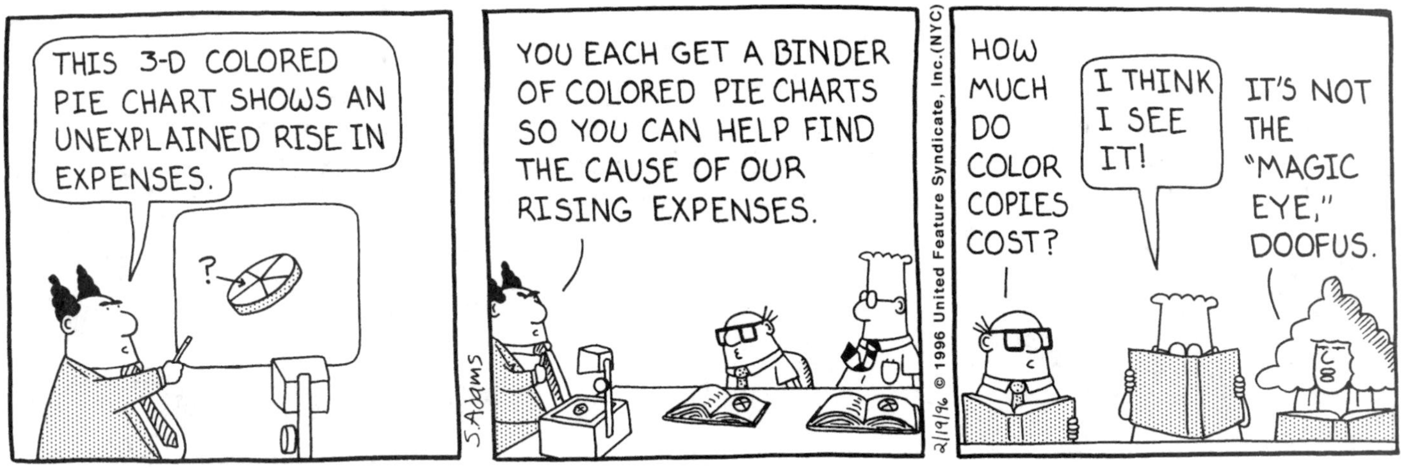
THIS 3-D COLORED PIE CHART SHOWS AN UNEXPLAINED RISE IN EXPENSES.
?
YOU EACH GET A BINDER OF COLORED PIE CHARTS SO YOU CAN HELP FIND THE CAUSE OF OUR RISING EXPENSES.
HOW MUCH DO COLOR COPIES COST?
I THINK I SEE IT!
IT'S NOT THE "MAGIC EYE," DOOFUS.
S.Adams
2/19/96 © 1996 United Feature Syndicate, Inc.(NYC)

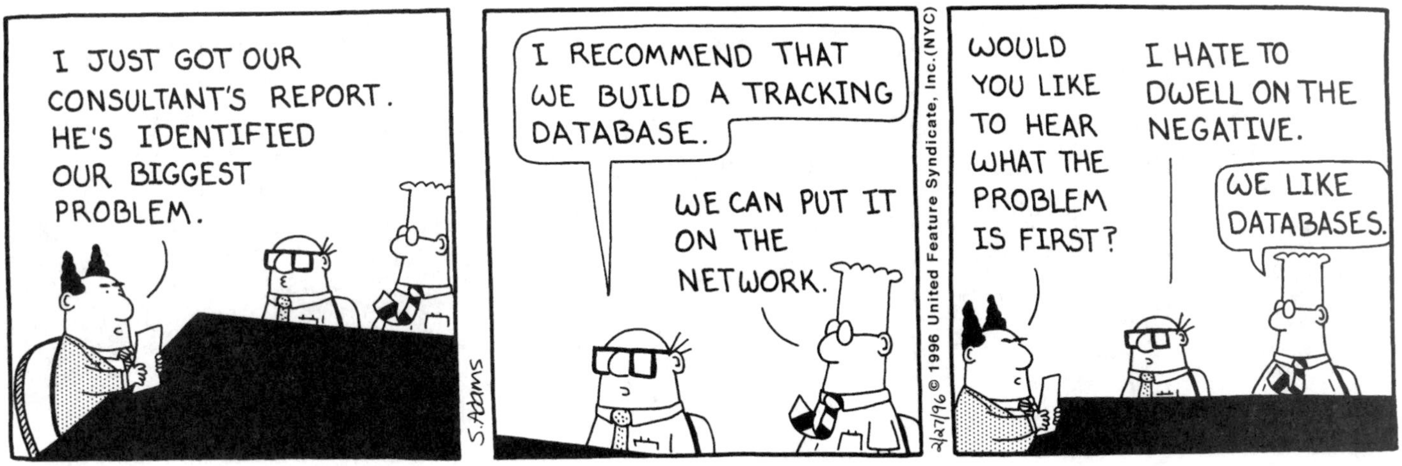
I JUST GOT OUR CONSULTANT'S REPORT. HE'S IDENTIFIED OUR BIGGEST PROBLEM.
I RECOMMEND THAT WE BUILD A TRACKING DATABASE.
WE CAN PUT IT ON THE NETWORK.
WOULD YOU LIKE TO HEAR WHAT THE PROBLEM IS FIRST?
I HATE TO DWELL ON THE NEGATIVE.
WE LIKE DATABASES.
S.Adams
2/27/96 © 1996 United Feature Syndicate, Inc.(NYC)

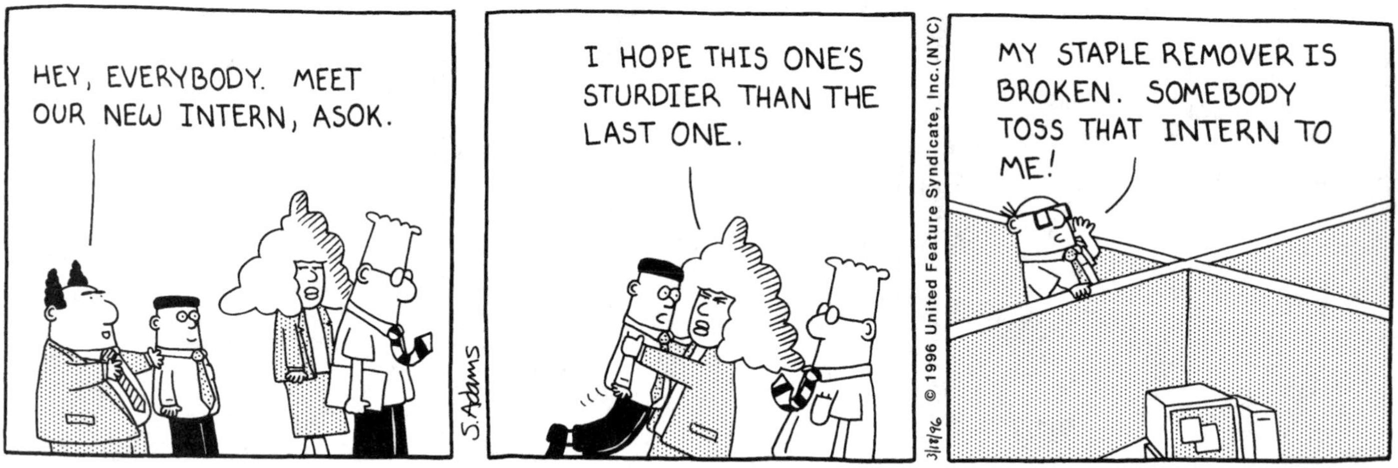
HEY, EVERYBODY. MEET OUR NEW INTERN, ASOK.
S. Adams
I HOPE THIS ONE'S STURDIER THAN THE LAST ONE.
3/18/96 © 1996 United Feature Syndicate, Inc.(NYC)
MY STAPLE REMOVER IS BROKEN. SOMEBODY TOSS THAT INTERN TO ME!

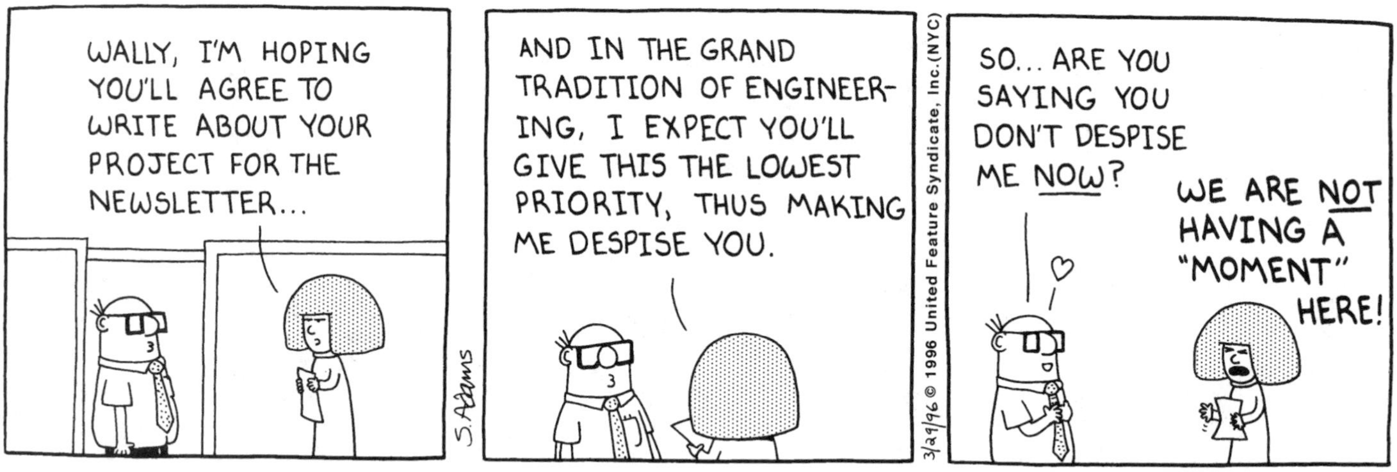
WALLY, I'M HOPING YOU'LL AGREE TO WRITE ABOUT YOUR PROJECT FOR THE NEWSLETTER...
S. Adams
AND IN THE GRAND TRADITION OF ENGINEERING, I EXPECT YOU'LL GIVE THIS THE LOWEST PRIORITY, THUS MAKING ME DESPISE YOU.
3/29/96 © 1996 United Feature Syndicate, Inc.(NYC)
SO... ARE YOU SAYING YOU DON'T DESPISE ME NOW?
WE ARE NOT HAVING A "MOMENT" HERE!

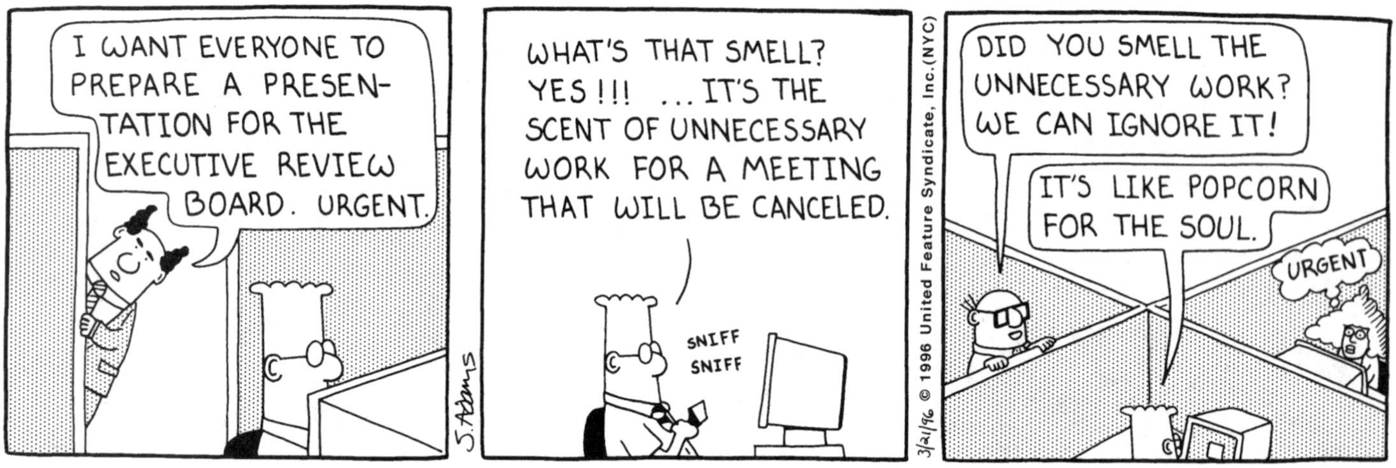
I WANT EVERYONE TO PREPARE A PRESENTATION FOR THE EXECUTIVE REVIEW BOARD. URGENT.
S. Adams
WHAT'S THAT SMELL? YES!!! ... IT'S THE SCENT OF UNNECESSARY WORK FOR A MEETING THAT WILL BE CANCELED.
SNIFF
SNIFF
3/21/96 © 1996 United Feature Syndicate, Inc.(NYC)
DID YOU SMELL THE UNNECESSARY WORK? WE CAN IGNORE IT!
IT'S LIKE POPCORN FOR THE SOUL.
URGENT

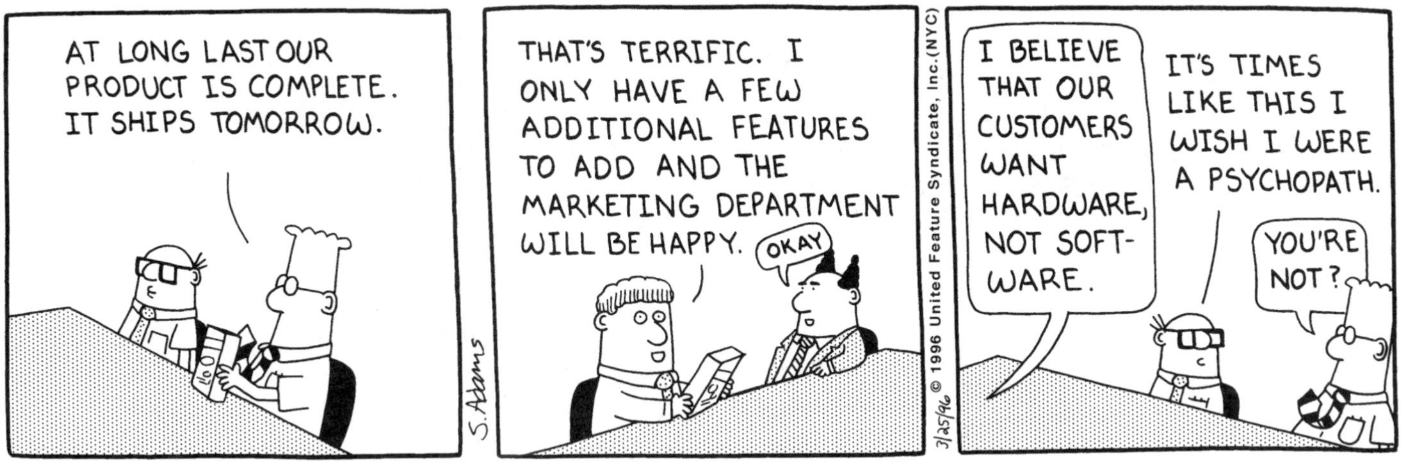
AT LONG LAST OUR PRODUCT IS COMPLETE. IT SHIPS TOMORROW.
THAT'S TERRIFIC. I ONLY HAVE A FEW ADDITIONAL FEATURES TO ADD AND THE MARKETING DEPARTMENT WILL BE HAPPY.
OKAY
I BELIEVE THAT OUR CUSTOMERS WANT HARDWARE, NOT SOFTWARE.
IT'S TIMES LIKE THIS I WISH I WERE A PSYCHOPATH.
YOU'RE NOT?
S. Adams
3/25/96 © 1996 United Feature Syndicate, Inc.(NYC)

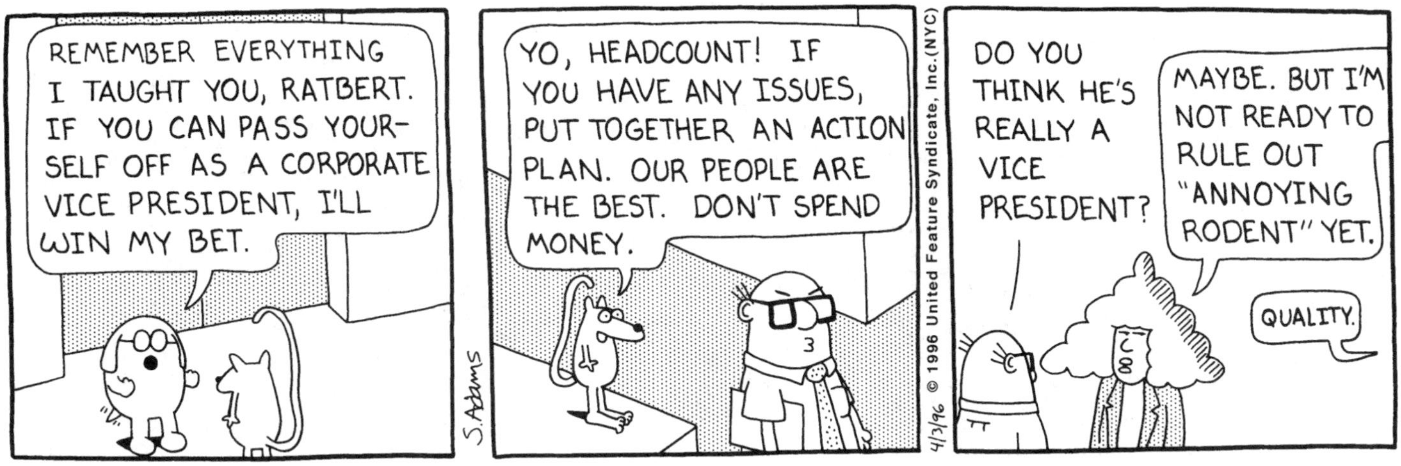
REMEMBER EVERYTHING I TAUGHT YOU, RATBERT. IF YOU CAN PASS YOURSELF OFF AS A CORPORATE VICE PRESIDENT, I'LL WIN MY BET.
YO, HEADCOUNT! IF YOU HAVE ANY ISSUES, PUT TOGETHER AN ACTION PLAN. OUR PEOPLE ARE THE BEST. DON'T SPEND MONEY.
DO YOU THINK HE'S REALLY A VICE PRESIDENT?
MAYBE. BUT I'M NOT READY TO RULE OUT "ANNOYING RODENT" YET.
QUALITY.
S. Adams
4/3/96 © 1996 United Feature Syndicate, Inc.(NYC)

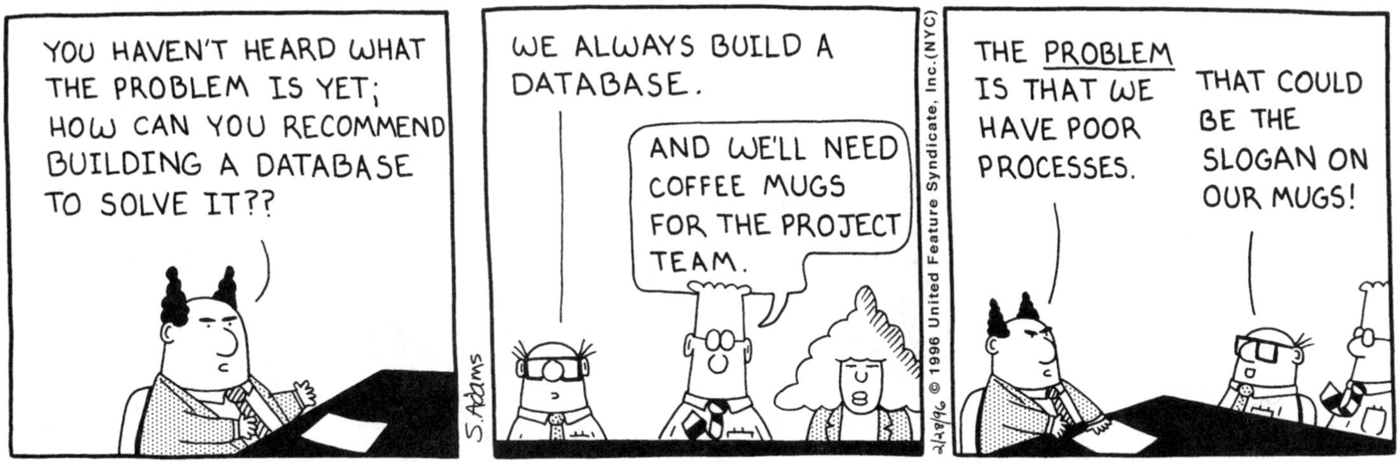
YOU HAVEN'T HEARD WHAT THE PROBLEM IS YET; HOW CAN YOU RECOMMEND BUILDING A DATABASE TO SOLVE IT??
WE ALWAYS BUILD A DATABASE.
AND WE'LL NEED COFFEE MUGS FOR THE PROJECT TEAM.
THE PROBLEM IS THAT WE HAVE POOR PROCESSES.
THAT COULD BE THE SLOGAN ON OUR MUGS!
S. Adams
2/28/96 © 1996 United Feature Syndicate, Inc.(NYC)

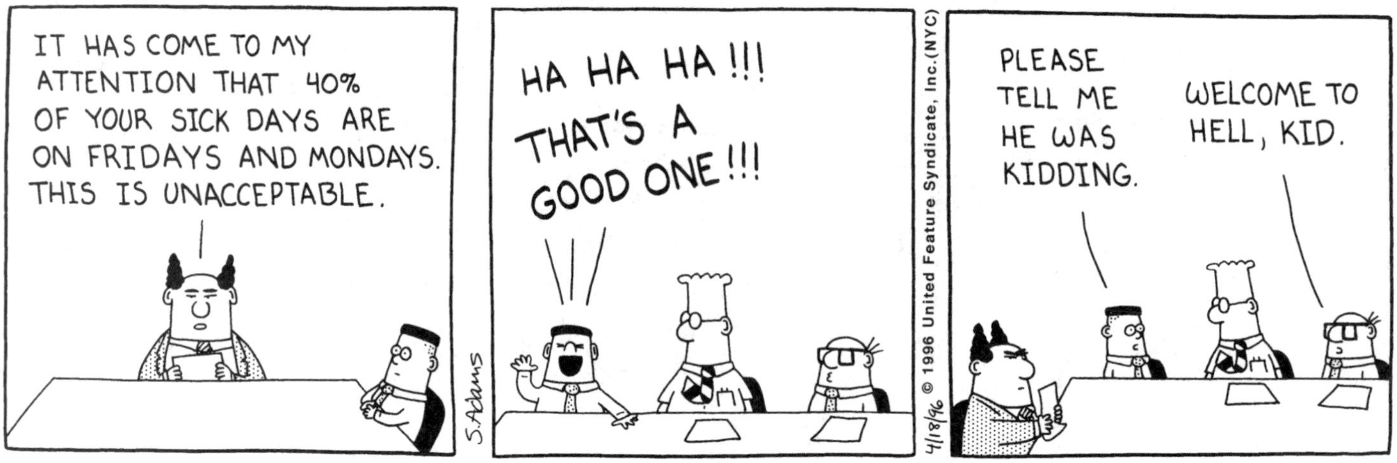
IT HAS COME TO MY ATTENTION THAT 40% OF YOUR SICK DAYS ARE ON FRIDAYS AND MONDAYS. THIS IS UNACCEPTABLE.
HA HA HA !!! THAT'S A GOOD ONE !!!
PLEASE TELL ME HE WAS KIDDING.
WELCOME TO HELL, KID.
4/18/96 © 1996 United Feature Syndicate, Inc.(NYC)

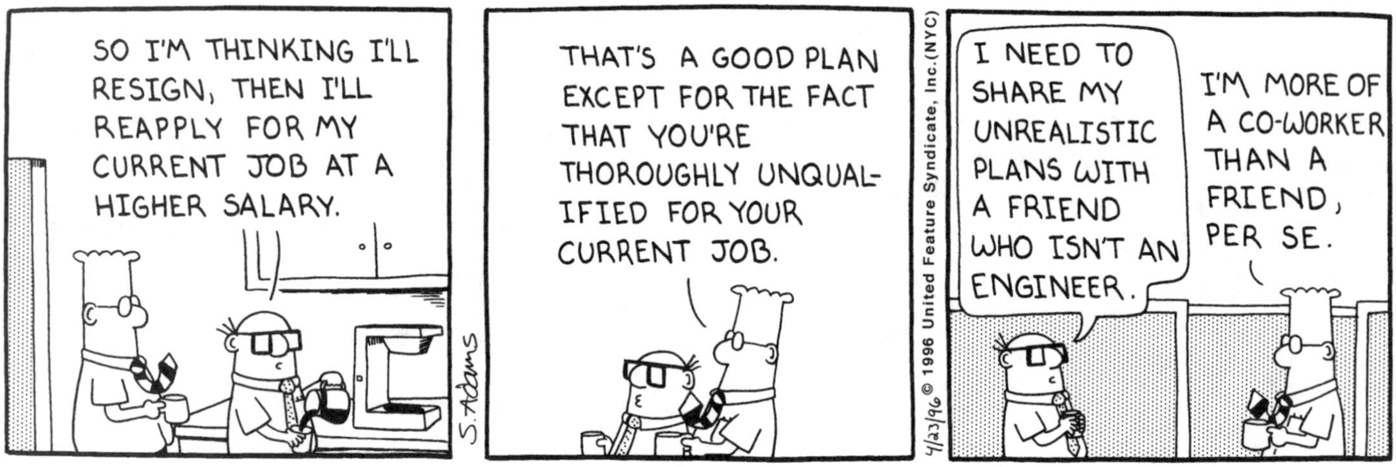
SO I'M THINKING I'LL RESIGN, THEN I'LL REAPPLY FOR MY CURRENT JOB AT A HIGHER SALARY.
THAT'S A GOOD PLAN EXCEPT FOR THE FACT THAT YOU'RE THOROUGHLY UNQUALIFIED FOR YOUR CURRENT JOB.
I NEED TO SHARE MY UNREALISTIC PLANS WITH A FRIEND WHO ISN'T AN ENGINEER.
I'M MORE OF A CO-WORKER THAN A FRIEND, PER SE.
4/23/96 © 1996 United Feature Syndicate, Inc.(NYC)

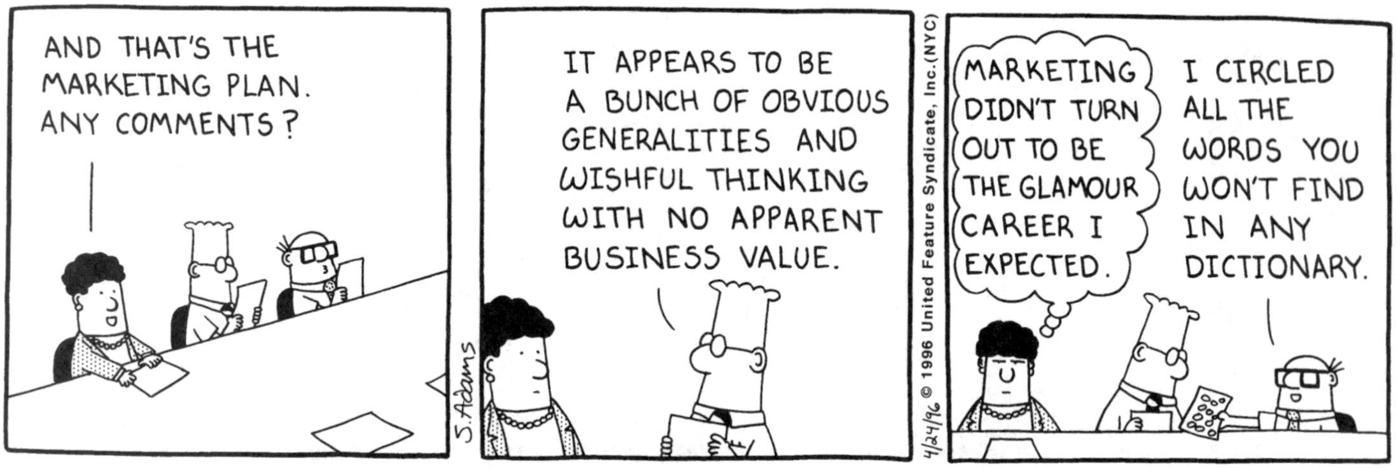
AND THAT'S THE MARKETING PLAN. ANY COMMENTS?
IT APPEARS TO BE A BUNCH OF OBVIOUS GENERALITIES AND WISHFUL THINKING WITH NO APPARENT BUSINESS VALUE.
MARKETING DIDN'T TURN OUT TO BE THE GLAMOUR CAREER I EXPECTED.
I CIRCLED ALL THE WORDS YOU WON'T FIND IN ANY DICTIONARY.
4/24/96 © 1996 United Feature Syndicate, Inc.(NYC)

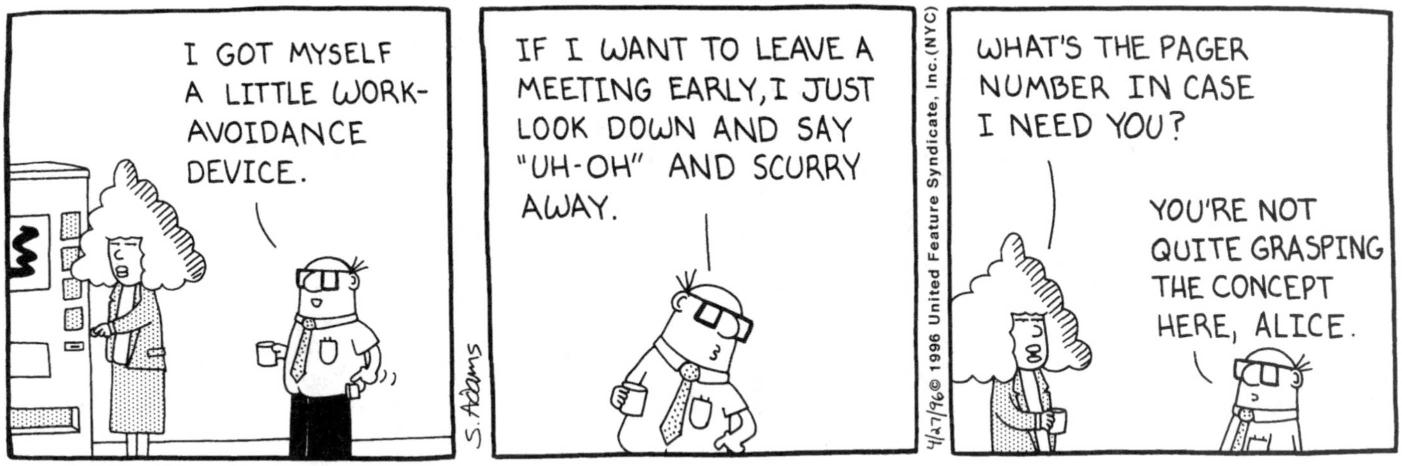
I GOT MYSELF A LITTLE WORK-AVOIDANCE DEVICE.
S. Adams
IF I WANT TO LEAVE A MEETING EARLY, I JUST LOOK DOWN AND SAY "UH-OH" AND SCURRY AWAY.
4/27/96 © 1996 United Feature Syndicate, Inc.(NYC)
WHAT'S THE PAGER NUMBER IN CASE I NEED YOU?
YOU'RE NOT QUITE GRASPING THE CONCEPT HERE, ALICE.

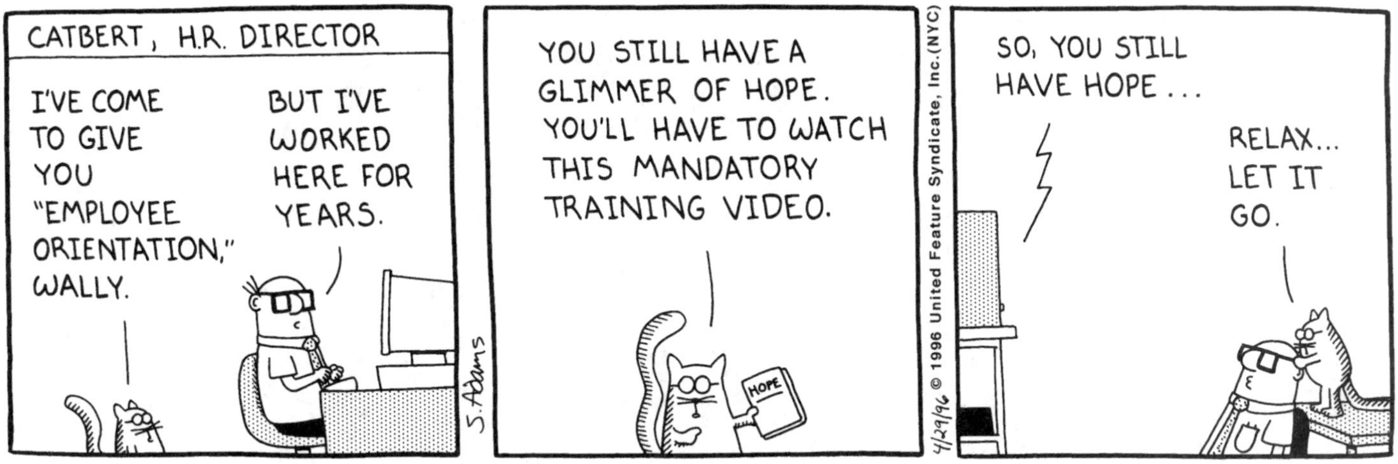
CATBERT, H.R. DIRECTOR
I'VE COME TO GIVE YOU "EMPLOYEE ORIENTATION," WALLY.
BUT I'VE WORKED HERE FOR YEARS.
S. Adams
YOU STILL HAVE A GLIMMER OF HOPE. YOU'LL HAVE TO WATCH THIS MANDATORY TRAINING VIDEO.
HOPE
4/29/96 © 1996 United Feature Syndicate, Inc.(NYC)
SO, YOU STILL HAVE HOPE...
RELAX... LET IT GO.

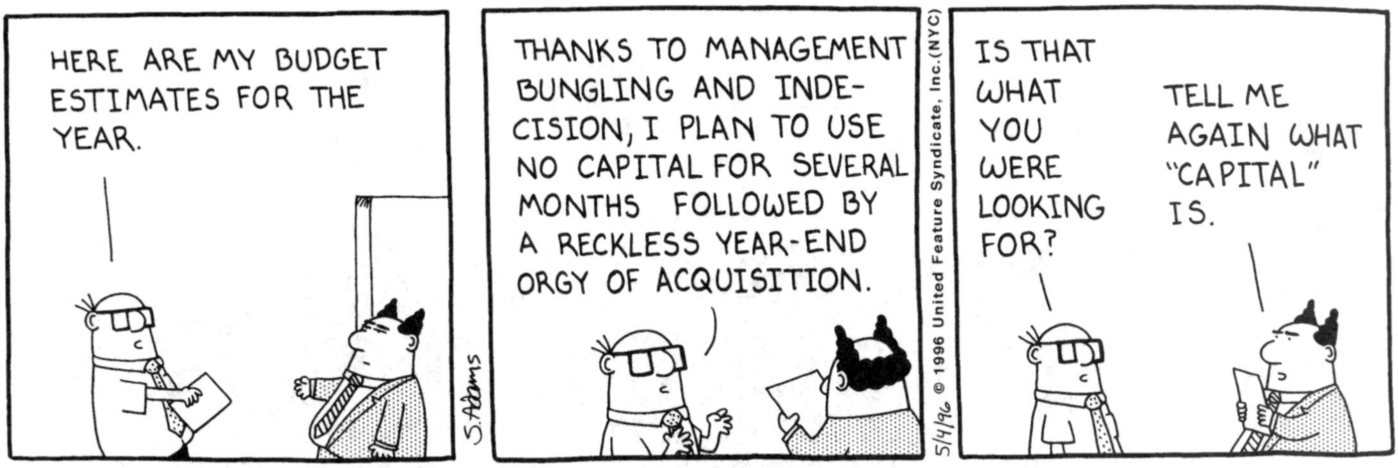
HERE ARE MY BUDGET ESTIMATES FOR THE YEAR.
S. Adams
THANKS TO MANAGEMENT BUNGLING AND INDECISION, I PLAN TO USE NO CAPITAL FOR SEVERAL MONTHS FOLLOWED BY A RECKLESS YEAR-END ORGY OF ACQUISITION.
5/4/96 © 1996 United Feature Syndicate, Inc.(NYC)
IS THAT WHAT YOU WERE LOOKING FOR?
TELL ME AGAIN WHAT "CAPITAL" IS.

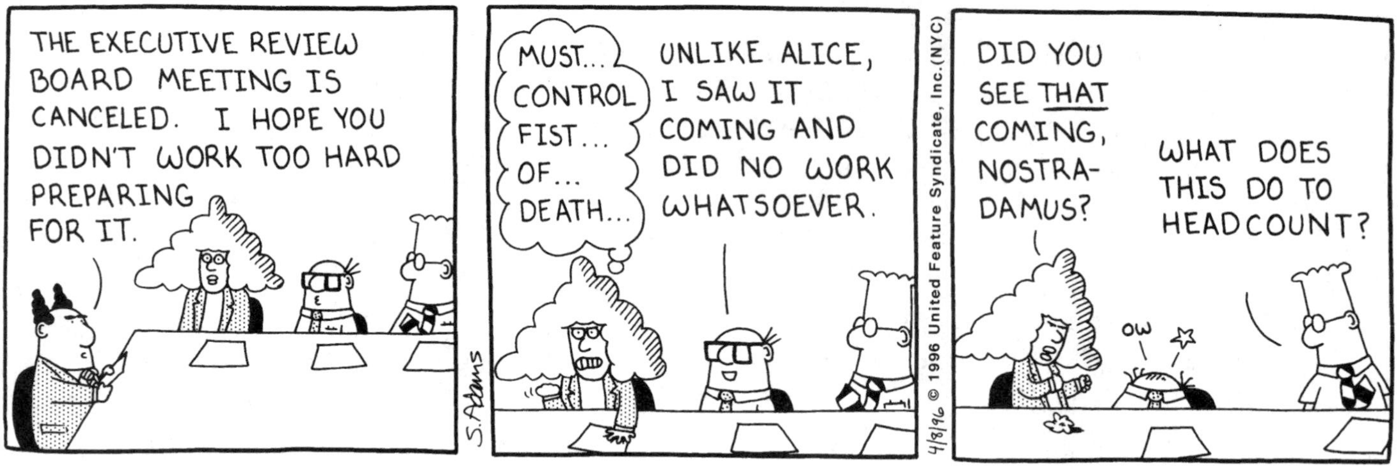
THE EXECUTIVE REVIEW BOARD MEETING IS CANCELED. I HOPE YOU DIDN'T WORK TOO HARD PREPARING FOR IT.
S. Adams
MUST... CONTROL FIST... OF... DEATH...
UNLIKE ALICE, I SAW IT COMING AND DID NO WORK WHATSOEVER.
4/8/96 © 1996 United Feature Syndicate, Inc.(NYC)
DID YOU SEE THAT COMING, NOSTRA-DAMUS?
OW
WHAT DOES THIS DO TO HEADCOUNT?

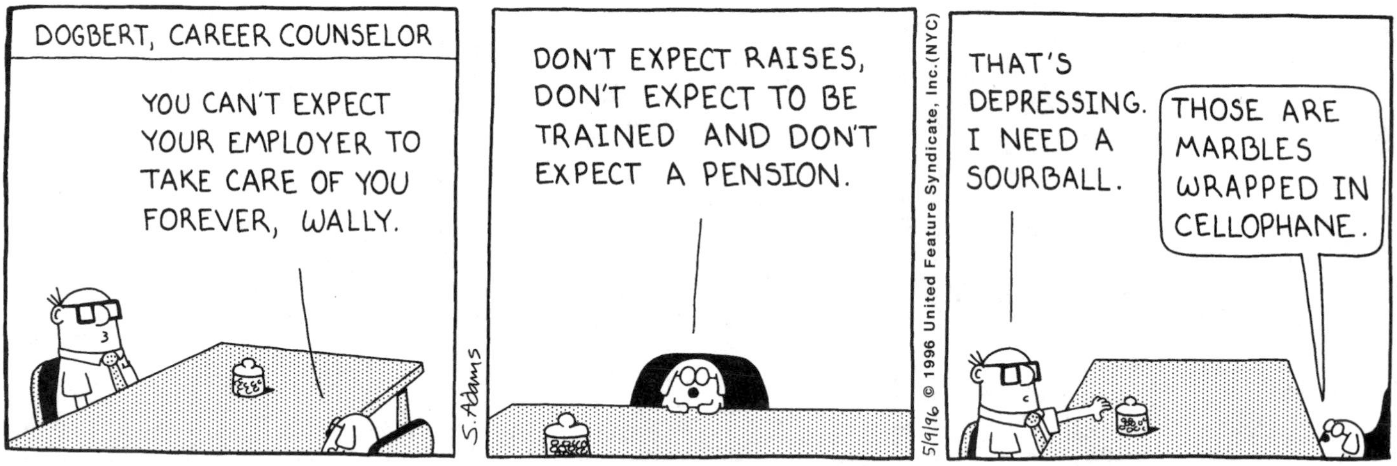
DOGBERT, CAREER COUNSELOR
YOU CAN'T EXPECT YOUR EMPLOYER TO TAKE CARE OF YOU FOREVER, WALLY.
S. Adams
DON'T EXPECT RAISES, DON'T EXPECT TO BE TRAINED AND DON'T EXPECT A PENSION.
5/9/96 © 1996 United Feature Syndicate, Inc.(NYC)
THAT'S DEPRESSING. I NEED A SOURBALL.
THOSE ARE MARBLES WRAPPED IN CELLOPHANE.

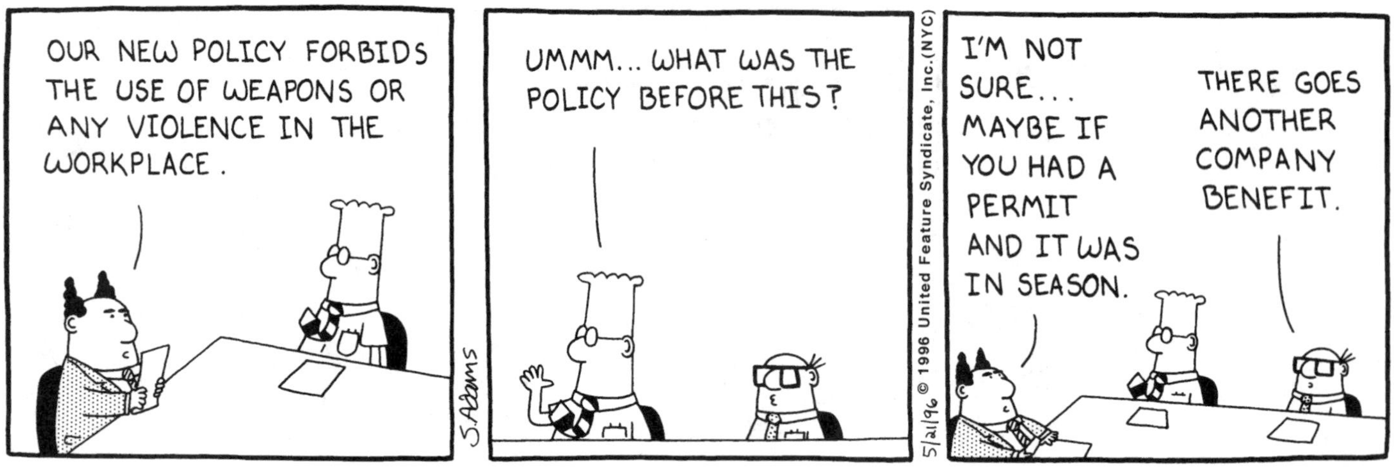
OUR NEW POLICY FORBIDS THE USE OF WEAPONS OR ANY VIOLENCE IN THE WORKPLACE.
S. Adams
UMMM... WHAT WAS THE POLICY BEFORE THIS?
5/21/96 © 1996 United Feature Syndicate, Inc.(NYC)
I'M NOT SURE... MAYBE IF YOU HAD A PERMIT AND IT WAS IN SEASON.
THERE GOES ANOTHER COMPANY BENEFIT.

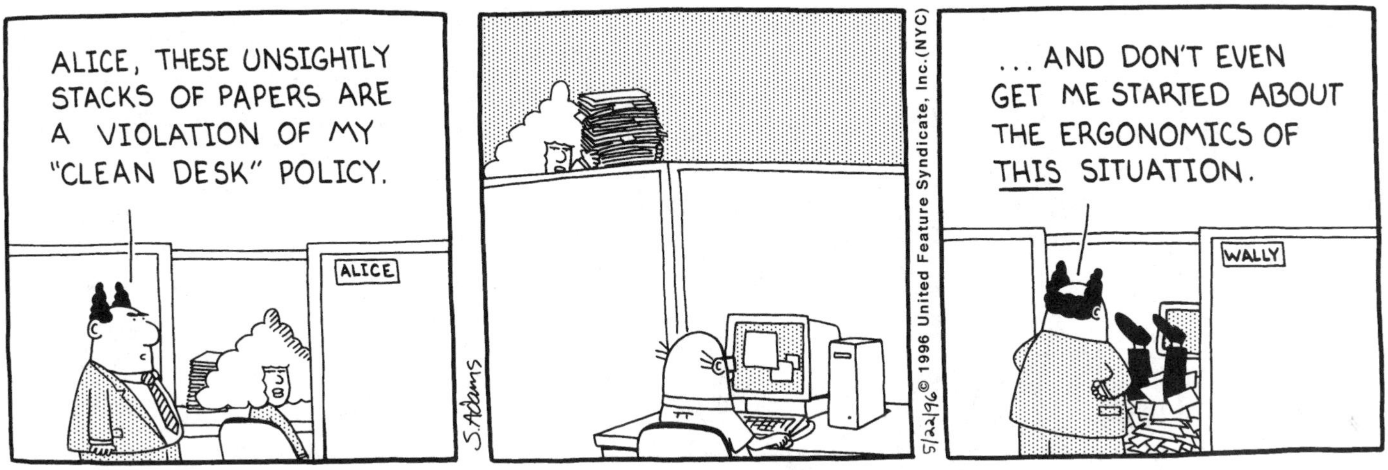
ALICE, THESE UNSIGHTLY STACKS OF PAPERS ARE A VIOLATION OF MY "CLEAN DESK" POLICY.
ALICE
S. Adams
5/22/96 © 1996 United Feature Syndicate, Inc.(NYC)
... AND DON'T EVEN GET ME STARTED ABOUT THE ERGONOMICS OF THIS SITUATION.
WALLY

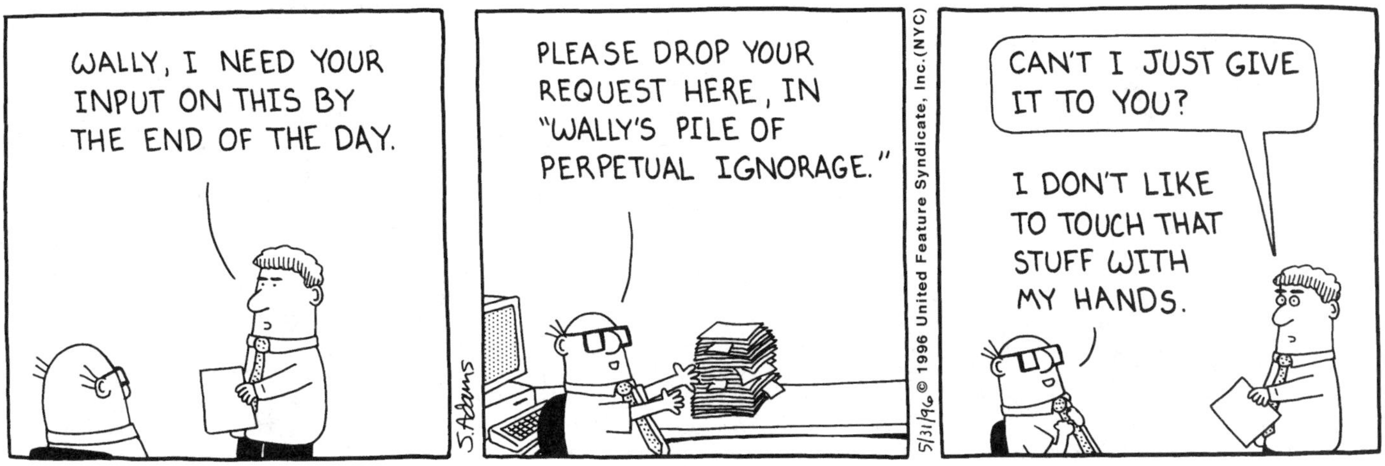
WALLY, I NEED YOUR INPUT ON THIS BY THE END OF THE DAY.
S. Adams
PLEASE DROP YOUR REQUEST HERE, IN "WALLY'S PILE OF PERPETUAL IGNORAGE."
5/31/96 © 1996 United Feature Syndicate, Inc.(NYC)
CAN'T I JUST GIVE IT TO YOU?
I DON'T LIKE TO TOUCH THAT STUFF WITH MY HANDS.

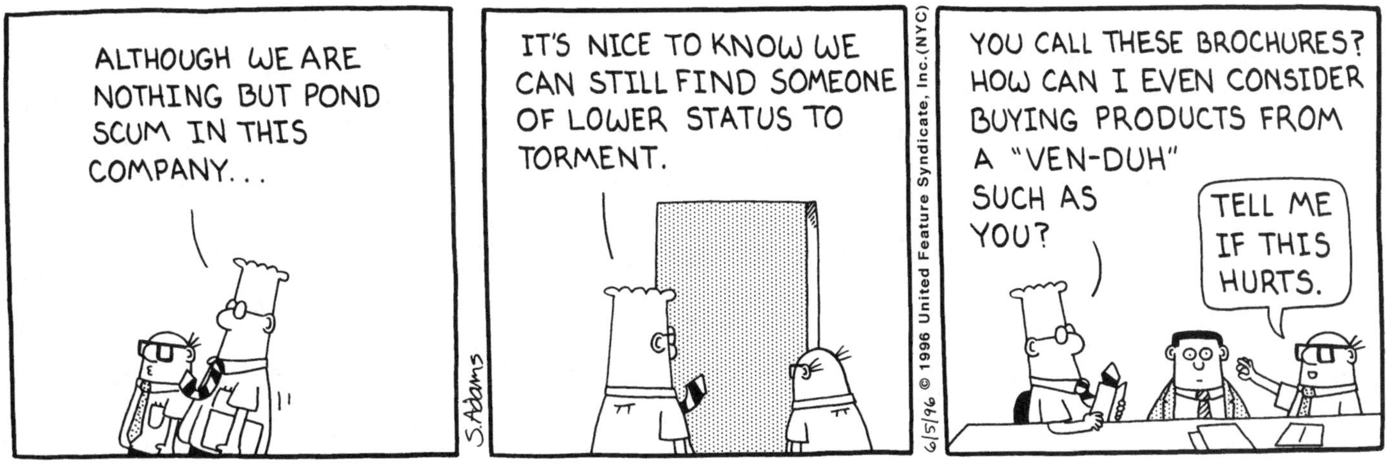
ALTHOUGH WE ARE NOTHING BUT POND SCUM IN THIS COMPANY...
S. Adams
IT'S NICE TO KNOW WE CAN STILL FIND SOMEONE OF LOWER STATUS TO TORMENT.
6/5/96 © 1996 United Feature Syndicate, Inc.(NYC)
YOU CALL THESE BROCHURES? HOW CAN I EVEN CONSIDER BUYING PRODUCTS FROM A "VEN-DUH" SUCH AS YOU?
TELL ME IF THIS HURTS.

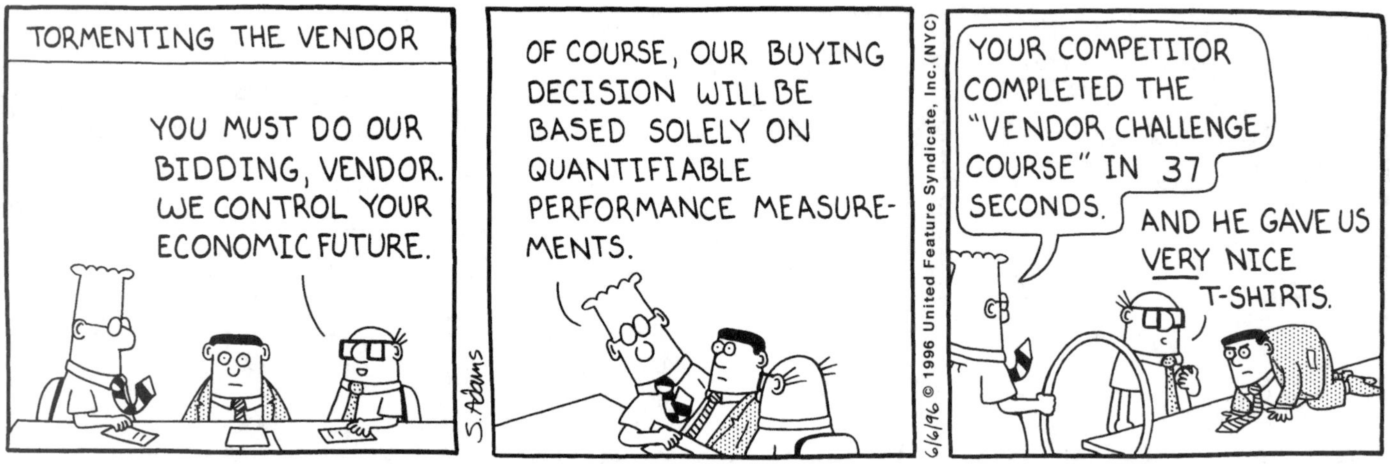
TORMENTING THE VENDOR
YOU MUST DO OUR BIDDING, VENDOR. WE CONTROL YOUR ECONOMIC FUTURE.
OF COURSE, OUR BUYING DECISION WILL BE BASED SOLELY ON QUANTIFIABLE PERFORMANCE MEASUREMENTS.
YOUR COMPETITOR COMPLETED THE "VENDOR CHALLENGE COURSE" IN 37 SECONDS.
AND HE GAVE US VERY NICE T-SHIRTS.
6/6/96 © 1996 United Feature Syndicate, Inc.(NYC)

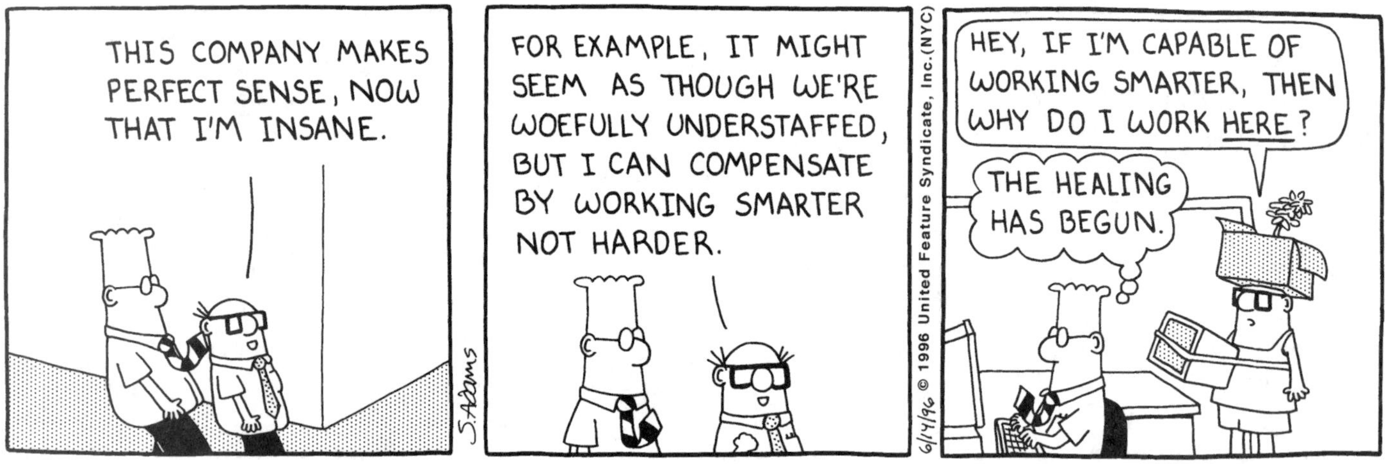
THIS COMPANY MAKES PERFECT SENSE, NOW THAT I'M INSANE.
FOR EXAMPLE, IT MIGHT SEEM AS THOUGH WE'RE WOEFULLY UNDERSTAFFED, BUT I CAN COMPENSATE BY WORKING SMARTER NOT HARDER.
HEY, IF I'M CAPABLE OF WORKING SMARTER, THEN WHY DO I WORK HERE?
THE HEALING HAS BEGUN.
6/4/96 © 1996 United Feature Syndicate, Inc.(NYC)

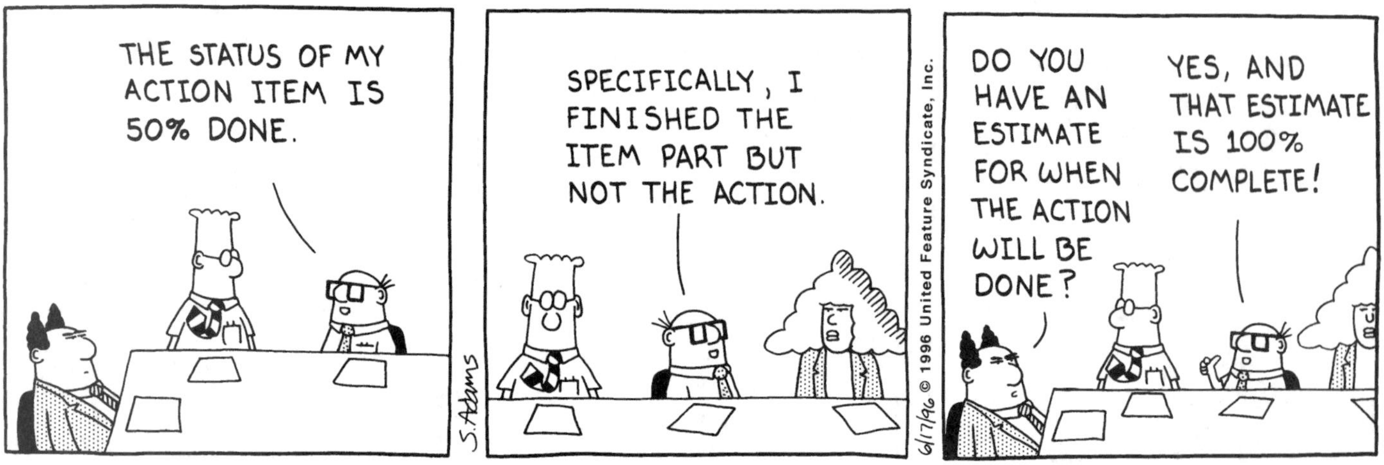
THE STATUS OF MY ACTION ITEM IS 50% DONE.
SPECIFICALLY, I FINISHED THE ITEM PART BUT NOT THE ACTION.
DO YOU HAVE AN ESTIMATE FOR WHEN THE ACTION WILL BE DONE?
YES, AND THAT ESTIMATE IS 100% COMPLETE!
6/17/96 © 1996 United Feature Syndicate, Inc.

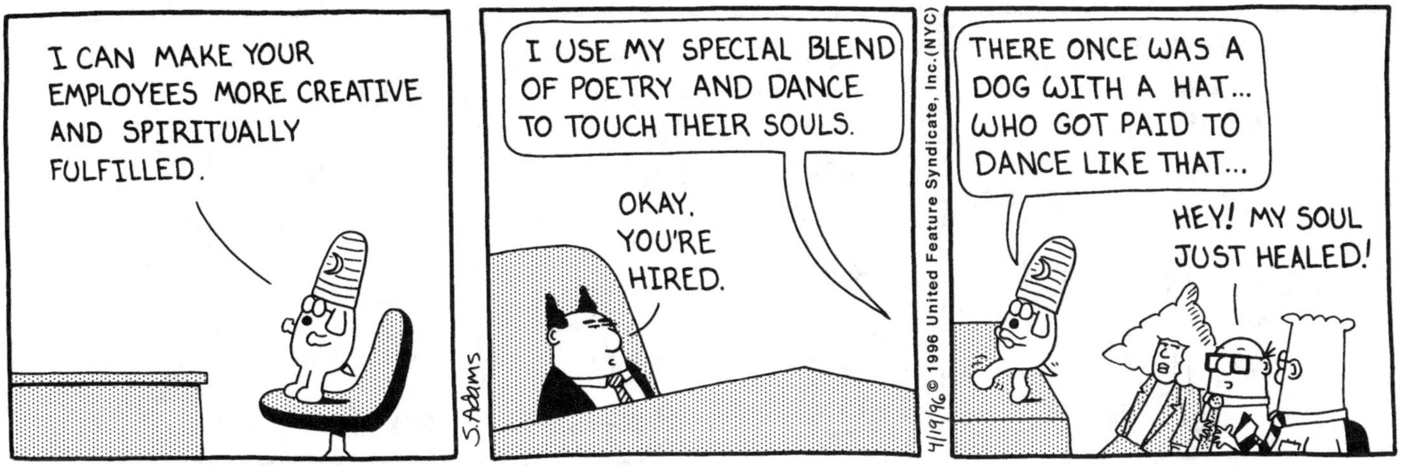
I CAN MAKE YOUR EMPLOYEES MORE CREATIVE AND SPIRITUALLY FULFILLED.
I USE MY SPECIAL BLEND OF POETRY AND DANCE TO TOUCH THEIR SOULS.
OKAY. YOU'RE HIRED.
THERE ONCE WAS A DOG WITH A HAT... WHO GOT PAID TO DANCE LIKE THAT...
HEY! MY SOUL JUST HEALED!
S.Adams
4/1/96 © 1996 United Feature Syndicate, Inc.(NYC)

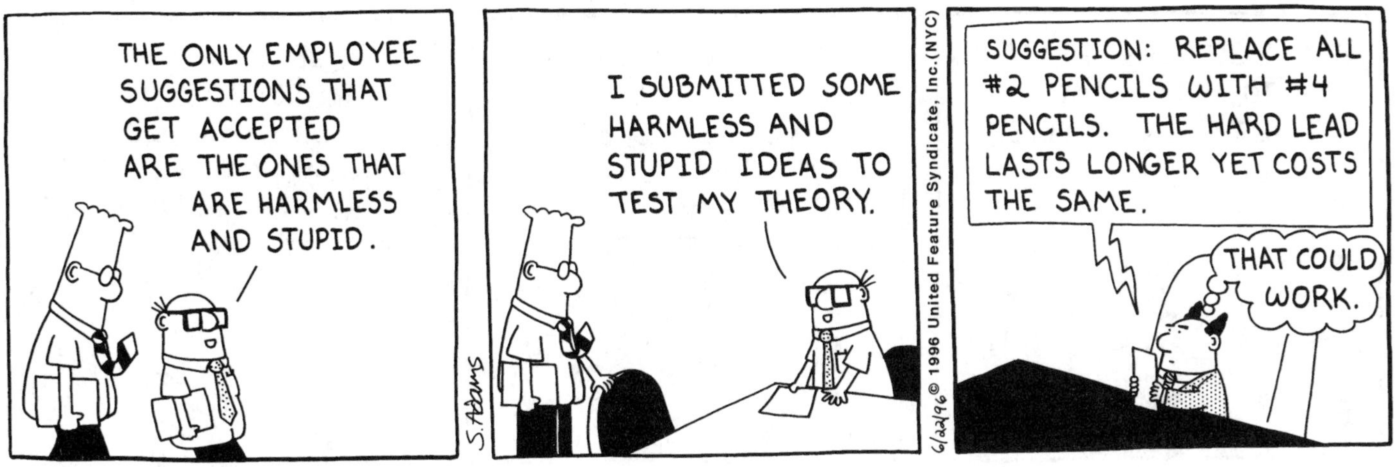
THE ONLY EMPLOYEE SUGGESTIONS THAT GET ACCEPTED ARE THE ONES THAT ARE HARMLESS AND STUPID.
I SUBMITTED SOME HARMLESS AND STUPID IDEAS TO TEST MY THEORY.
SUGGESTION: REPLACE ALL #2 PENCILS WITH #4 PENCILS. THE HARD LEAD LASTS LONGER YET COSTS THE SAME.
THAT COULD WORK.
S.Adams
6/22/96 © 1996 United Feature Syndicate, Inc.(NYC)

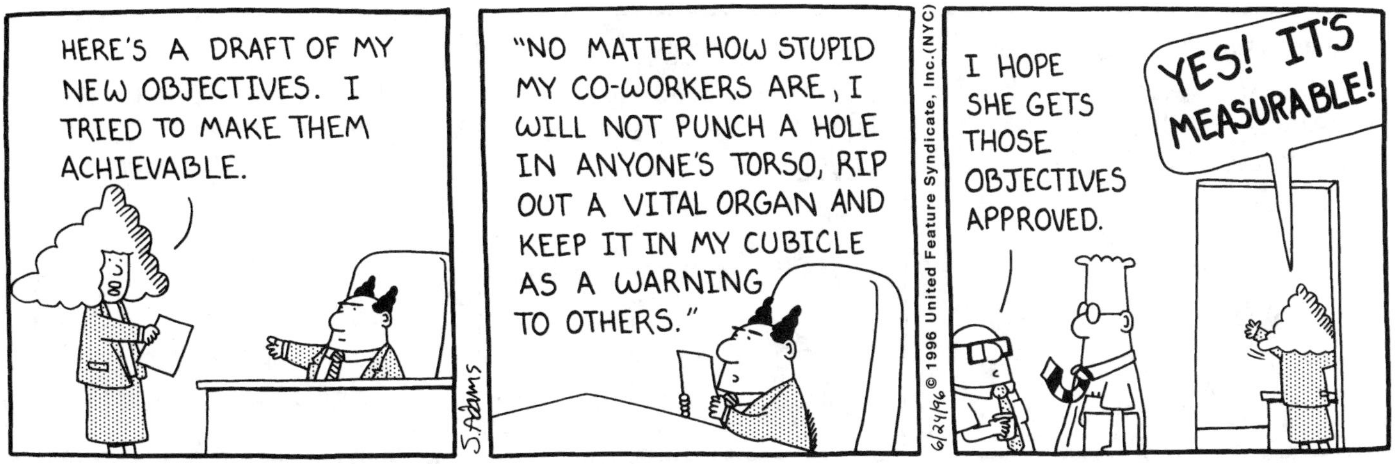
HERE'S A DRAFT OF MY NEW OBJECTIVES. I TRIED TO MAKE THEM ACHIEVABLE.
"NO MATTER HOW STUPID MY CO-WORKERS ARE, I WILL NOT PUNCH A HOLE IN ANYONE'S TORSO, RIP OUT A VITAL ORGAN AND KEEP IT IN MY CUBICLE AS A WARNING TO OTHERS."
I HOPE SHE GETS THOSE OBJECTIVES APPROVED.
YES! IT'S MEASURABLE!
S.Adams
6/24/96 © 1996 United Feature Syndicate, Inc.(NYC)

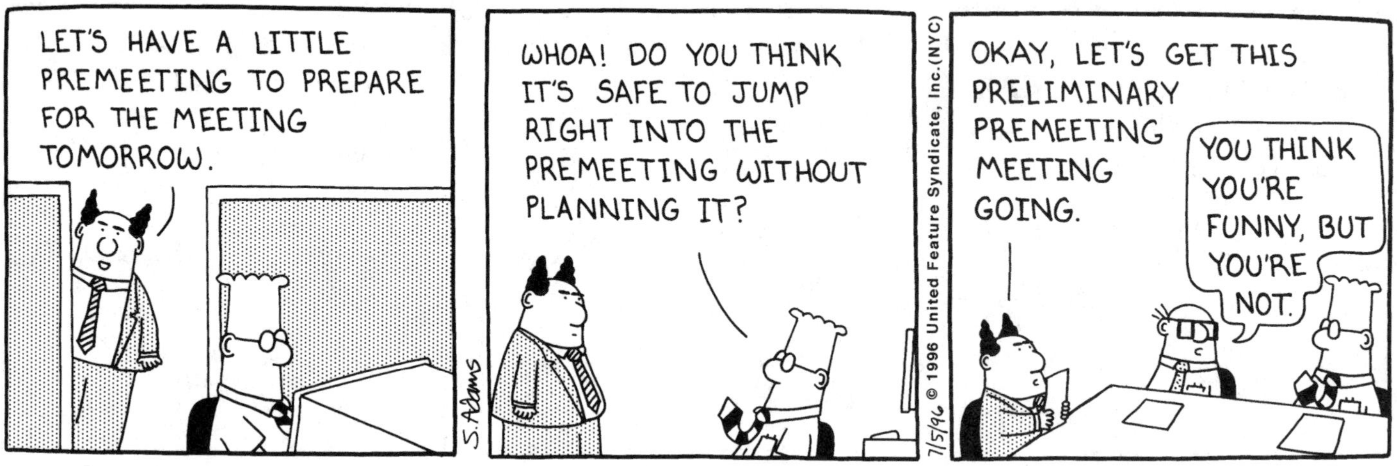
LET'S HAVE A LITTLE PREMEETING TO PREPARE FOR THE MEETING TOMORROW.
S. Adams
WHOA! DO YOU THINK IT'S SAFE TO JUMP RIGHT INTO THE PREMEETING WITHOUT PLANNING IT?
7/5/96 © 1996 United Feature Syndicate, Inc.(NYC)
OKAY, LET'S GET THIS PRELIMINARY PREMEETING MEETING GOING.
YOU THINK YOU'RE FUNNY, BUT YOU'RE NOT.

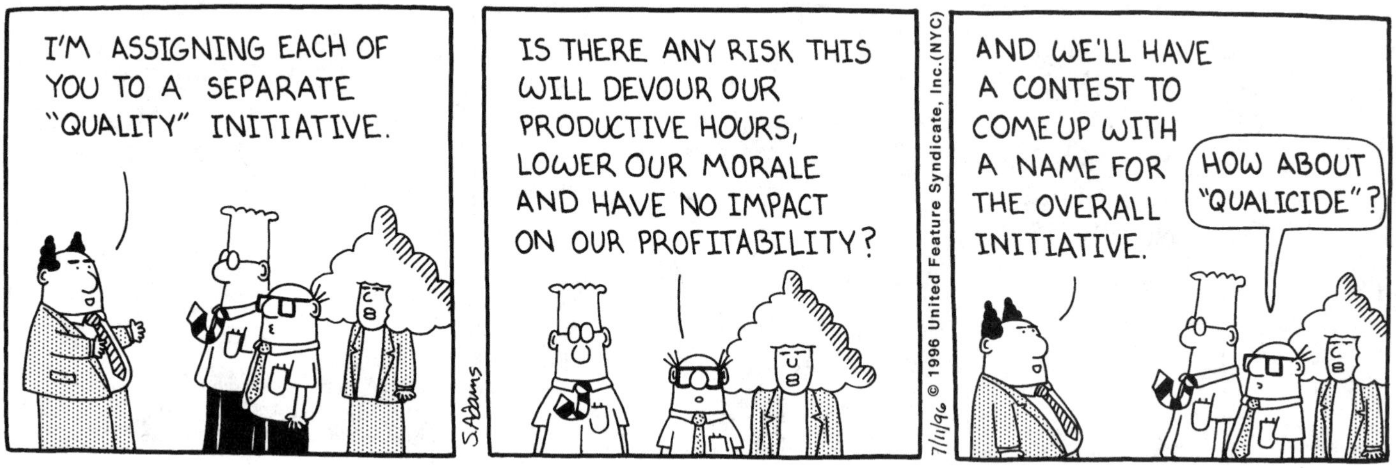
I'M ASSIGNING EACH OF YOU TO A SEPARATE "QUALITY" INITIATIVE.
S. Adams
IS THERE ANY RISK THIS WILL DEVOUR OUR PRODUCTIVE HOURS, LOWER OUR MORALE AND HAVE NO IMPACT ON OUR PROFITABILITY?
7/11/96 © 1996 United Feature Syndicate, Inc.(NYC)
AND WE'LL HAVE A CONTEST TO COME UP WITH A NAME FOR THE OVERALL INITIATIVE.
HOW ABOUT "QUALICIDE"?

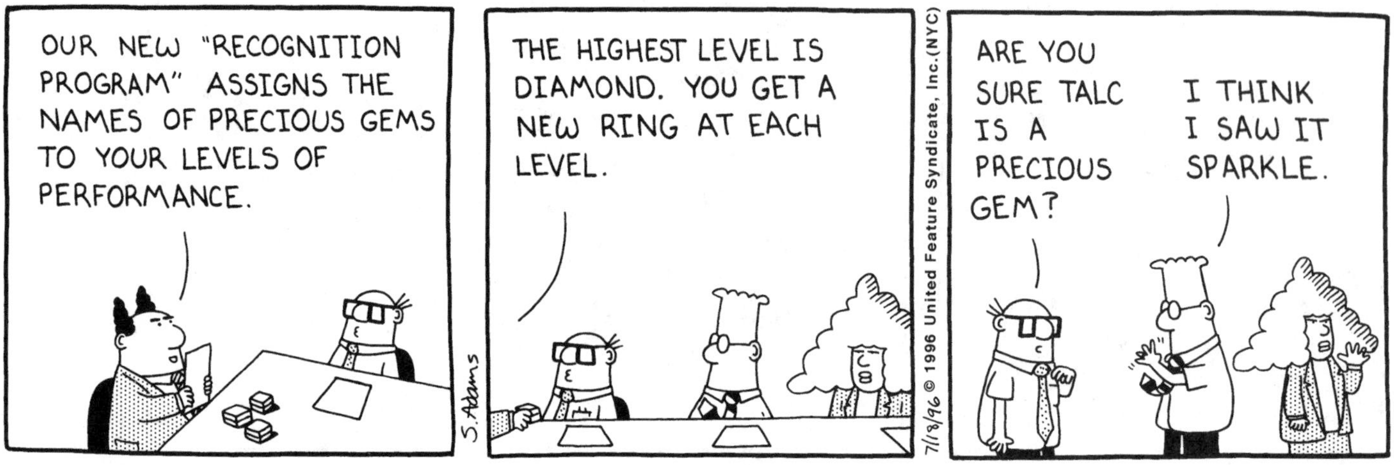
OUR NEW "RECOGNITION PROGRAM" ASSIGNS THE NAMES OF PRECIOUS GEMS TO YOUR LEVELS OF PERFORMANCE.
S. Adams
THE HIGHEST LEVEL IS DIAMOND. YOU GET A NEW RING AT EACH LEVEL.
7/18/96 © 1996 United Feature Syndicate, Inc.(NYC)
ARE YOU SURE TALC IS A PRECIOUS GEM?
I THINK I SAW IT SPARKLE.

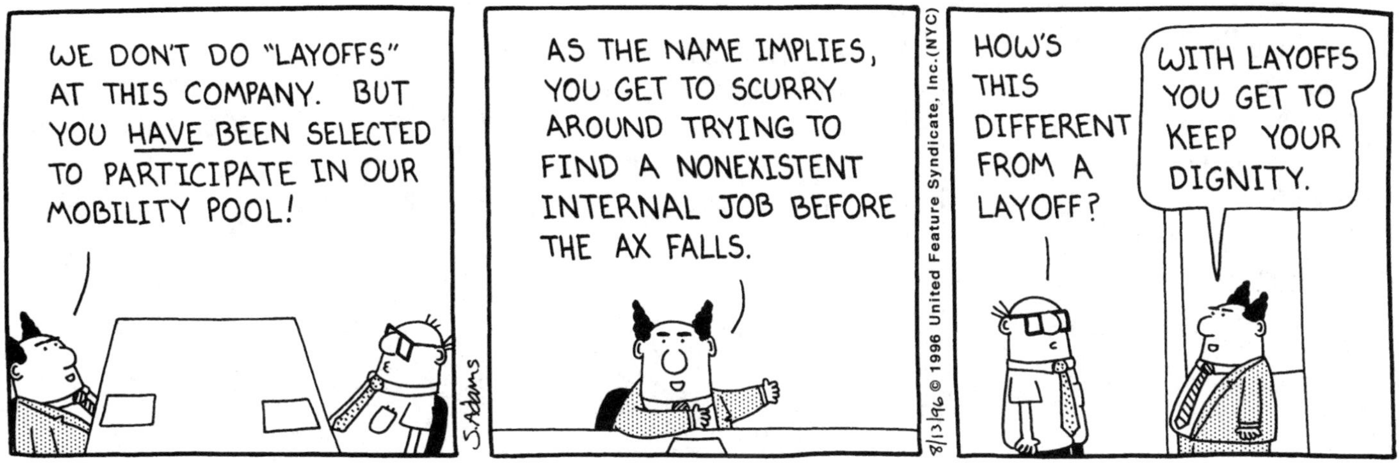
WE DON'T DO "LAYOFFS" AT THIS COMPANY. BUT YOU HAVE BEEN SELECTED TO PARTICIPATE IN OUR MOBILITY POOL!
S. Adams
AS THE NAME IMPLIES, YOU GET TO SCURRY AROUND TRYING TO FIND A NONEXISTENT INTERNAL JOB BEFORE THE AX FALLS.
8/13/96 © 1996 United Feature Syndicate, Inc.(NYC)
HOW'S THIS DIFFERENT FROM A LAYOFF?
WITH LAYOFFS YOU GET TO KEEP YOUR DIGNITY.

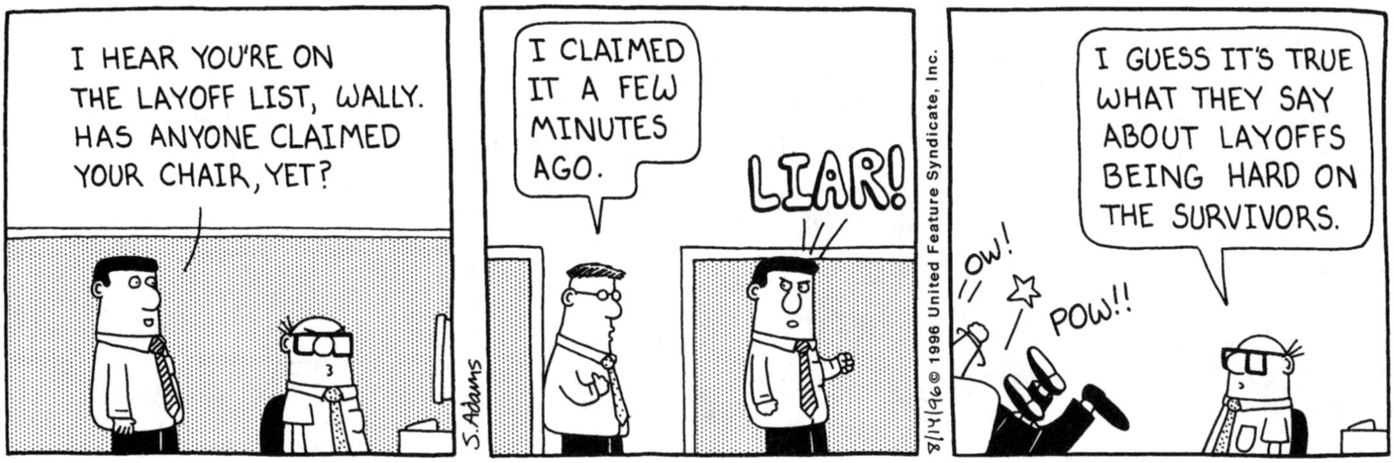
I HEAR YOU'RE ON THE LAYOFF LIST, WALLY. HAS ANYONE CLAIMED YOUR CHAIR, YET?
S. Adams
I CLAIMED IT A FEW MINUTES AGO.
LIAR!
8/14/96 © 1996 United Feature Syndicate, Inc.
OW!
POW!!
I GUESS IT'S TRUE WHAT THEY SAY ABOUT LAYOFFS BEING HARD ON THE SURVIVORS.

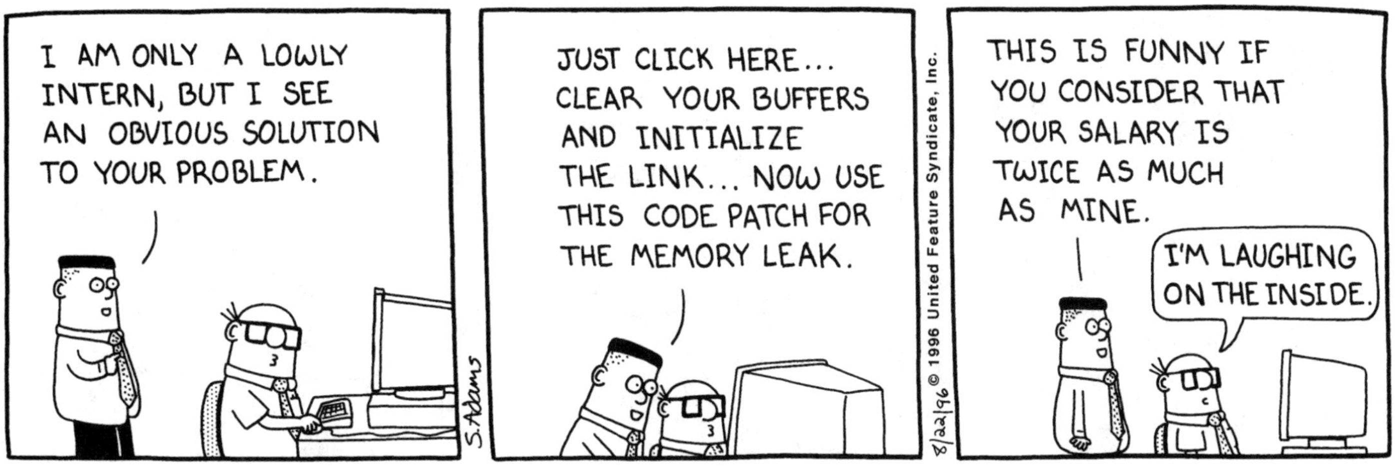
I AM ONLY A LOWLY INTERN, BUT I SEE AN OBVIOUS SOLUTION TO YOUR PROBLEM.
S. Adams
JUST CLICK HERE... CLEAR YOUR BUFFERS AND INITIALIZE THE LINK... NOW USE THIS CODE PATCH FOR THE MEMORY LEAK.
8/22/96 © 1996 United Feature Syndicate, Inc.
THIS IS FUNNY IF YOU CONSIDER THAT YOUR SALARY IS TWICE AS MUCH AS MINE.
I'M LAUGHING ON THE INSIDE.

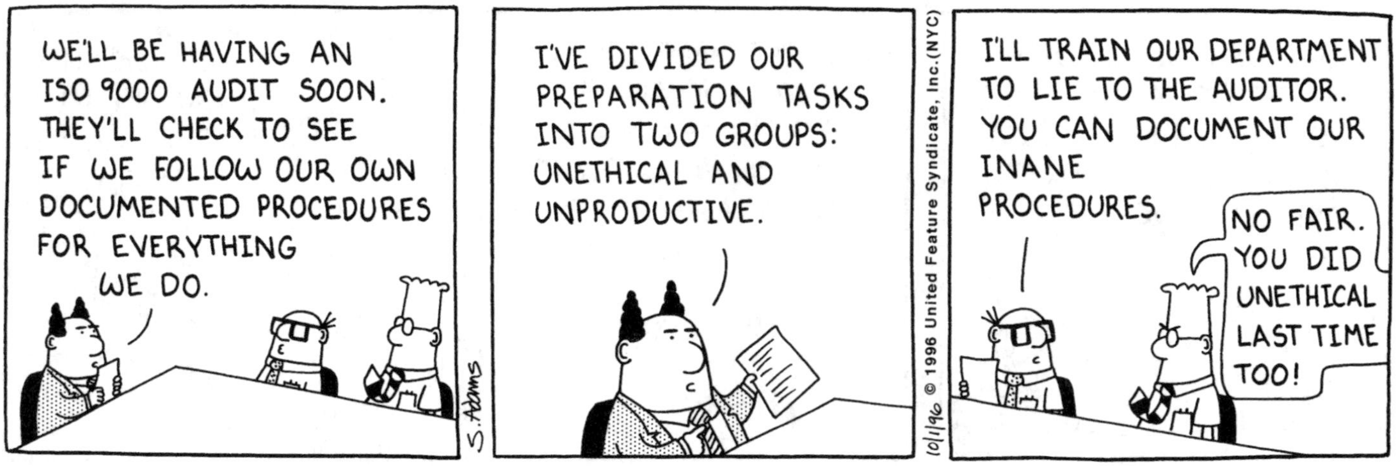
WE'LL BE HAVING AN ISO 9000 AUDIT SOON. THEY'LL CHECK TO SEE IF WE FOLLOW OUR OWN DOCUMENTED PROCEDURES FOR EVERYTHING WE DO.
S. Adams
I'VE DIVIDED OUR PREPARATION TASKS INTO TWO GROUPS: UNETHICAL AND UNPRODUCTIVE.
10/1/96 © 1996 United Feature Syndicate, Inc.(NYC)
I'LL TRAIN OUR DEPARTMENT TO LIE TO THE AUDITOR. YOU CAN DOCUMENT OUR INANE PROCEDURES.
NO FAIR. YOU DID UNETHICAL LAST TIME TOO!

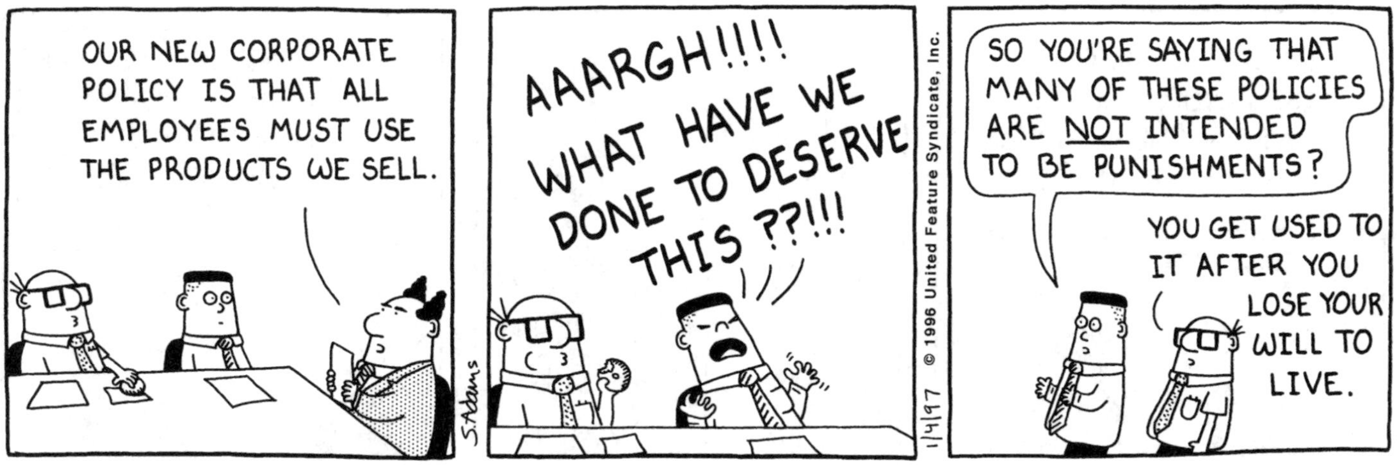
OUR NEW CORPORATE POLICY IS THAT ALL EMPLOYEES MUST USE THE PRODUCTS WE SELL.
S. Adams
AAARGH!!!! WHAT HAVE WE DONE TO DESERVE THIS ??!!!
1/4/97 © 1996 United Feature Syndicate, Inc.
SO YOU'RE SAYING THAT MANY OF THESE POLICIES ARE NOT INTENDED TO BE PUNISHMENTS?
YOU GET USED TO IT AFTER YOU LOSE YOUR WILL TO LIVE.

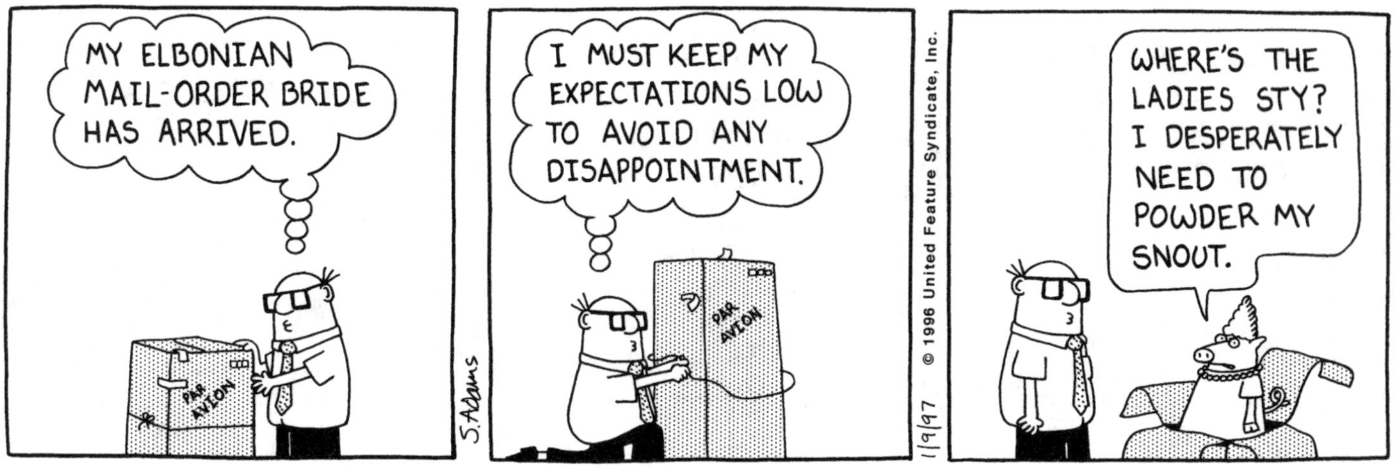
MY ELBONIAN MAIL-ORDER BRIDE HAS ARRIVED.
PAR AVION
S. Adams
I MUST KEEP MY EXPECTATIONS LOW TO AVOID ANY DISAPPOINTMENT.
PAR AVION
1/9/97 © 1996 United Feature Syndicate, Inc.
WHERE'S THE LADIES STY? I DESPERATELY NEED TO POWDER MY SNOUT.

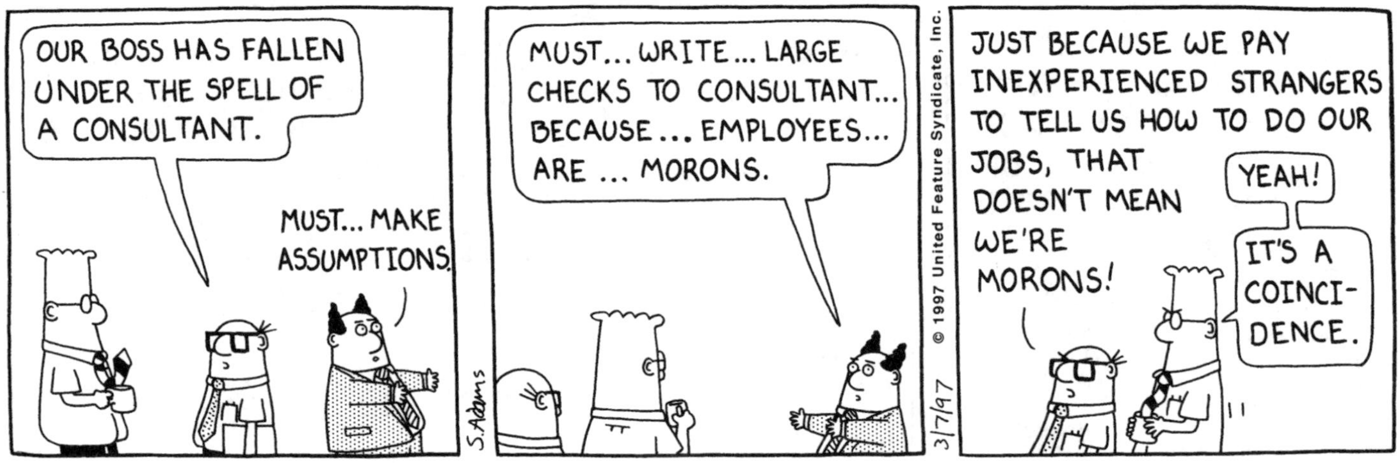
OUR BOSS HAS FALLEN UNDER THE SPELL OF A CONSULTANT.
MUST... MAKE ASSUMPTIONS.
S. Adams
MUST... WRITE... LARGE CHECKS TO CONSULTANT... BECAUSE... EMPLOYEES... ARE ... MORONS.
3/7/97
© 1997 United Feature Syndicate, Inc.
JUST BECAUSE WE PAY INEXPERIENCED STRANGERS TO TELL US HOW TO DO OUR JOBS, THAT DOESN'T MEAN WE'RE MORONS!
YEAH!
IT'S A COINCI-DENCE.

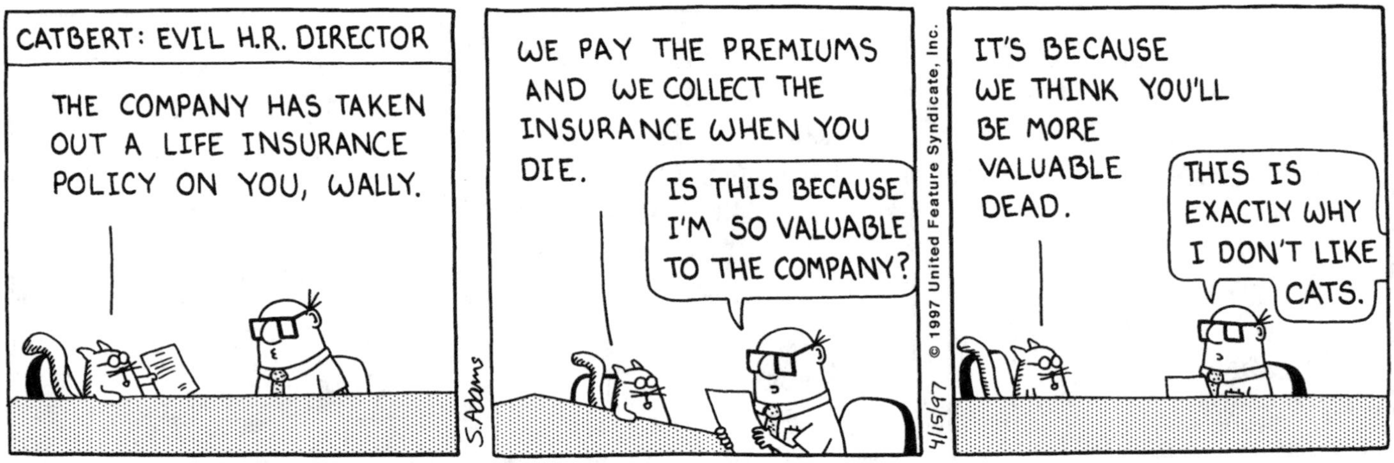
CATBERT: EVIL H.R. DIRECTOR
THE COMPANY HAS TAKEN OUT A LIFE INSURANCE POLICY ON YOU, WALLY.
S. Adams
WE PAY THE PREMIUMS AND WE COLLECT THE INSURANCE WHEN YOU DIE.
IS THIS BECAUSE I'M SO VALUABLE TO THE COMPANY?
4/15/97
© 1997 United Feature Syndicate, Inc.
IT'S BECAUSE WE THINK YOU'LL BE MORE VALUABLE DEAD.
THIS IS EXACTLY WHY I DON'T LIKE CATS.

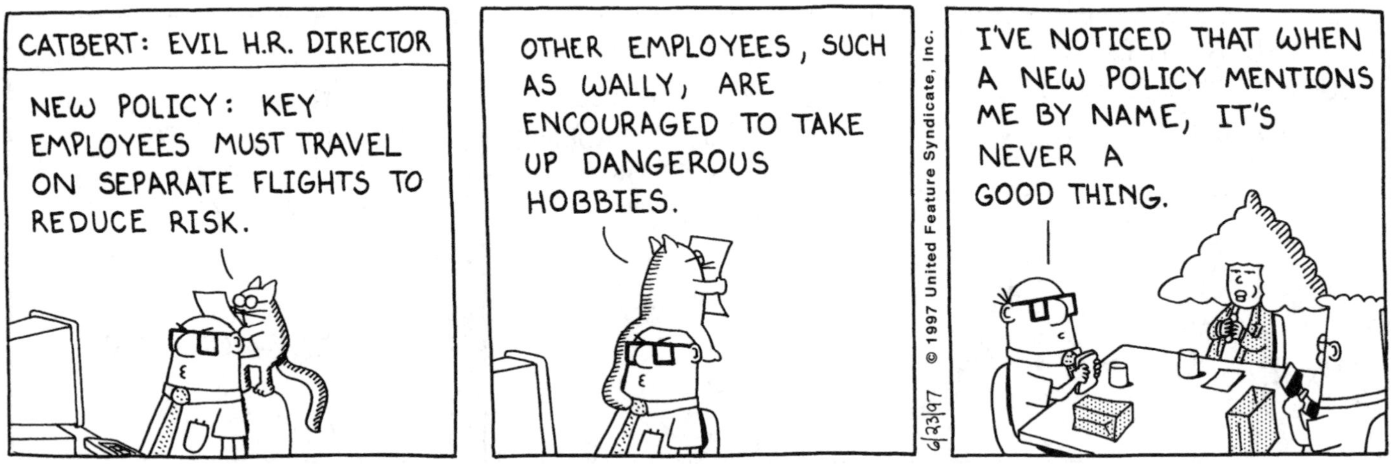
CATBERT: EVIL H.R. DIRECTOR
NEW POLICY: KEY EMPLOYEES MUST TRAVEL ON SEPARATE FLIGHTS TO REDUCE RISK.
OTHER EMPLOYEES, SUCH AS WALLY, ARE ENCOURAGED TO TAKE UP DANGEROUS HOBBIES.
6/23/97
© 1997 United Feature Syndicate, Inc.
I'VE NOTICED THAT WHEN A NEW POLICY MENTIONS ME BY NAME, IT'S NEVER A GOOD THING.

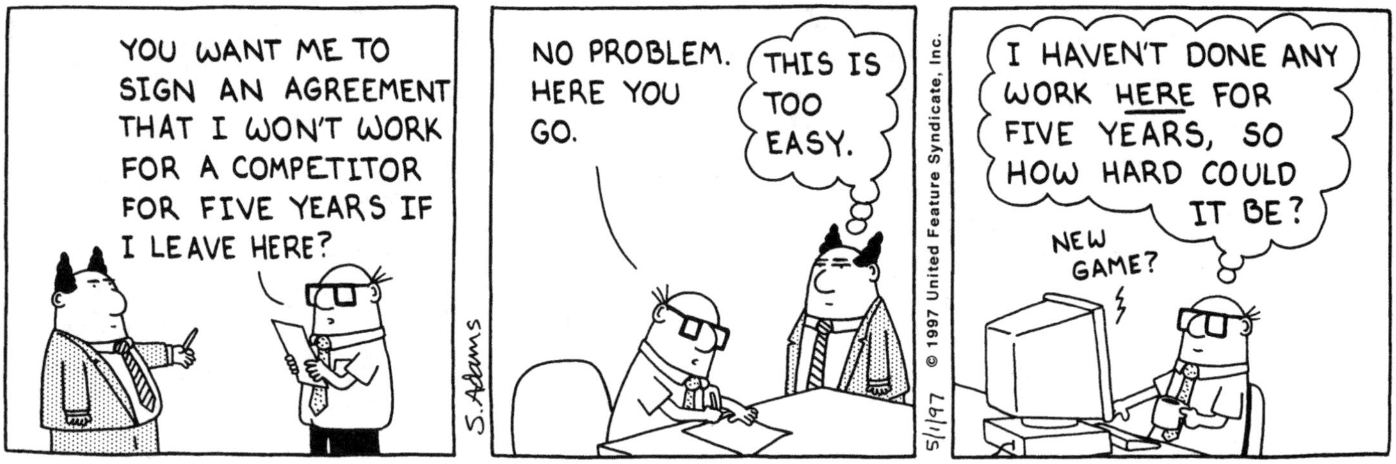
YOU WANT ME TO SIGN AN AGREEMENT THAT I WON'T WORK FOR A COMPETITOR FOR FIVE YEARS IF I LEAVE HERE?
S. Adams
NO PROBLEM. HERE YOU GO.
THIS IS TOO EASY.
5/1/97 © 1997 United Feature Syndicate, Inc.
I HAVEN'T DONE ANY WORK HERE FOR FIVE YEARS, SO HOW HARD COULD IT BE?
NEW GAME?

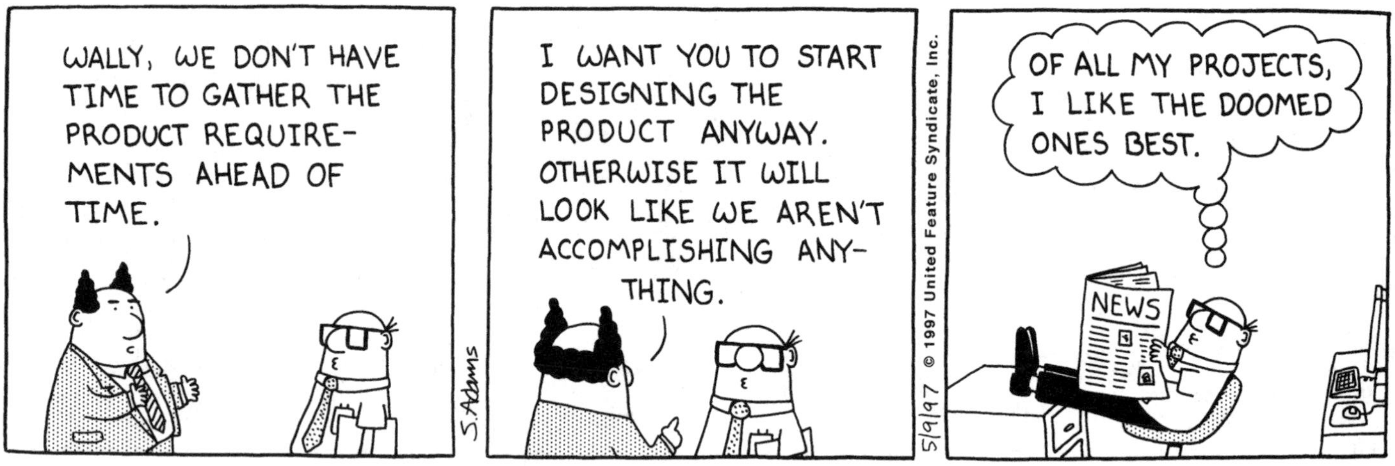
WALLY, WE DON'T HAVE TIME TO GATHER THE PRODUCT REQUIREMENTS AHEAD OF TIME.
S. Adams
I WANT YOU TO START DESIGNING THE PRODUCT ANYWAY. OTHERWISE IT WILL LOOK LIKE WE AREN'T ACCOMPLISHING ANYTHING.
5/9/97 © 1997 United Feature Syndicate, Inc.
OF ALL MY PROJECTS, I LIKE THE DOOMED ONES BEST.
NEWS

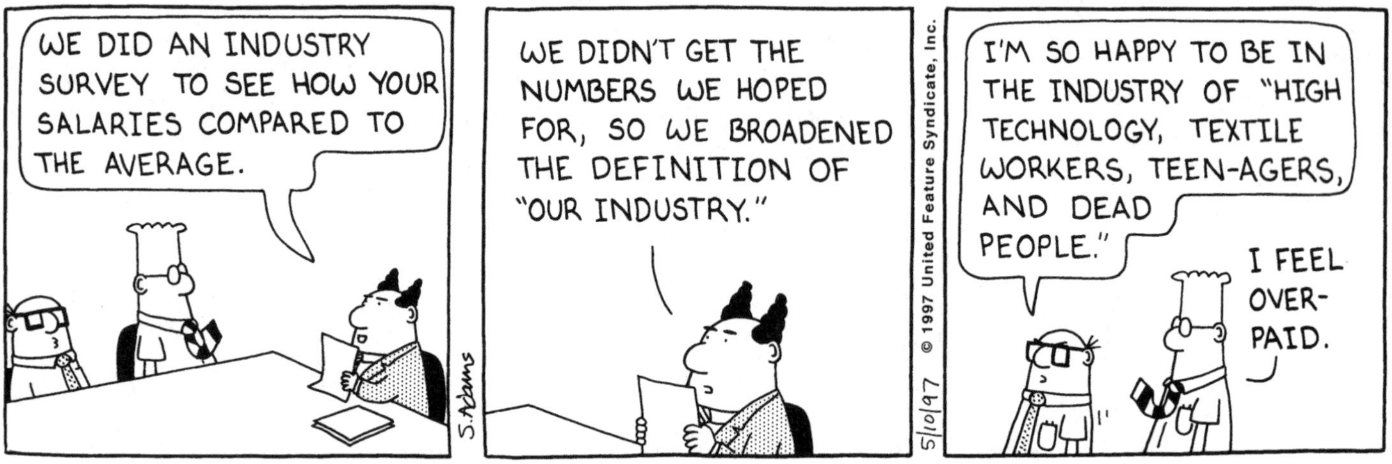
WE DID AN INDUSTRY SURVEY TO SEE HOW YOUR SALARIES COMPARED TO THE AVERAGE.
S. Adams
WE DIDN'T GET THE NUMBERS WE HOPED FOR, SO WE BROADENED THE DEFINITION OF "OUR INDUSTRY."
5/10/97 © 1997 United Feature Syndicate, Inc.
I'M SO HAPPY TO BE IN THE INDUSTRY OF "HIGH TECHNOLOGY, TEXTILE WORKERS, TEEN-AGERS, AND DEAD PEOPLE."
I FEEL OVERPAID.

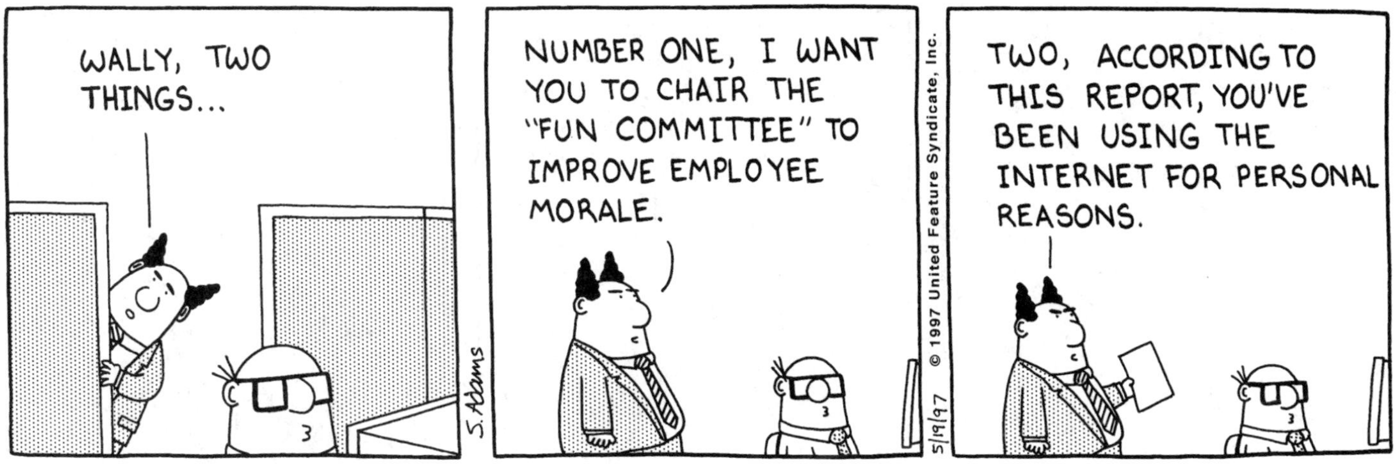
WALLY, TWO THINGS...
NUMBER ONE, I WANT YOU TO CHAIR THE "FUN COMMITTEE" TO IMPROVE EMPLOYEE MORALE.
TWO, ACCORDING TO THIS REPORT, YOU'VE BEEN USING THE INTERNET FOR PERSONAL REASONS.
S. Adams
5/19/97 © 1997 United Feature Syndicate, Inc.

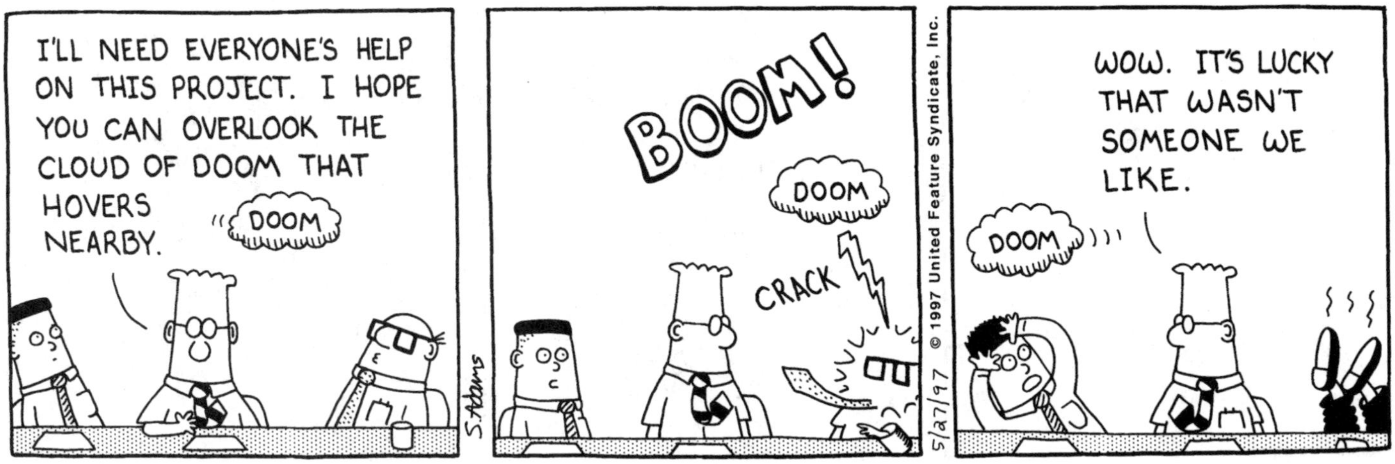
I'LL NEED EVERYONE'S HELP ON THIS PROJECT. I HOPE YOU CAN OVERLOOK THE CLOUD OF DOOM THAT HOVERS NEARBY.
DOOM
BOOM!
DOOM
CRACK
WOW. IT'S LUCKY THAT WASN'T SOMEONE WE LIKE.
DOOM
S. Adams
5/27/97 © 1997 United Feature Syndicate, Inc.

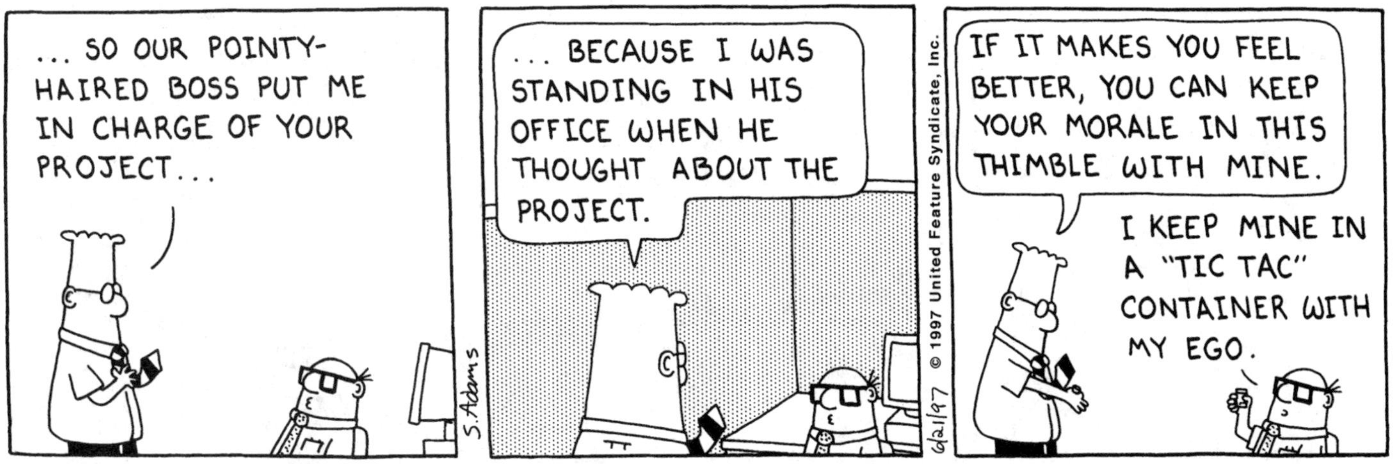
... SO OUR POINTY-HAIRED BOSS PUT ME IN CHARGE OF YOUR PROJECT...
... BECAUSE I WAS STANDING IN HIS OFFICE WHEN HE THOUGHT ABOUT THE PROJECT.
IF IT MAKES YOU FEEL BETTER, YOU CAN KEEP YOUR MORALE IN THIS THIMBLE WITH MINE.
I KEEP MINE IN A "TIC TAC" CONTAINER WITH MY EGO.
S. Adams
6/21/97 © 1997 United Feature Syndicate, Inc.

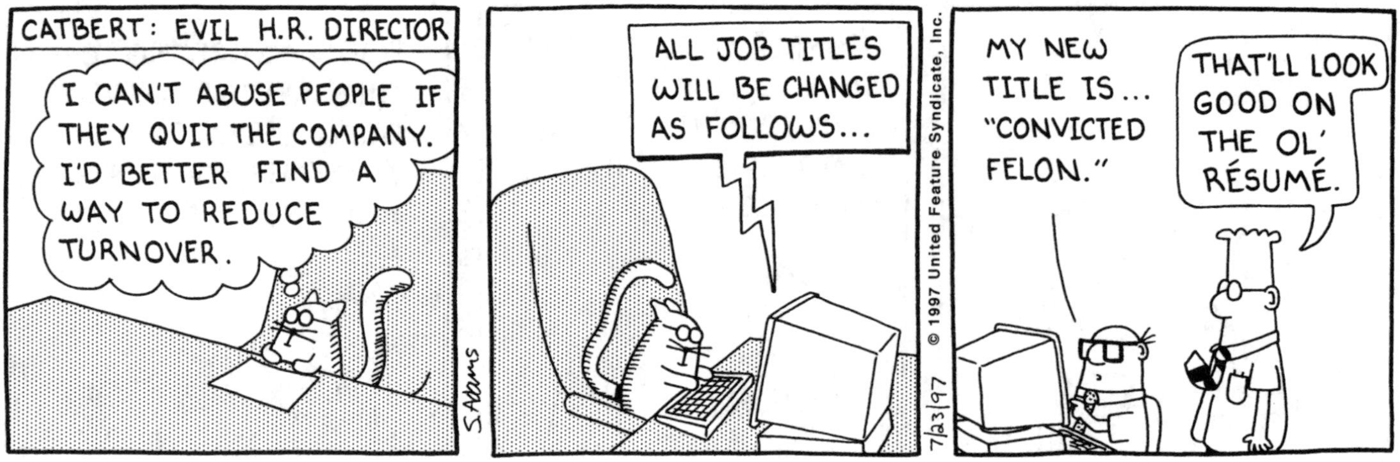
CATBERT: EVIL H.R. DIRECTOR
I CAN'T ABUSE PEOPLE IF THEY QUIT THE COMPANY. I'D BETTER FIND A WAY TO REDUCE TURNOVER.
S. Adams
ALL JOB TITLES WILL BE CHANGED AS FOLLOWS...
7/23/97 © 1997 United Feature Syndicate, Inc.
MY NEW TITLE IS... "CONVICTED FELON."
THAT'LL LOOK GOOD ON THE OL' RÉSUMÉ.

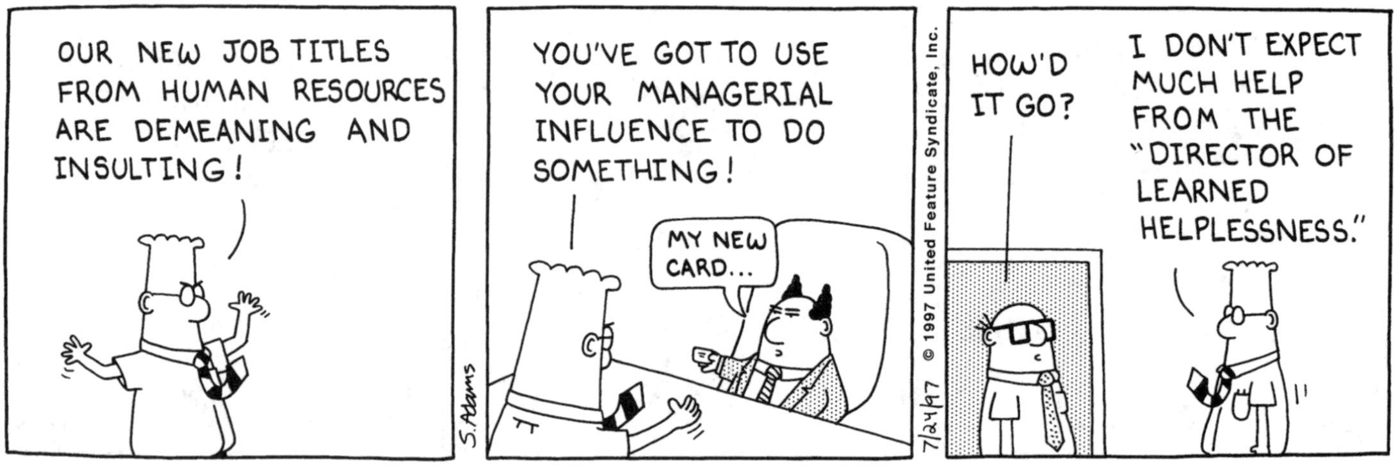
OUR NEW JOB TITLES FROM HUMAN RESOURCES ARE DEMEANING AND INSULTING!
S. Adams
YOU'VE GOT TO USE YOUR MANAGERIAL INFLUENCE TO DO SOMETHING!
MY NEW CARD...
7/24/97 © 1997 United Feature Syndicate, Inc.
HOW'D IT GO?
I DON'T EXPECT MUCH HELP FROM THE "DIRECTOR OF LEARNED HELPLESSNESS."

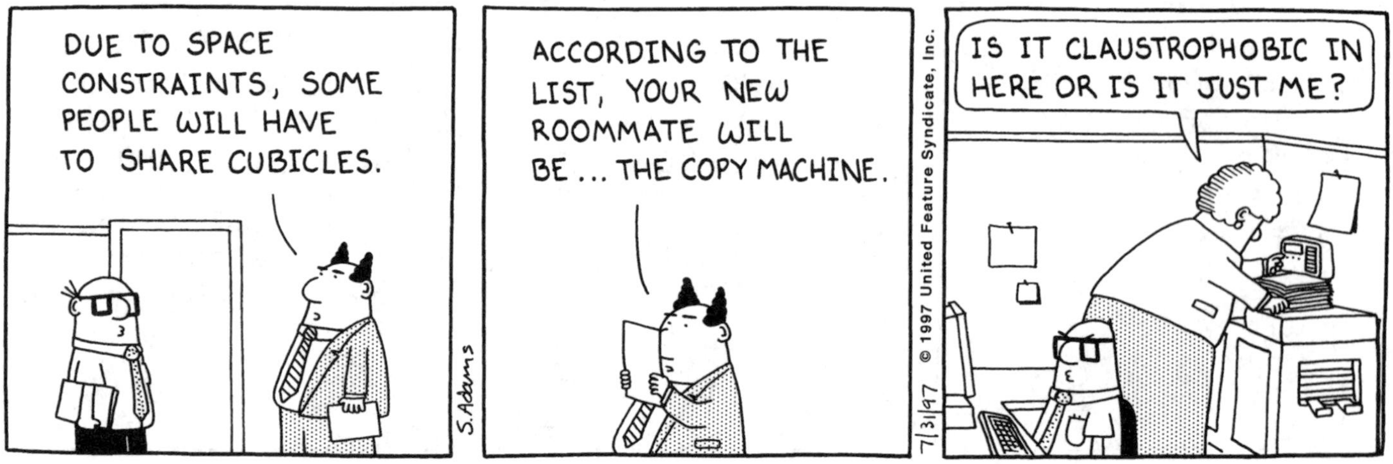
DUE TO SPACE CONSTRAINTS, SOME PEOPLE WILL HAVE TO SHARE CUBICLES.
S. Adams
ACCORDING TO THE LIST, YOUR NEW ROOMMATE WILL BE... THE COPY MACHINE.
7/31/97 © 1997 United Feature Syndicate, Inc.
IS IT CLAUSTROPHOBIC IN HERE OR IS IT JUST ME?

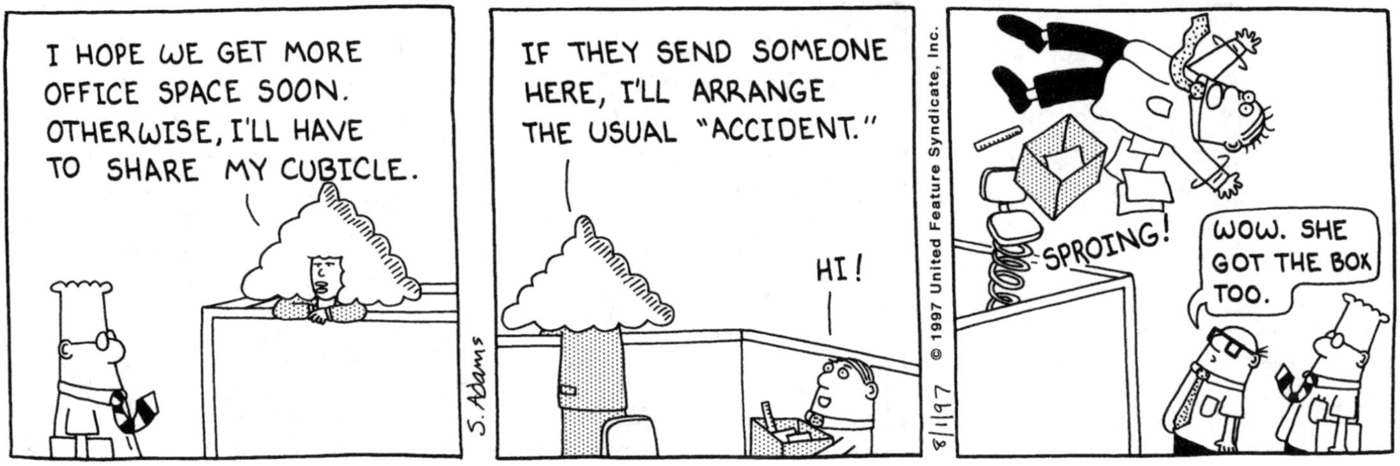
I HOPE WE GET MORE OFFICE SPACE SOON. OTHERWISE, I'LL HAVE TO SHARE MY CUBICLE.
S. Adams
IF THEY SEND SOMEONE HERE, I'LL ARRANGE THE USUAL "ACCIDENT."
HI!
8/1/97
© 1997 United Feature Syndicate, Inc.
SPROING!
WOW. SHE GOT THE BOX TOO.

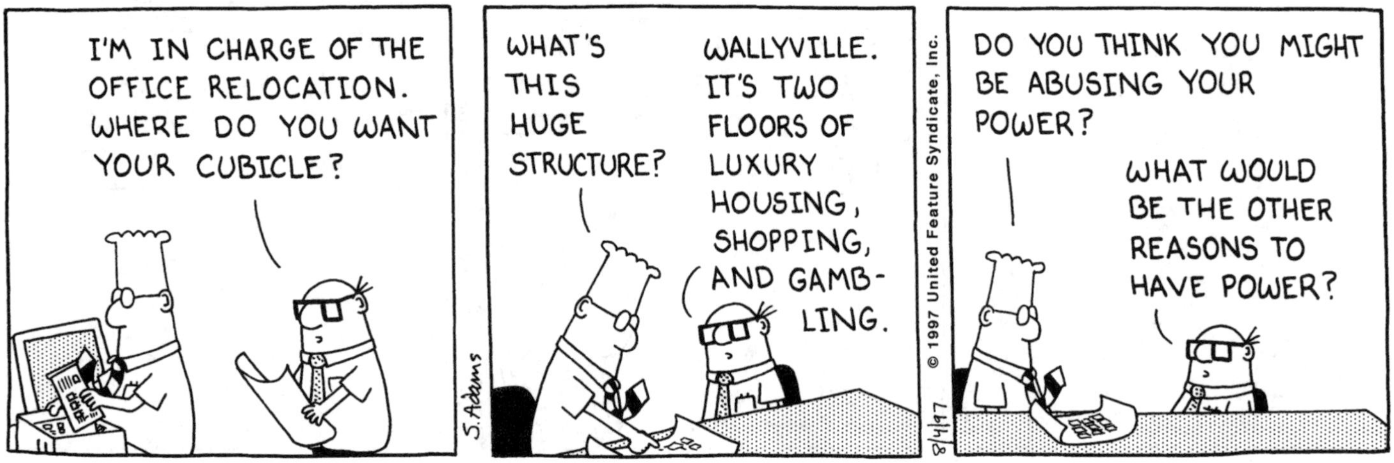
I'M IN CHARGE OF THE OFFICE RELOCATION. WHERE DO YOU WANT YOUR CUBICLE?
S. Adams
WHAT'S THIS HUGE STRUCTURE?
WALLYVILLE. IT'S TWO FLOORS OF LUXURY HOUSING, SHOPPING, AND GAMBLING.
8/4/97
© 1997 United Feature Syndicate, Inc.
DO YOU THINK YOU MIGHT BE ABUSING YOUR POWER?
WHAT WOULD BE THE OTHER REASONS TO HAVE POWER?

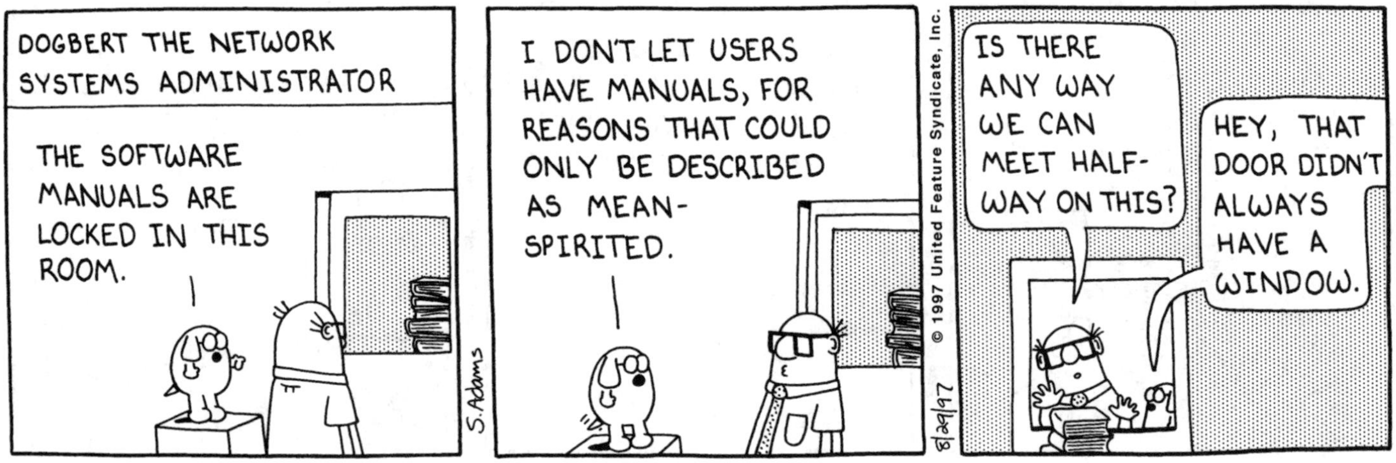
DOGBERT THE NETWORK SYSTEMS ADMINISTRATOR
THE SOFTWARE MANUALS ARE LOCKED IN THIS ROOM.
S. Adams
I DON'T LET USERS HAVE MANUALS, FOR REASONS THAT COULD ONLY BE DESCRIBED AS MEAN-SPIRITED.
8/29/97
© 1997 United Feature Syndicate, Inc.
IS THERE ANY WAY WE CAN MEET HALF-WAY ON THIS?
HEY, THAT DOOR DIDN'T ALWAYS HAVE A WINDOW.

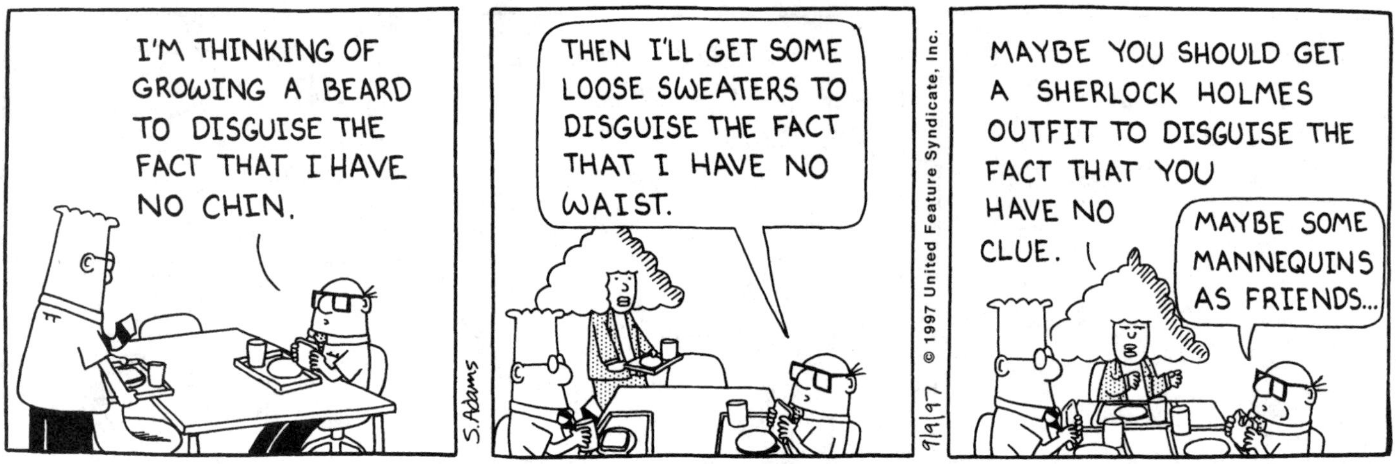
I'M THINKING OF GROWING A BEARD TO DISGUISE THE FACT THAT I HAVE NO CHIN.
S. Adams
THEN I'LL GET SOME LOOSE SWEATERS TO DISGUISE THE FACT THAT I HAVE NO WAIST.
9/9/97 © 1997 United Feature Syndicate, Inc.
MAYBE YOU SHOULD GET A SHERLOCK HOLMES OUTFIT TO DISGUISE THE FACT THAT YOU HAVE NO CLUE.
MAYBE SOME MANNEQUINS AS FRIENDS...

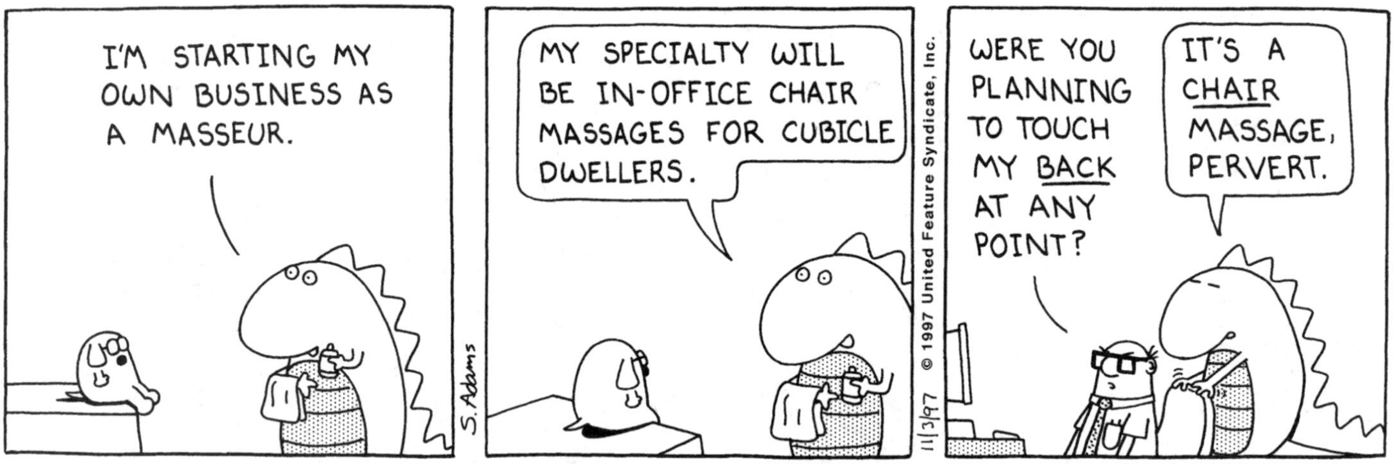
I'M STARTING MY OWN BUSINESS AS A MASSEUR.
S. Adams
MY SPECIALTY WILL BE IN-OFFICE CHAIR MASSAGES FOR CUBICLE DWELLERS.
11/3/97 © 1997 United Feature Syndicate, Inc.
WERE YOU PLANNING TO TOUCH MY BACK AT ANY POINT?
IT'S A CHAIR MASSAGE, PERVERT.

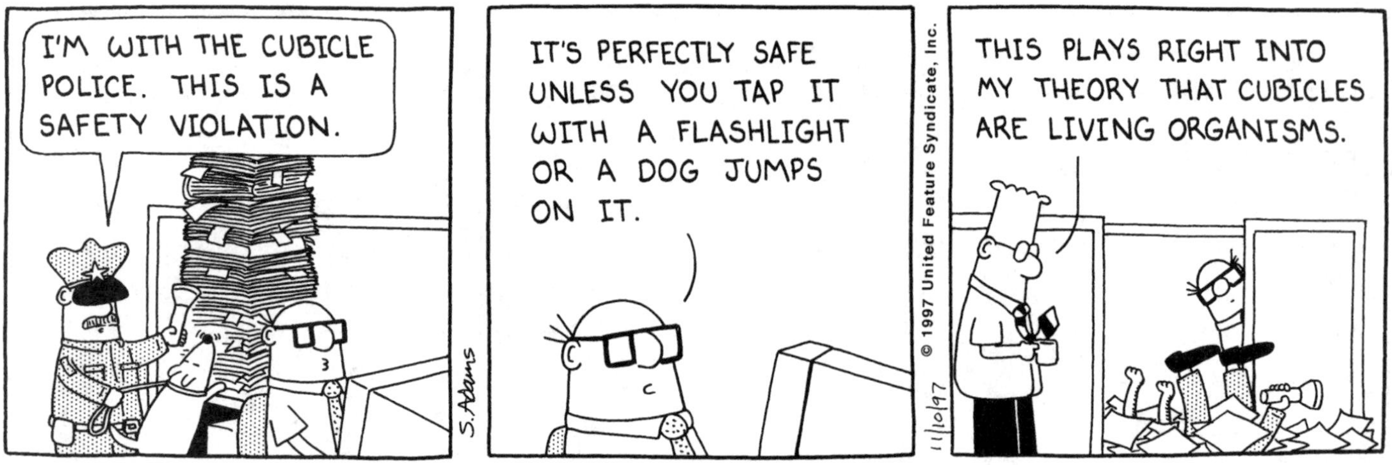
I'M WITH THE CUBICLE POLICE. THIS IS A SAFETY VIOLATION.
S. Adams
IT'S PERFECTLY SAFE UNLESS YOU TAP IT WITH A FLASHLIGHT OR A DOG JUMPS ON IT.
11/10/97 © 1997 United Feature Syndicate, Inc.
THIS PLAYS RIGHT INTO MY THEORY THAT CUBICLES ARE LIVING ORGANISMS.

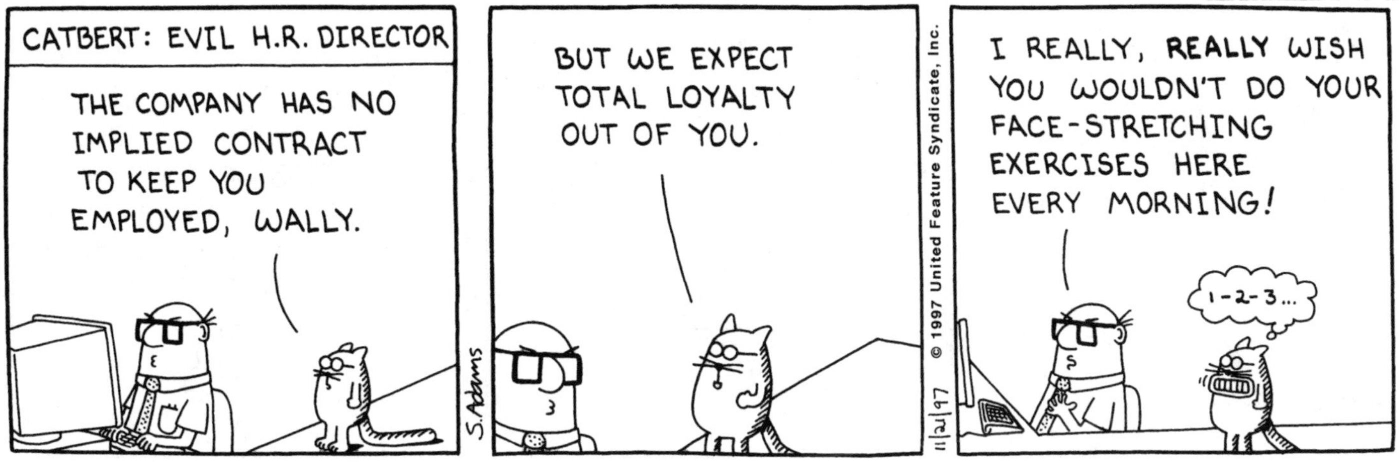
CATBERT: EVIL H.R. DIRECTOR
THE COMPANY HAS NO IMPLIED CONTRACT TO KEEP YOU EMPLOYED, WALLY.
BUT WE EXPECT TOTAL LOYALTY OUT OF YOU.
I REALLY, **REALLY** WISH YOU WOULDN'T DO YOUR FACE-STRETCHING EXERCISES HERE EVERY MORNING!
1-2-3...
S. Adams
11/21/97
© 1997 United Feature Syndicate, Inc.

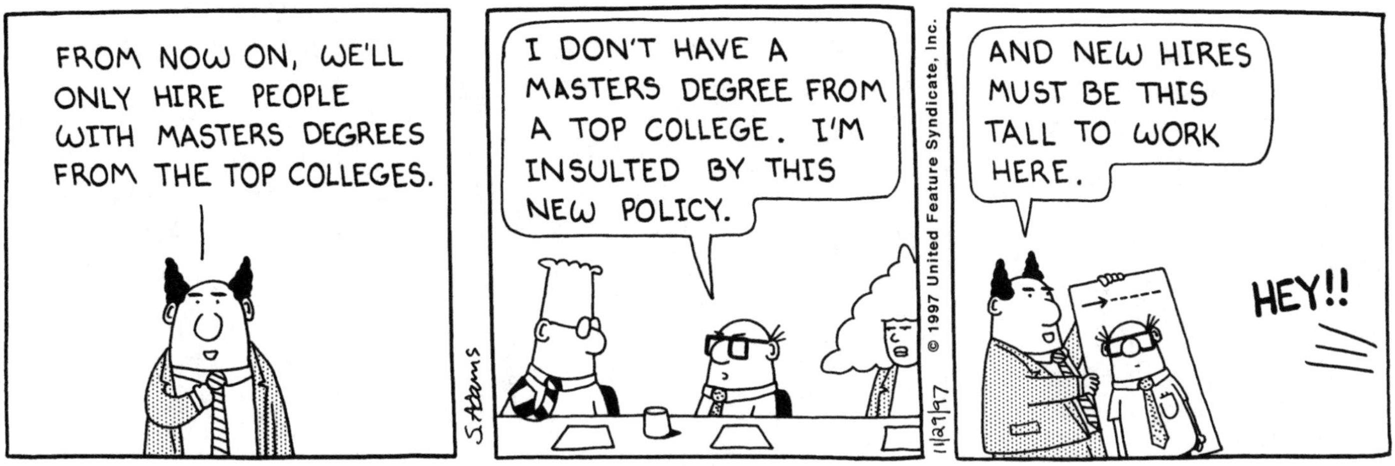
FROM NOW ON, WE'LL ONLY HIRE PEOPLE WITH MASTERS DEGREES FROM THE TOP COLLEGES.
I DON'T HAVE A MASTERS DEGREE FROM A TOP COLLEGE. I'M INSULTED BY THIS NEW POLICY.
AND NEW HIRES MUST BE THIS TALL TO WORK HERE.
HEY!!
S. Adams
11/29/97
© 1997 United Feature Syndicate, Inc.

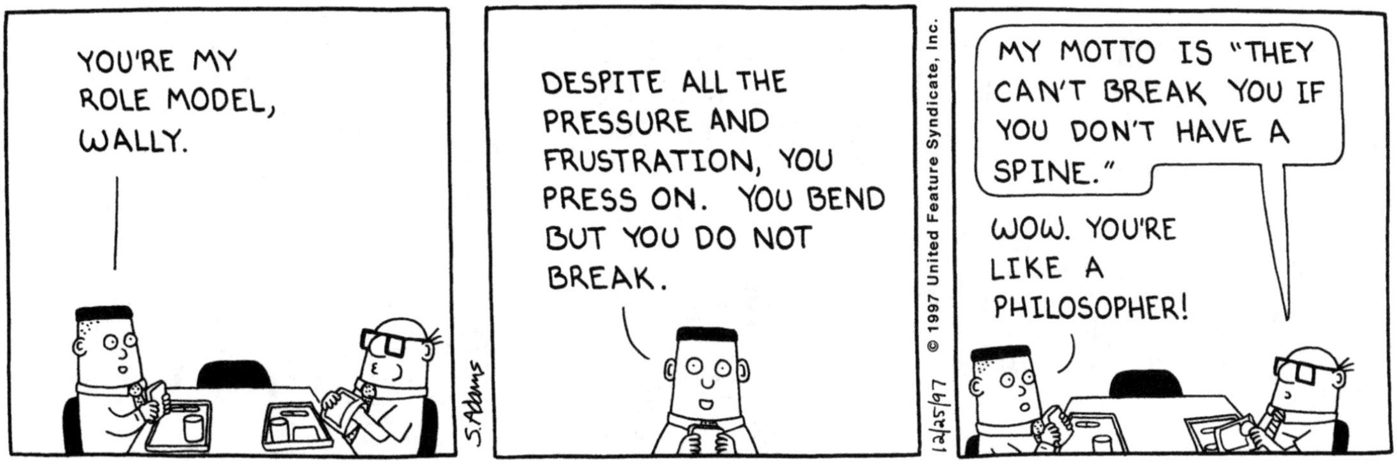
YOU'RE MY ROLE MODEL, WALLY.
DESPITE ALL THE PRESSURE AND FRUSTRATION, YOU PRESS ON. YOU BEND BUT YOU DO NOT BREAK.
MY MOTTO IS "THEY CAN'T BREAK YOU IF YOU DON'T HAVE A SPINE."
WOW. YOU'RE LIKE A PHILOSOPHER!
S. Adams
12/25/97
© 1997 United Feature Syndicate, Inc.

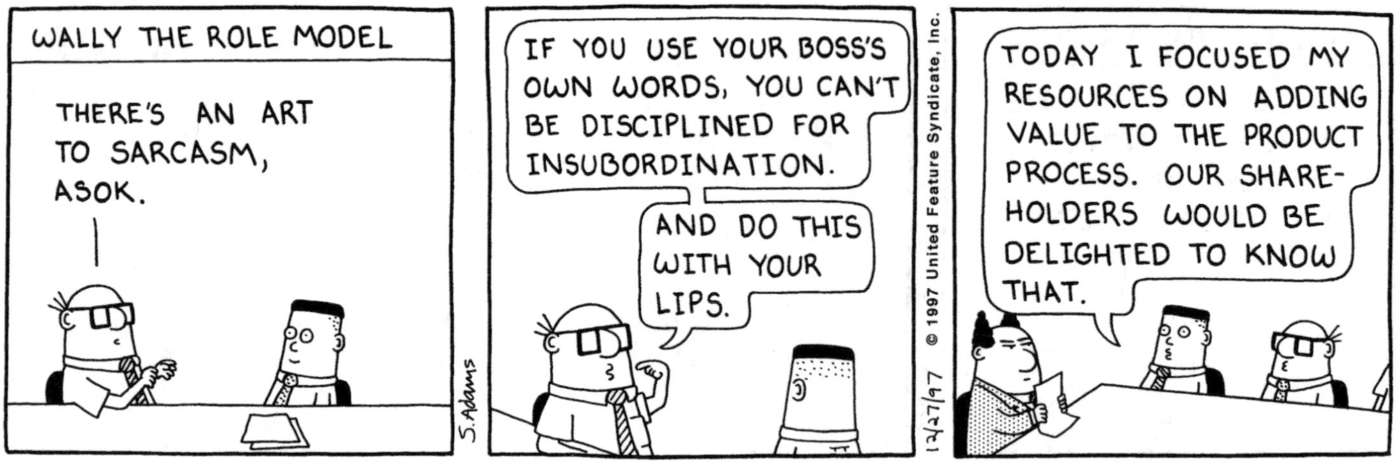
WALLY THE ROLE MODEL
THERE'S AN ART TO SARCASM, ASOK.
IF YOU USE YOUR BOSS'S OWN WORDS, YOU CAN'T BE DISCIPLINED FOR INSUBORDINATION.
AND DO THIS WITH YOUR LIPS.
TODAY I FOCUSED MY RESOURCES ON ADDING VALUE TO THE PRODUCT PROCESS. OUR SHARE-HOLDERS WOULD BE DELIGHTED TO KNOW THAT.
S. Adams
12/27/97 © 1997 United Feature Syndicate, Inc.

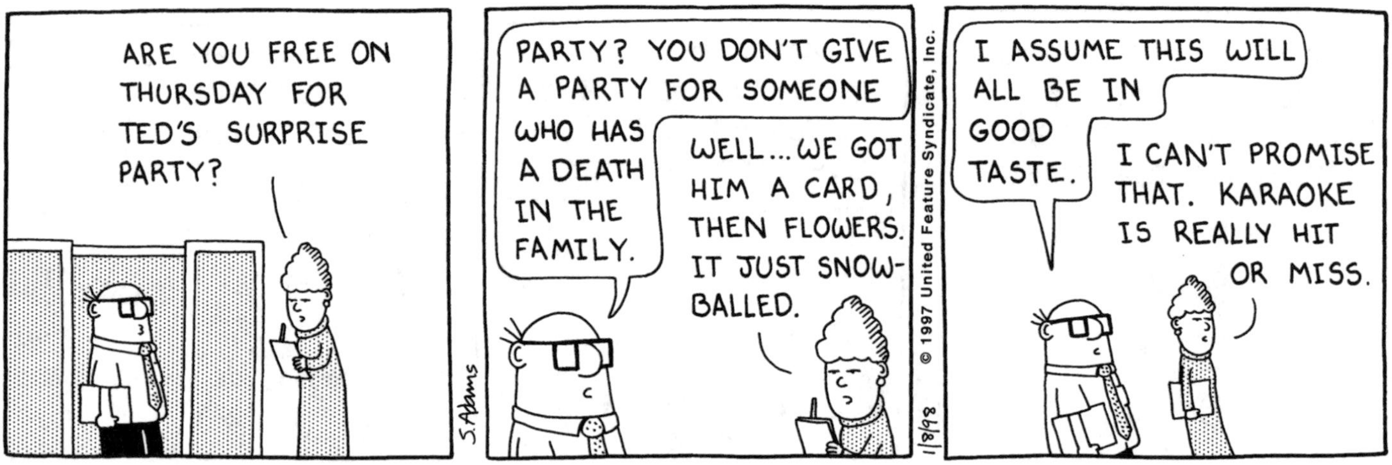
ARE YOU FREE ON THURSDAY FOR TED'S SURPRISE PARTY?
PARTY? YOU DON'T GIVE A PARTY FOR SOMEONE WHO HAS A DEATH IN THE FAMILY.
WELL... WE GOT HIM A CARD, THEN FLOWERS. IT JUST SNOW-BALLED.
I ASSUME THIS WILL ALL BE IN GOOD TASTE.
I CAN'T PROMISE THAT. KARAOKE IS REALLY HIT OR MISS.
S. Adams
1/8/98 © 1997 United Feature Syndicate, Inc.

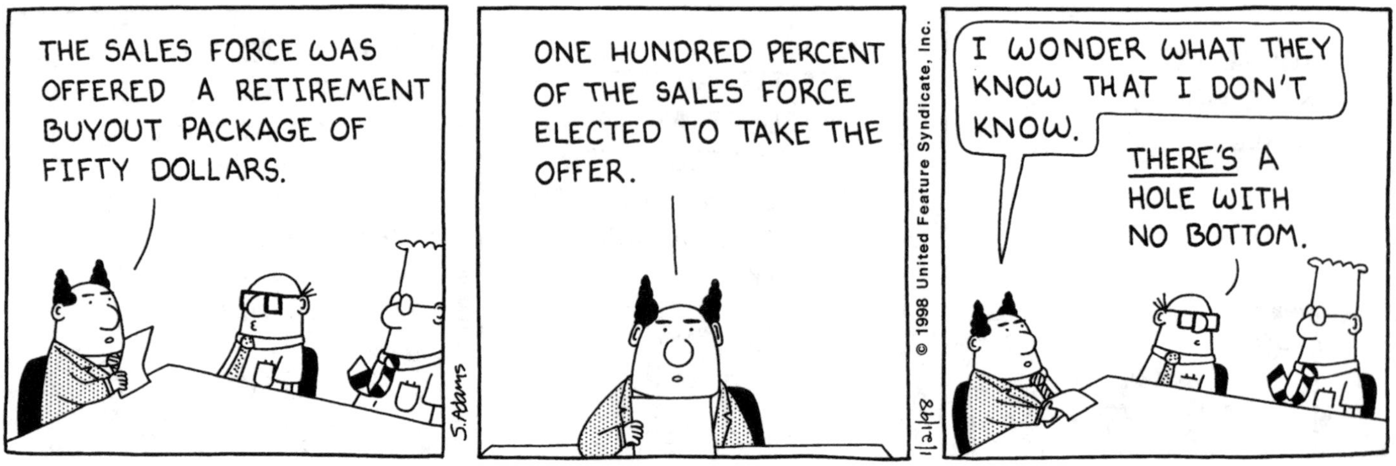
THE SALES FORCE WAS OFFERED A RETIREMENT BUYOUT PACKAGE OF FIFTY DOLLARS.
ONE HUNDRED PERCENT OF THE SALES FORCE ELECTED TO TAKE THE OFFER.
I WONDER WHAT THEY KNOW THAT I DON'T KNOW.
THERE'S A HOLE WITH NO BOTTOM.
S. Adams
1/21/98 © 1998 United Feature Syndicate, Inc.

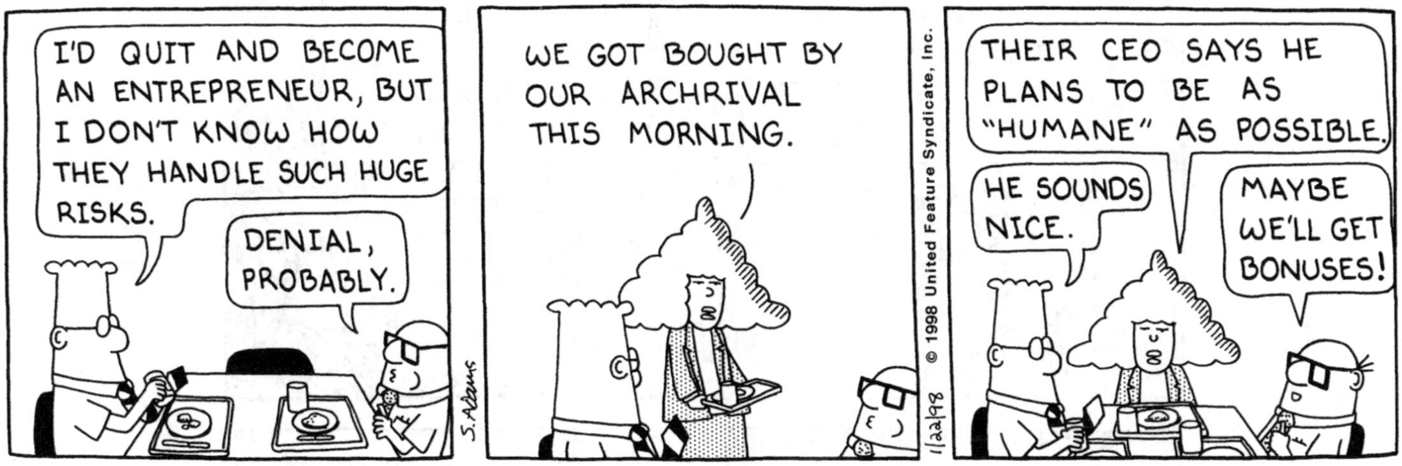
I'D QUIT AND BECOME AN ENTREPRENEUR, BUT I DON'T KNOW HOW THEY HANDLE SUCH HUGE RISKS.
DENIAL, PROBABLY.
S. Adams
WE GOT BOUGHT BY OUR ARCHRIVAL THIS MORNING.
1/22/98 © 1998 United Feature Syndicate, Inc.
THEIR CEO SAYS HE PLANS TO BE AS "HUMANE" AS POSSIBLE.
HE SOUNDS NICE.
MAYBE WE'LL GET BONUSES!

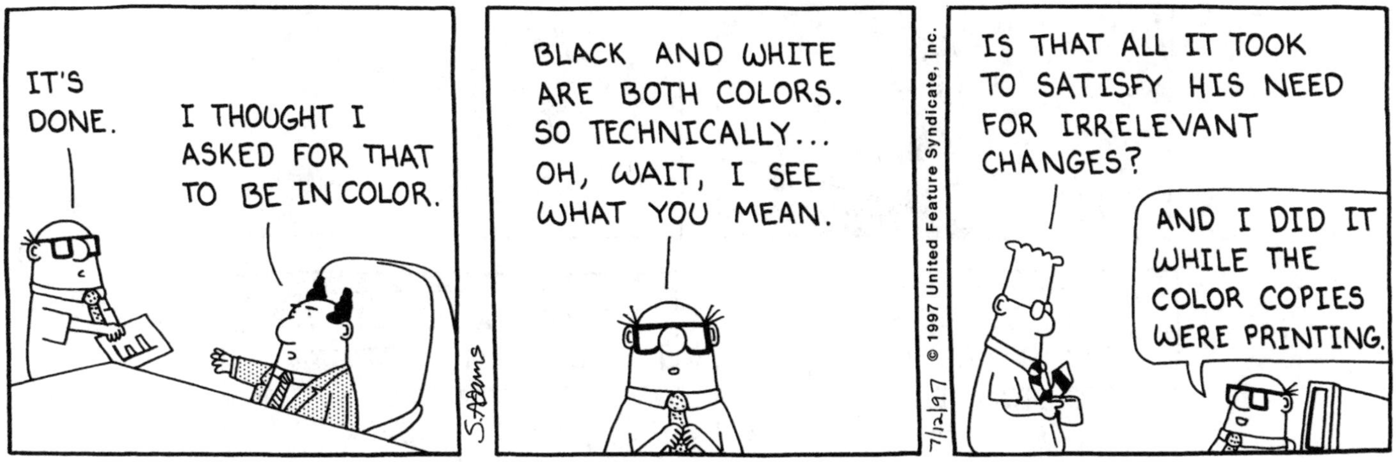
IT'S DONE.
I THOUGHT I ASKED FOR THAT TO BE IN COLOR.
S. Adams
BLACK AND WHITE ARE BOTH COLORS. SO TECHNICALLY... OH, WAIT, I SEE WHAT YOU MEAN.
7/12/97 © 1997 United Feature Syndicate, Inc.
IS THAT ALL IT TOOK TO SATISFY HIS NEED FOR IRRELEVANT CHANGES?
AND I DID IT WHILE THE COLOR COPIES WERE PRINTING.

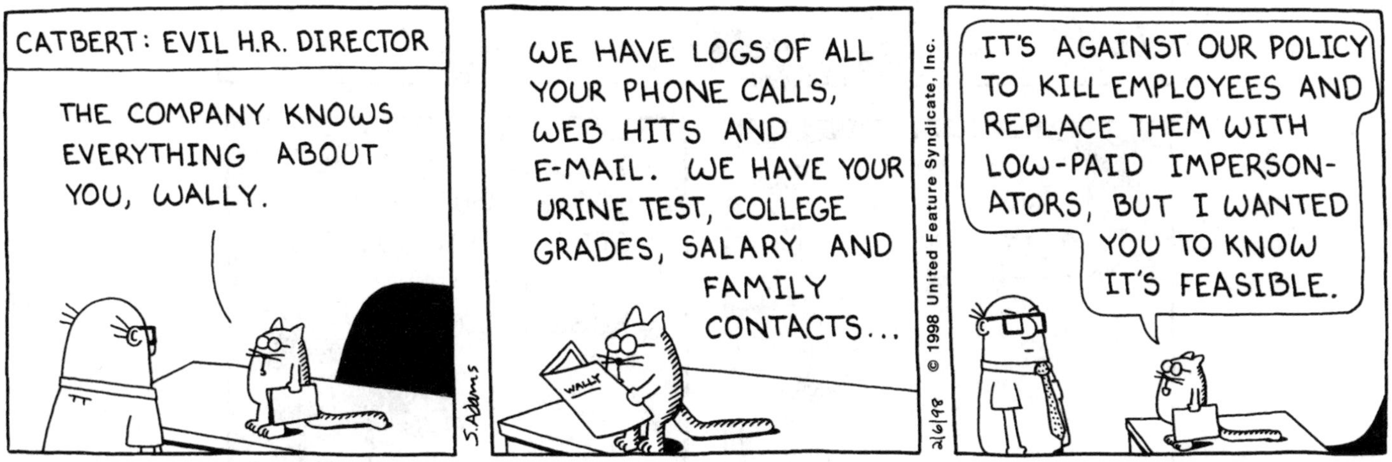
CATBERT: EVIL H.R. DIRECTOR
THE COMPANY KNOWS EVERYTHING ABOUT YOU, WALLY.
S. Adams
WE HAVE LOGS OF ALL YOUR PHONE CALLS, WEB HITS AND E-MAIL. WE HAVE YOUR URINE TEST, COLLEGE GRADES, SALARY AND FAMILY CONTACTS...
WALLY
2/6/98 © 1998 United Feature Syndicate, Inc.
IT'S AGAINST OUR POLICY TO KILL EMPLOYEES AND REPLACE THEM WITH LOW-PAID IMPERSON-ATORS, BUT I WANTED YOU TO KNOW IT'S FEASIBLE.

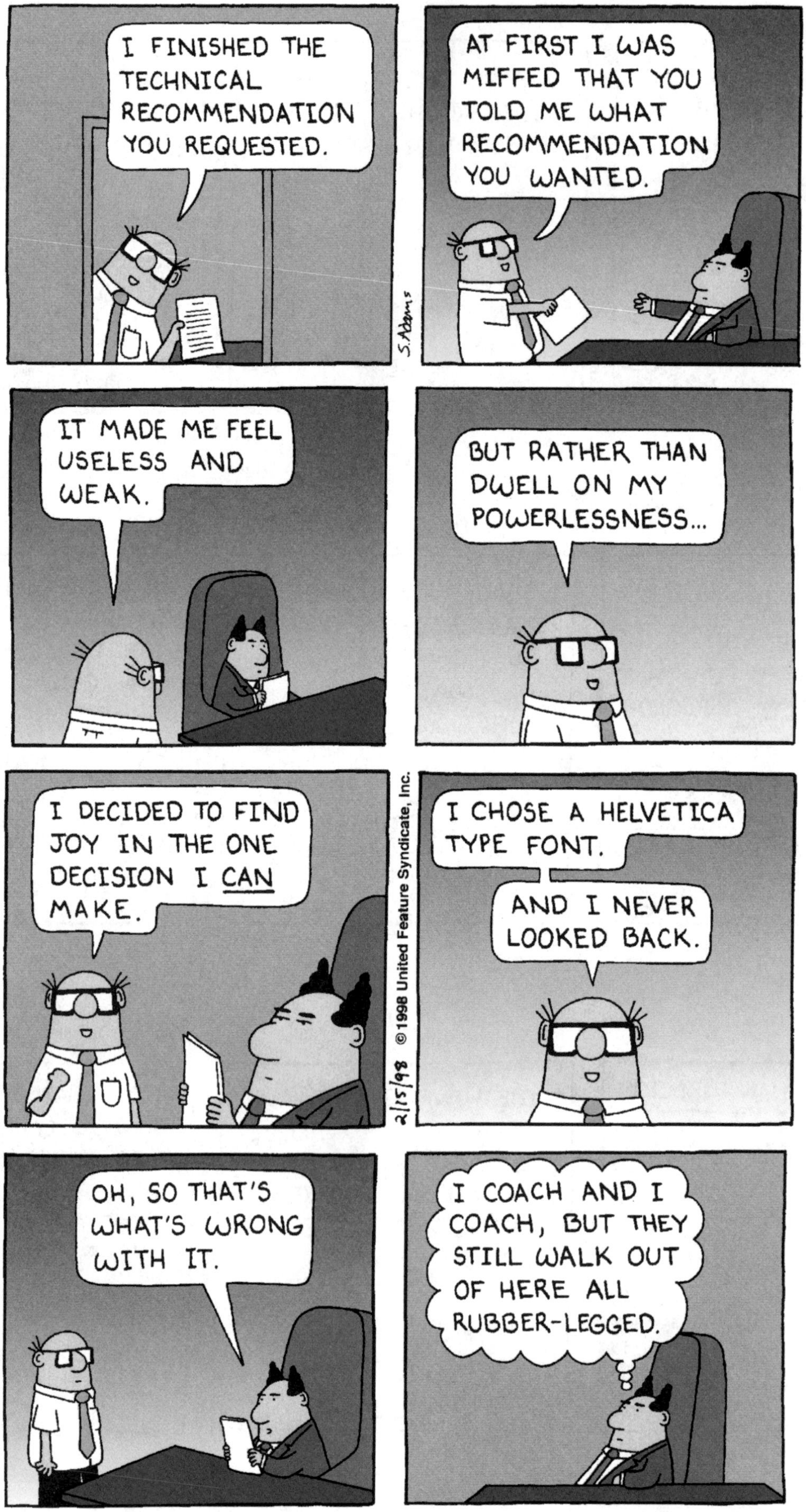
I FINISHED THE TECHNICAL RECOMMENDATION YOU REQUESTED.
AT FIRST I WAS MIFFED THAT YOU TOLD ME WHAT RECOMMENDATION YOU WANTED.
S. Adams
IT MADE ME FEEL USELESS AND WEAK.
BUT RATHER THAN DWELL ON MY POWERLESSNESS...
I DECIDED TO FIND JOY IN THE ONE DECISION I CAN MAKE.
©1998 United Feature Syndicate, Inc.
2/15/98
I CHOSE A HELVETICA TYPE FONT.
AND I NEVER LOOKED BACK.
OH, SO THAT'S WHAT'S WRONG WITH IT.
I COACH AND I COACH, BUT THEY STILL WALK OUT OF HERE ALL RUBBER-LEGGED.

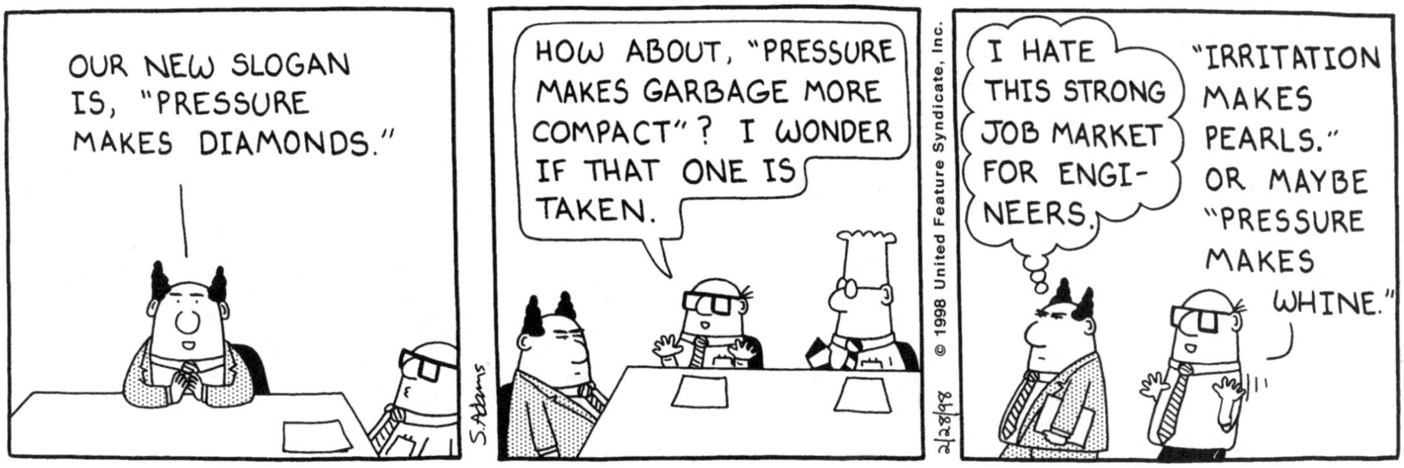
OUR NEW SLOGAN IS, "PRESSURE MAKES DIAMONDS."
S. Adams
HOW ABOUT, "PRESSURE MAKES GARBAGE MORE COMPACT"? I WONDER IF THAT ONE IS TAKEN.
© 1998 United Feature Syndicate, Inc.
2/28/98
I HATE THIS STRONG JOB MARKET FOR ENGINEERS.
"IRRITATION MAKES PEARLS." OR MAYBE "PRESSURE MAKES WHINE."

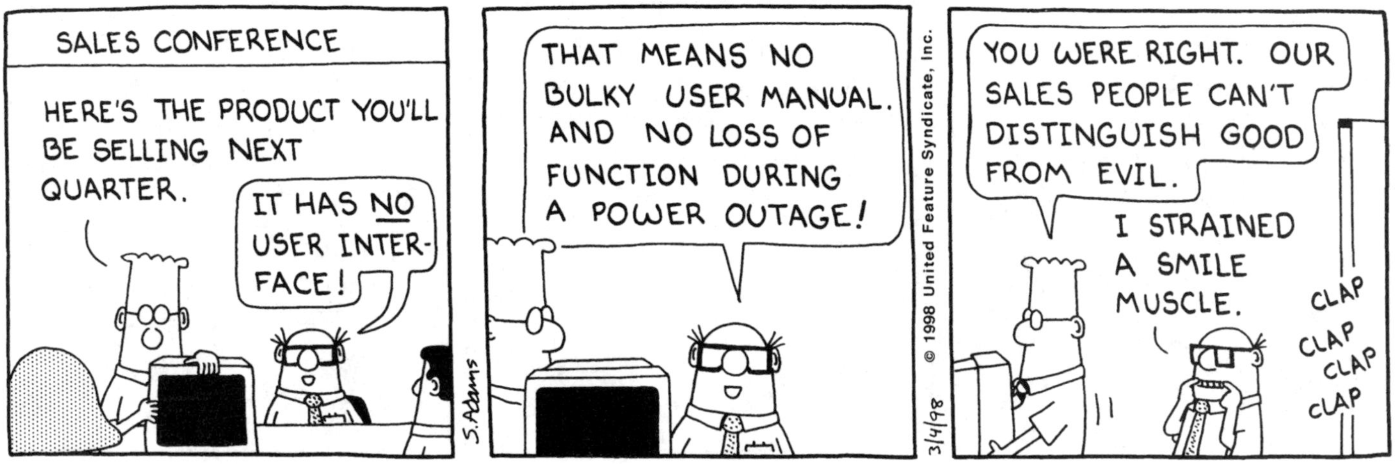
SALES CONFERENCE
HERE'S THE PRODUCT YOU'LL BE SELLING NEXT QUARTER.
IT HAS NO USER INTERFACE!
S. Adams
THAT MEANS NO BULKY USER MANUAL. AND NO LOSS OF FUNCTION DURING A POWER OUTAGE!
© 1998 United Feature Syndicate, Inc.
3/4/98
YOU WERE RIGHT. OUR SALES PEOPLE CAN'T DISTINGUISH GOOD FROM EVIL.
I STRAINED A SMILE MUSCLE.
CLAP
CLAP
CLAP
CLAP

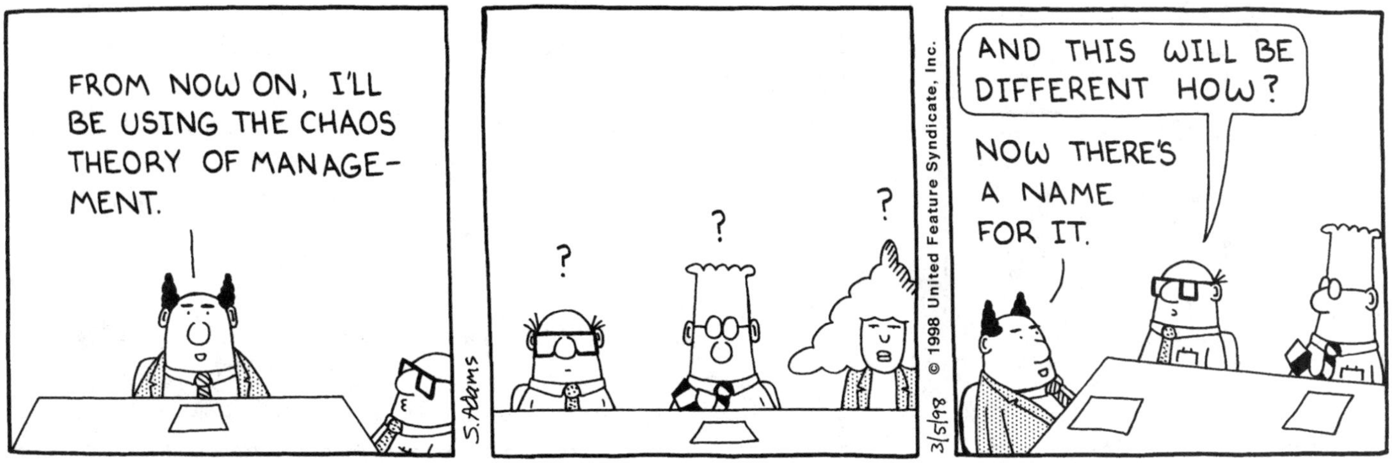
FROM NOW ON, I'LL BE USING THE CHAOS THEORY OF MANAGEMENT.
S. Adams
?
?
?
© 1998 United Feature Syndicate, Inc.
3/5/98
AND THIS WILL BE DIFFERENT HOW?
NOW THERE'S A NAME FOR IT.

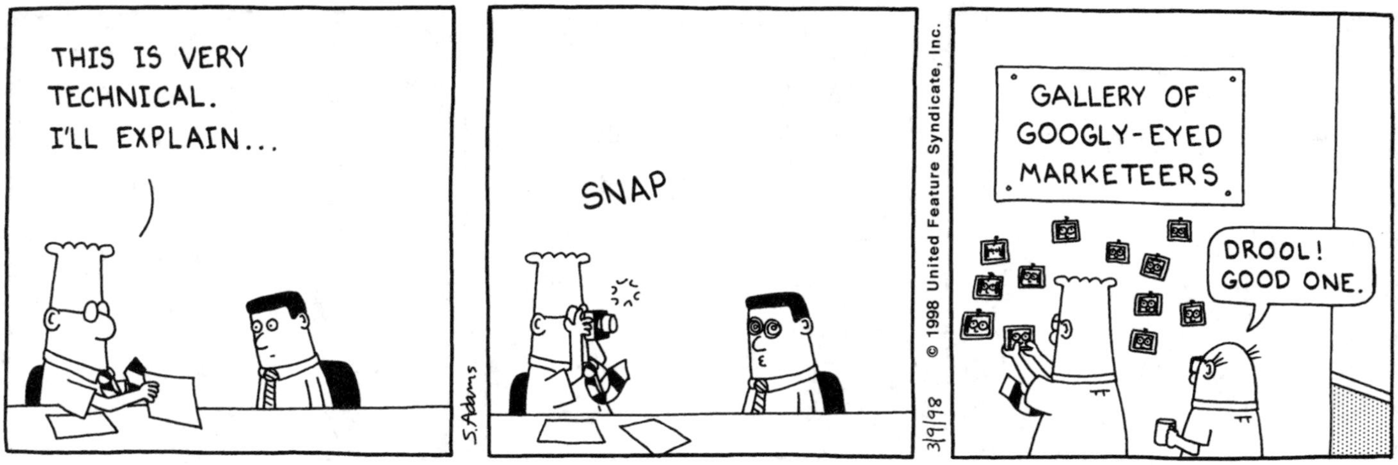
THIS IS VERY TECHNICAL. I'LL EXPLAIN...
SNAP
GALLERY OF GOOGLY-EYED MARKETEERS
DROOL! GOOD ONE.
© 1998 United Feature Syndicate, Inc.

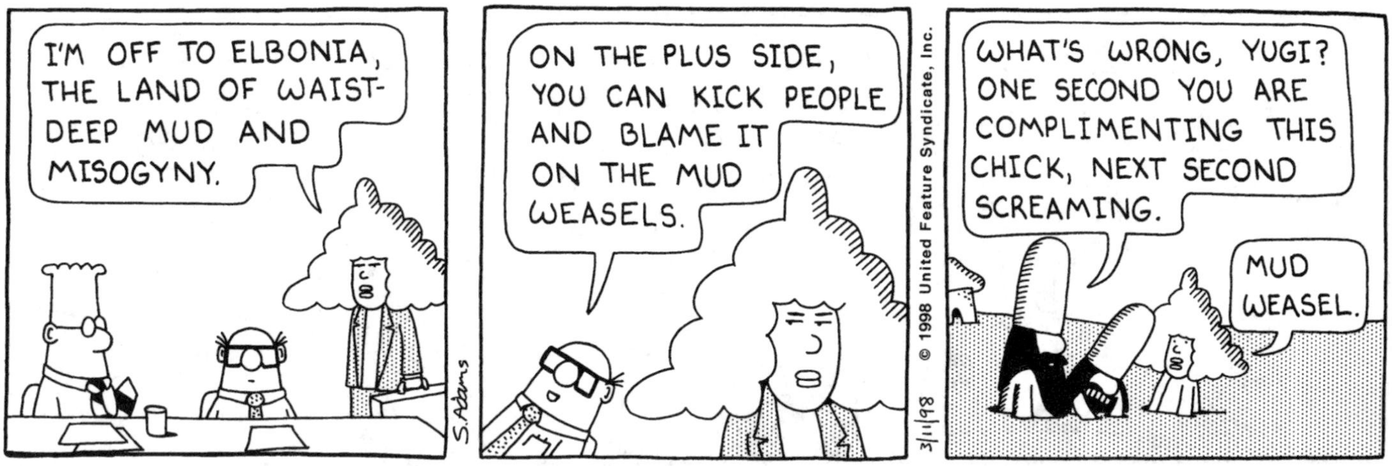
I'M OFF TO ELBONIA, THE LAND OF WAIST-DEEP MUD AND MISOGYNY.
ON THE PLUS SIDE, YOU CAN KICK PEOPLE AND BLAME IT ON THE MUD WEASELS.
WHAT'S WRONG, YUGI? ONE SECOND YOU ARE COMPLIMENTING THIS CHICK, NEXT SECOND SCREAMING.
MUD WEASEL.
© 1998 United Feature Syndicate, Inc.

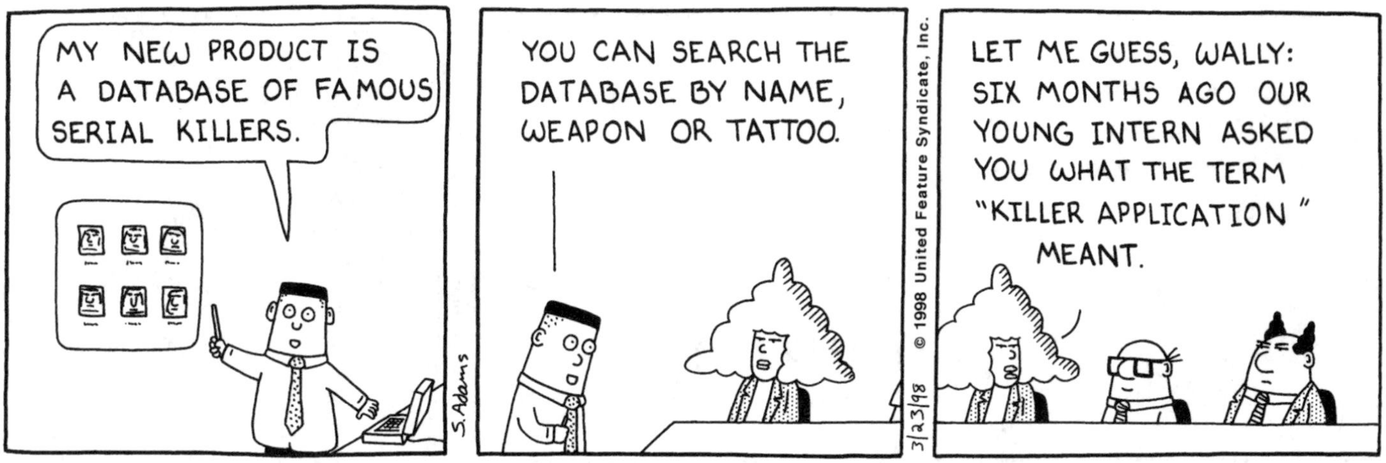
MY NEW PRODUCT IS A DATABASE OF FAMOUS SERIAL KILLERS.
YOU CAN SEARCH THE DATABASE BY NAME, WEAPON OR TATTOO.
LET ME GUESS, WALLY: SIX MONTHS AGO OUR YOUNG INTERN ASKED YOU WHAT THE TERM "KILLER APPLICATION" MEANT.
© 1998 United Feature Syndicate, Inc.

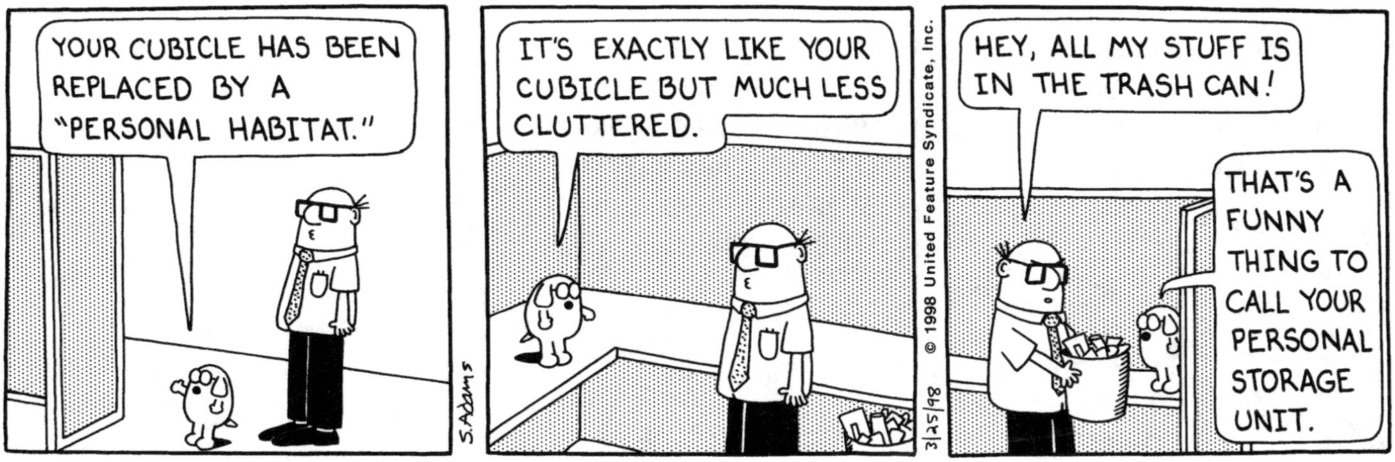
YOUR CUBICLE HAS BEEN REPLACED BY A "PERSONAL HABITAT."
S. Adams
IT'S EXACTLY LIKE YOUR CUBICLE BUT MUCH LESS CLUTTERED.
3/25/98 © 1998 United Feature Syndicate, Inc.
HEY, ALL MY STUFF IS IN THE TRASH CAN!
THAT'S A FUNNY THING TO CALL YOUR PERSONAL STORAGE UNIT.

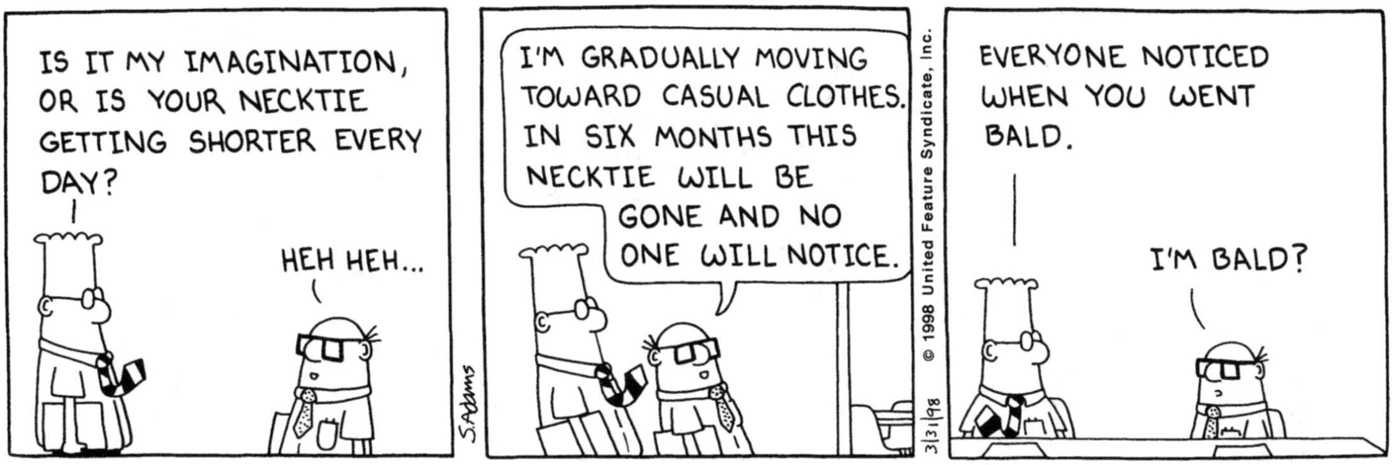
IS IT MY IMAGINATION, OR IS YOUR NECKTIE GETTING SHORTER EVERY DAY?
HEH HEH...
S. Adams
I'M GRADUALLY MOVING TOWARD CASUAL CLOTHES. IN SIX MONTHS THIS NECKTIE WILL BE GONE AND NO ONE WILL NOTICE.
3/31/98 © 1998 United Feature Syndicate, Inc.
EVERYONE NOTICED WHEN YOU WENT BALD.
I'M BALD?

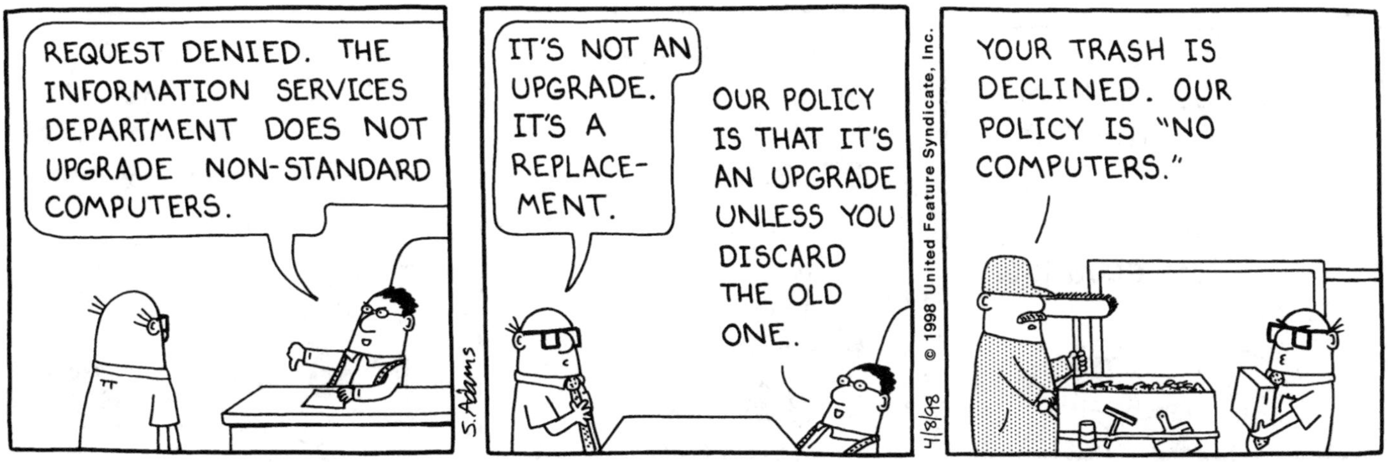
REQUEST DENIED. THE INFORMATION SERVICES DEPARTMENT DOES NOT UPGRADE NON-STANDARD COMPUTERS.
S. Adams
IT'S NOT AN UPGRADE. IT'S A REPLACE-MENT.
OUR POLICY IS THAT IT'S AN UPGRADE UNLESS YOU DISCARD THE OLD ONE.
4/8/98 © 1998 United Feature Syndicate, Inc.
YOUR TRASH IS DECLINED. OUR POLICY IS "NO COMPUTERS."

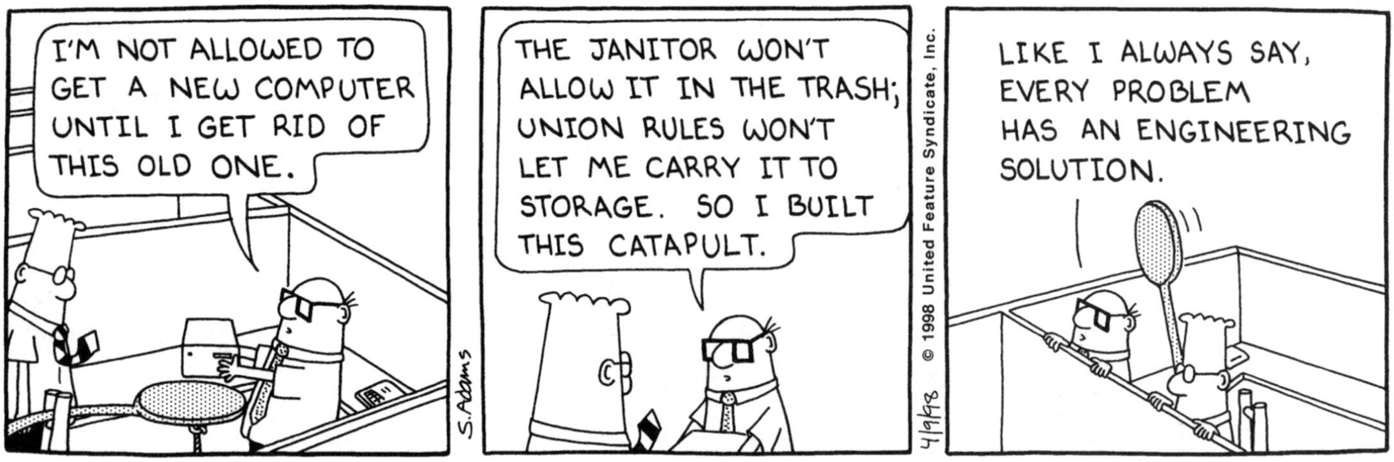
I'M NOT ALLOWED TO GET A NEW COMPUTER UNTIL I GET RID OF THIS OLD ONE.
S. Adams
THE JANITOR WON'T ALLOW IT IN THE TRASH; UNION RULES WON'T LET ME CARRY IT TO STORAGE. SO I BUILT THIS CATAPULT.
4/9/98 © 1998 United Feature Syndicate, Inc.
LIKE I ALWAYS SAY, EVERY PROBLEM HAS AN ENGINEERING SOLUTION.

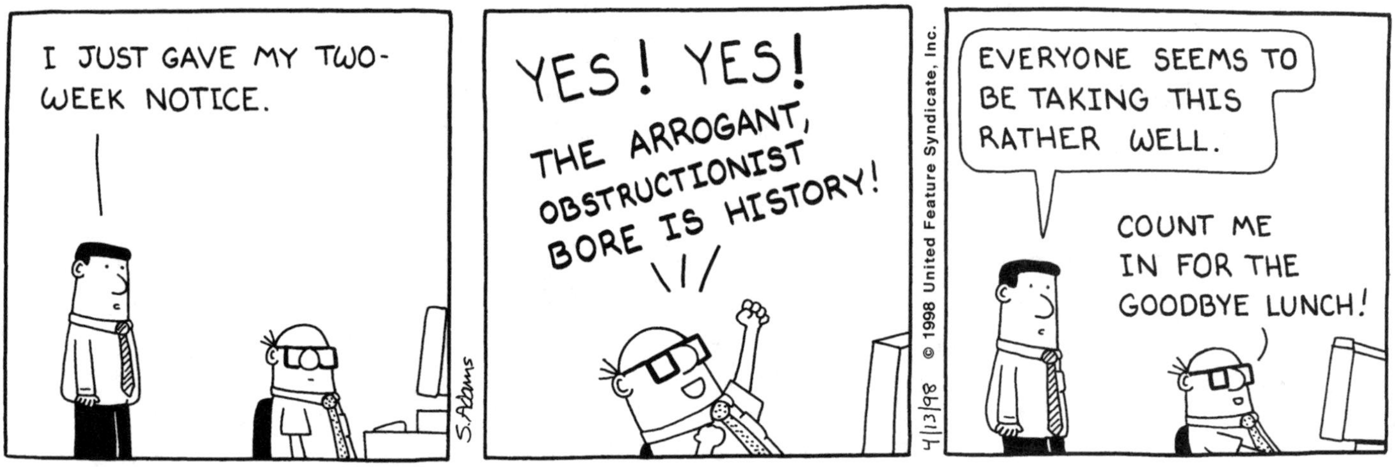
I JUST GAVE MY TWO-WEEK NOTICE.
S. Adams
YES! YES!
THE ARROGANT, OBSTRUCTIONIST BORE IS HISTORY!
4/13/98 © 1998 United Feature Syndicate, Inc.
EVERYONE SEEMS TO BE TAKING THIS RATHER WELL.
COUNT ME IN FOR THE GOODBYE LUNCH!

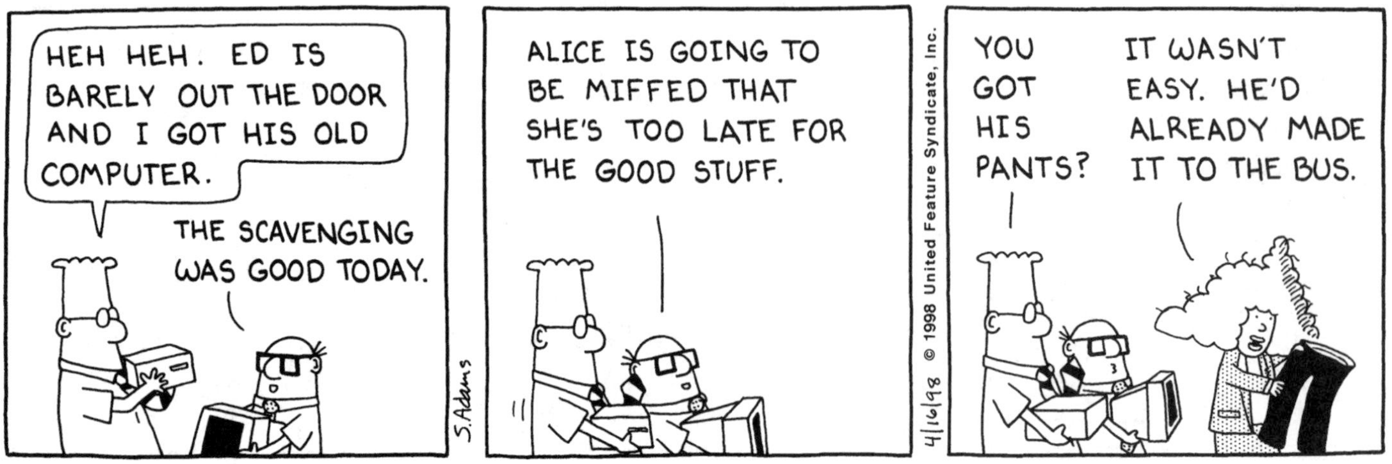
HEH HEH. ED IS BARELY OUT THE DOOR AND I GOT HIS OLD COMPUTER.
THE SCAVENGING WAS GOOD TODAY.
S. Adams
ALICE IS GOING TO BE MIFFED THAT SHE'S TOO LATE FOR THE GOOD STUFF.
4/16/98 © 1998 United Feature Syndicate, Inc.
YOU GOT HIS PANTS?
IT WASN'T EASY. HE'D ALREADY MADE IT TO THE BUS.

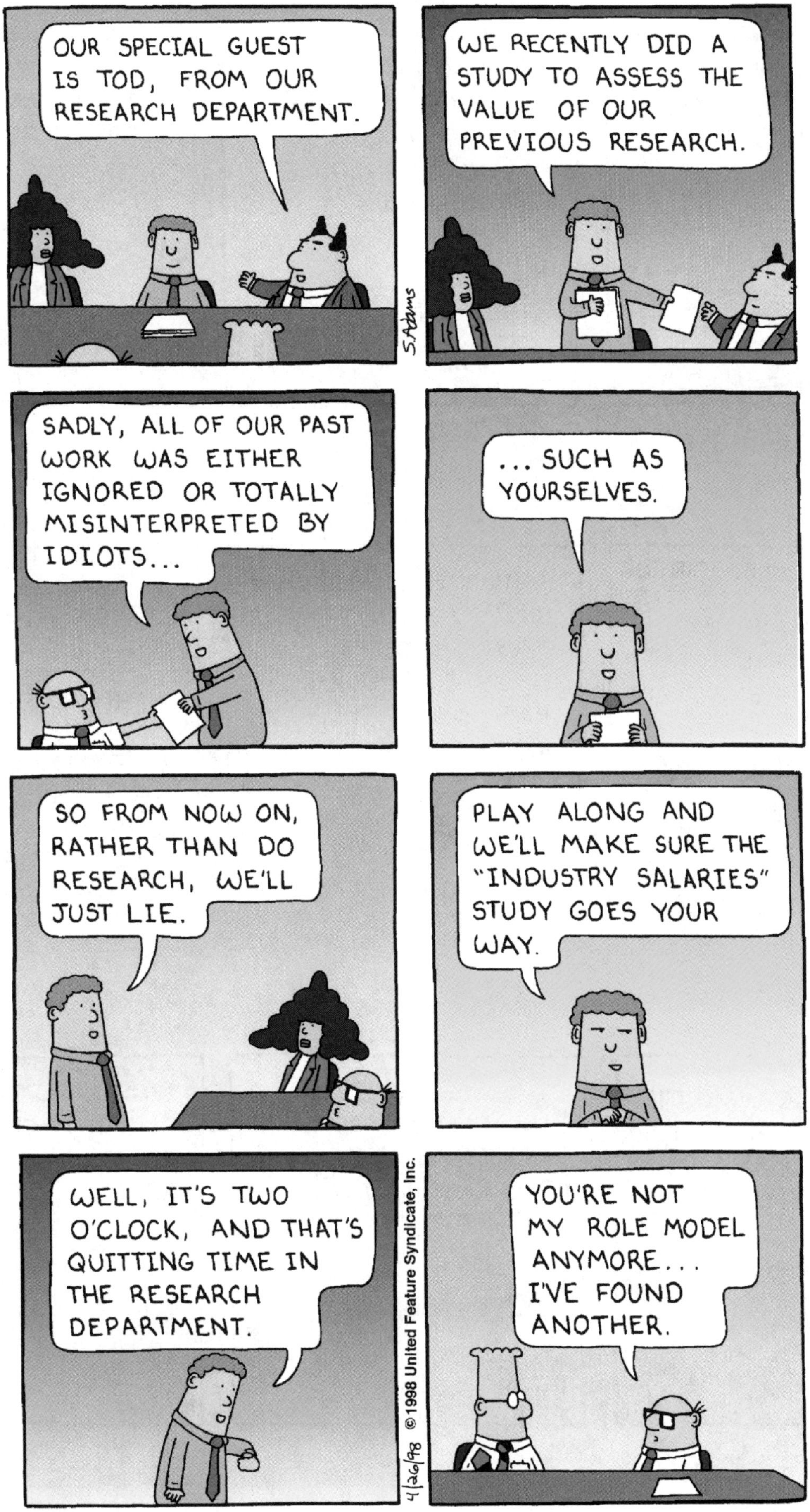
OUR SPECIAL GUEST IS TOD, FROM OUR RESEARCH DEPARTMENT.
WE RECENTLY DID A STUDY TO ASSESS THE VALUE OF OUR PREVIOUS RESEARCH.
S. Adams
SADLY, ALL OF OUR PAST WORK WAS EITHER IGNORED OR TOTALLY MISINTERPRETED BY IDIOTS...
... SUCH AS YOURSELVES.
SO FROM NOW ON, RATHER THAN DO RESEARCH, WE'LL JUST LIE.
PLAY ALONG AND WE'LL MAKE SURE THE "INDUSTRY SALARIES" STUDY GOES YOUR WAY.
WELL, IT'S TWO O'CLOCK, AND THAT'S QUITTING TIME IN THE RESEARCH DEPARTMENT.
4/26/98 © 1998 United Feature Syndicate, Inc.
YOU'RE NOT MY ROLE MODEL ANYMORE... I'VE FOUND ANOTHER.

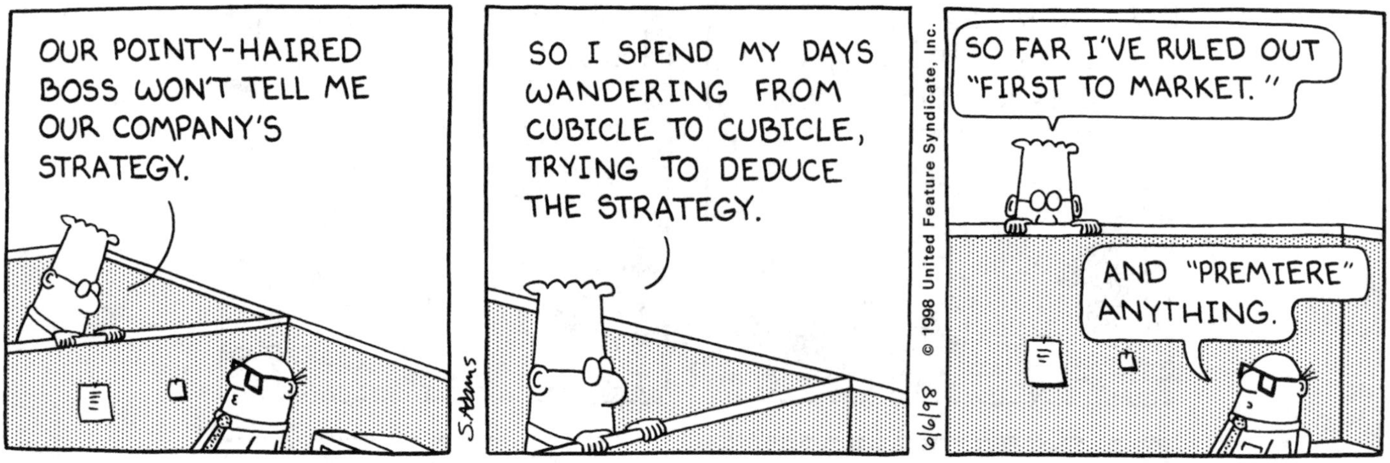
OUR POINTY-HAIRED BOSS WON'T TELL ME OUR COMPANY'S STRATEGY.
SO I SPEND MY DAYS WANDERING FROM CUBICLE TO CUBICLE, TRYING TO DEDUCE THE STRATEGY.
SO FAR I'VE RULED OUT "FIRST TO MARKET."
AND "PREMIERE" ANYTHING.
S.Adams
6/6/98
© 1998 United Feature Syndicate, Inc.

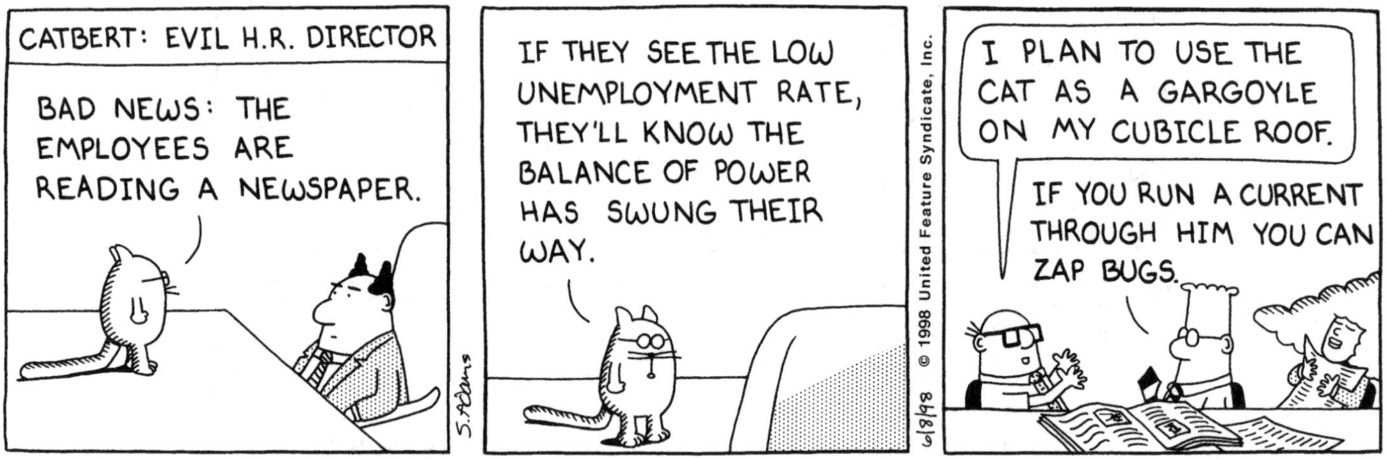
CATBERT: EVIL H.R. DIRECTOR
BAD NEWS: THE EMPLOYEES ARE READING A NEWSPAPER.
IF THEY SEE THE LOW UNEMPLOYMENT RATE, THEY'LL KNOW THE BALANCE OF POWER HAS SWUNG THEIR WAY.
I PLAN TO USE THE CAT AS A GARGOYLE ON MY CUBICLE ROOF.
IF YOU RUN A CURRENT THROUGH HIM YOU CAN ZAP BUGS.
S.Adams
6/8/98
© 1998 United Feature Syndicate, Inc.

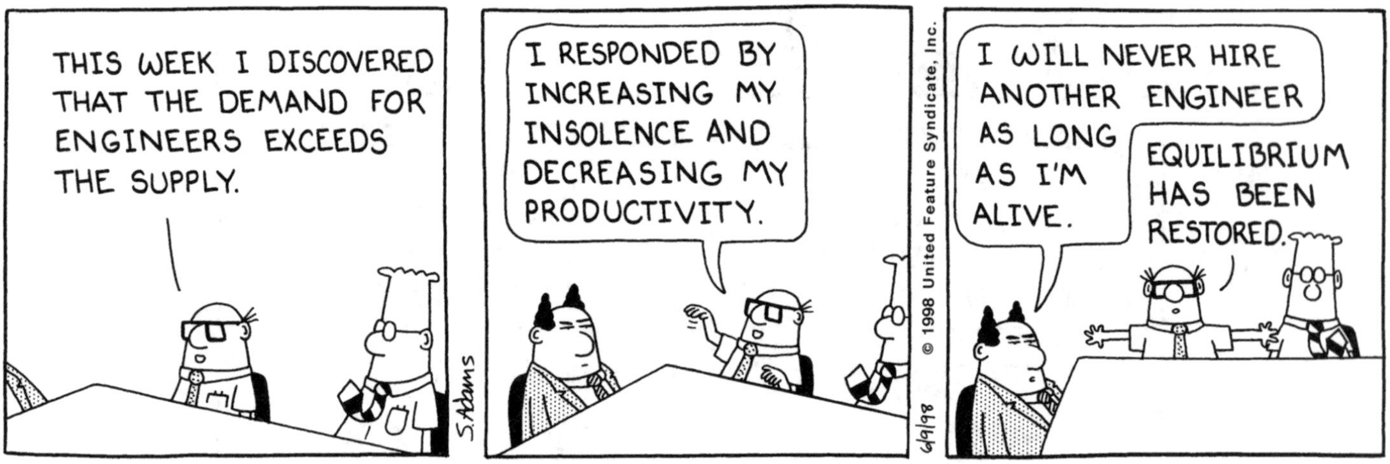
THIS WEEK I DISCOVERED THAT THE DEMAND FOR ENGINEERS EXCEEDS THE SUPPLY.
I RESPONDED BY INCREASING MY INSOLENCE AND DECREASING MY PRODUCTIVITY.
I WILL NEVER HIRE ANOTHER ENGINEER AS LONG AS I'M ALIVE.
EQUILIBRIUM HAS BEEN RESTORED.
S.Adams
6/9/98
© 1998 United Feature Syndicate, Inc.

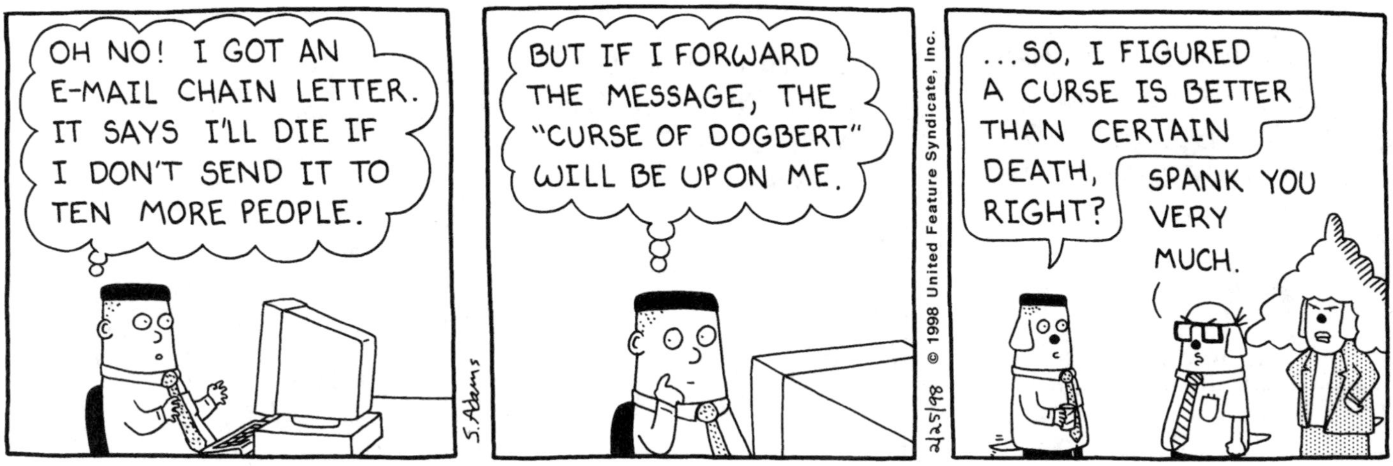
OH NO! I GOT AN E-MAIL CHAIN LETTER. IT SAYS I'LL DIE IF I DON'T SEND IT TO TEN MORE PEOPLE.
BUT IF I FORWARD THE MESSAGE, THE "CURSE OF DOGBERT" WILL BE UPON ME.
...SO, I FIGURED A CURSE IS BETTER THAN CERTAIN DEATH, RIGHT?
SPANK YOU VERY MUCH.
© 1998 United Feature Syndicate, Inc.

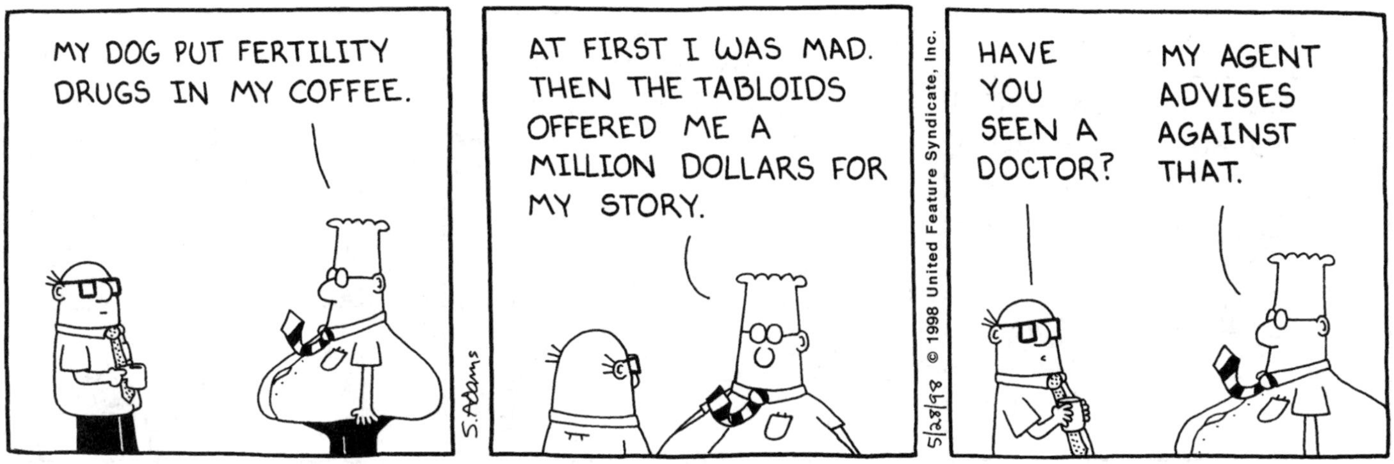
MY DOG PUT FERTILITY DRUGS IN MY COFFEE.
AT FIRST I WAS MAD. THEN THE TABLOIDS OFFERED ME A MILLION DOLLARS FOR MY STORY.
HAVE YOU SEEN A DOCTOR?
MY AGENT ADVISES AGAINST THAT.
© 1998 United Feature Syndicate, Inc.

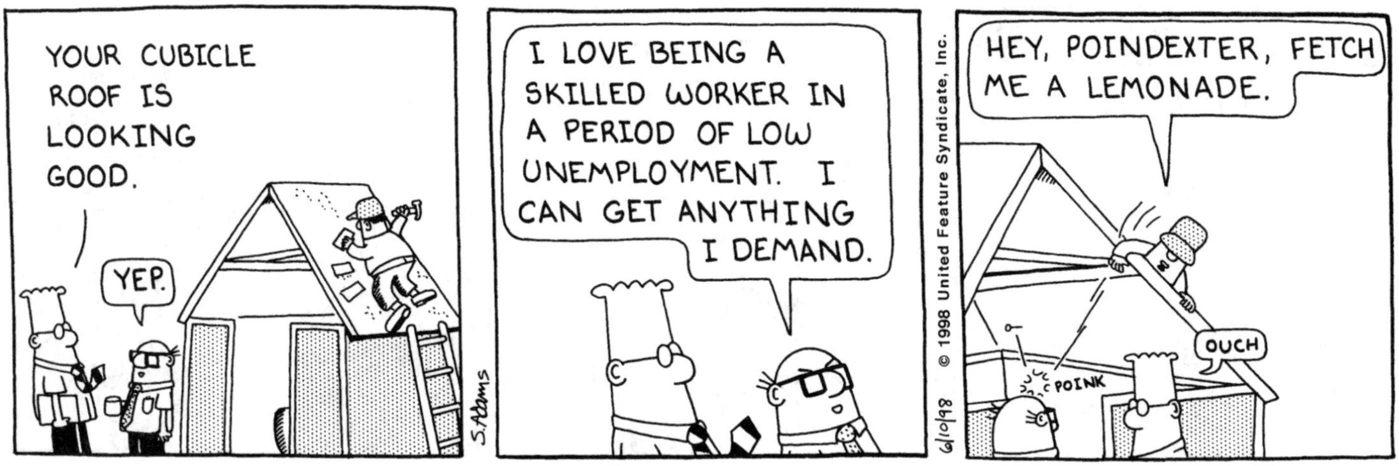
YOUR CUBICLE ROOF IS LOOKING GOOD.
YEP.
I LOVE BEING A SKILLED WORKER IN A PERIOD OF LOW UNEMPLOYMENT. I CAN GET ANYTHING I DEMAND.
HEY, POINDEXTER, FETCH ME A LEMONADE.
POINK
OUCH
© 1998 United Feature Syndicate, Inc.

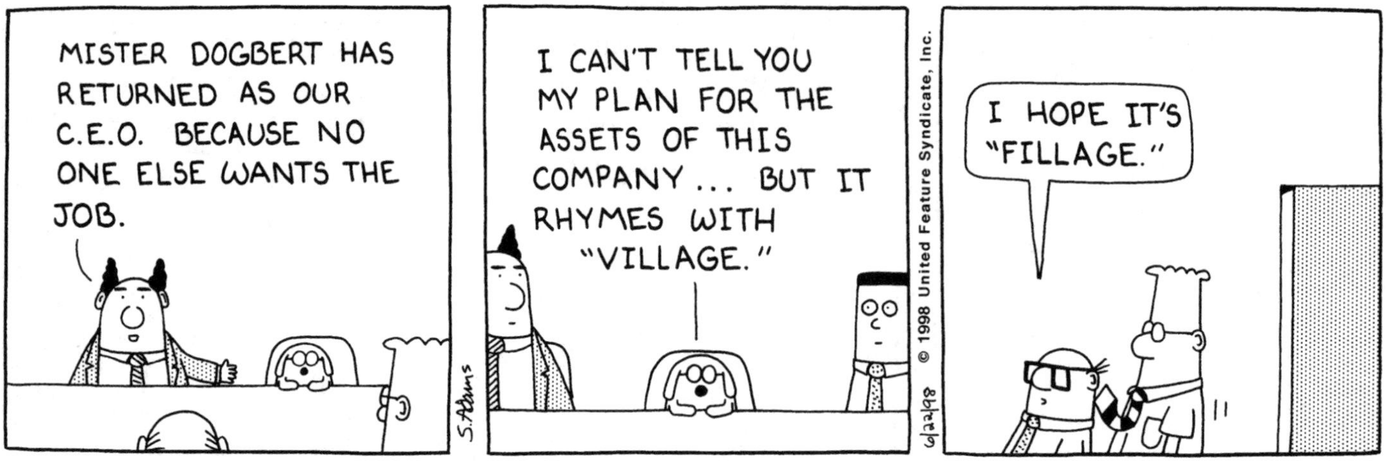
MISTER DOGBERT HAS RETURNED AS OUR C.E.O. BECAUSE NO ONE ELSE WANTS THE JOB.
I CAN'T TELL YOU MY PLAN FOR THE ASSETS OF THIS COMPANY ... BUT IT RHYMES WITH "VILLAGE."
I HOPE IT'S "FILLAGE."
S. Adams
6/22/98 © 1998 United Feature Syndicate, Inc.

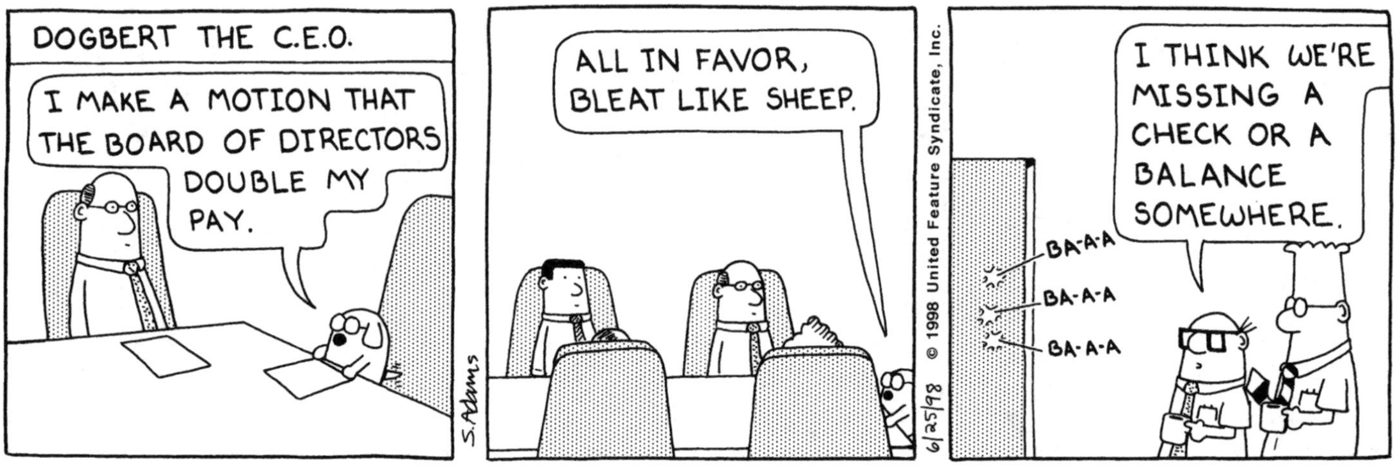
DOGBERT THE C.E.O.
I MAKE A MOTION THAT THE BOARD OF DIRECTORS DOUBLE MY PAY.
ALL IN FAVOR, BLEAT LIKE SHEEP.
BA-A-A
BA-A-A
BA-A-A
I THINK WE'RE MISSING A CHECK OR A BALANCE SOMEWHERE.
S. Adams
6/25/98 © 1998 United Feature Syndicate, Inc.

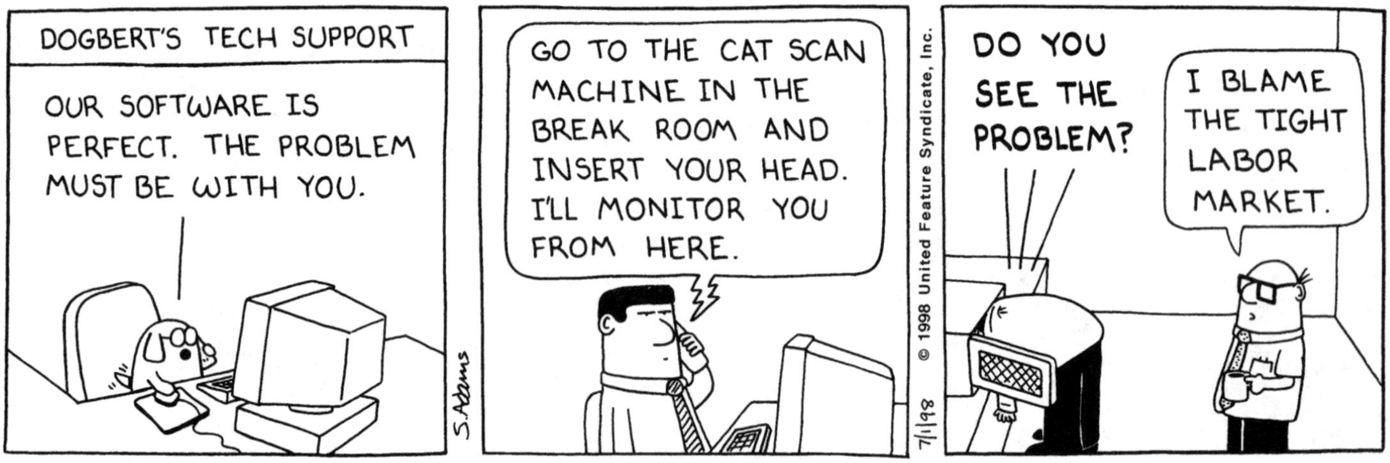
DOGBERT'S TECH SUPPORT
OUR SOFTWARE IS PERFECT. THE PROBLEM MUST BE WITH YOU.
GO TO THE CAT SCAN MACHINE IN THE BREAK ROOM AND INSERT YOUR HEAD. I'LL MONITOR YOU FROM HERE.
DO YOU SEE THE PROBLEM?
I BLAME THE TIGHT LABOR MARKET.
S. Adams
7/1/98 © 1998 United Feature Syndicate, Inc.

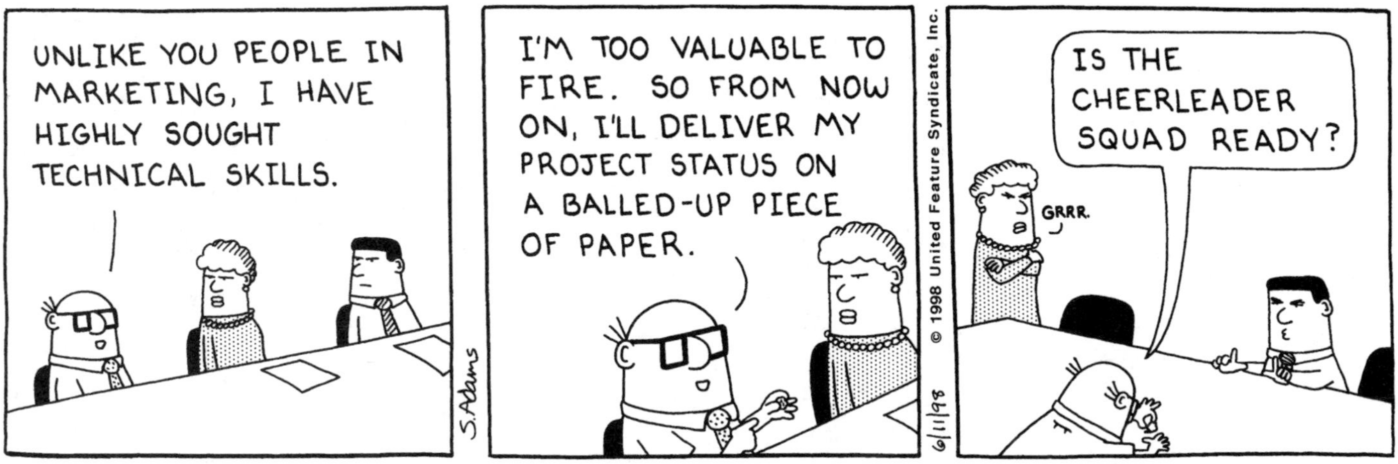
UNLIKE YOU PEOPLE IN MARKETING, I HAVE HIGHLY SOUGHT TECHNICAL SKILLS.
S. Adams
I'M TOO VALUABLE TO FIRE. SO FROM NOW ON, I'LL DELIVER MY PROJECT STATUS ON A BALLED-UP PIECE OF PAPER.
6/11/98
© 1998 United Feature Syndicate, Inc.
IS THE CHEERLEADER SQUAD READY?
GRRR.

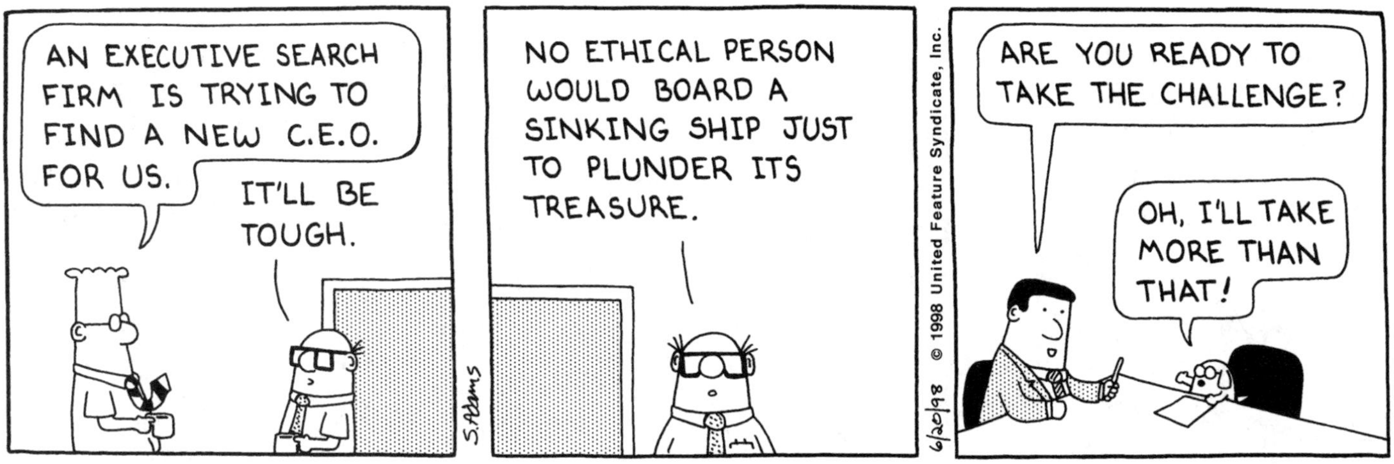
AN EXECUTIVE SEARCH FIRM IS TRYING TO FIND A NEW C.E.O. FOR US.
IT'LL BE TOUGH.
S. Adams
NO ETHICAL PERSON WOULD BOARD A SINKING SHIP JUST TO PLUNDER ITS TREASURE.
6/20/98
© 1998 United Feature Syndicate, Inc.
ARE YOU READY TO TAKE THE CHALLENGE?
OH, I'LL TAKE MORE THAN THAT!

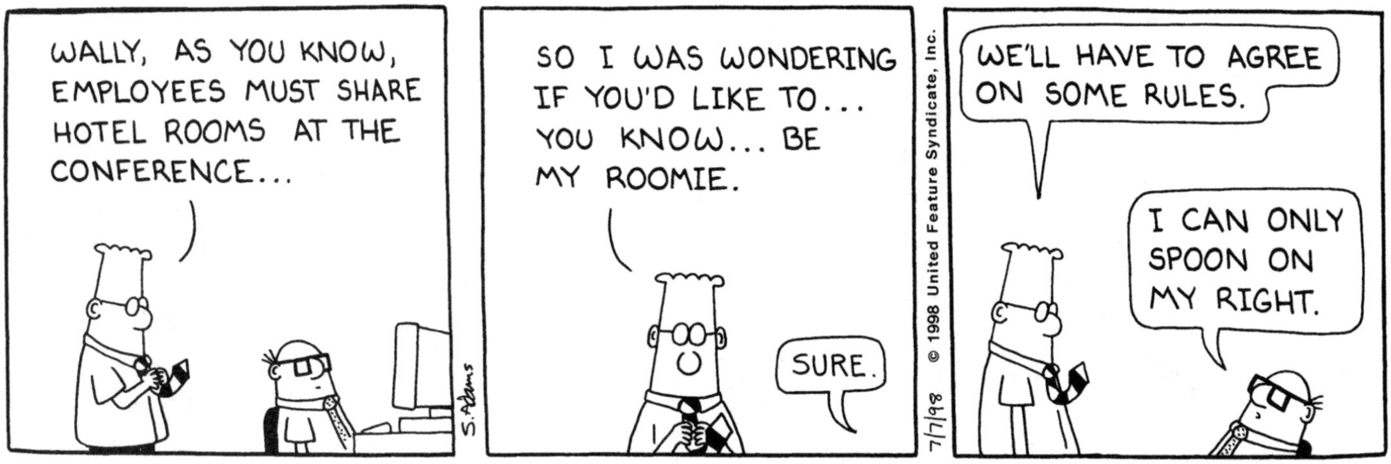
WALLY, AS YOU KNOW, EMPLOYEES MUST SHARE HOTEL ROOMS AT THE CONFERENCE...
S. Adams
SO I WAS WONDERING IF YOU'D LIKE TO... YOU KNOW... BE MY ROOMIE.
SURE.
7/7/98
© 1998 United Feature Syndicate, Inc.
WE'LL HAVE TO AGREE ON SOME RULES.
I CAN ONLY SPOON ON MY RIGHT.

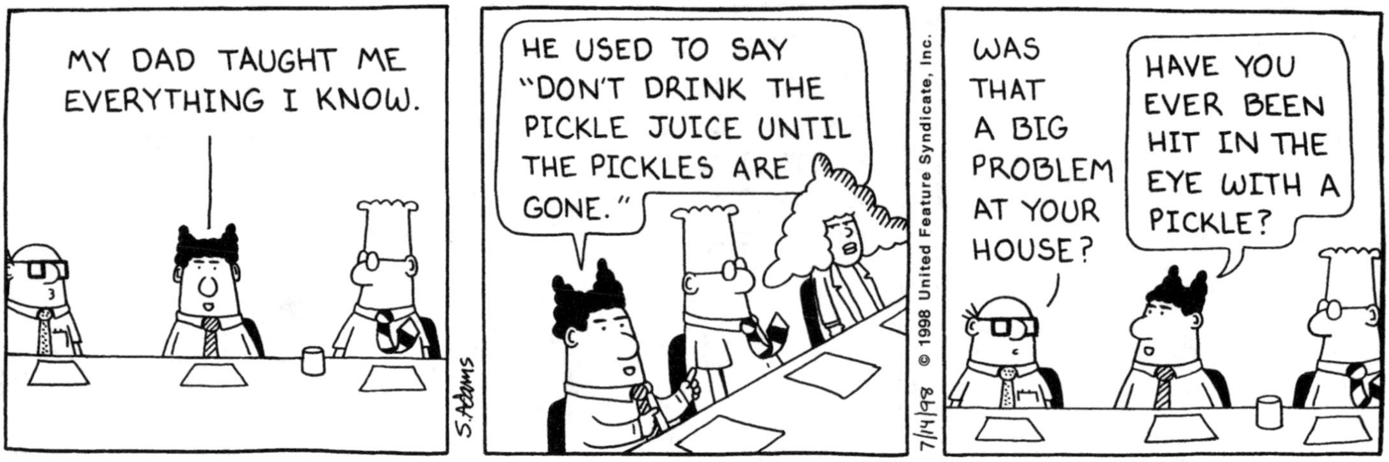
MY DAD TAUGHT ME EVERYTHING I KNOW.
S. Adams
HE USED TO SAY "DON'T DRINK THE PICKLE JUICE UNTIL THE PICKLES ARE GONE."
7/14/98 © 1998 United Feature Syndicate, Inc.
WAS THAT A BIG PROBLEM AT YOUR HOUSE?
HAVE YOU EVER BEEN HIT IN THE EYE WITH A PICKLE?

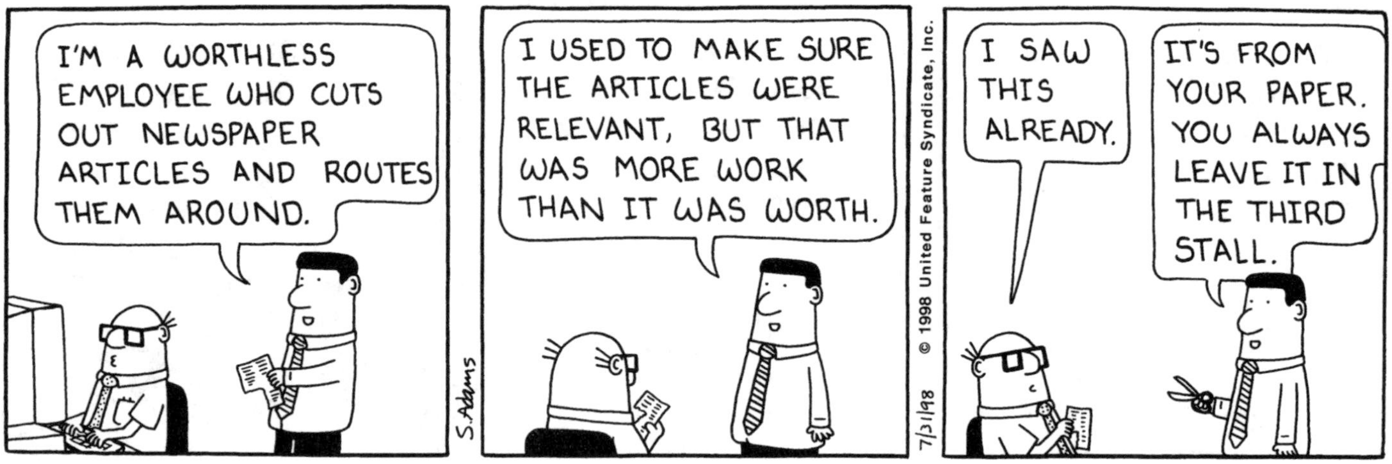
I'M A WORTHLESS EMPLOYEE WHO CUTS OUT NEWSPAPER ARTICLES AND ROUTES THEM AROUND.
S. Adams
I USED TO MAKE SURE THE ARTICLES WERE RELEVANT, BUT THAT WAS MORE WORK THAN IT WAS WORTH.
7/31/98 © 1998 United Feature Syndicate, Inc.
I SAW THIS ALREADY.
IT'S FROM YOUR PAPER. YOU ALWAYS LEAVE IT IN THE THIRD STALL.

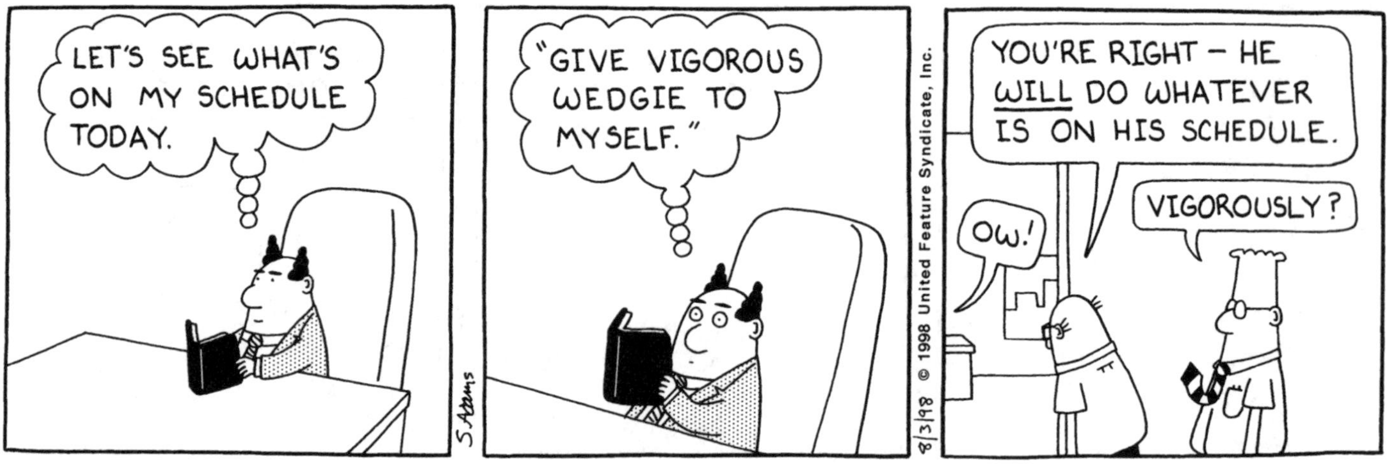
LET'S SEE WHAT'S ON MY SCHEDULE TODAY.
S. Adams
"GIVE VIGOROUS WEDGIE TO MYSELF."
8/3/98 © 1998 United Feature Syndicate, Inc.
YOU'RE RIGHT – HE WILL DO WHATEVER IS ON HIS SCHEDULE.
OW!
VIGOROUSLY?

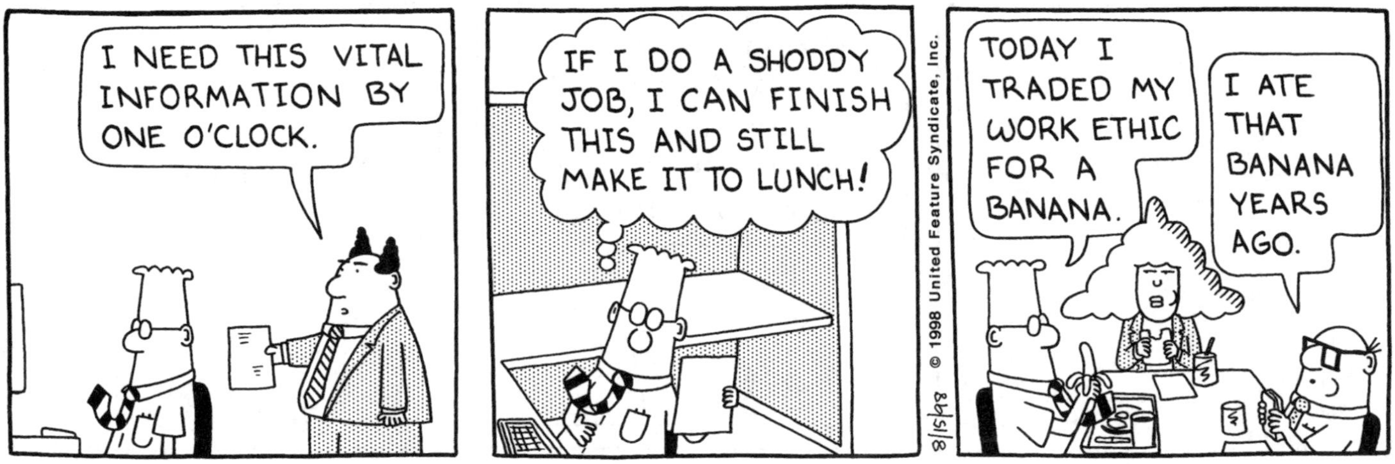
I NEED THIS VITAL INFORMATION BY ONE O'CLOCK.
IF I DO A SHODDY JOB, I CAN FINISH THIS AND STILL MAKE IT TO LUNCH!
8/15/98
© 1998 United Feature Syndicate, Inc.
TODAY I TRADED MY WORK ETHIC FOR A BANANA.
I ATE THAT BANANA YEARS AGO.

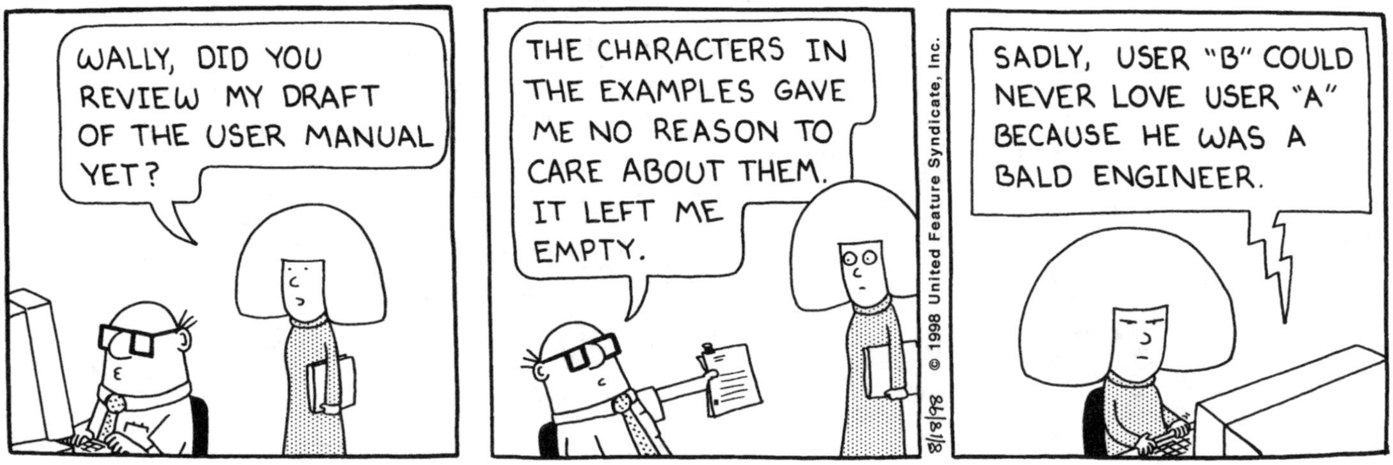
WALLY, DID YOU REVIEW MY DRAFT OF THE USER MANUAL YET?
THE CHARACTERS IN THE EXAMPLES GAVE ME NO REASON TO CARE ABOUT THEM. IT LEFT ME EMPTY.
8/18/98
© 1998 United Feature Syndicate, Inc.
SADLY, USER "B" COULD NEVER LOVE USER "A" BECAUSE HE WAS A BALD ENGINEER.

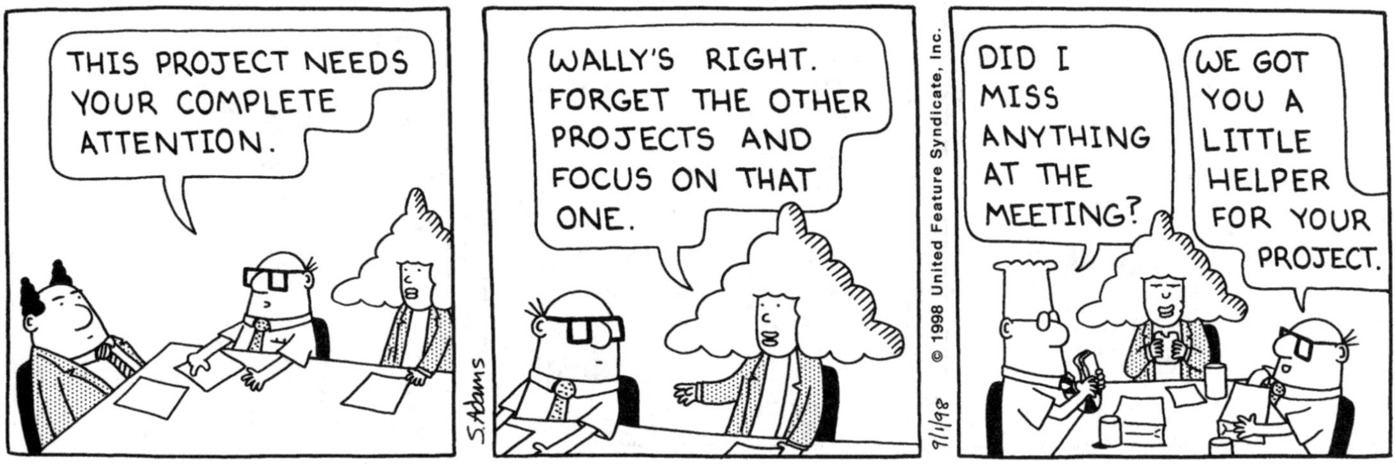
THIS PROJECT NEEDS YOUR COMPLETE ATTENTION.
S.Adams
WALLY'S RIGHT. FORGET THE OTHER PROJECTS AND FOCUS ON THAT ONE.
9/1/98
© 1998 United Feature Syndicate, Inc.
DID I MISS ANYTHING AT THE MEETING?
WE GOT YOU A LITTLE HELPER FOR YOUR PROJECT.

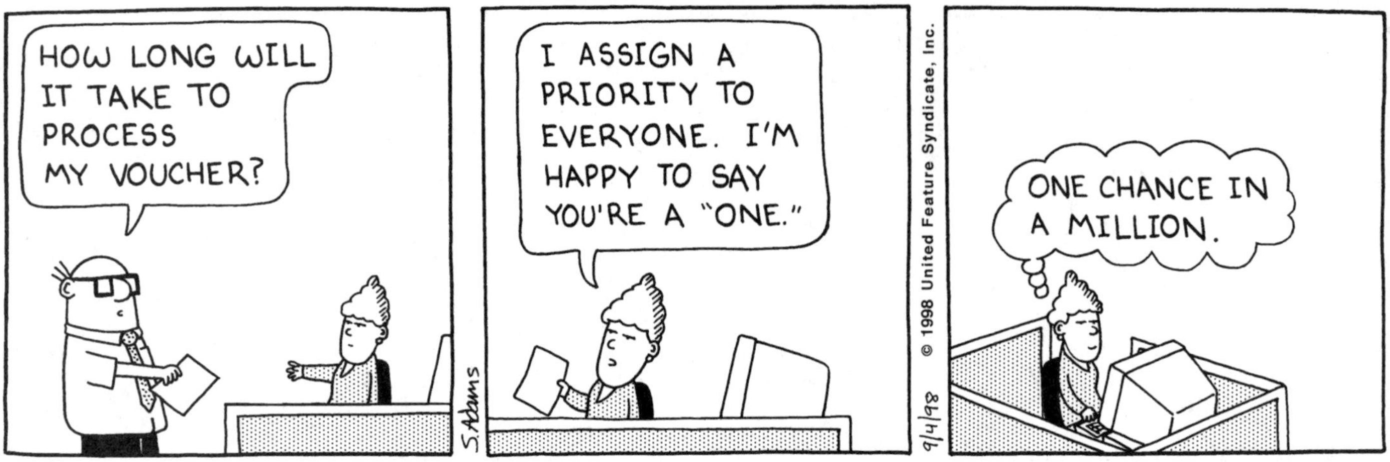
HOW LONG WILL IT TAKE TO PROCESS MY VOUCHER?
I ASSIGN A PRIORITY TO EVERYONE. I'M HAPPY TO SAY YOU'RE A "ONE."
ONE CHANCE IN A MILLION.
S. Adams
9/4/98
© 1998 United Feature Syndicate, Inc.

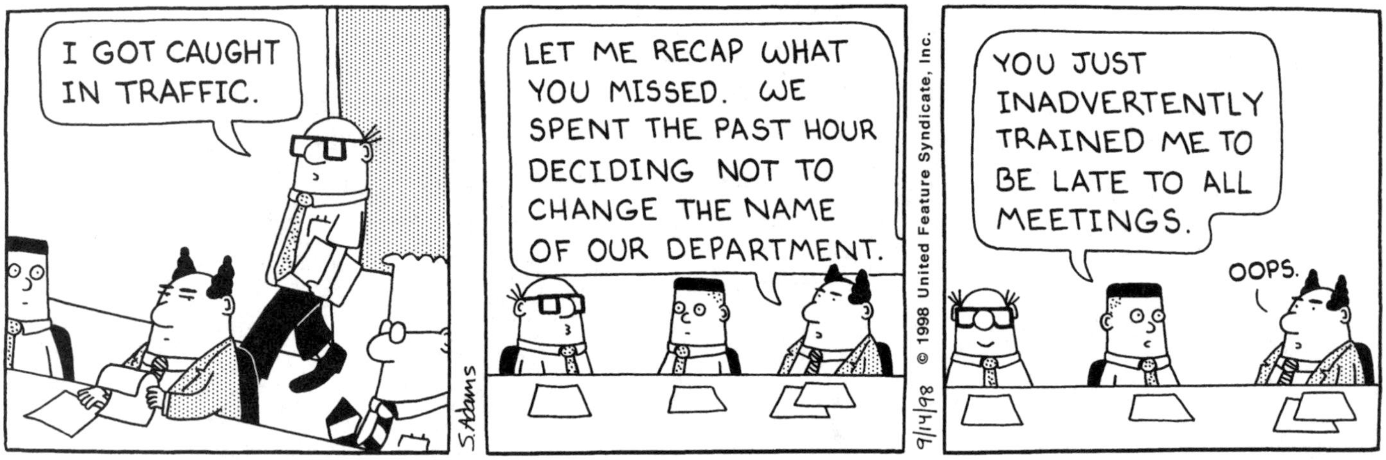
I GOT CAUGHT IN TRAFFIC.
LET ME RECAP WHAT YOU MISSED. WE SPENT THE PAST HOUR DECIDING NOT TO CHANGE THE NAME OF OUR DEPARTMENT.
YOU JUST INADVERTENTLY TRAINED ME TO BE LATE TO ALL MEETINGS.
OOPS.
S. Adams
9/14/98
© 1998 United Feature Syndicate, Inc.

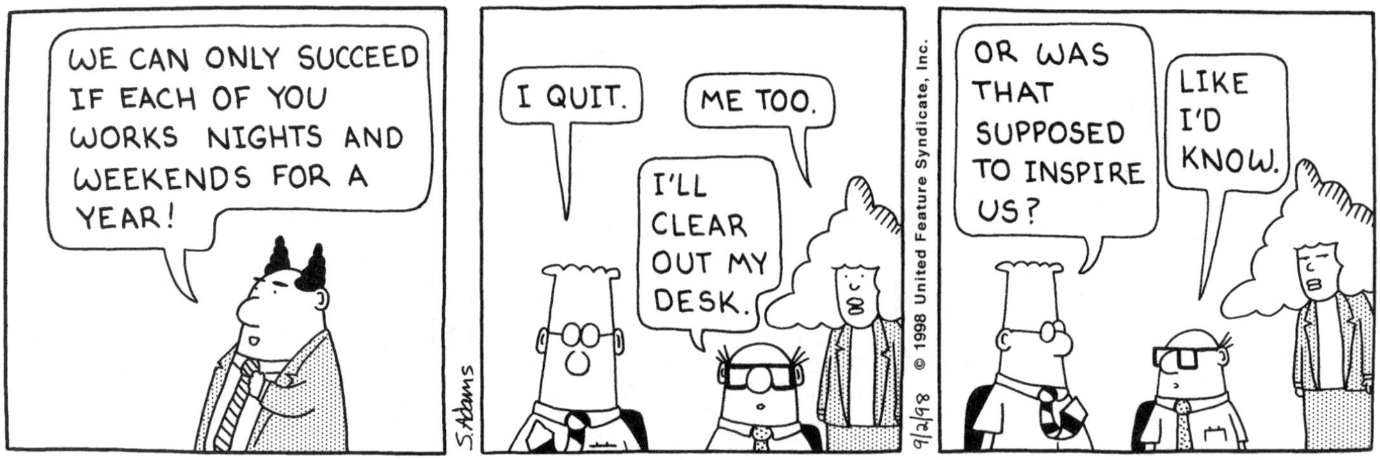
WE CAN ONLY SUCCEED IF EACH OF YOU WORKS NIGHTS AND WEEKENDS FOR A YEAR!
I QUIT.
ME TOO.
I'LL CLEAR OUT MY DESK.
OR WAS THAT SUPPOSED TO INSPIRE US?
LIKE I'D KNOW.
S. Adams
9/2/98
© 1998 United Feature Syndicate, Inc.

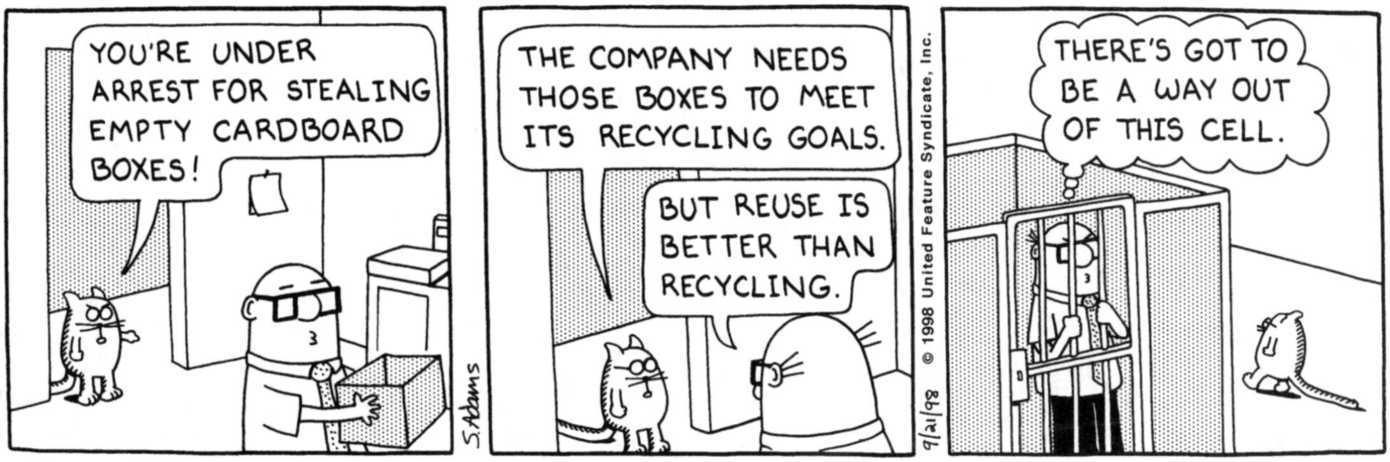
YOU'RE UNDER ARREST FOR STEALING EMPTY CARDBOARD BOXES!
THE COMPANY NEEDS THOSE BOXES TO MEET ITS RECYCLING GOALS.
BUT REUSE IS BETTER THAN RECYCLING.
THERE'S GOT TO BE A WAY OUT OF THIS CELL.
S.Adams
9/21/98 © 1998 United Feature Syndicate, Inc.

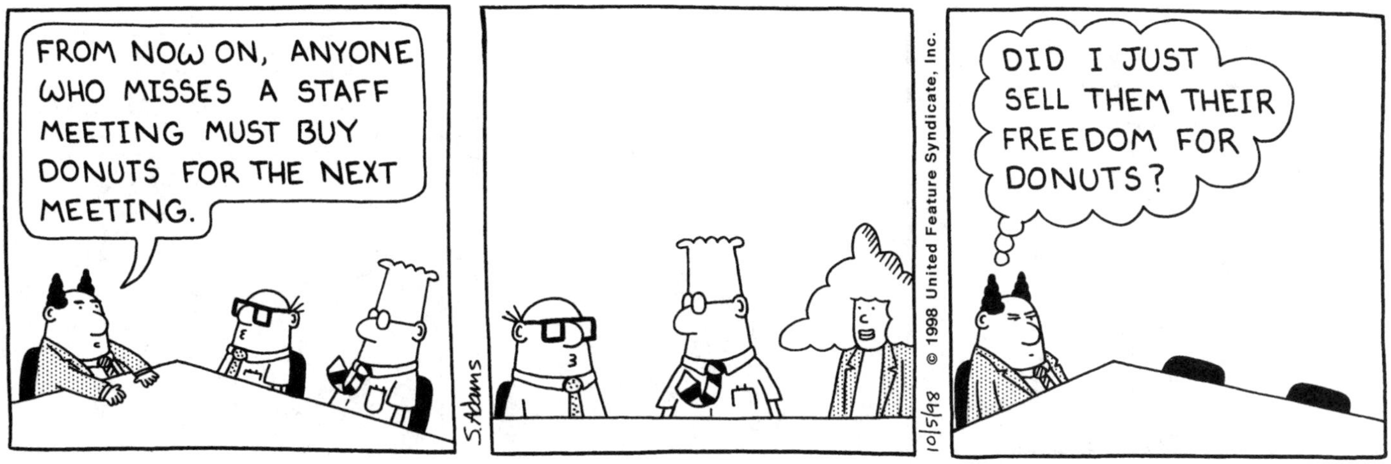
FROM NOW ON, ANYONE WHO MISSES A STAFF MEETING MUST BUY DONUTS FOR THE NEXT MEETING.
DID I JUST SELL THEM THEIR FREEDOM FOR DONUTS?
S.Adams
10/5/98 © 1998 United Feature Syndicate, Inc.

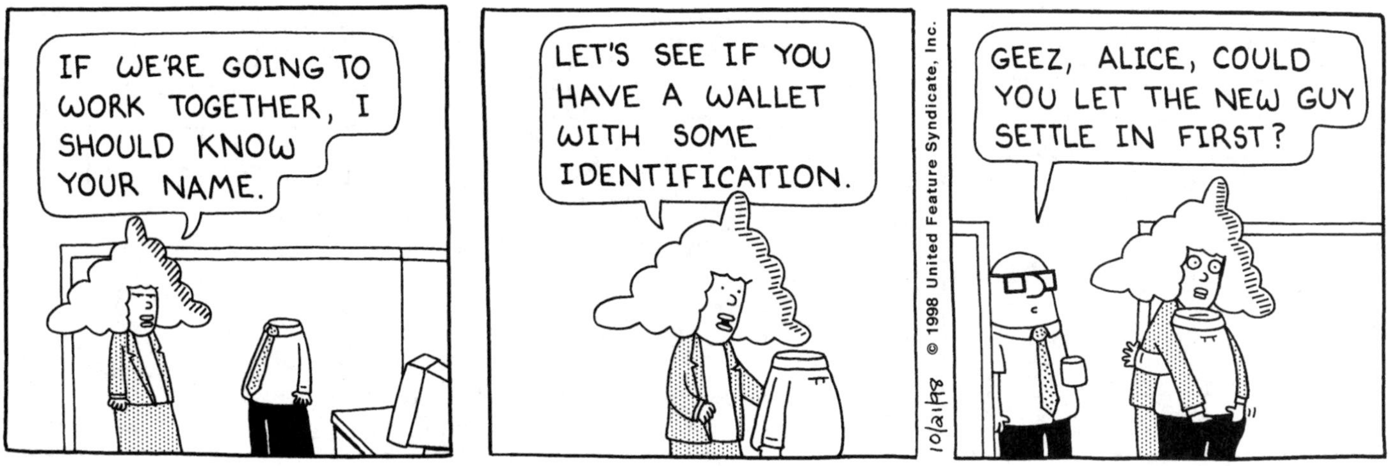
IF WE'RE GOING TO WORK TOGETHER, I SHOULD KNOW YOUR NAME.
LET'S SEE IF YOU HAVE A WALLET WITH SOME IDENTIFICATION.
GEEZ, ALICE, COULD YOU LET THE NEW GUY SETTLE IN FIRST?
10/21/98 © 1998 United Feature Syndicate, Inc.

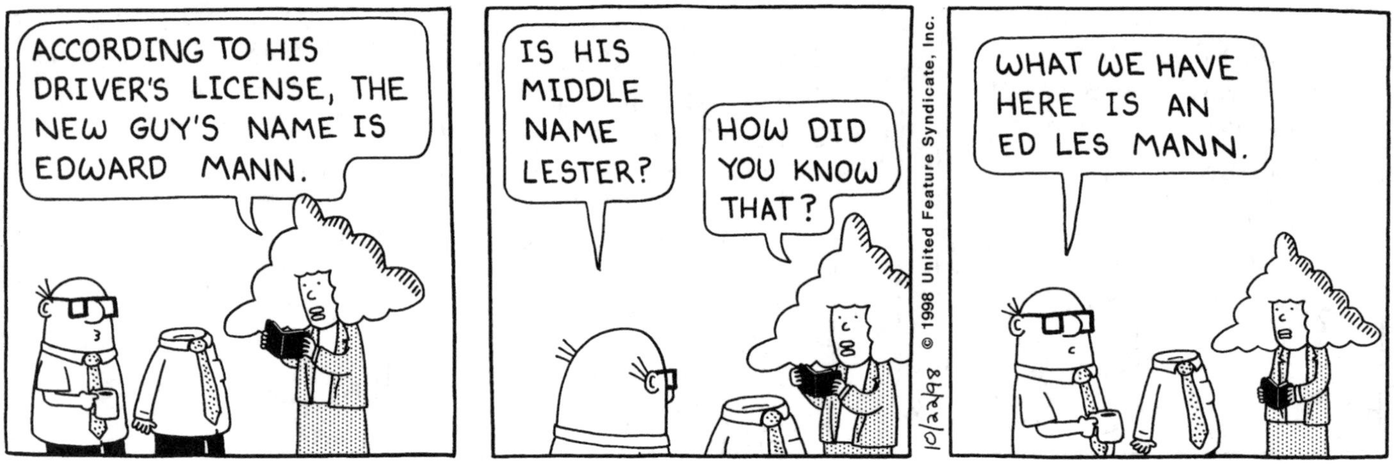
ACCORDING TO HIS DRIVER'S LICENSE, THE NEW GUY'S NAME IS EDWARD MANN.
IS HIS MIDDLE NAME LESTER?
HOW DID YOU KNOW THAT?
WHAT WE HAVE HERE IS AN ED LES MANN.
10/22/98 © 1998 United Feature Syndicate, Inc.

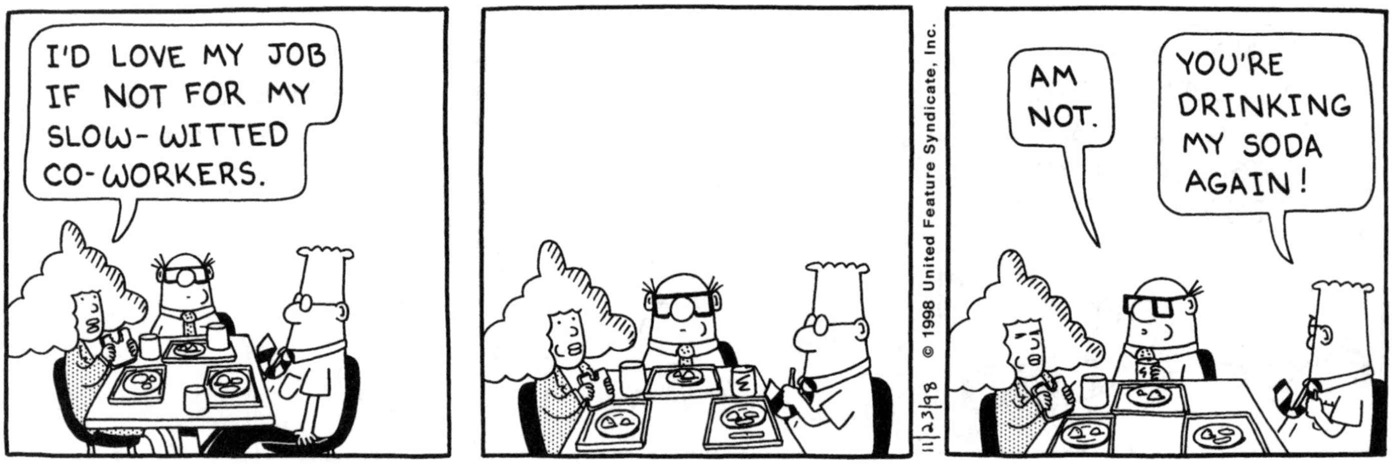
I'D LOVE MY JOB IF NOT FOR MY SLOW-WITTED CO-WORKERS.
AM NOT.
YOU'RE DRINKING MY SODA AGAIN!
11/23/98 © 1998 United Feature Syndicate, Inc.

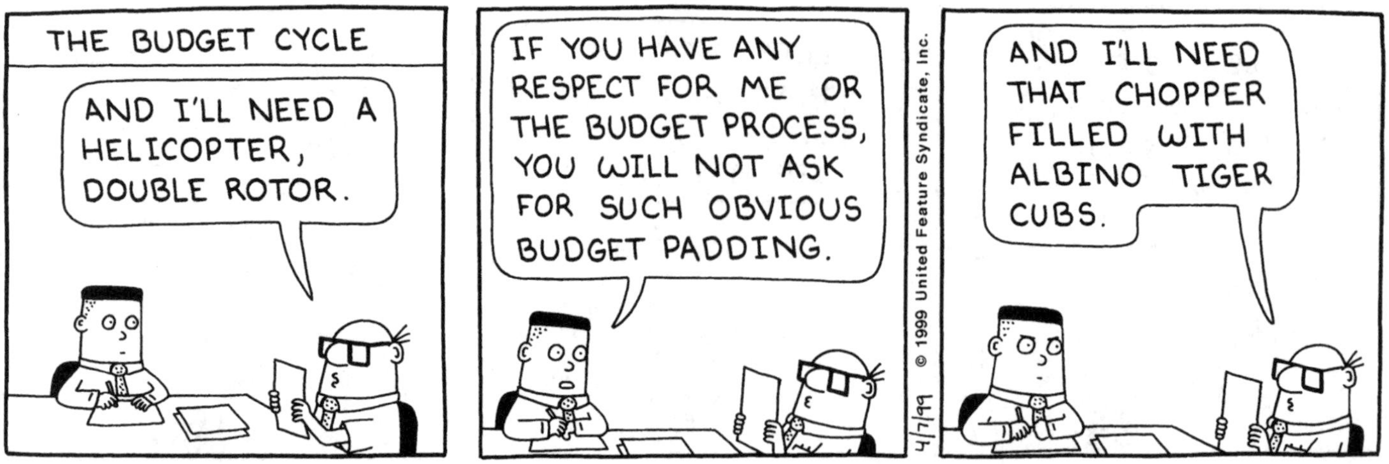
THE BUDGET CYCLE
AND I'LL NEED A HELICOPTER, DOUBLE ROTOR.
IF YOU HAVE ANY RESPECT FOR ME OR THE BUDGET PROCESS, YOU WILL NOT ASK FOR SUCH OBVIOUS BUDGET PADDING.
AND I'LL NEED THAT CHOPPER FILLED WITH ALBINO TIGER CUBS.
4/7/99 © 1999 United Feature Syndicate, Inc.

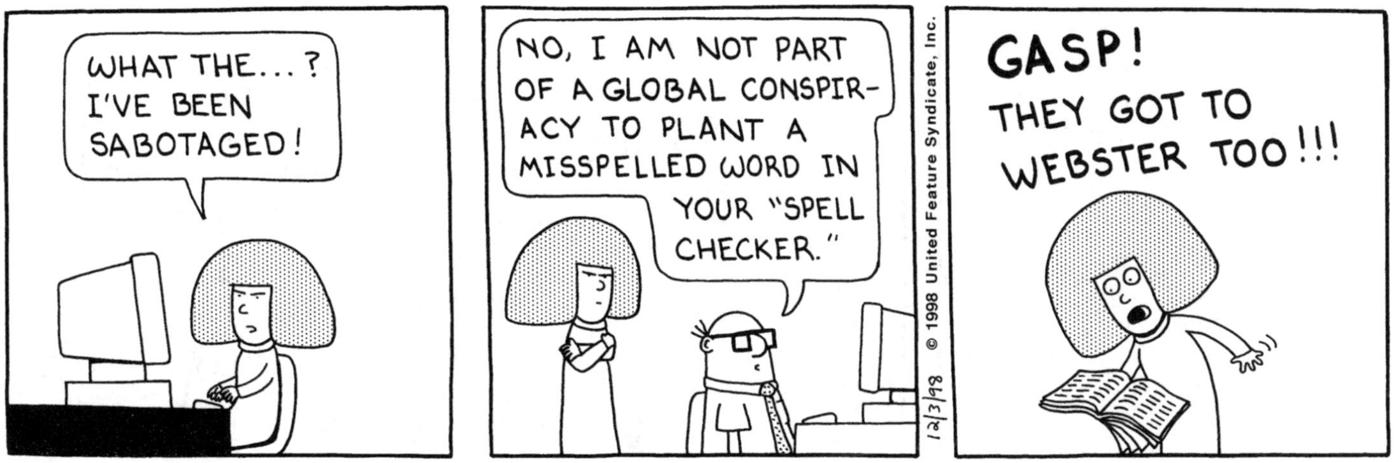
WHAT THE...? I'VE BEEN SABOTAGED!
NO, I AM NOT PART OF A GLOBAL CONSPIR-ACY TO PLANT A MISSPELLED WORD IN YOUR "SPELL CHECKER."
12/3/98 © 1998 United Feature Syndicate, Inc.
GASP! THEY GOT TO WEBSTER TOO!!!

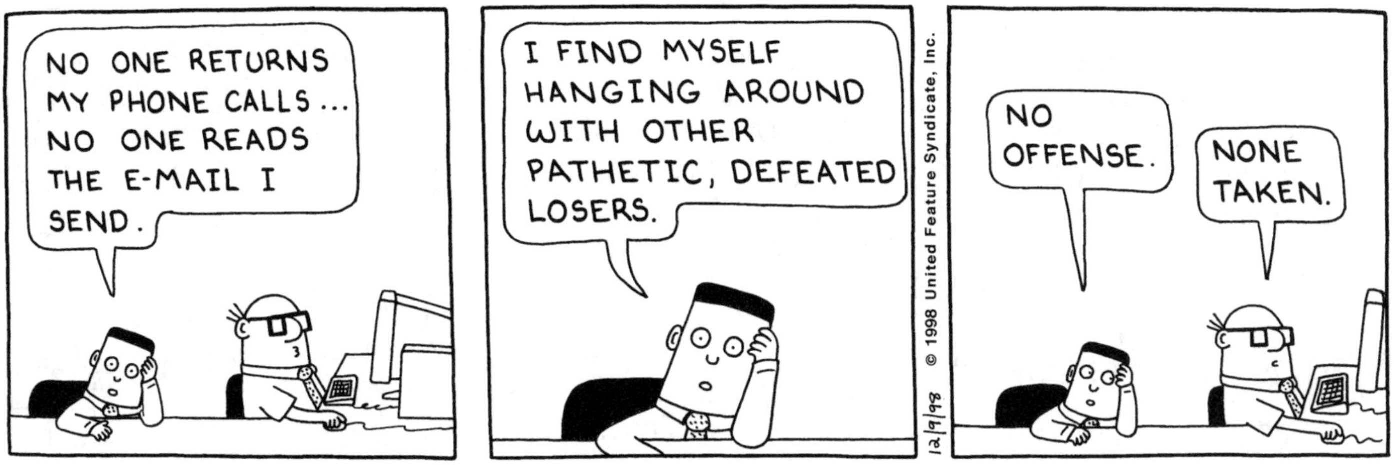
NO ONE RETURNS MY PHONE CALLS... NO ONE READS THE E-MAIL I SEND.
I FIND MYSELF HANGING AROUND WITH OTHER PATHETIC, DEFEATED LOSERS.
12/9/98 © 1998 United Feature Syndicate, Inc.
NO OFFENSE.
NONE TAKEN.

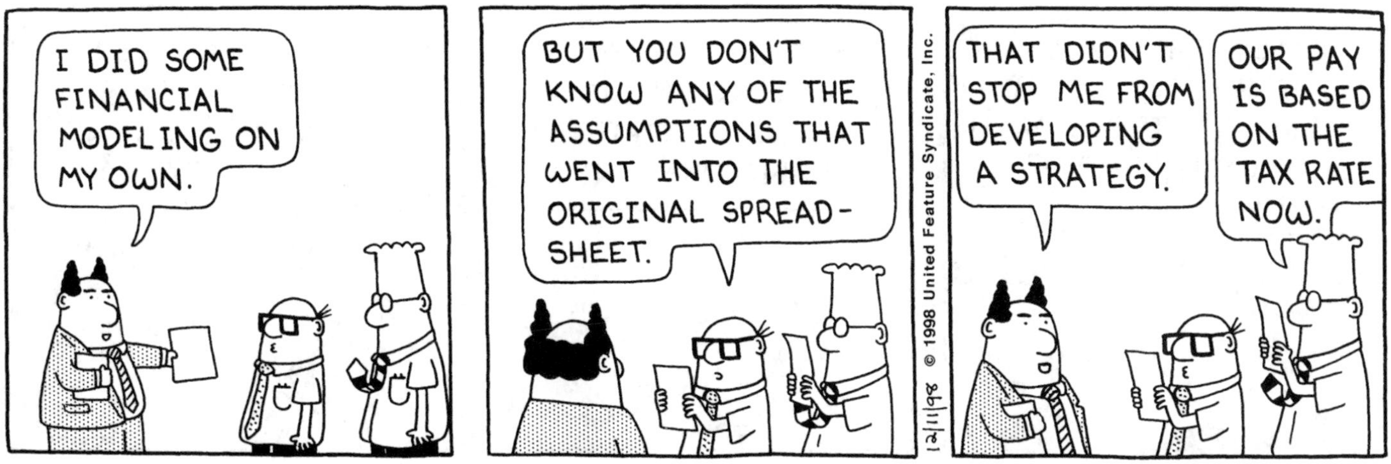
I DID SOME FINANCIAL MODELING ON MY OWN.
BUT YOU DON'T KNOW ANY OF THE ASSUMPTIONS THAT WENT INTO THE ORIGINAL SPREAD-SHEET.
12/11/98 © 1998 United Feature Syndicate, Inc.
THAT DIDN'T STOP ME FROM DEVELOPING A STRATEGY.
OUR PAY IS BASED ON THE TAX RATE NOW.

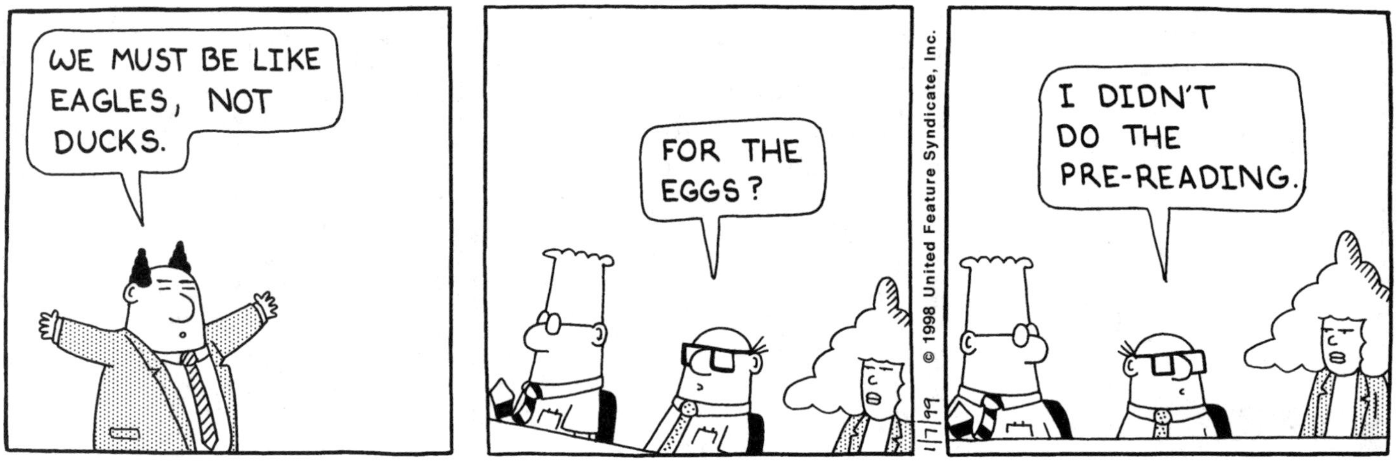
WE MUST BE LIKE EAGLES, NOT DUCKS.
FOR THE EGGS?
I DIDN'T DO THE PRE-READING.
1/7/99
© 1998 United Feature Syndicate, Inc.

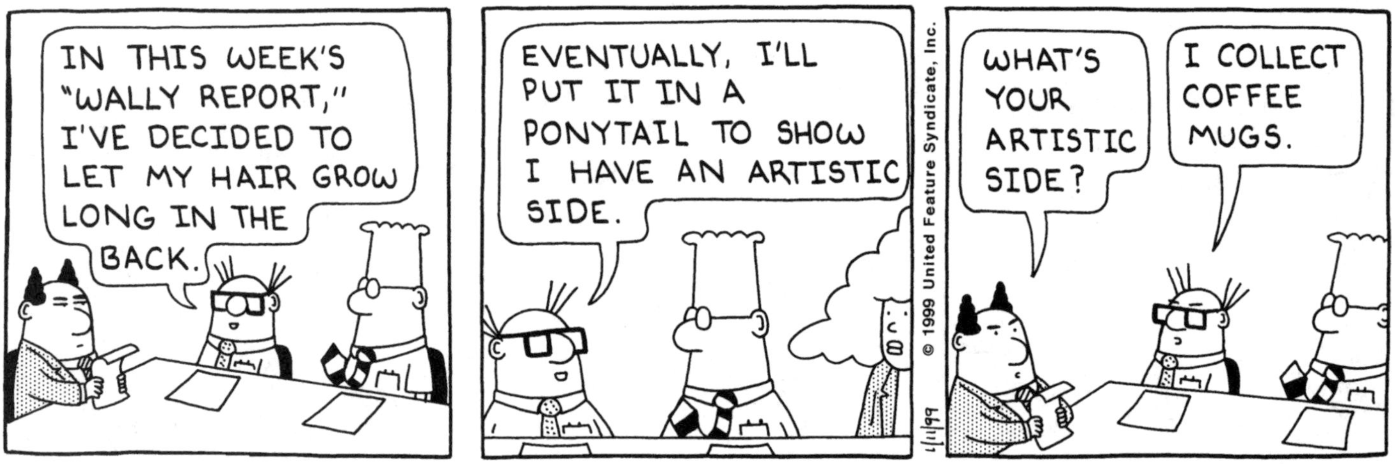
IN THIS WEEK'S "WALLY REPORT," I'VE DECIDED TO LET MY HAIR GROW LONG IN THE BACK.
EVENTUALLY, I'LL PUT IT IN A PONYTAIL TO SHOW I HAVE AN ARTISTIC SIDE.
WHAT'S YOUR ARTISTIC SIDE?
I COLLECT COFFEE MUGS.
1/11/99
© 1999 United Feature Syndicate, Inc.

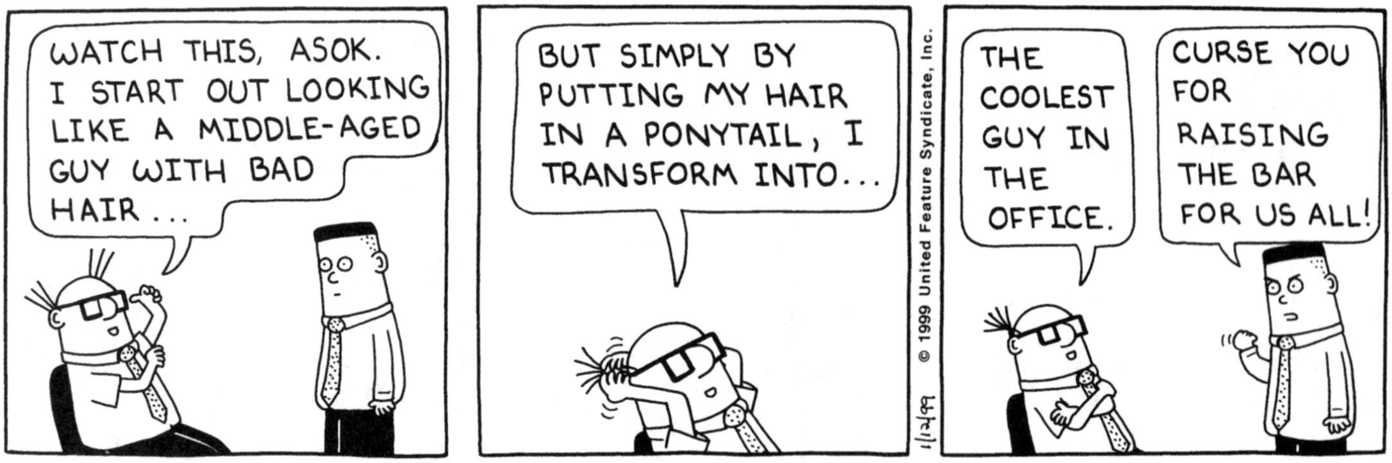
WATCH THIS, ASOK. I START OUT LOOKING LIKE A MIDDLE-AGED GUY WITH BAD HAIR...
BUT SIMPLY BY PUTTING MY HAIR IN A PONYTAIL, I TRANSFORM INTO...
THE COOLEST GUY IN THE OFFICE.
CURSE YOU FOR RAISING THE BAR FOR US ALL!
1/12/99
© 1999 United Feature Syndicate, Inc.

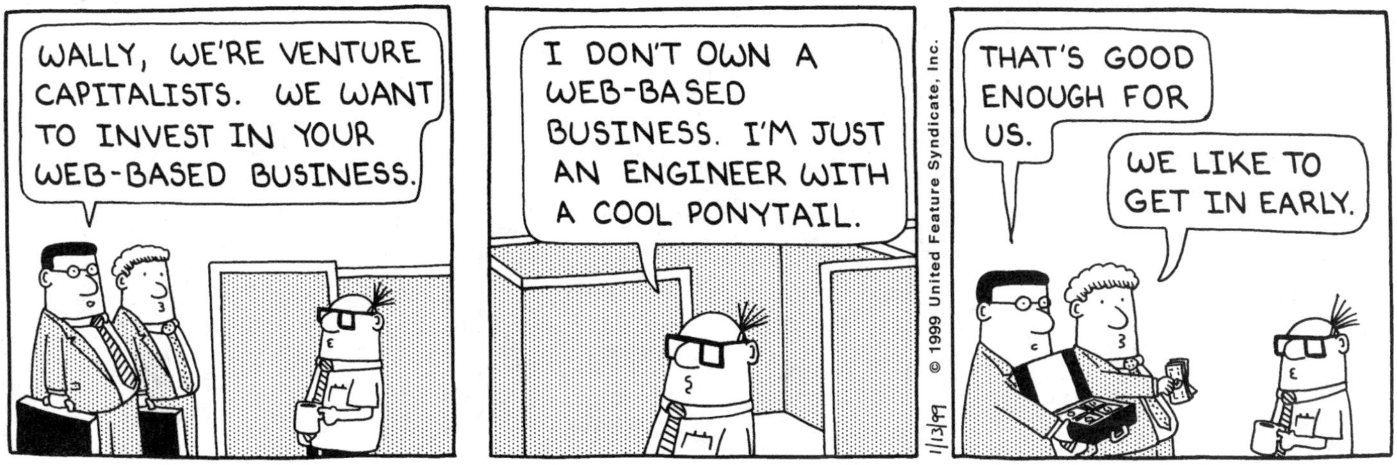
WALLY, WE'RE VENTURE CAPITALISTS. WE WANT TO INVEST IN YOUR WEB-BASED BUSINESS.
I DON'T OWN A WEB-BASED BUSINESS. I'M JUST AN ENGINEER WITH A COOL PONYTAIL.
1/13/99 © 1999 United Feature Syndicate, Inc.
THAT'S GOOD ENOUGH FOR US.
WE LIKE TO GET IN EARLY.

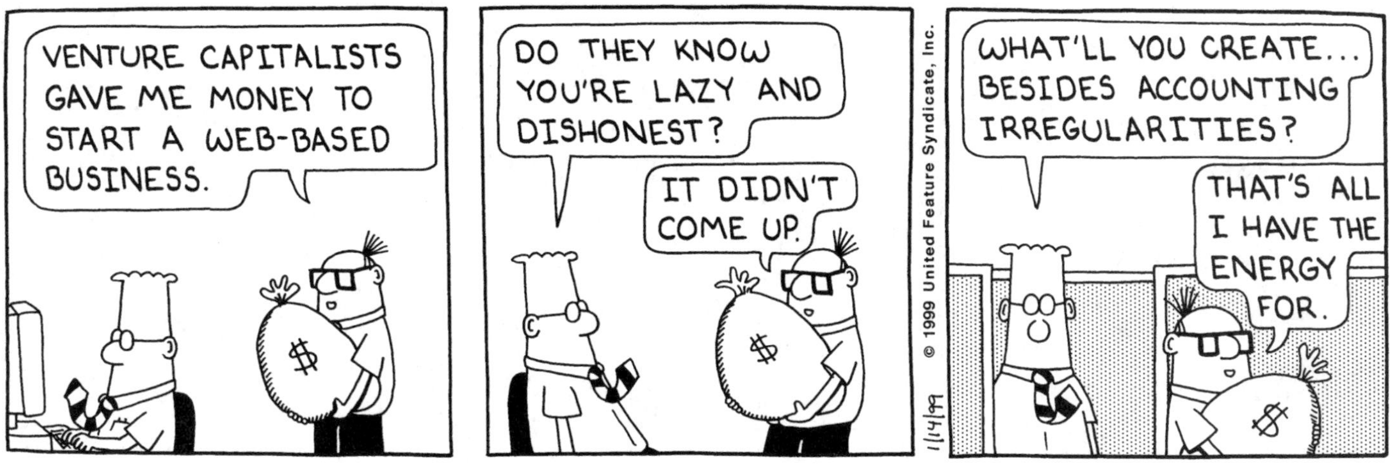
VENTURE CAPITALISTS GAVE ME MONEY TO START A WEB-BASED BUSINESS.
DO THEY KNOW YOU'RE LAZY AND DISHONEST?
IT DIDN'T COME UP.
1/14/99 © 1999 United Feature Syndicate, Inc.
WHAT'LL YOU CREATE... BESIDES ACCOUNTING IRREGULARITIES?
THAT'S ALL I HAVE THE ENERGY FOR.

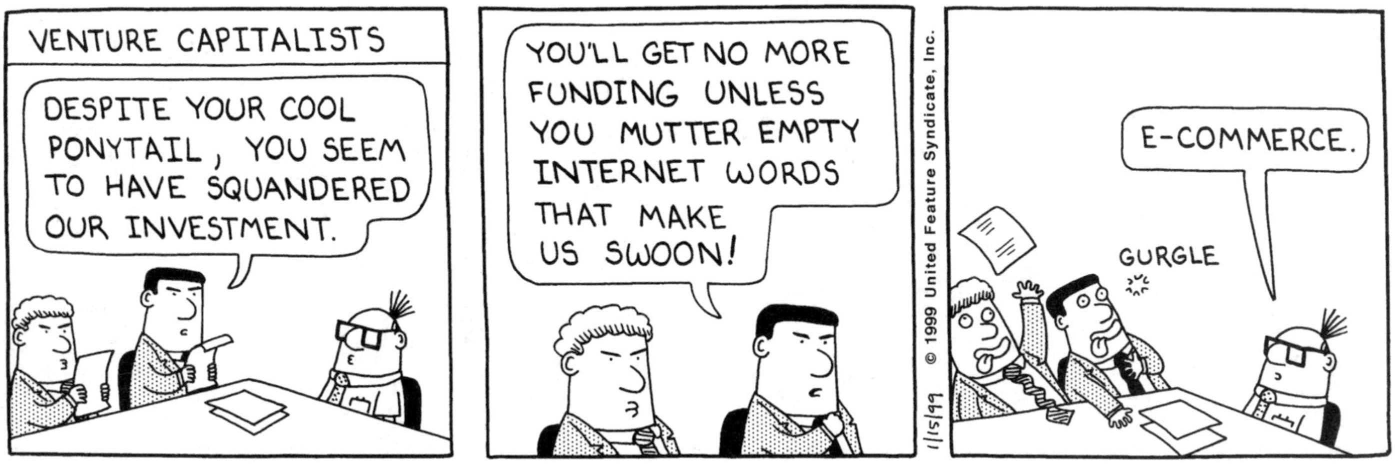
VENTURE CAPITALISTS
DESPITE YOUR COOL PONYTAIL, YOU SEEM TO HAVE SQUANDERED OUR INVESTMENT.
YOU'LL GET NO MORE FUNDING UNLESS YOU MUTTER EMPTY INTERNET WORDS THAT MAKE US SWOON!
1/15/99 © 1999 United Feature Syndicate, Inc.
E-COMMERCE.
GURGLE

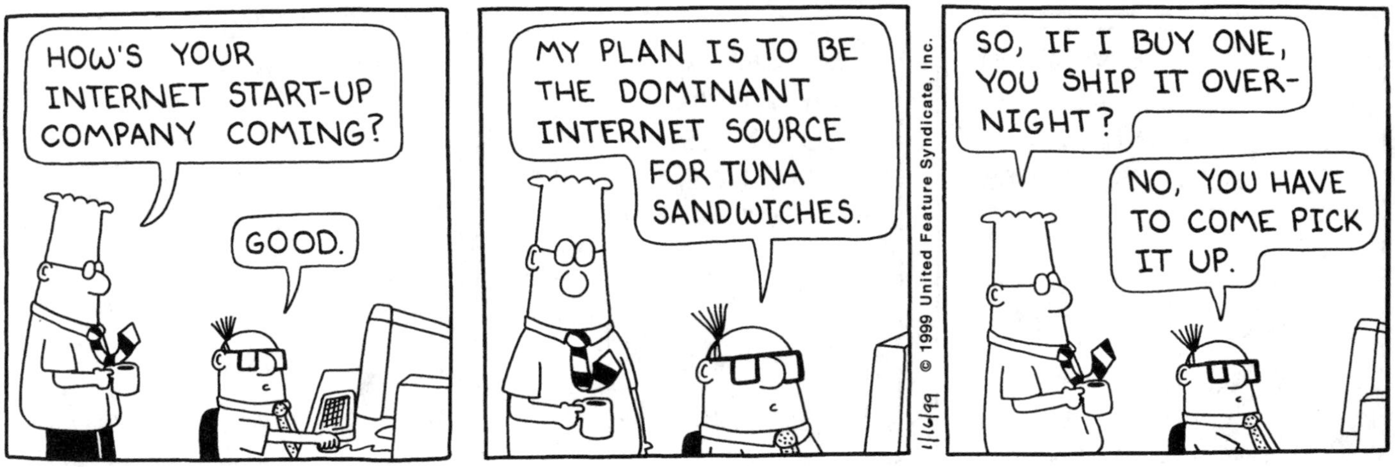
HOW'S YOUR INTERNET START-UP COMPANY COMING?
GOOD.
MY PLAN IS TO BE THE DOMINANT INTERNET SOURCE FOR TUNA SANDWICHES.
1/16/99 © 1999 United Feature Syndicate, Inc.
SO, IF I BUY ONE, YOU SHIP IT OVER-NIGHT?
NO, YOU HAVE TO COME PICK IT UP.

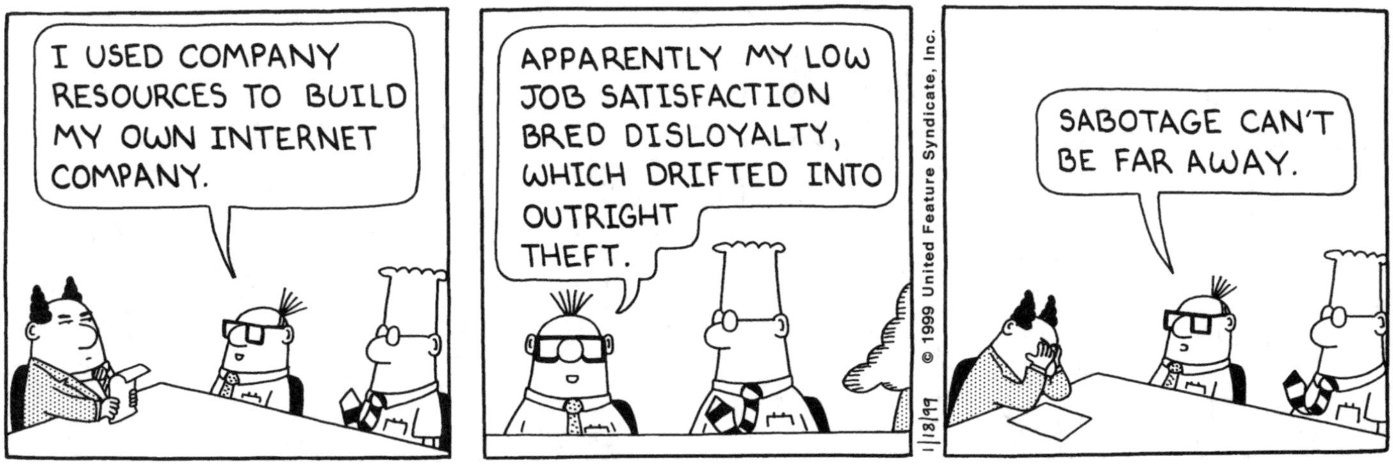
I USED COMPANY RESOURCES TO BUILD MY OWN INTERNET COMPANY.
APPARENTLY MY LOW JOB SATISFACTION BRED DISLOYALTY, WHICH DRIFTED INTO OUTRIGHT THEFT.
1/18/99 © 1999 United Feature Syndicate, Inc.
SABOTAGE CAN'T BE FAR AWAY.

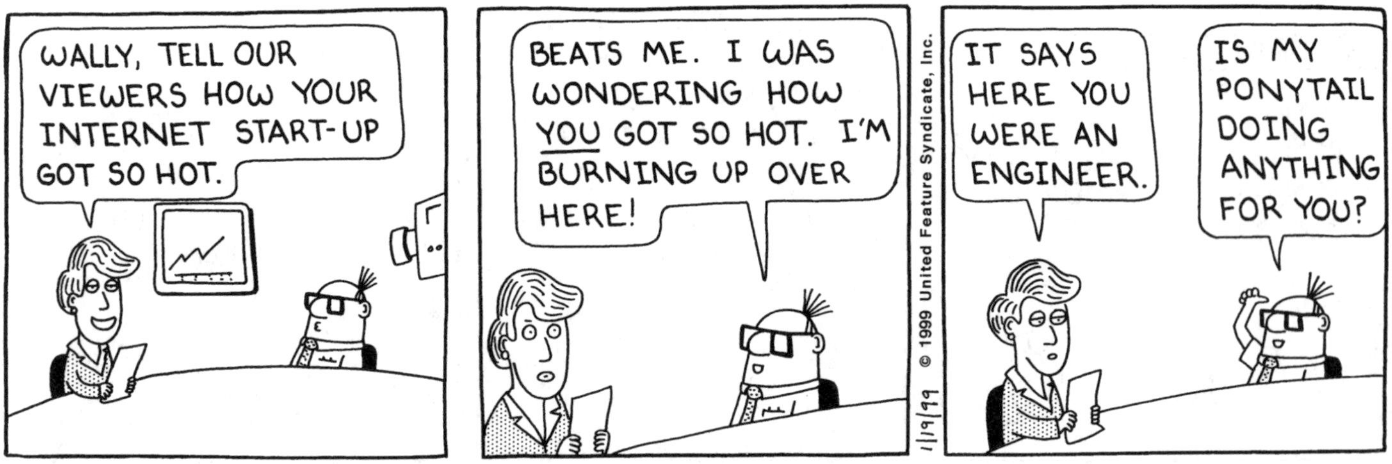
WALLY, TELL OUR VIEWERS HOW YOUR INTERNET START-UP GOT SO HOT.
BEATS ME. I WAS WONDERING HOW YOU GOT SO HOT. I'M BURNING UP OVER HERE!
1/19/99 © 1999 United Feature Syndicate, Inc.
IT SAYS HERE YOU WERE AN ENGINEER.
IS MY PONYTAIL DOING ANYTHING FOR YOU?

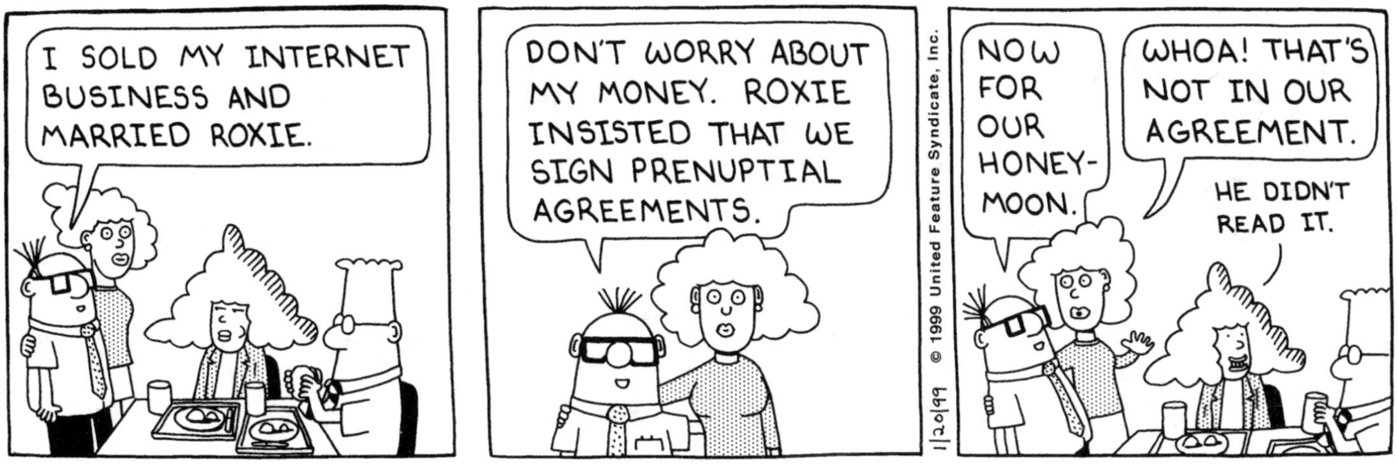
I SOLD MY INTERNET BUSINESS AND MARRIED ROXIE.
DON'T WORRY ABOUT MY MONEY. ROXIE INSISTED THAT WE SIGN PRENUPTIAL AGREEMENTS.
1/20/99 © 1999 United Feature Syndicate, Inc.
NOW FOR OUR HONEY-MOON.
WHOA! THAT'S NOT IN OUR AGREEMENT.
HE DIDN'T READ IT.

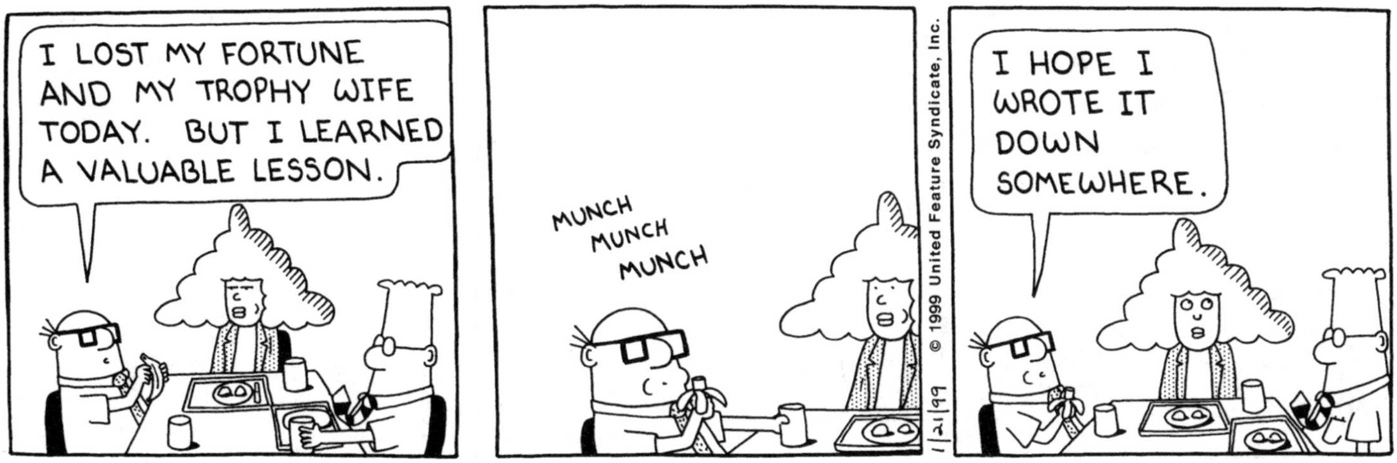
I LOST MY FORTUNE AND MY TROPHY WIFE TODAY. BUT I LEARNED A VALUABLE LESSON.
MUNCH MUNCH MUNCH
1/21/99 © 1999 United Feature Syndicate, Inc.
I HOPE I WROTE IT DOWN SOMEWHERE.

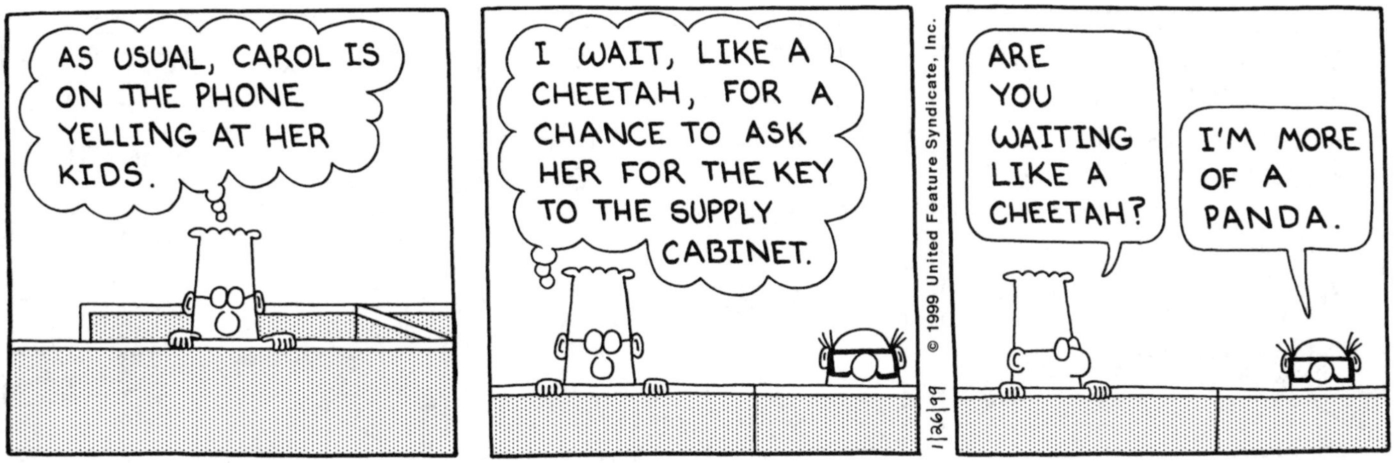
AS USUAL, CAROL IS ON THE PHONE YELLING AT HER KIDS.
I WAIT, LIKE A CHEETAH, FOR A CHANCE TO ASK HER FOR THE KEY TO THE SUPPLY CABINET.
1/26/99 © 1999 United Feature Syndicate, Inc.
ARE YOU WAITING LIKE A CHEETAH?
I'M MORE OF A PANDA.

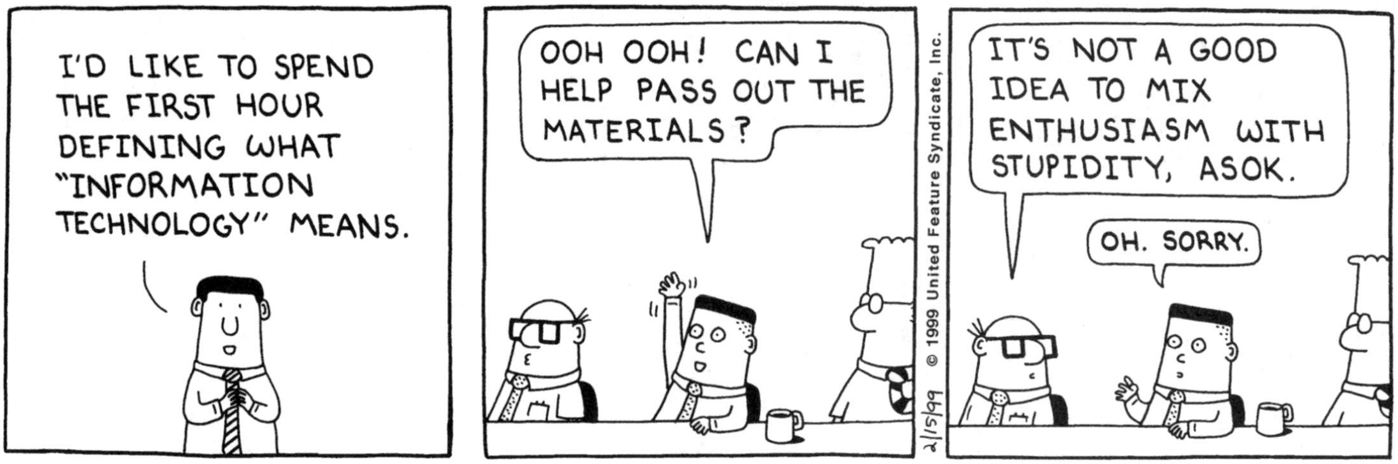
I'D LIKE TO SPEND THE FIRST HOUR DEFINING WHAT "INFORMATION TECHNOLOGY" MEANS.
OOH OOH! CAN I HELP PASS OUT THE MATERIALS?
2/15/99 © 1999 United Feature Syndicate, Inc.
IT'S NOT A GOOD IDEA TO MIX ENTHUSIASM WITH STUPIDITY, ASOK.
OH. SORRY.

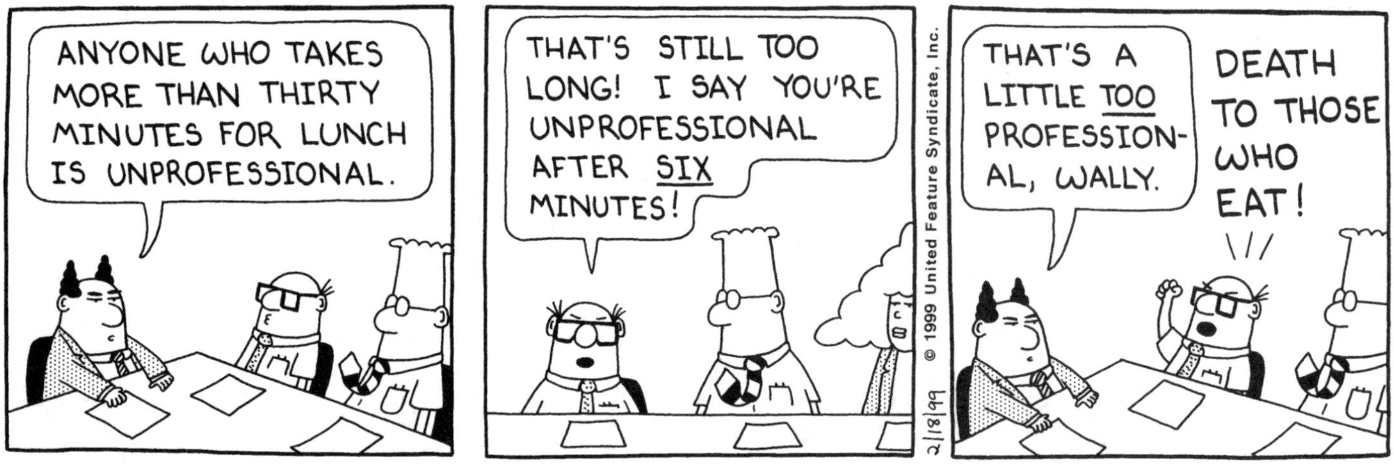
ANYONE WHO TAKES MORE THAN THIRTY MINUTES FOR LUNCH IS UNPROFESSIONAL.
THAT'S STILL TOO LONG! I SAY YOU'RE UNPROFESSIONAL AFTER SIX MINUTES!
2/18/99 © 1999 United Feature Syndicate, Inc.
THAT'S A LITTLE TOO PROFESSIONAL, WALLY.
DEATH TO THOSE WHO EAT!

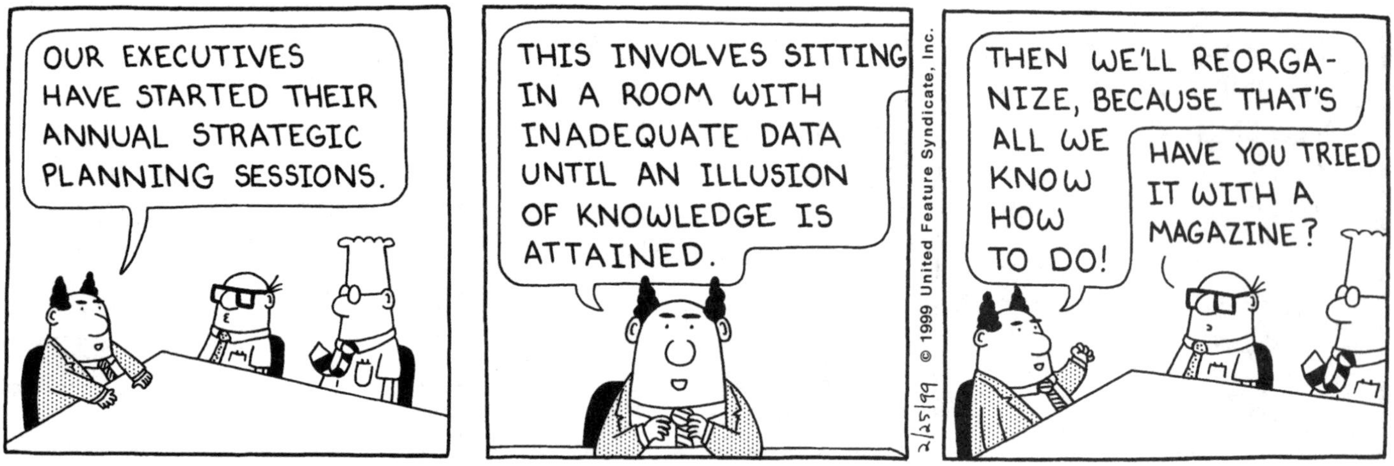
OUR EXECUTIVES HAVE STARTED THEIR ANNUAL STRATEGIC PLANNING SESSIONS.
THIS INVOLVES SITTING IN A ROOM WITH INADEQUATE DATA UNTIL AN ILLUSION OF KNOWLEDGE IS ATTAINED.
2/25/99 © 1999 United Feature Syndicate, Inc.
THEN WE'LL REORGANIZE, BECAUSE THAT'S ALL WE KNOW HOW TO DO!
HAVE YOU TRIED IT WITH A MAGAZINE?

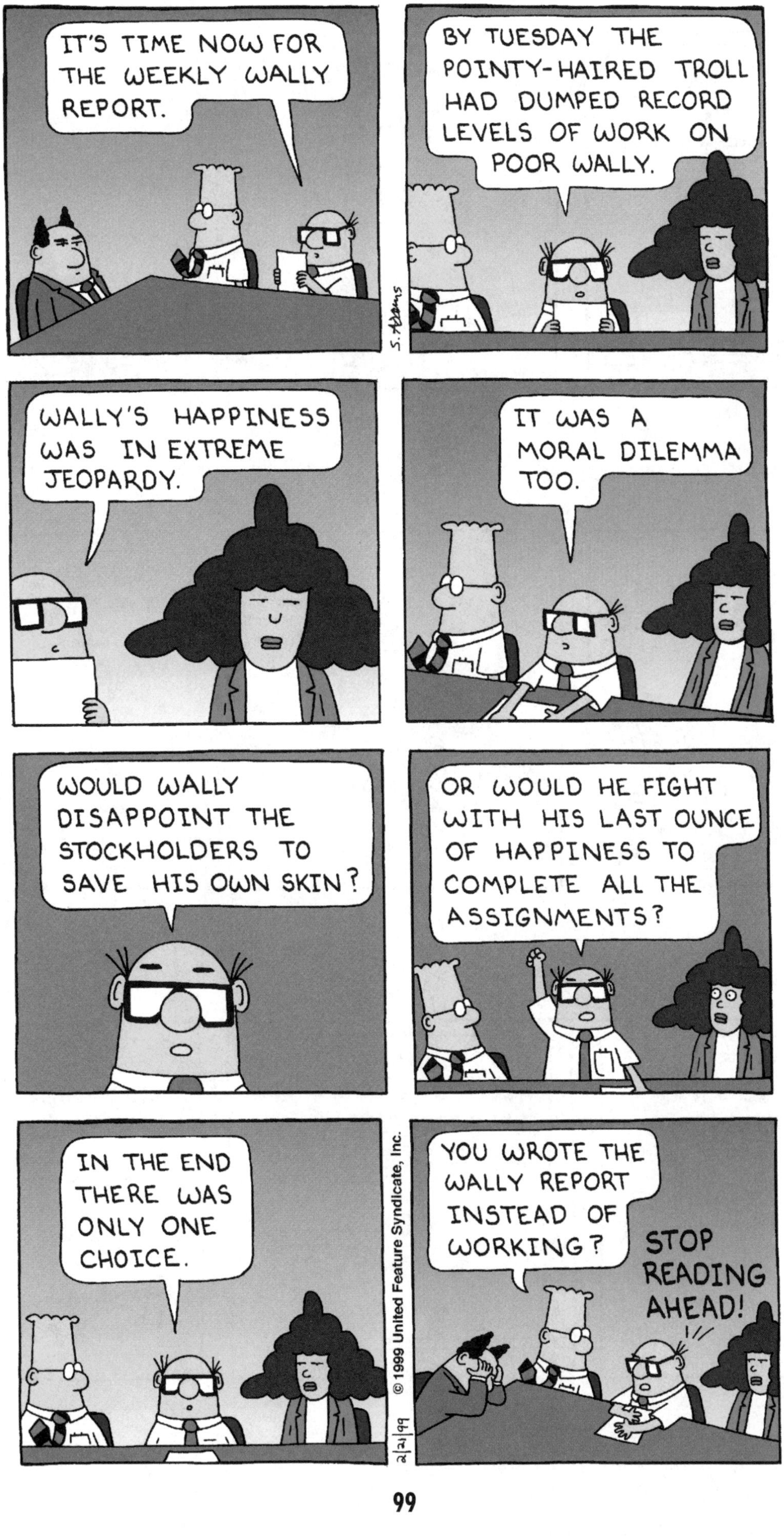
IT'S TIME NOW FOR THE WEEKLY WALLY REPORT.
S. Adams
BY TUESDAY THE POINTY-HAIRED TROLL HAD DUMPED RECORD LEVELS OF WORK ON POOR WALLY.
WALLY'S HAPPINESS WAS IN EXTREME JEOPARDY.
IT WAS A MORAL DILEMMA TOO.
WOULD WALLY DISAPPOINT THE STOCKHOLDERS TO SAVE HIS OWN SKIN?
OR WOULD HE FIGHT WITH HIS LAST OUNCE OF HAPPINESS TO COMPLETE ALL THE ASSIGNMENTS?
IN THE END THERE WAS ONLY ONE CHOICE.
2/21/99 © 1999 United Feature Syndicate, Inc.
YOU WROTE THE WALLY REPORT INSTEAD OF WORKING?
STOP READING AHEAD!

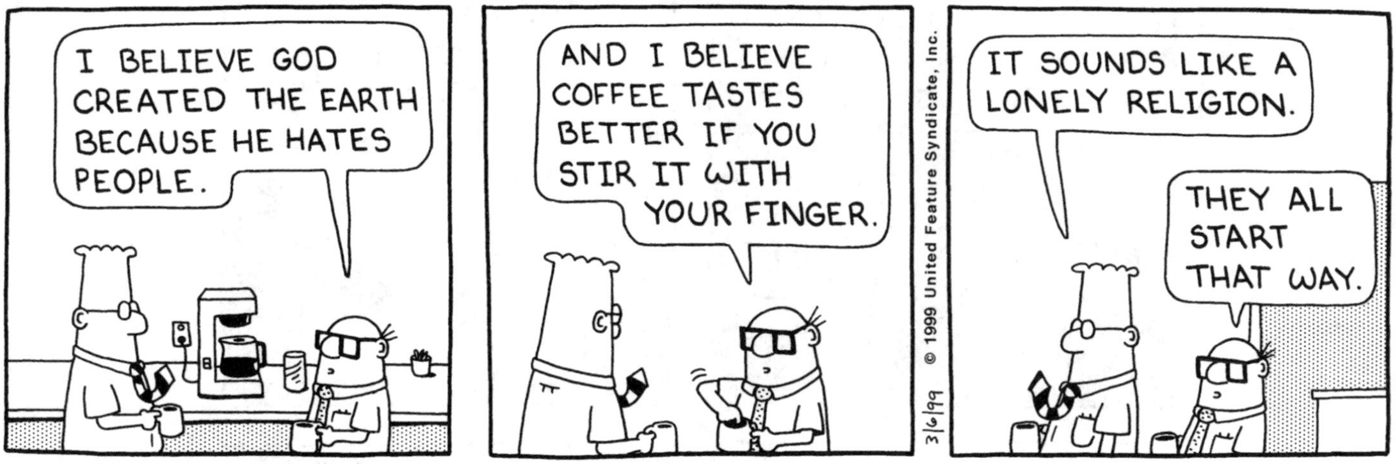
I BELIEVE GOD CREATED THE EARTH BECAUSE HE HATES PEOPLE.
AND I BELIEVE COFFEE TASTES BETTER IF YOU STIR IT WITH YOUR FINGER.
3/6/99 © 1999 United Feature Syndicate, Inc.
IT SOUNDS LIKE A LONELY RELIGION.
THEY ALL START THAT WAY.

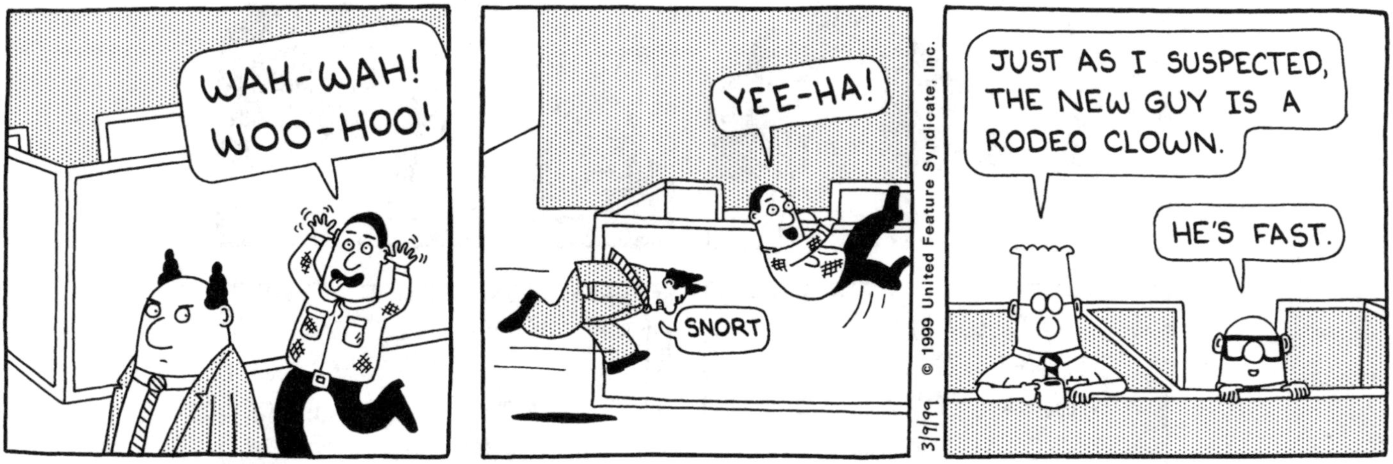
WAH-WAH! WOO-HOO!
YEE-HA!
SNORT
3/9/99 © 1999 United Feature Syndicate, Inc.
JUST AS I SUSPECTED, THE NEW GUY IS A RODEO CLOWN.
HE'S FAST.

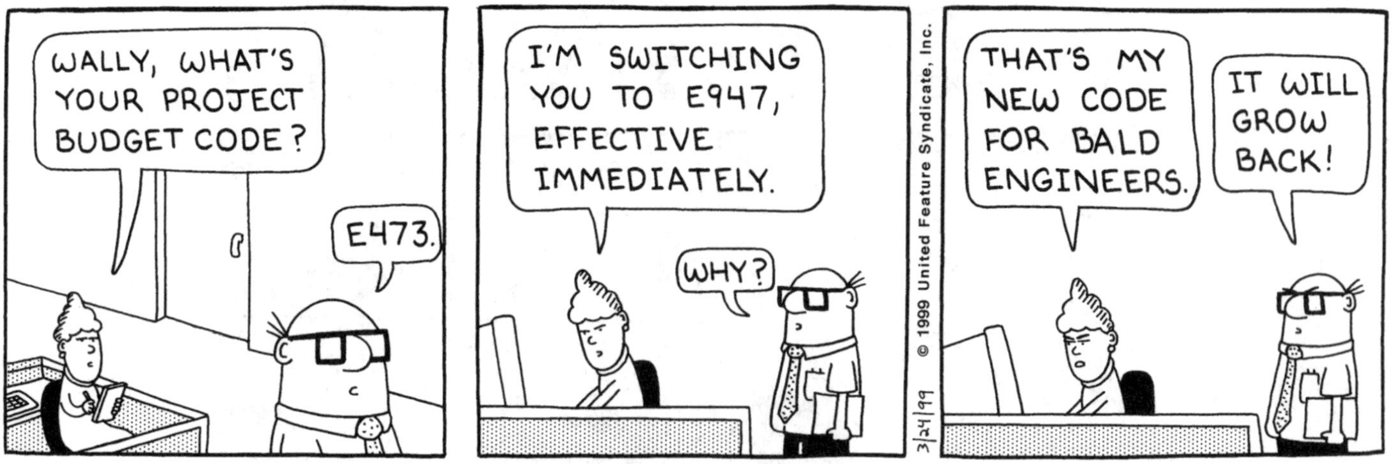
WALLY, WHAT'S YOUR PROJECT BUDGET CODE?
E473.
I'M SWITCHING YOU TO E947, EFFECTIVE IMMEDIATELY.
WHY?
3/24/99 © 1999 United Feature Syndicate, Inc.
THAT'S MY NEW CODE FOR BALD ENGINEERS.
IT WILL GROW BACK!

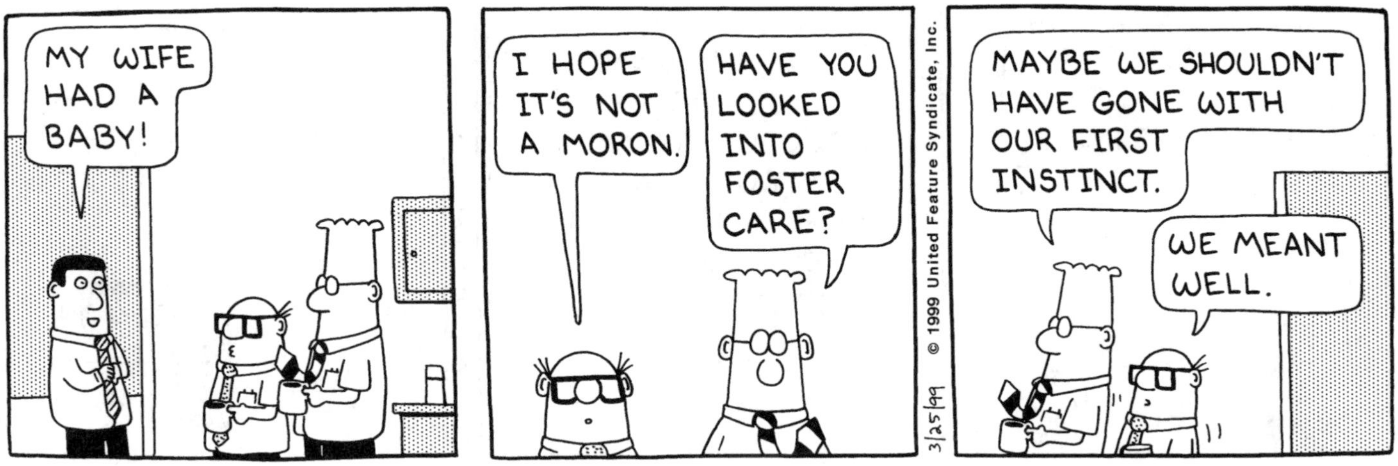
MY WIFE HAD A BABY!
I HOPE IT'S NOT A MORON.
HAVE YOU LOOKED INTO FOSTER CARE?
3/25/99 © 1999 United Feature Syndicate, Inc.
MAYBE WE SHOULDN'T HAVE GONE WITH OUR FIRST INSTINCT.
WE MEANT WELL.

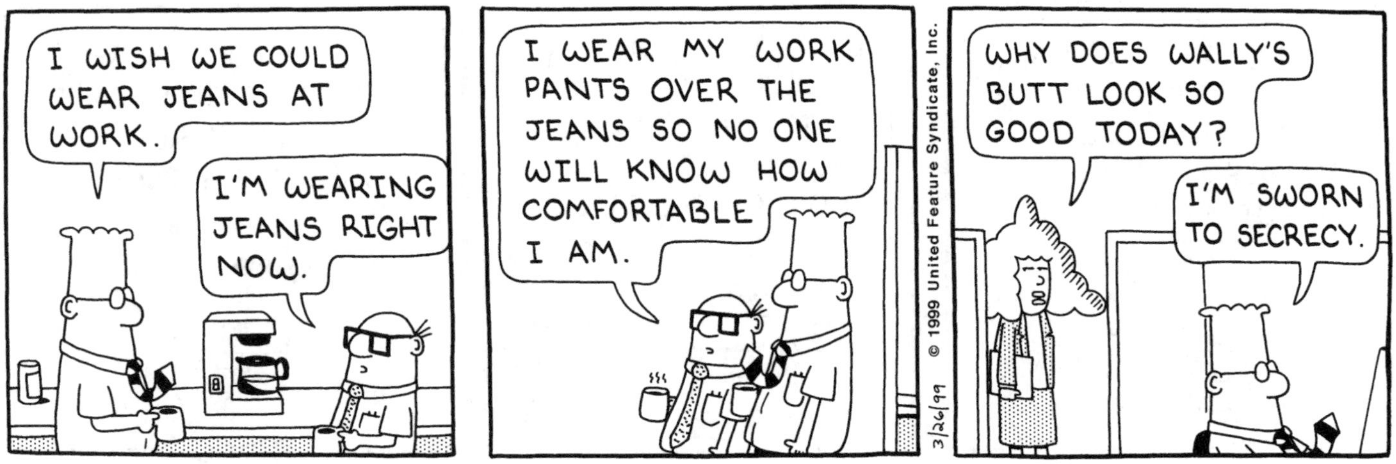
I WISH WE COULD WEAR JEANS AT WORK.
I'M WEARING JEANS RIGHT NOW.
I WEAR MY WORK PANTS OVER THE JEANS SO NO ONE WILL KNOW HOW COMFORTABLE I AM.
3/26/99 © 1999 United Feature Syndicate, Inc.
WHY DOES WALLY'S BUTT LOOK SO GOOD TODAY?
I'M SWORN TO SECRECY.

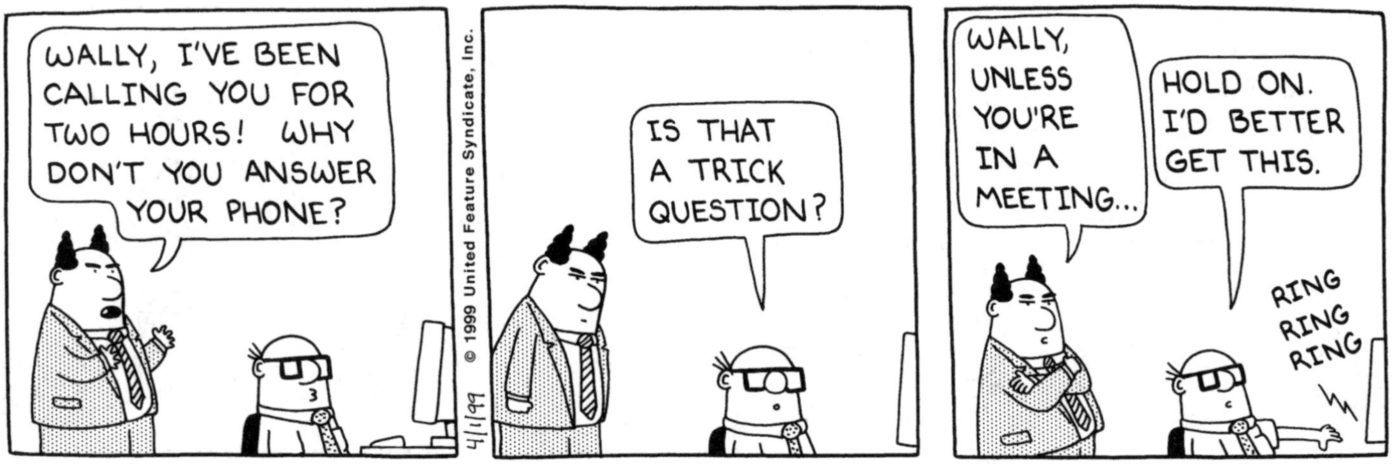
WALLY, I'VE BEEN CALLING YOU FOR TWO HOURS! WHY DON'T YOU ANSWER YOUR PHONE?
4/1/99 © 1999 United Feature Syndicate, Inc.
IS THAT A TRICK QUESTION?
WALLY, UNLESS YOU'RE IN A MEETING...
HOLD ON. I'D BETTER GET THIS.
RING RING RING

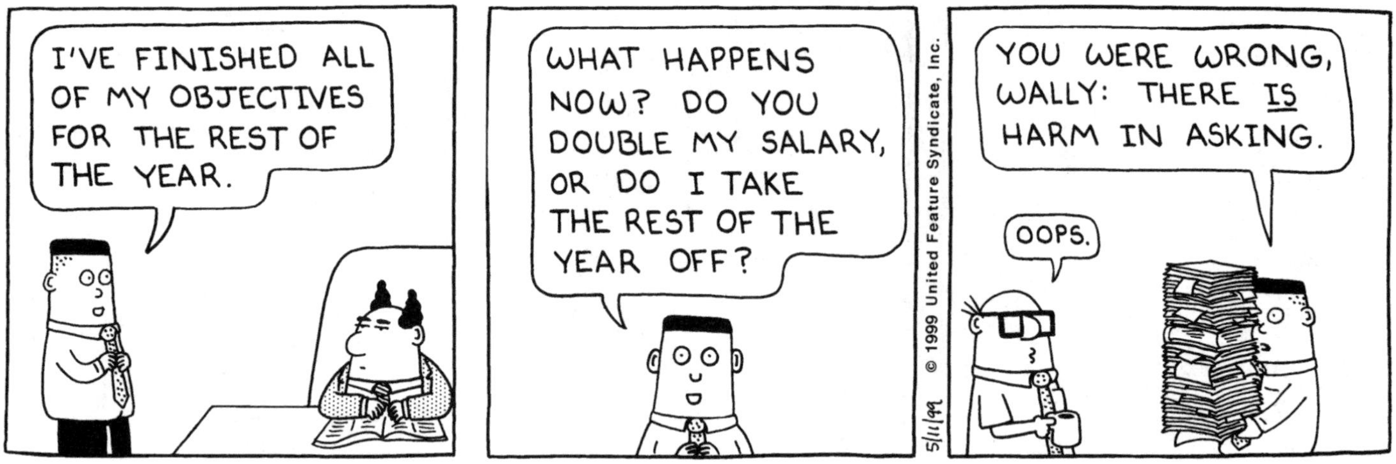
I'VE FINISHED ALL OF MY OBJECTIVES FOR THE REST OF THE YEAR.
WHAT HAPPENS NOW? DO YOU DOUBLE MY SALARY, OR DO I TAKE THE REST OF THE YEAR OFF?
5/11/99 © 1999 United Feature Syndicate, Inc.
YOU WERE WRONG, WALLY: THERE IS HARM IN ASKING.
OOPS.

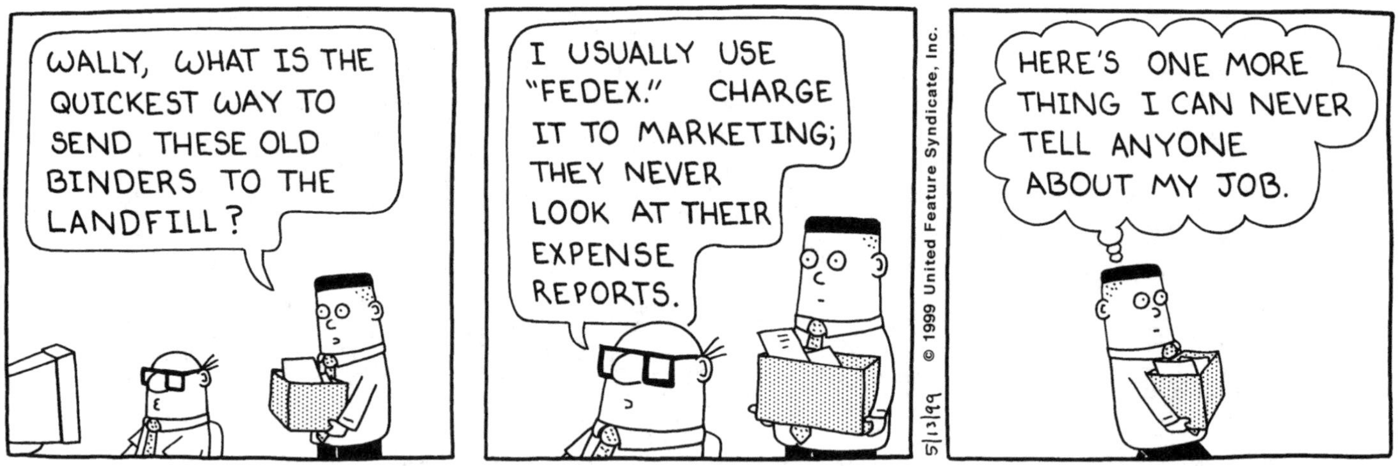
WALLY, WHAT IS THE QUICKEST WAY TO SEND THESE OLD BINDERS TO THE LANDFILL?
I USUALLY USE "FEDEX." CHARGE IT TO MARKETING; THEY NEVER LOOK AT THEIR EXPENSE REPORTS.
5/13/99 © 1999 United Feature Syndicate, Inc.
HERE'S ONE MORE THING I CAN NEVER TELL ANYONE ABOUT MY JOB.

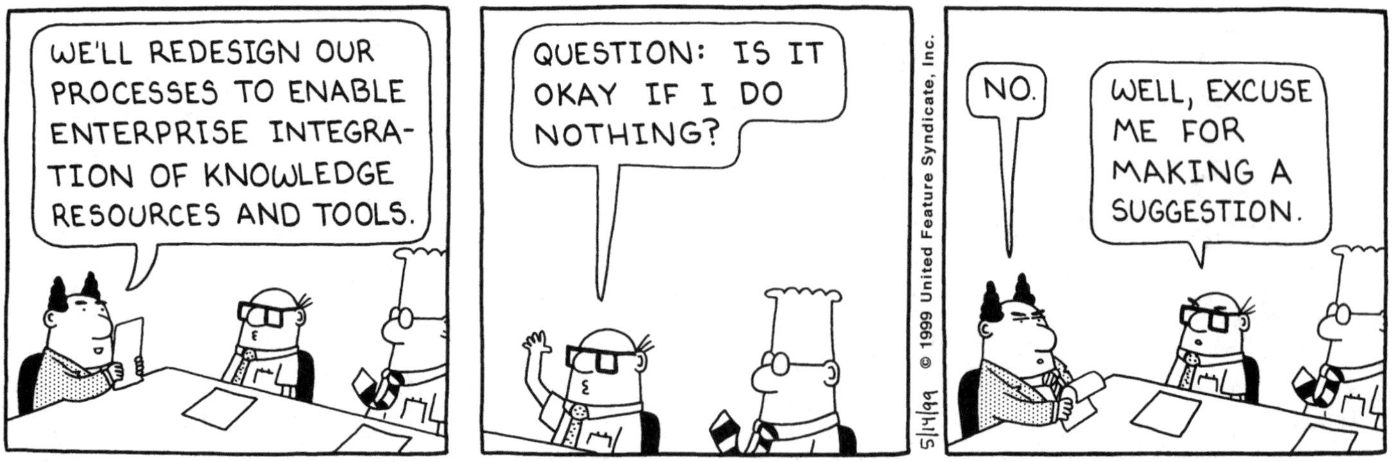
WE'LL REDESIGN OUR PROCESSES TO ENABLE ENTERPRISE INTEGRATION OF KNOWLEDGE RESOURCES AND TOOLS.
QUESTION: IS IT OKAY IF I DO NOTHING?
5/14/99 © 1999 United Feature Syndicate, Inc.
NO.
WELL, EXCUSE ME FOR MAKING A SUGGESTION.

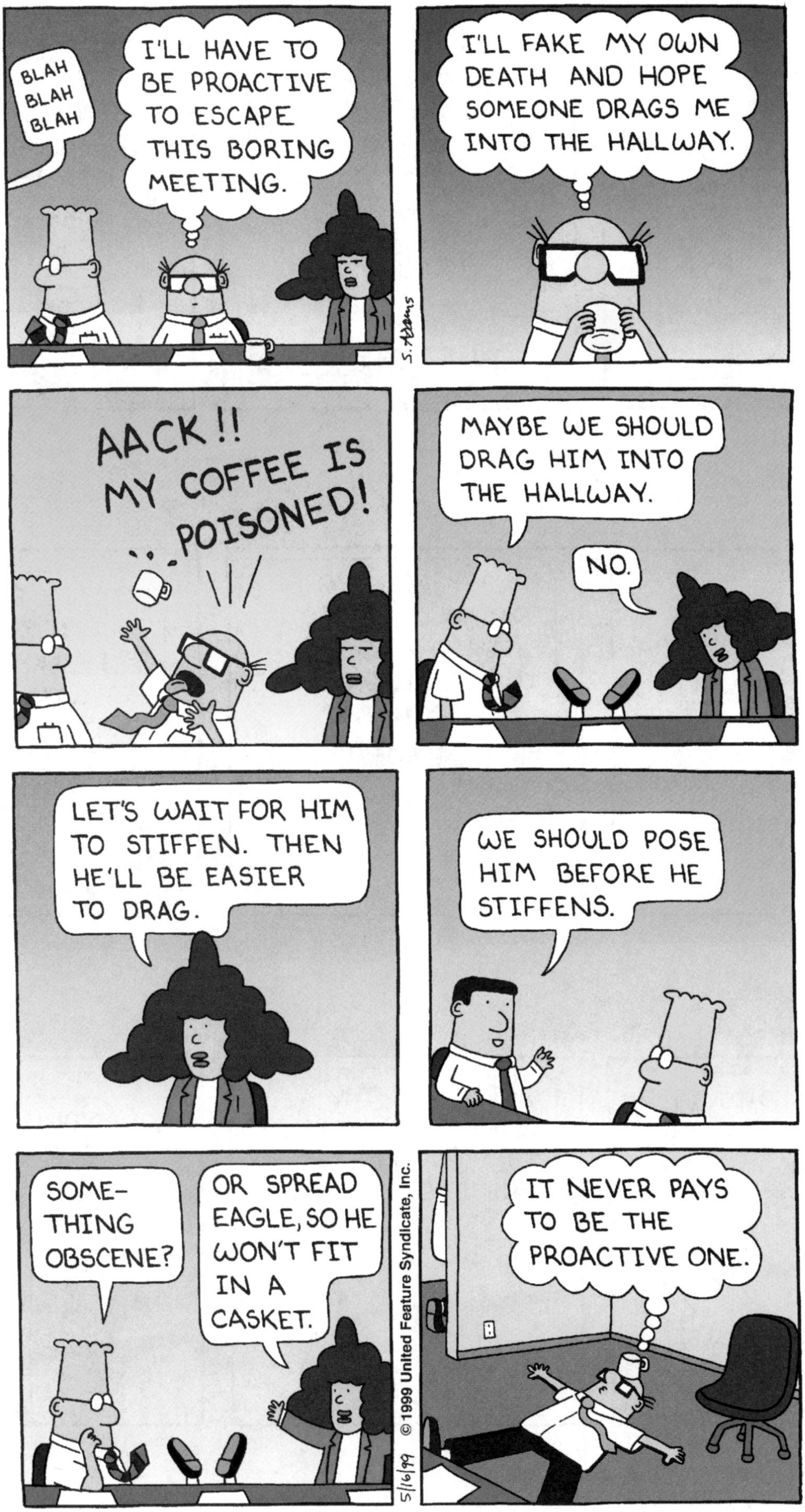
BLAH BLAH BLAH
I'LL HAVE TO BE PROACTIVE TO ESCAPE THIS BORING MEETING.
S. Adams
I'LL FAKE MY OWN DEATH AND HOPE SOMEONE DRAGS ME INTO THE HALLWAY.
AACK!! MY COFFEE IS POISONED!
MAYBE WE SHOULD DRAG HIM INTO THE HALLWAY.
NO.
LET'S WAIT FOR HIM TO STIFFEN. THEN HE'LL BE EASIER TO DRAG.
WE SHOULD POSE HIM BEFORE HE STIFFENS.
SOME-THING OBSCENE?
OR SPREAD EAGLE, SO HE WON'T FIT IN A CASKET.
5/16/99
© 1999 United Feature Syndicate, Inc.
IT NEVER PAYS TO BE THE PROACTIVE ONE.

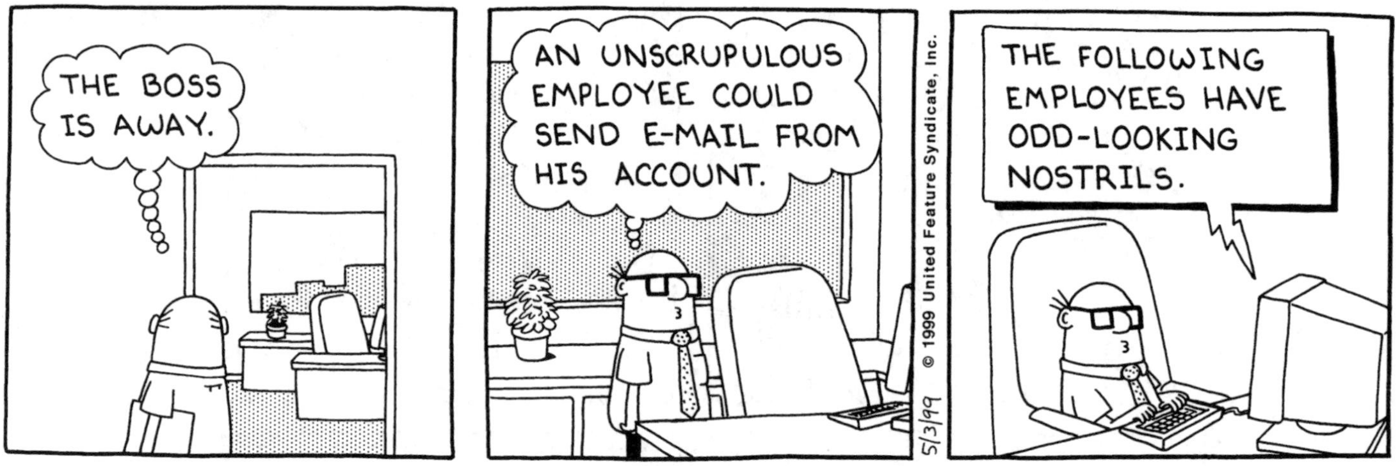
THE BOSS IS AWAY.
AN UNSCRUPULOUS EMPLOYEE COULD SEND E-MAIL FROM HIS ACCOUNT.
5/3/99 © 1999 United Feature Syndicate, Inc.
THE FOLLOWING EMPLOYEES HAVE ODD-LOOKING NOSTRILS.

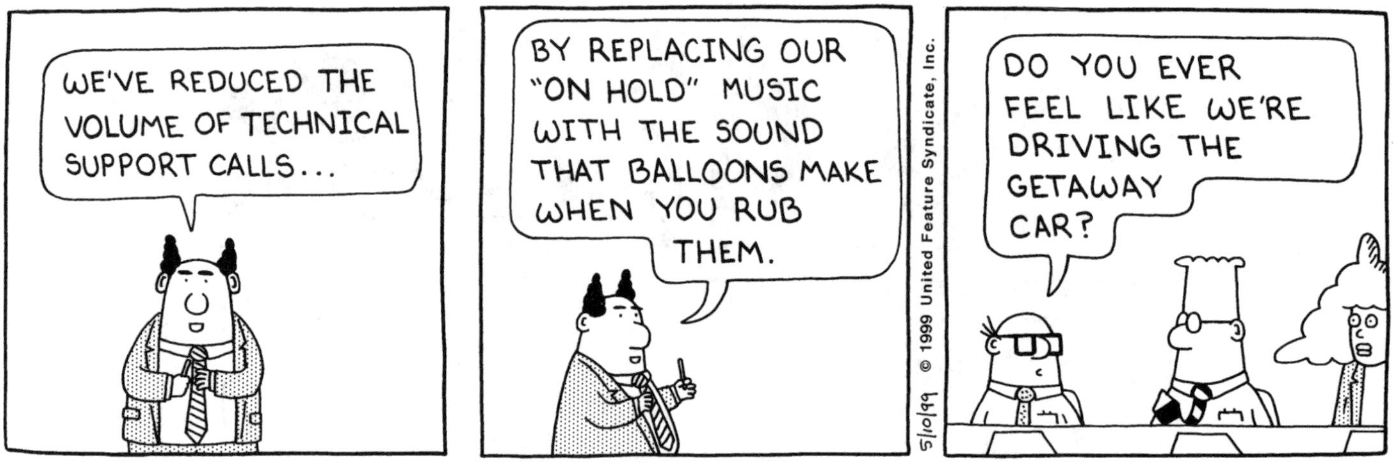
WE'VE REDUCED THE VOLUME OF TECHNICAL SUPPORT CALLS...
BY REPLACING OUR "ON HOLD" MUSIC WITH THE SOUND THAT BALLOONS MAKE WHEN YOU RUB THEM.
5/10/99 © 1999 United Feature Syndicate, Inc.
DO YOU EVER FEEL LIKE WE'RE DRIVING THE GETAWAY CAR?

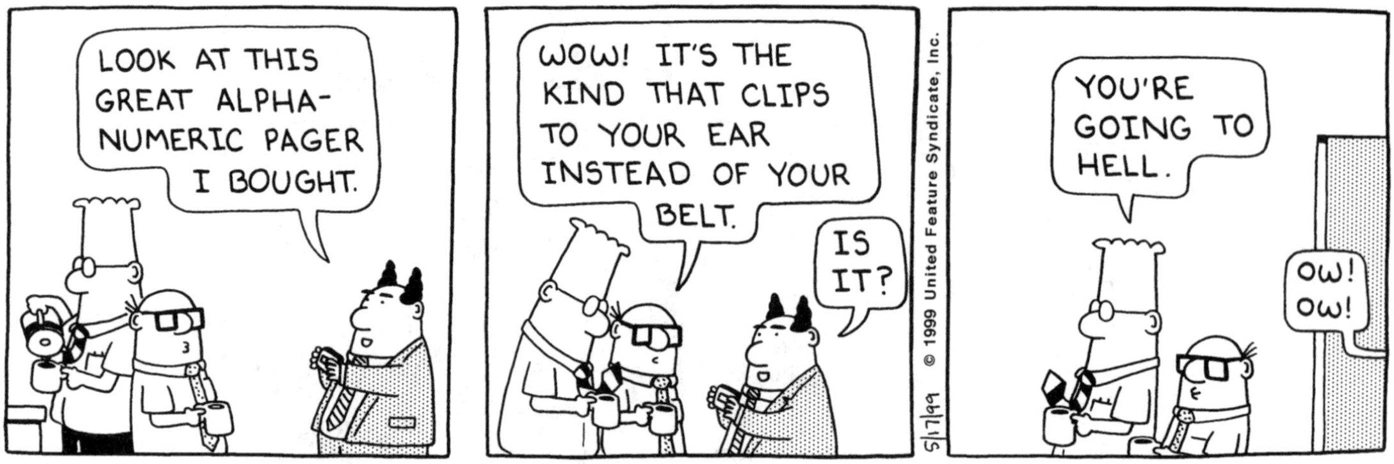
LOOK AT THIS GREAT ALPHA-NUMERIC PAGER I BOUGHT.
WOW! IT'S THE KIND THAT CLIPS TO YOUR EAR INSTEAD OF YOUR BELT.
IS IT?
5/17/99 © 1999 United Feature Syndicate, Inc.
YOU'RE GOING TO HELL.
OW! OW!

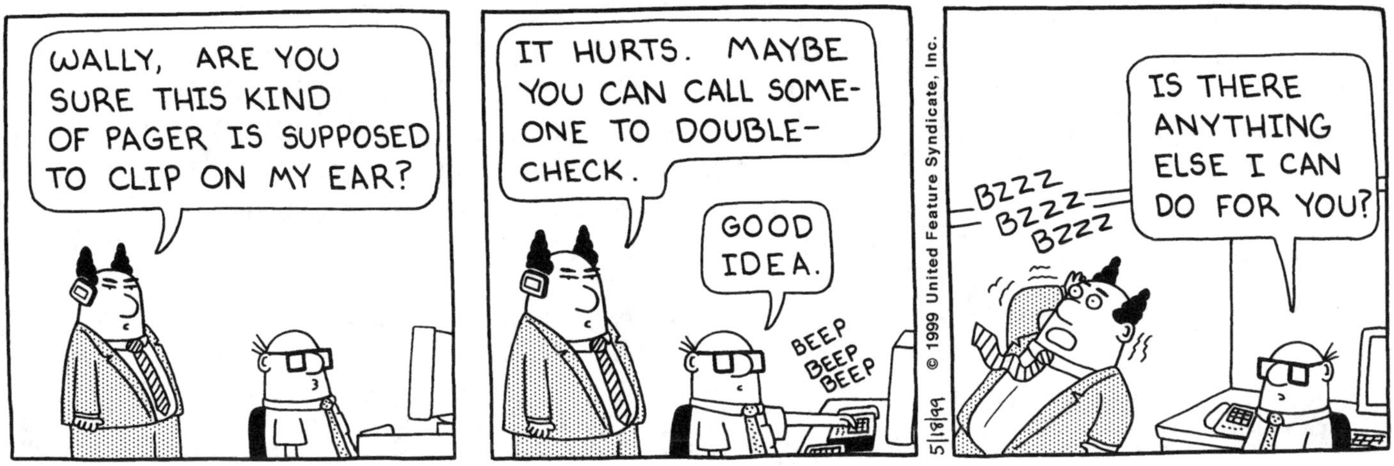
WALLY, ARE YOU SURE THIS KIND OF PAGER IS SUPPOSED TO CLIP ON MY EAR?
IT HURTS. MAYBE YOU CAN CALL SOME-ONE TO DOUBLE-CHECK.
GOOD IDEA.
BEEP BEEP BEEP
5/18/99 © 1999 United Feature Syndicate, Inc.
BZZZ BZZZ BZZZ
IS THERE ANYTHING ELSE I CAN DO FOR YOU?

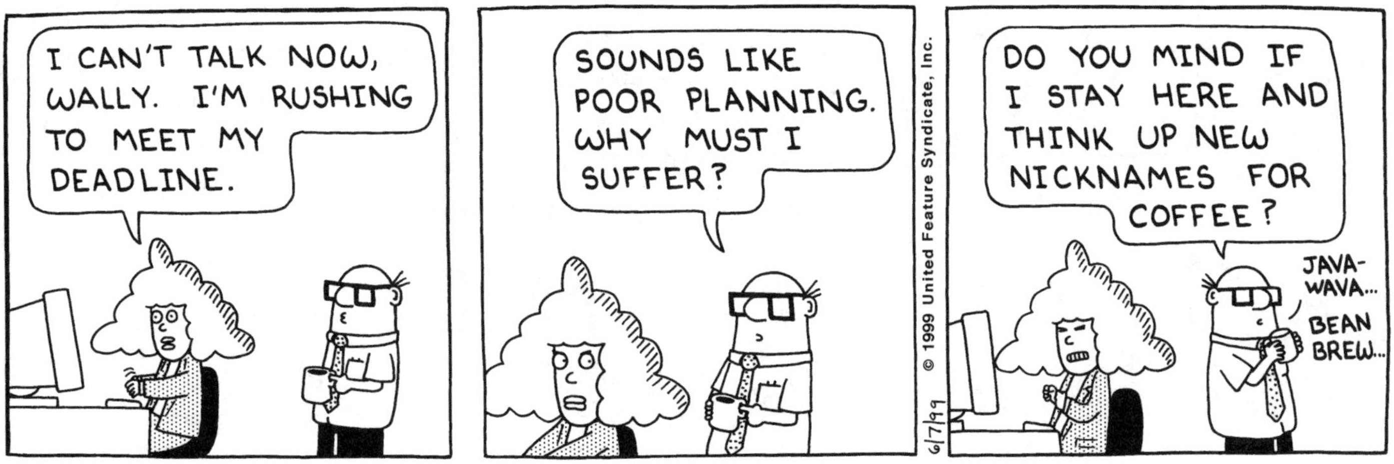
I CAN'T TALK NOW, WALLY. I'M RUSHING TO MEET MY DEADLINE.
SOUNDS LIKE POOR PLANNING. WHY MUST I SUFFER?
6/7/99 © 1999 United Feature Syndicate, Inc.
DO YOU MIND IF I STAY HERE AND THINK UP NEW NICKNAMES FOR COFFEE?
JAVA-WAVA...
BEAN BREW...

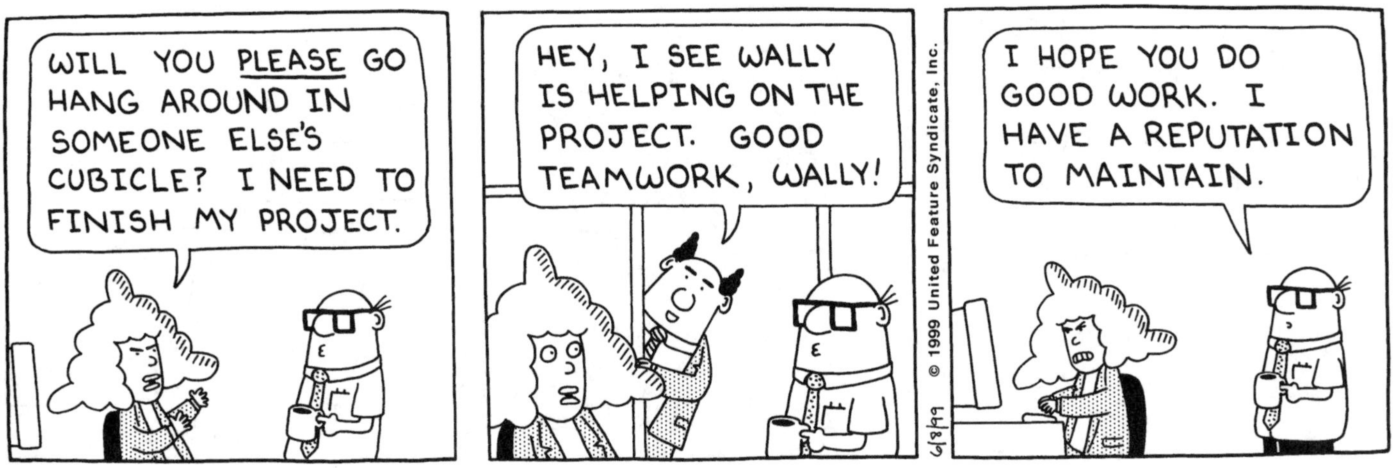
WILL YOU PLEASE GO HANG AROUND IN SOMEONE ELSE'S CUBICLE? I NEED TO FINISH MY PROJECT.
HEY, I SEE WALLY IS HELPING ON THE PROJECT. GOOD TEAMWORK, WALLY!
6/8/99 © 1999 United Feature Syndicate, Inc.
I HOPE YOU DO GOOD WORK. I HAVE A REPUTATION TO MAINTAIN.

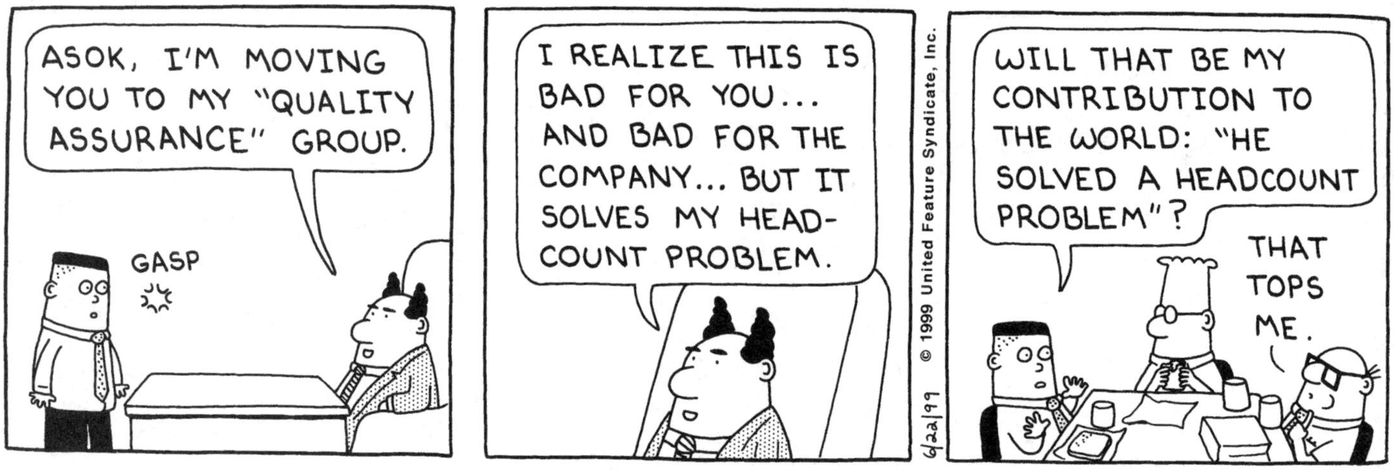
ASOK, I'M MOVING YOU TO MY "QUALITY ASSURANCE" GROUP.
GASP
I REALIZE THIS IS BAD FOR YOU... AND BAD FOR THE COMPANY... BUT IT SOLVES MY HEAD-COUNT PROBLEM.
6/22/99 © 1999 United Feature Syndicate, Inc.
WILL THAT BE MY CONTRIBUTION TO THE WORLD: "HE SOLVED A HEADCOUNT PROBLEM"?
THAT TOPS ME.

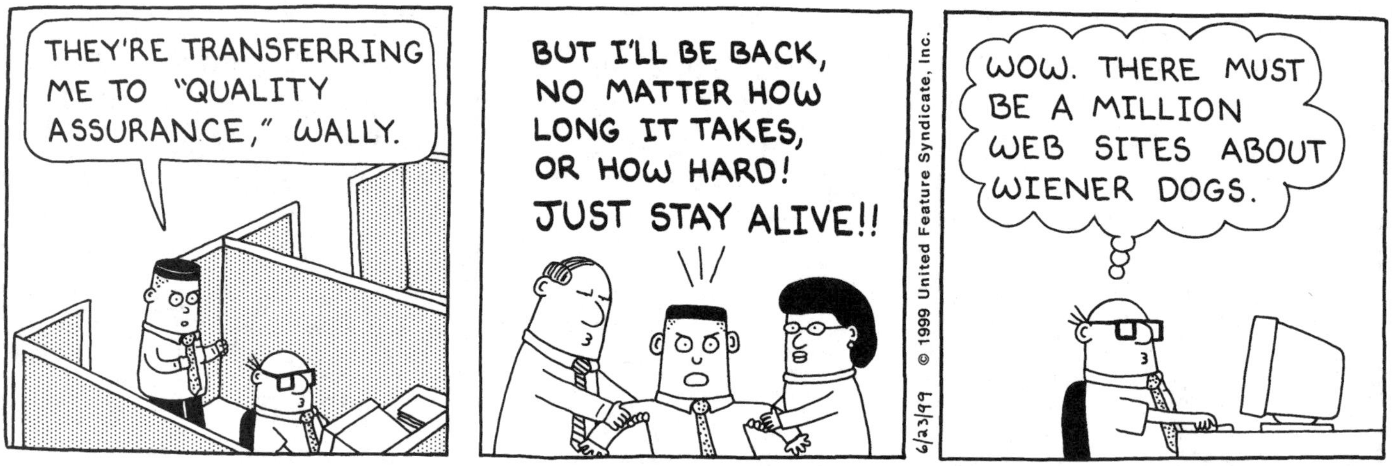
THEY'RE TRANSFERRING ME TO "QUALITY ASSURANCE," WALLY.
BUT I'LL BE BACK, NO MATTER HOW LONG IT TAKES, OR HOW HARD! JUST STAY ALIVE!!
6/23/99 © 1999 United Feature Syndicate, Inc.
WOW. THERE MUST BE A MILLION WEB SITES ABOUT WIENER DOGS.

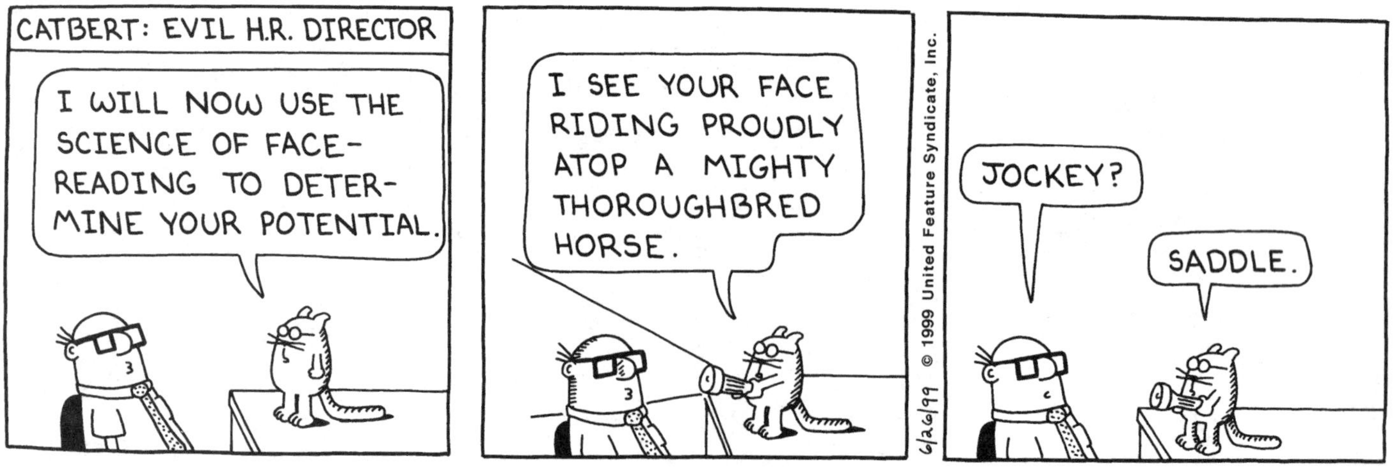
CATBERT: EVIL H.R. DIRECTOR
I WILL NOW USE THE SCIENCE OF FACE-READING TO DETER-MINE YOUR POTENTIAL.
I SEE YOUR FACE RIDING PROUDLY ATOP A MIGHTY THOROUGHBRED HORSE.
6/26/99 © 1999 United Feature Syndicate, Inc.
JOCKEY?
SADDLE.

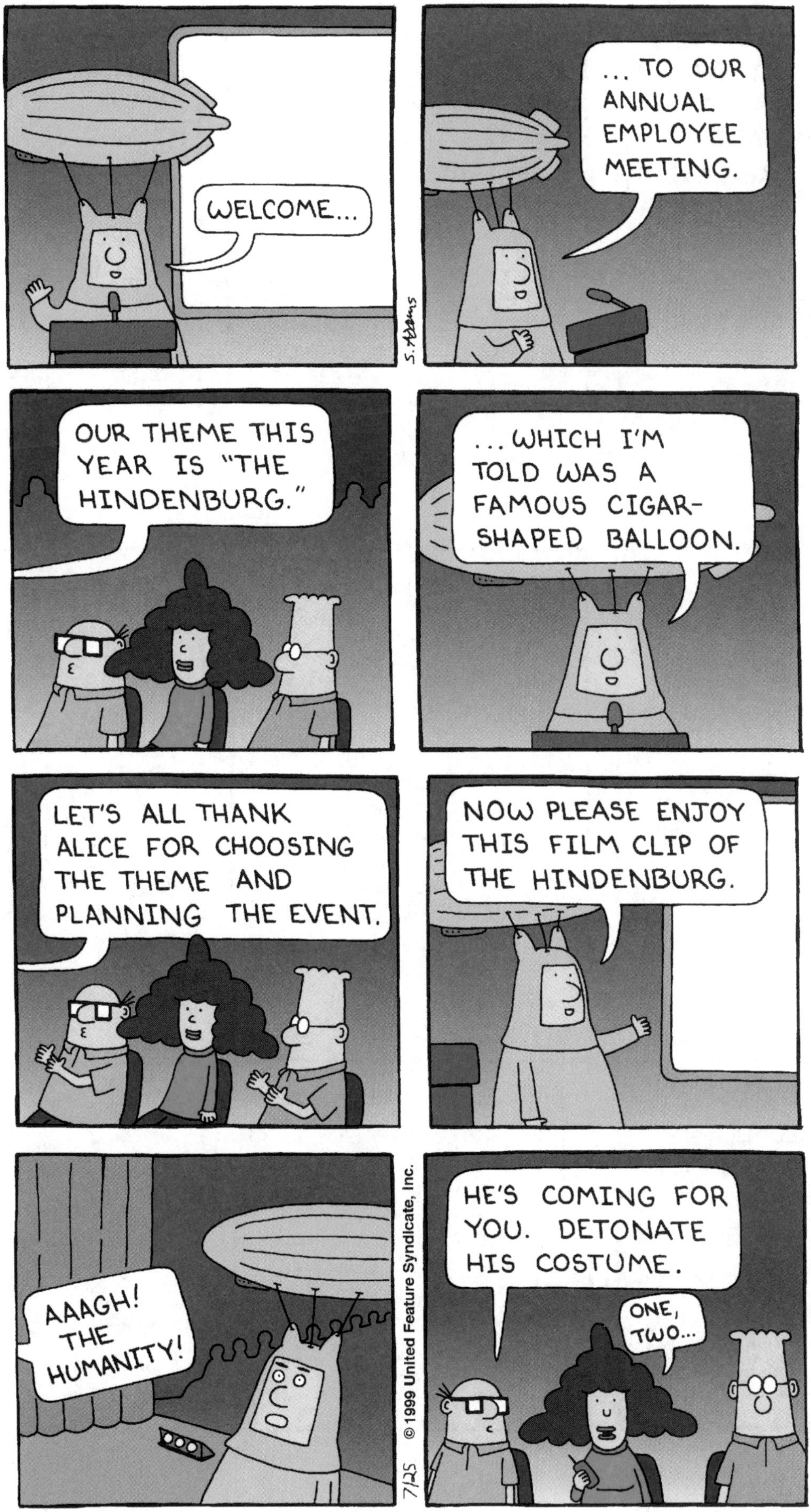
WELCOME...
... TO OUR ANNUAL EMPLOYEE MEETING.
OUR THEME THIS YEAR IS "THE HINDENBURG."
...WHICH I'M TOLD WAS A FAMOUS CIGAR-SHAPED BALLOON.
LET'S ALL THANK ALICE FOR CHOOSING THE THEME AND PLANNING THE EVENT.
NOW PLEASE ENJOY THIS FILM CLIP OF THE HINDENBURG.
AAAGH! THE HUMANITY!
HE'S COMING FOR YOU. DETONATE HIS COSTUME.
ONE, TWO...
S. Adams
7/25
© 1999 United Feature Syndicate, Inc.

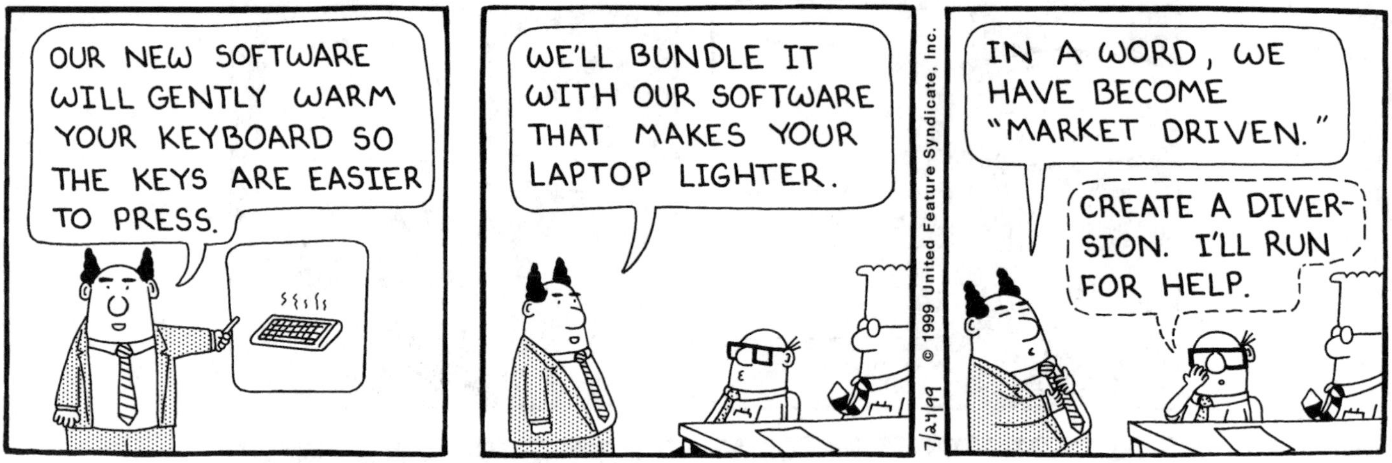
OUR NEW SOFTWARE WILL GENTLY WARM YOUR KEYBOARD SO THE KEYS ARE EASIER TO PRESS.
WE'LL BUNDLE IT WITH OUR SOFTWARE THAT MAKES YOUR LAPTOP LIGHTER.
7/24/99 © 1999 United Feature Syndicate, Inc.
IN A WORD, WE HAVE BECOME "MARKET DRIVEN."
CREATE A DIVERSION. I'LL RUN FOR HELP.

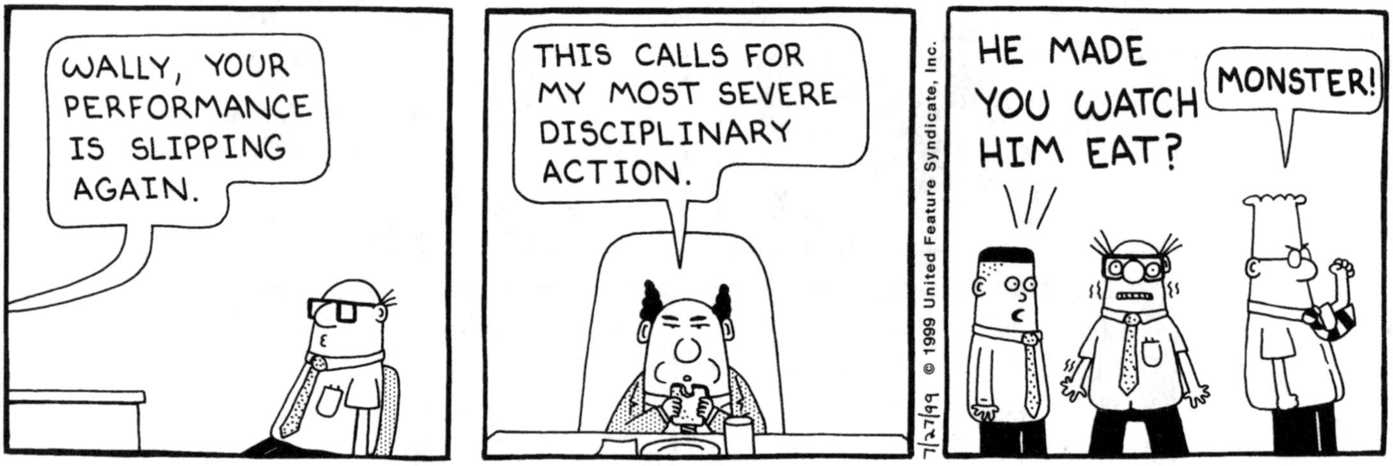
WALLY, YOUR PERFORMANCE IS SLIPPING AGAIN.
THIS CALLS FOR MY MOST SEVERE DISCIPLINARY ACTION.
7/27/99 © 1999 United Feature Syndicate, Inc.
HE MADE YOU WATCH HIM EAT?
MONSTER!

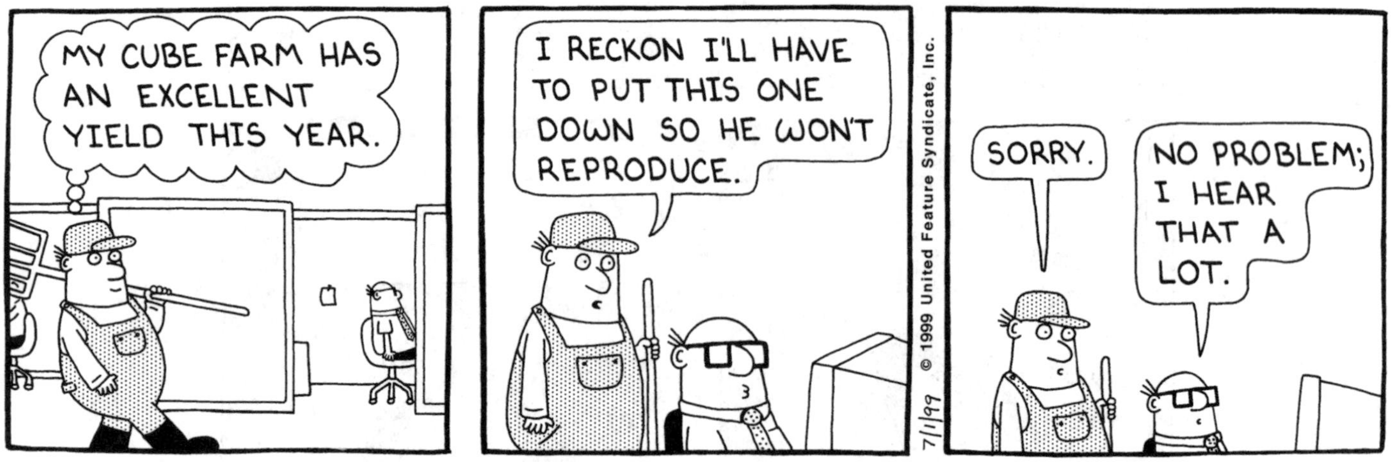
MY CUBE FARM HAS AN EXCELLENT YIELD THIS YEAR.
I RECKON I'LL HAVE TO PUT THIS ONE DOWN SO HE WON'T REPRODUCE.
7/1/99 © 1999 United Feature Syndicate, Inc.
SORRY.
NO PROBLEM; I HEAR THAT A LOT.

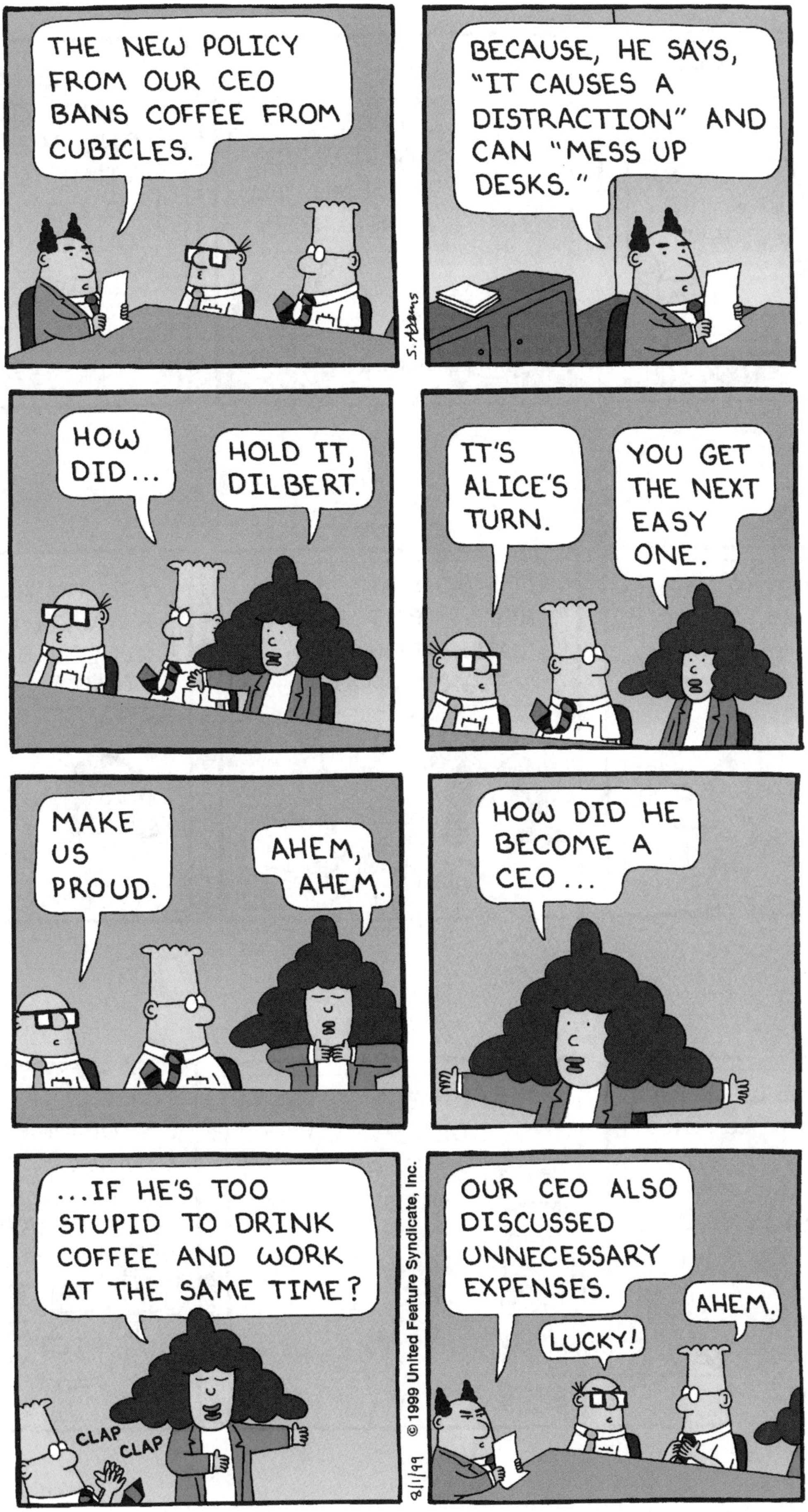
THE NEW POLICY FROM OUR CEO BANS COFFEE FROM CUBICLES.
BECAUSE, HE SAYS, "IT CAUSES A DISTRACTION" AND CAN "MESS UP DESKS."
S. ADAMS
HOW DID...
HOLD IT, DILBERT.
IT'S ALICE'S TURN.
YOU GET THE NEXT EASY ONE.
MAKE US PROUD.
AHEM, AHEM.
HOW DID HE BECOME A CEO...
...IF HE'S TOO STUPID TO DRINK COFFEE AND WORK AT THE SAME TIME?
CLAP
CLAP
© 1999 United Feature Syndicate, Inc.
8/1/99
OUR CEO ALSO DISCUSSED UNNECESSARY EXPENSES.
LUCKY!
AHEM.

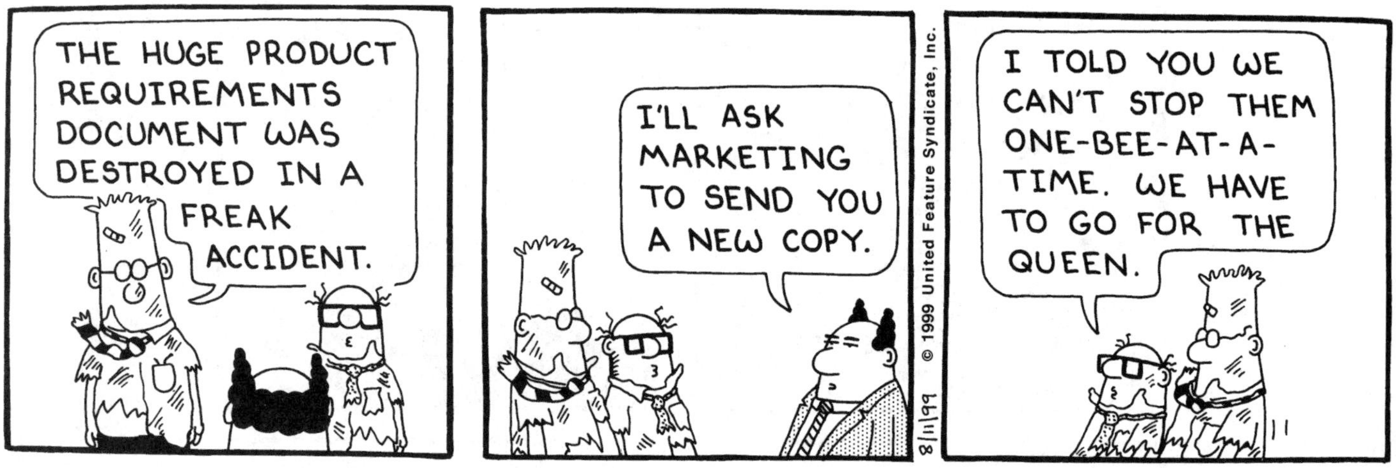
THE HUGE PRODUCT REQUIREMENTS DOCUMENT WAS DESTROYED IN A FREAK ACCIDENT.
I'LL ASK MARKETING TO SEND YOU A NEW COPY.
8/11/99 © 1999 United Feature Syndicate, Inc.
I TOLD YOU WE CAN'T STOP THEM ONE-BEE-AT-A-TIME. WE HAVE TO GO FOR THE QUEEN.

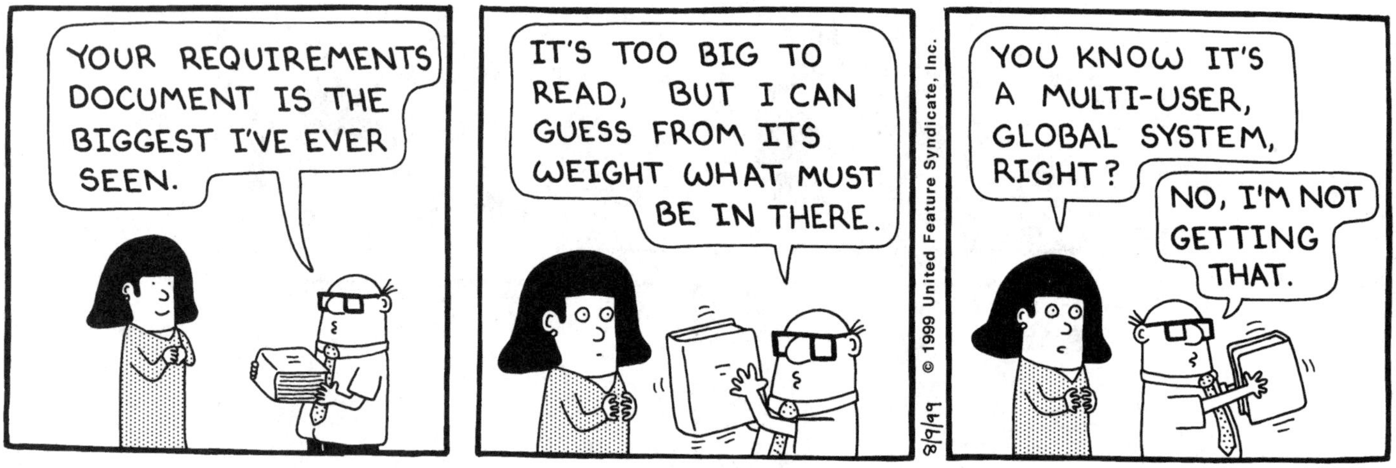
YOUR REQUIREMENTS DOCUMENT IS THE BIGGEST I'VE EVER SEEN.
IT'S TOO BIG TO READ, BUT I CAN GUESS FROM ITS WEIGHT WHAT MUST BE IN THERE.
8/9/99 © 1999 United Feature Syndicate, Inc.
YOU KNOW IT'S A MULTI-USER, GLOBAL SYSTEM, RIGHT?
NO, I'M NOT GETTING THAT.

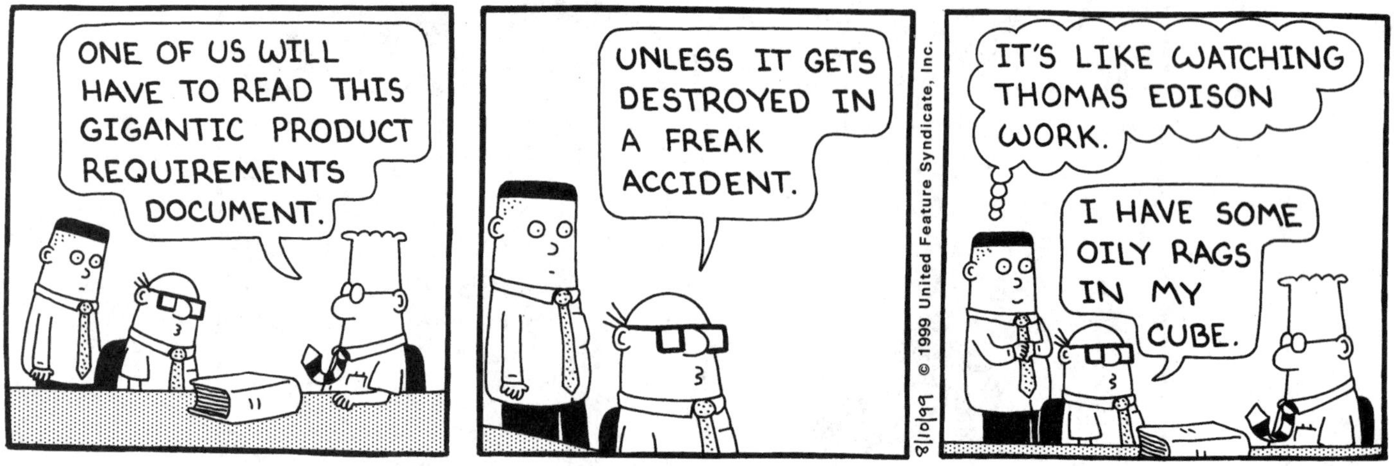
ONE OF US WILL HAVE TO READ THIS GIGANTIC PRODUCT REQUIREMENTS DOCUMENT.
UNLESS IT GETS DESTROYED IN A FREAK ACCIDENT.
8/10/99 © 1999 United Feature Syndicate, Inc.
IT'S LIKE WATCHING THOMAS EDISON WORK.
I HAVE SOME OILY RAGS IN MY CUBE.

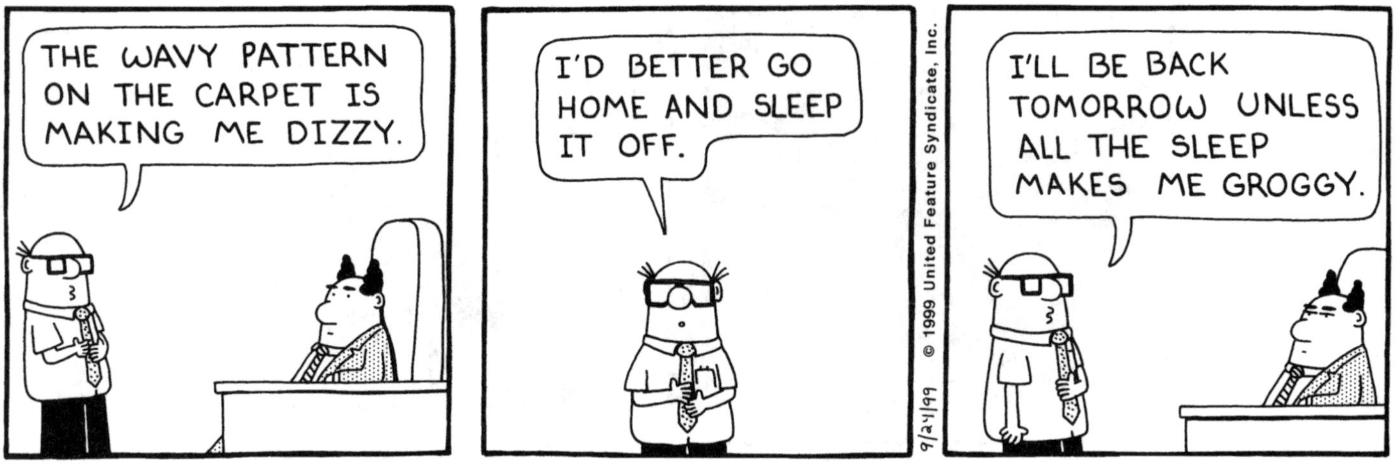
THE WAVY PATTERN ON THE CARPET IS MAKING ME DIZZY.
I'D BETTER GO HOME AND SLEEP IT OFF.
9/24/99 © 1999 United Feature Syndicate, Inc.
I'LL BE BACK TOMORROW UNLESS ALL THE SLEEP MAKES ME GROGGY.

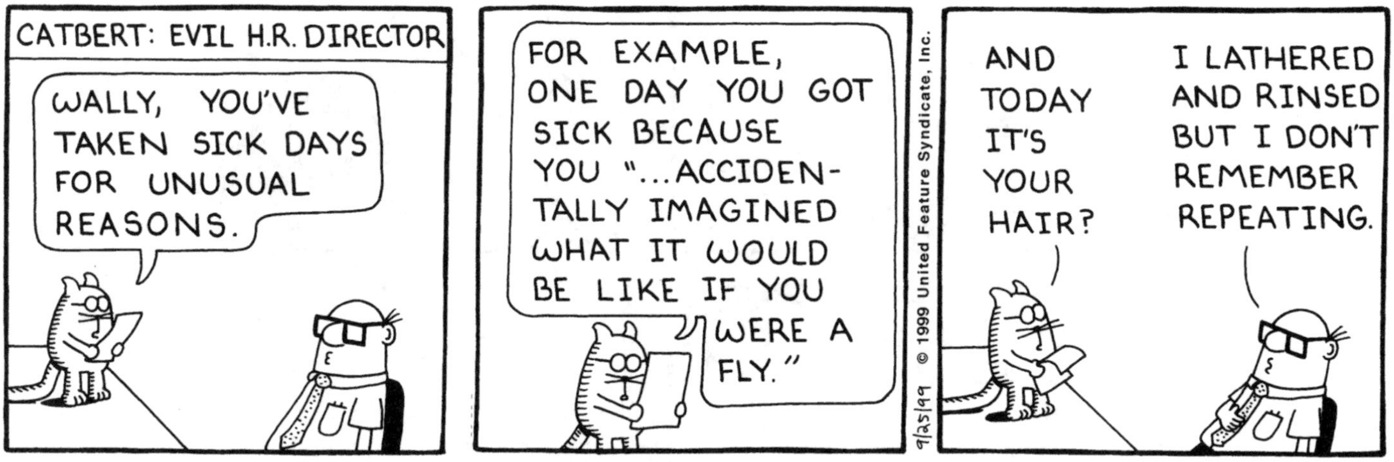
CATBERT: EVIL H.R. DIRECTOR
WALLY, YOU'VE TAKEN SICK DAYS FOR UNUSUAL REASONS.
FOR EXAMPLE, ONE DAY YOU GOT SICK BECAUSE YOU "...ACCIDENTALLY IMAGINED WHAT IT WOULD BE LIKE IF YOU WERE A FLY."
9/25/99 © 1999 United Feature Syndicate, Inc.
AND TODAY IT'S YOUR HAIR?
I LATHERED AND RINSED BUT I DON'T REMEMBER REPEATING.

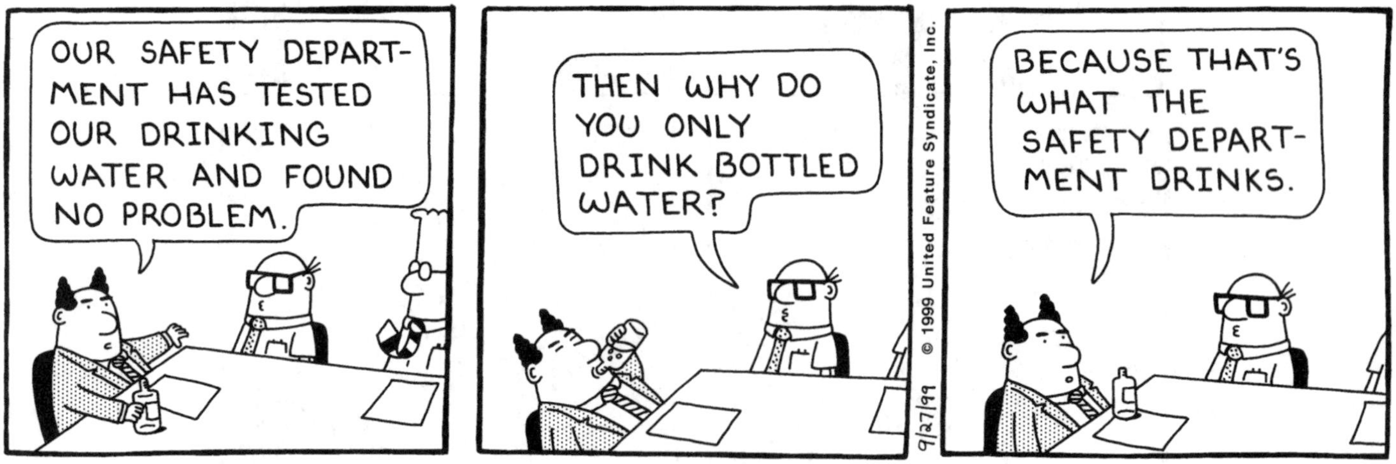
OUR SAFETY DEPARTMENT HAS TESTED OUR DRINKING WATER AND FOUND NO PROBLEM.
THEN WHY DO YOU ONLY DRINK BOTTLED WATER?
9/27/99 © 1999 United Feature Syndicate, Inc.
BECAUSE THAT'S WHAT THE SAFETY DEPARTMENT DRINKS.

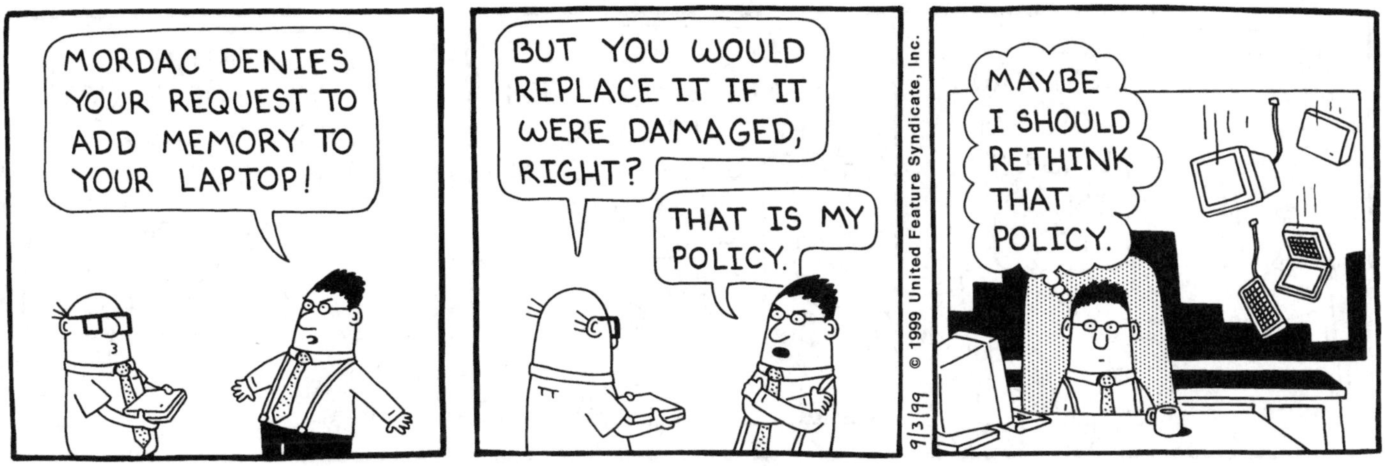
MORDAC DENIES YOUR REQUEST TO ADD MEMORY TO YOUR LAPTOP!
BUT YOU WOULD REPLACE IT IF IT WERE DAMAGED, RIGHT?
THAT IS MY POLICY.
9/3/99 © 1999 United Feature Syndicate, Inc.
MAYBE I SHOULD RETHINK THAT POLICY.

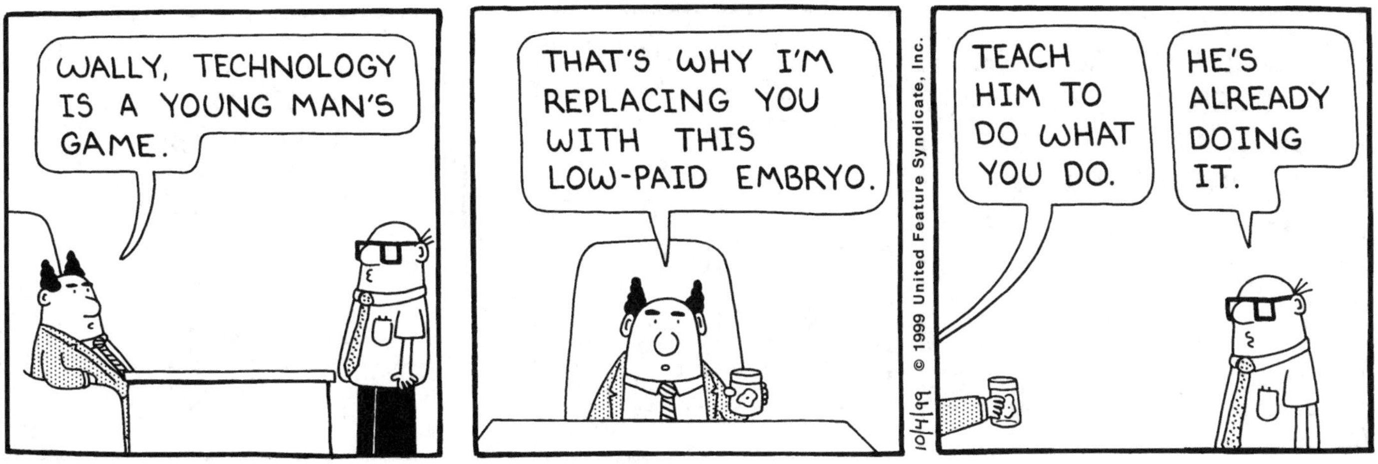
WALLY, TECHNOLOGY IS A YOUNG MAN'S GAME.
THAT'S WHY I'M REPLACING YOU WITH THIS LOW-PAID EMBRYO.
10/4/99 © 1999 United Feature Syndicate, Inc.
TEACH HIM TO DO WHAT YOU DO.
HE'S ALREADY DOING IT.

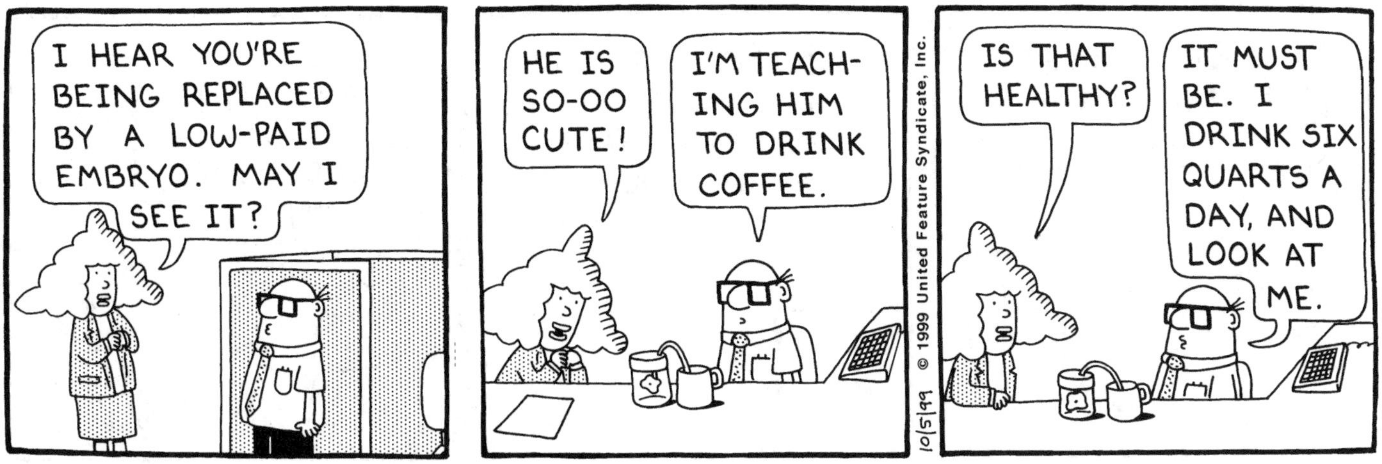
I HEAR YOU'RE BEING REPLACED BY A LOW-PAID EMBRYO. MAY I SEE IT?
HE IS SO-OO CUTE!
I'M TEACH-ING HIM TO DRINK COFFEE.
10/5/99 © 1999 United Feature Syndicate, Inc.
IS THAT HEALTHY?
IT MUST BE. I DRINK SIX QUARTS A DAY, AND LOOK AT ME.

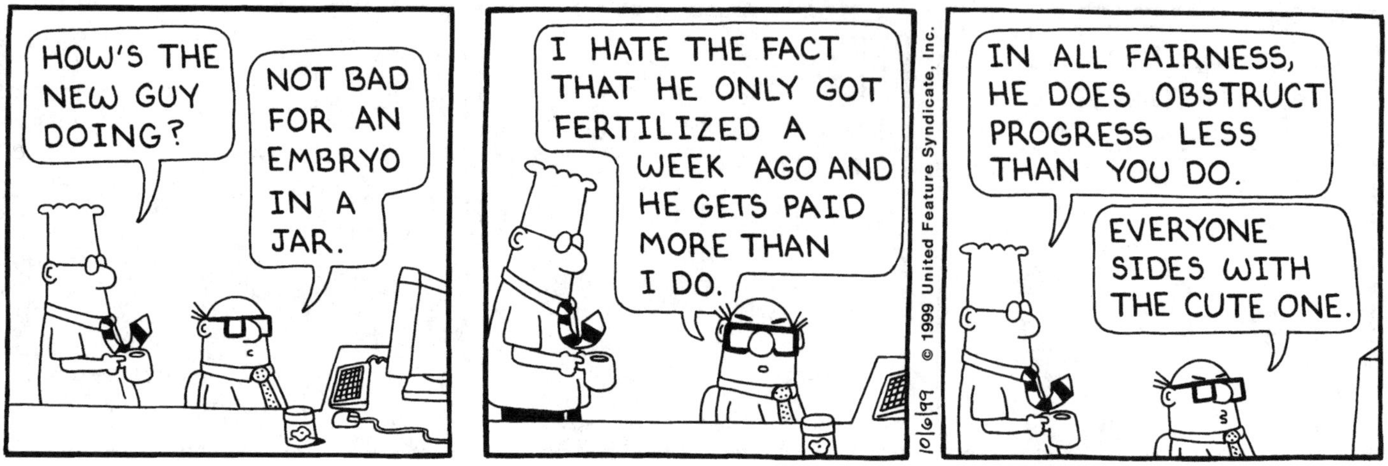
HOW'S THE NEW GUY DOING?
NOT BAD FOR AN EMBRYO IN A JAR.
I HATE THE FACT THAT HE ONLY GOT FERTILIZED A WEEK AGO AND HE GETS PAID MORE THAN I DO.
© 1999 United Feature Syndicate, Inc.
10/6/99
IN ALL FAIRNESS, HE DOES OBSTRUCT PROGRESS LESS THAN YOU DO.
EVERYONE SIDES WITH THE CUTE ONE.

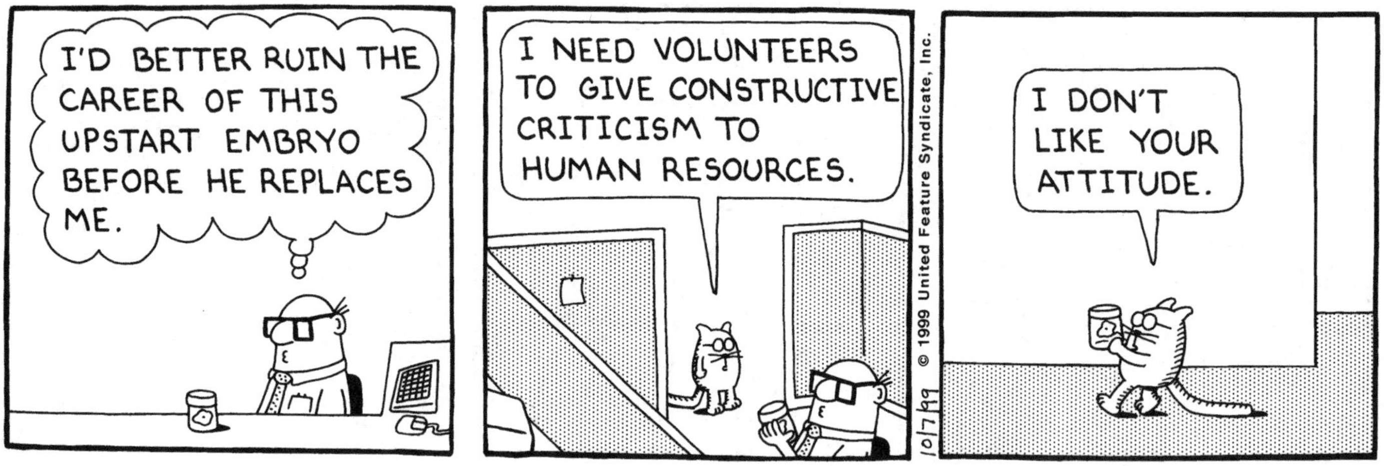
I'D BETTER RUIN THE CAREER OF THIS UPSTART EMBRYO BEFORE HE REPLACES ME.
I NEED VOLUNTEERS TO GIVE CONSTRUCTIVE CRITICISM TO HUMAN RESOURCES.
© 1999 United Feature Syndicate, Inc.
10/7/99
I DON'T LIKE YOUR ATTITUDE.

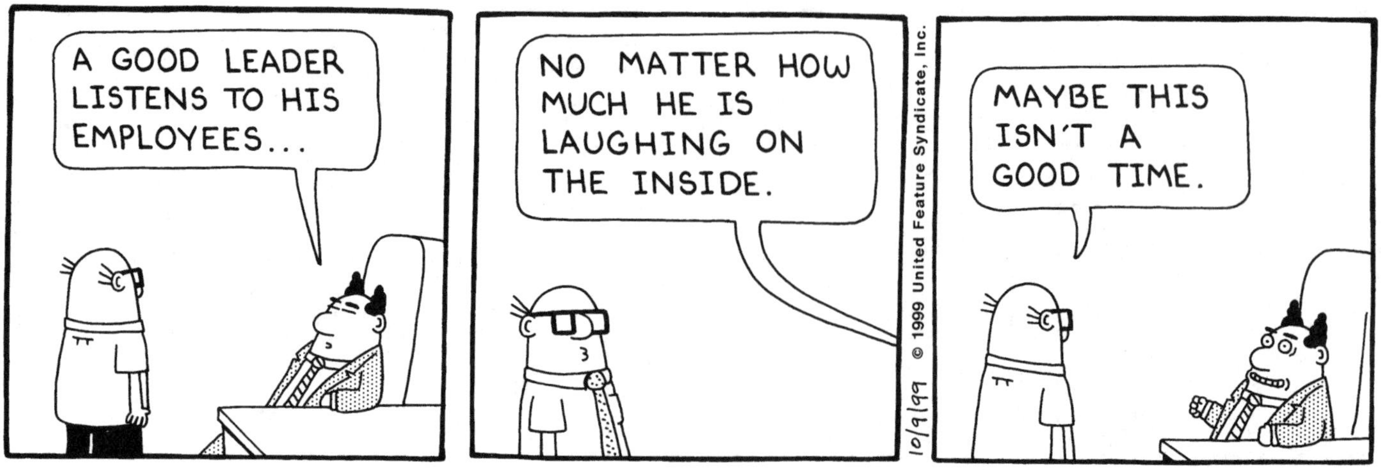
A GOOD LEADER LISTENS TO HIS EMPLOYEES...
NO MATTER HOW MUCH HE IS LAUGHING ON THE INSIDE.
© 1999 United Feature Syndicate, Inc.
10/9/99
MAYBE THIS ISN'T A GOOD TIME.

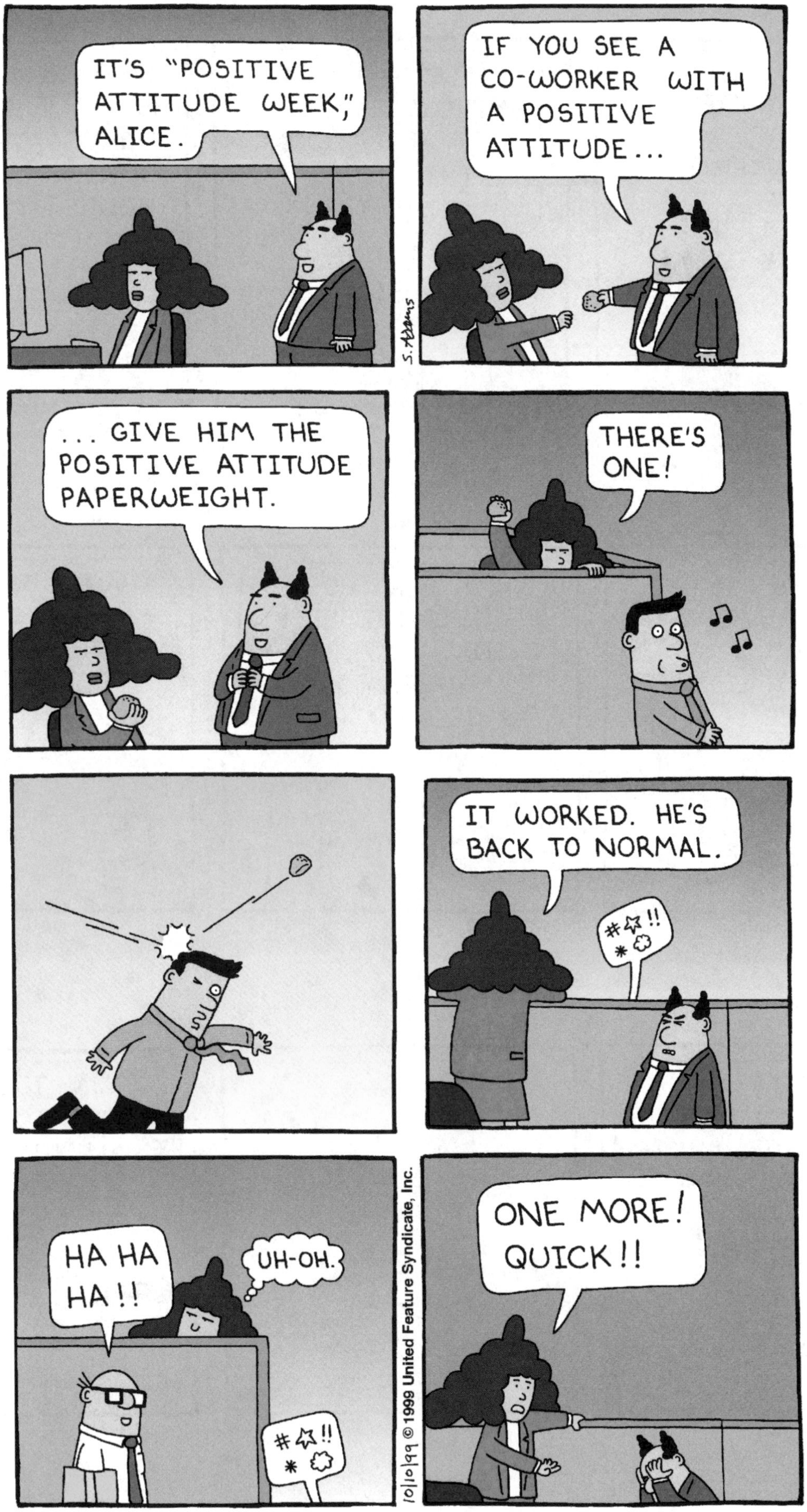
IT'S "POSITIVE ATTITUDE WEEK," ALICE.
IF YOU SEE A CO-WORKER WITH A POSITIVE ATTITUDE...
... GIVE HIM THE POSITIVE ATTITUDE PAPERWEIGHT.
THERE'S ONE!
IT WORKED. HE'S BACK TO NORMAL.
#☆!! * ✿
HA HA HA!!
UH-OH.
#☆!! * ✿
ONE MORE! QUICK!!

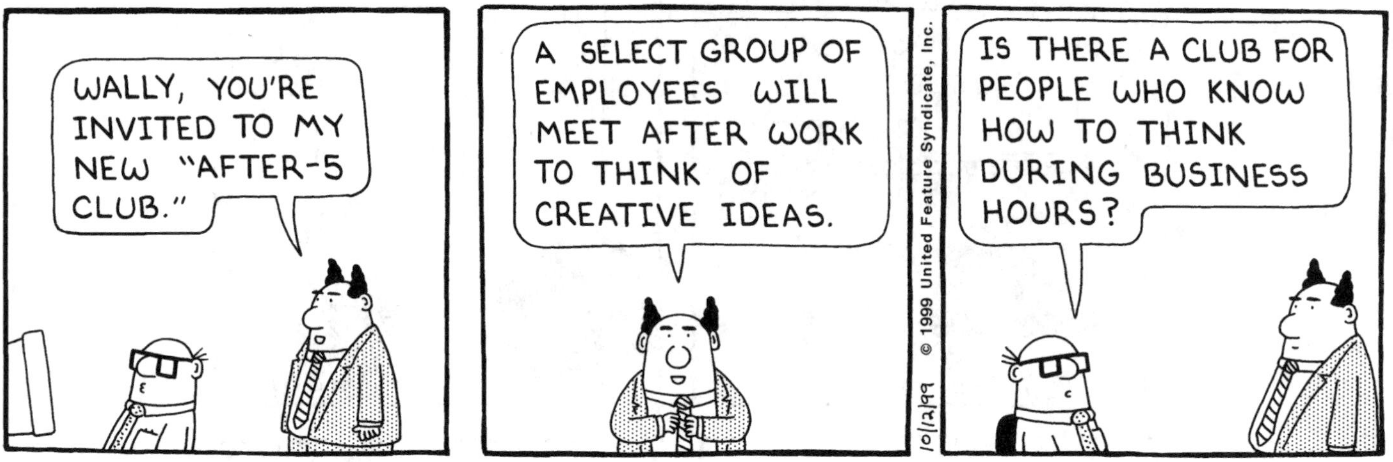
WALLY, YOU'RE INVITED TO MY NEW "AFTER-5 CLUB."
A SELECT GROUP OF EMPLOYEES WILL MEET AFTER WORK TO THINK OF CREATIVE IDEAS.
10/2/99 © 1999 United Feature Syndicate, Inc.
IS THERE A CLUB FOR PEOPLE WHO KNOW HOW TO THINK DURING BUSINESS HOURS?

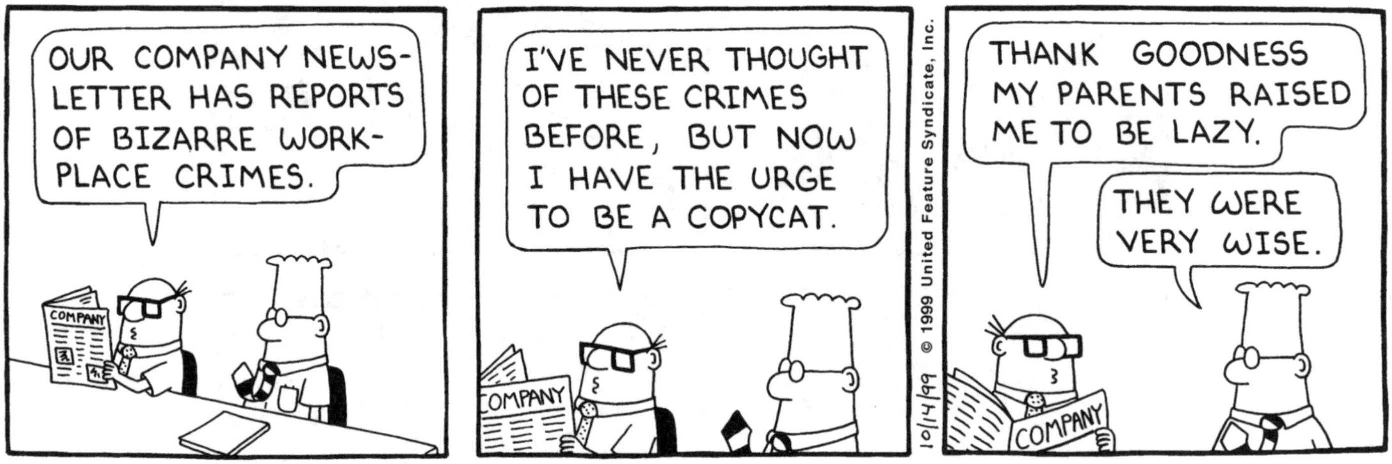
OUR COMPANY NEWS-LETTER HAS REPORTS OF BIZARRE WORK-PLACE CRIMES.
COMPANY
I'VE NEVER THOUGHT OF THESE CRIMES BEFORE, BUT NOW I HAVE THE URGE TO BE A COPYCAT.
COMPANY
10/14/99 © 1999 United Feature Syndicate, Inc.
THANK GOODNESS MY PARENTS RAISED ME TO BE LAZY.
THEY WERE VERY WISE.
COMPANY

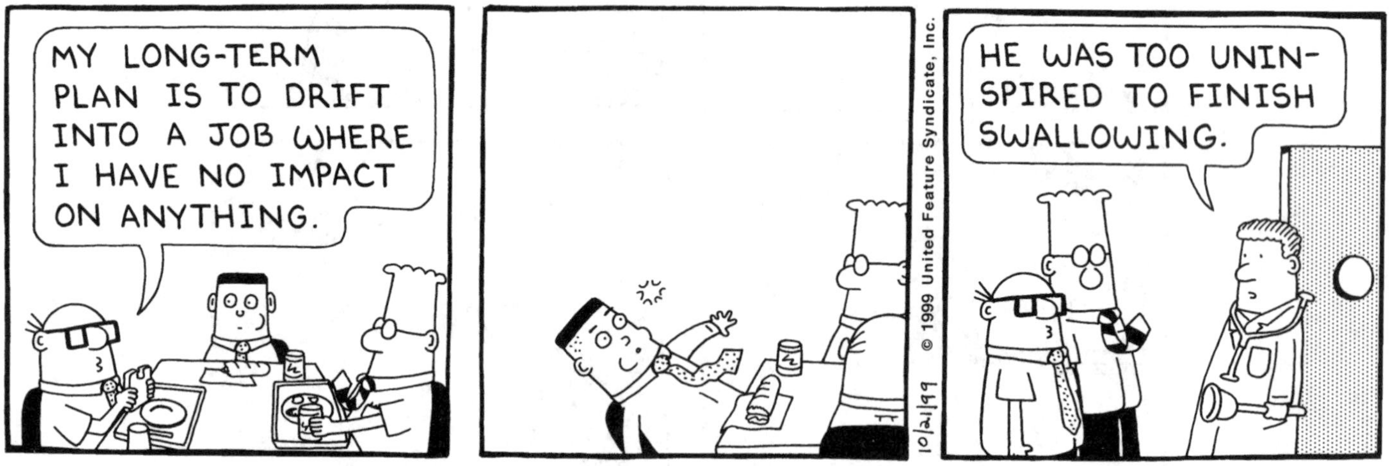
MY LONG-TERM PLAN IS TO DRIFT INTO A JOB WHERE I HAVE NO IMPACT ON ANYTHING.
10/21/99 © 1999 United Feature Syndicate, Inc.
HE WAS TOO UNIN-SPIRED TO FINISH SWALLOWING.

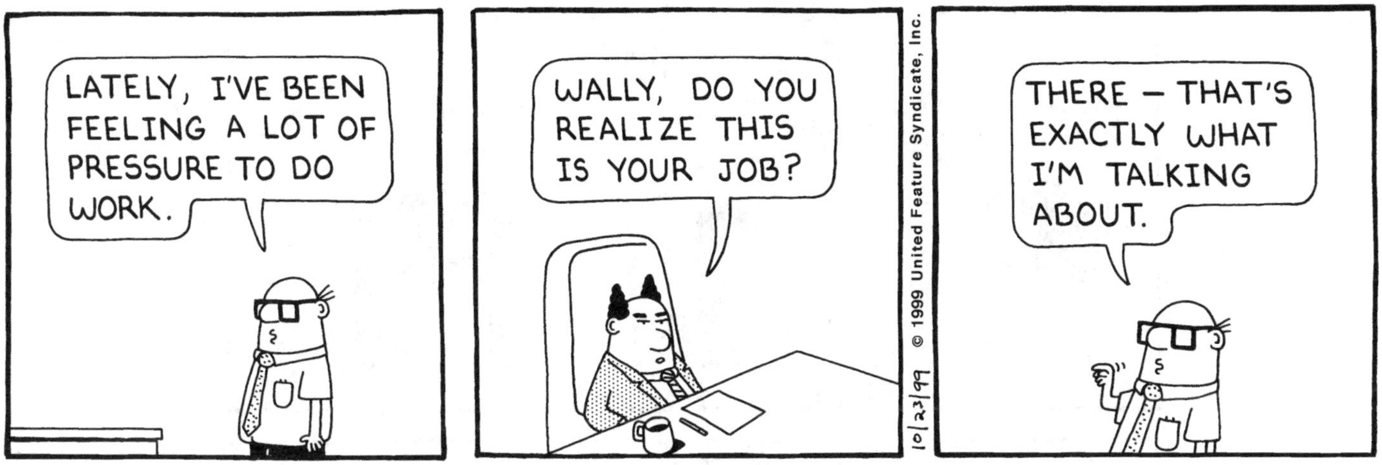
LATELY, I'VE BEEN FEELING A LOT OF PRESSURE TO DO WORK.
WALLY, DO YOU REALIZE THIS IS YOUR JOB?
THERE — THAT'S EXACTLY WHAT I'M TALKING ABOUT.
10/23/99 © 1999 United Feature Syndicate, Inc.

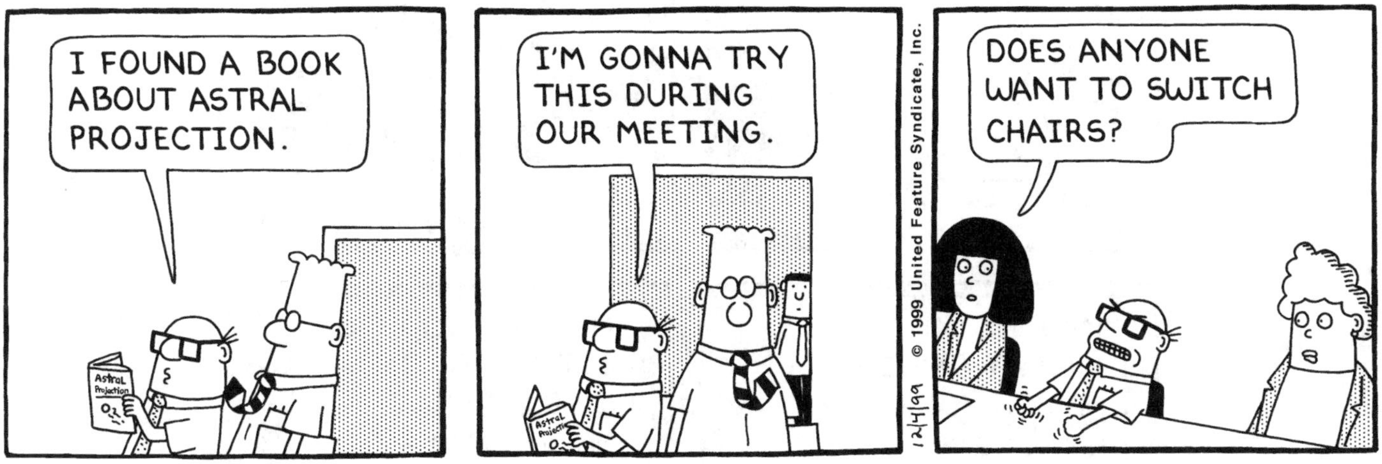
I FOUND A BOOK ABOUT ASTRAL PROJECTION.
Astral Projection
I'M GONNA TRY THIS DURING OUR MEETING.
DOES ANYONE WANT TO SWITCH CHAIRS?
12/4/99 © 1999 United Feature Syndicate, Inc.

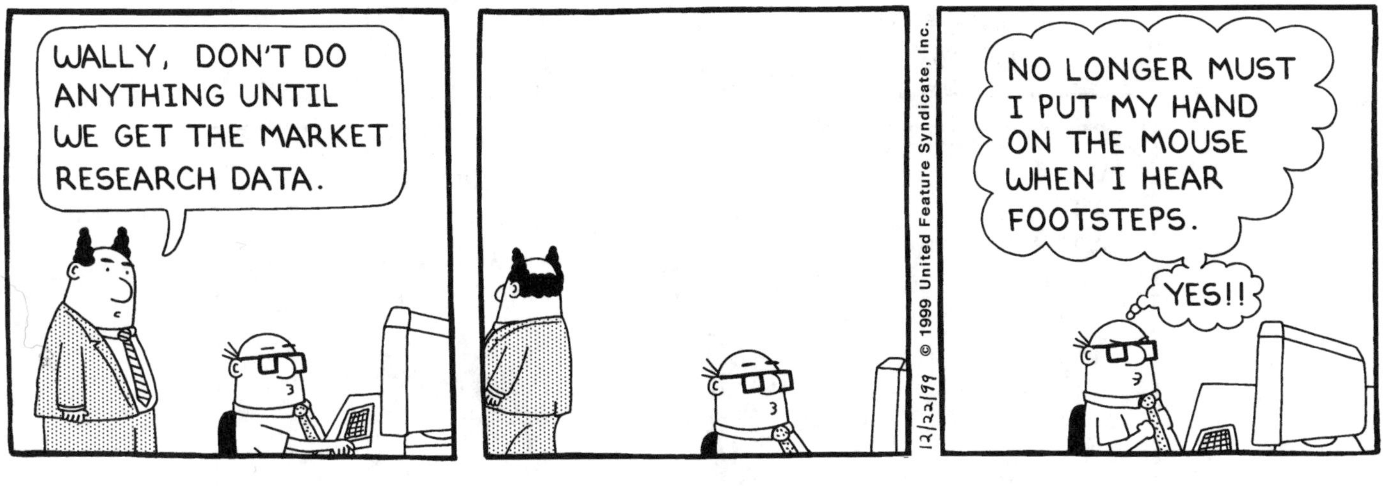
WALLY, DON'T DO ANYTHING UNTIL WE GET THE MARKET RESEARCH DATA.
NO LONGER MUST I PUT MY HAND ON THE MOUSE WHEN I HEAR FOOTSTEPS.
YES!!
12/22/99 © 1999 United Feature Syndicate, Inc.

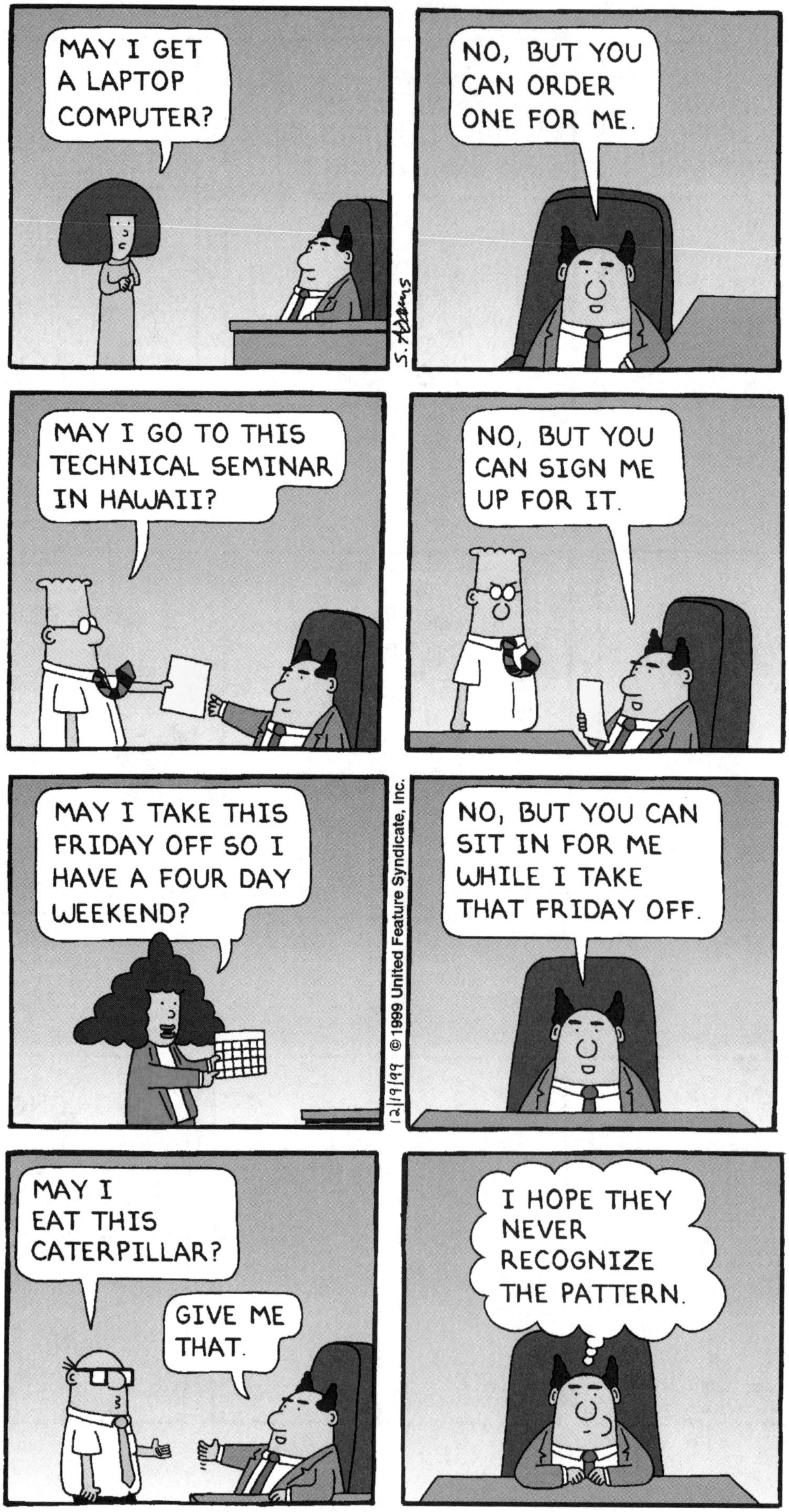
MAY I GET A LAPTOP COMPUTER?
NO, BUT YOU CAN ORDER ONE FOR ME.
MAY I GO TO THIS TECHNICAL SEMINAR IN HAWAII?
NO, BUT YOU CAN SIGN ME UP FOR IT.
MAY I TAKE THIS FRIDAY OFF SO I HAVE A FOUR DAY WEEKEND?
NO, BUT YOU CAN SIT IN FOR ME WHILE I TAKE THAT FRIDAY OFF.
MAY I EAT THIS CATERPILLAR?
GIVE ME THAT.
I HOPE THEY NEVER RECOGNIZE THE PATTERN.
S. Adams
12/19/99 © 1999 United Feature Syndicate, Inc.

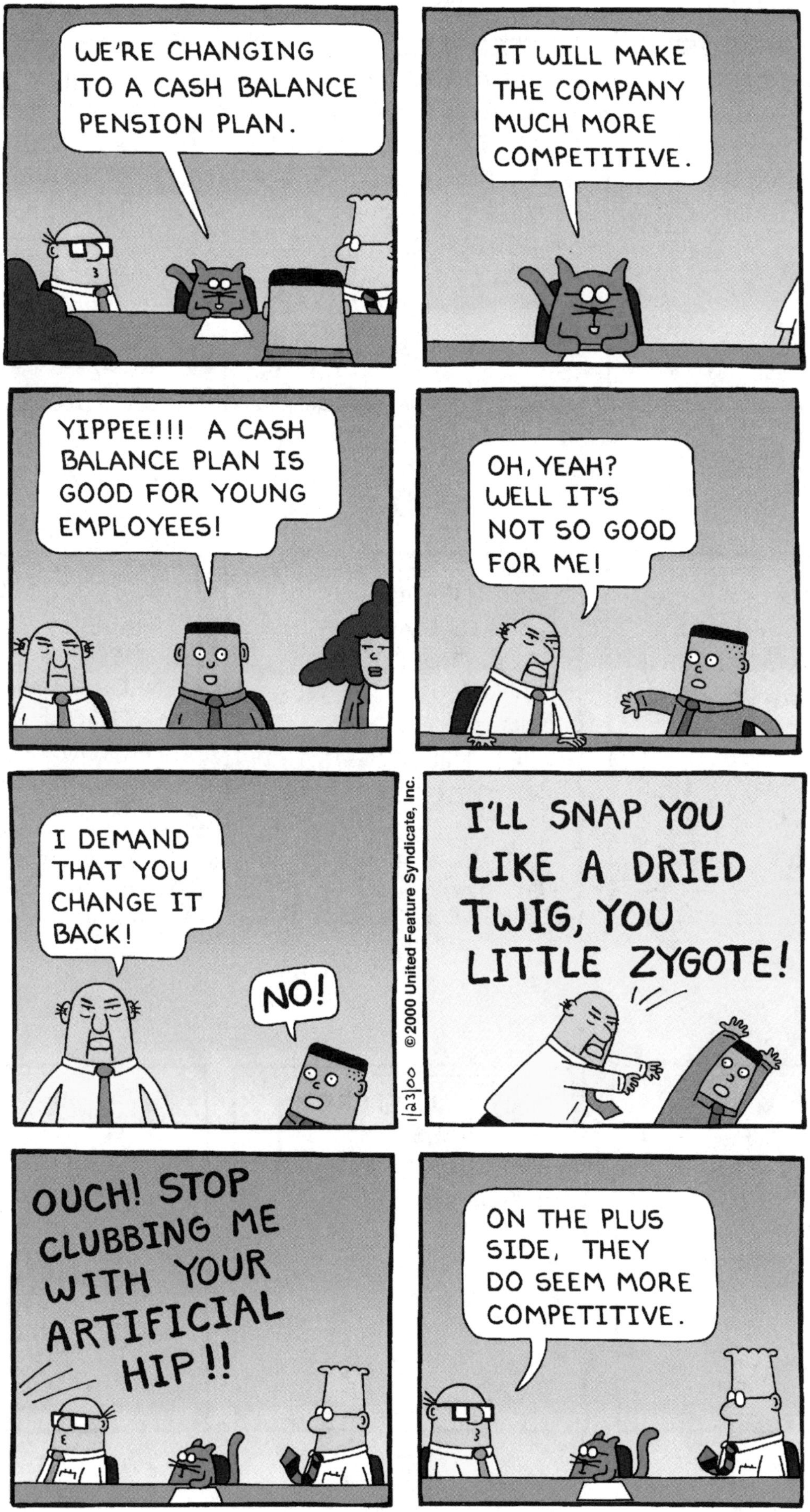
WE'RE CHANGING TO A CASH BALANCE PENSION PLAN.
IT WILL MAKE THE COMPANY MUCH MORE COMPETITIVE.
YIPPEE!!! A CASH BALANCE PLAN IS GOOD FOR YOUNG EMPLOYEES!
OH, YEAH? WELL IT'S NOT SO GOOD FOR ME!
I DEMAND THAT YOU CHANGE IT BACK!
NO!
©2000 United Feature Syndicate, Inc.
1/23/00
I'LL SNAP YOU LIKE A DRIED TWIG, YOU LITTLE ZYGOTE!
OUCH! STOP CLUBBING ME WITH YOUR ARTIFICIAL HIP!!
ON THE PLUS SIDE, THEY DO SEEM MORE COMPETITIVE.

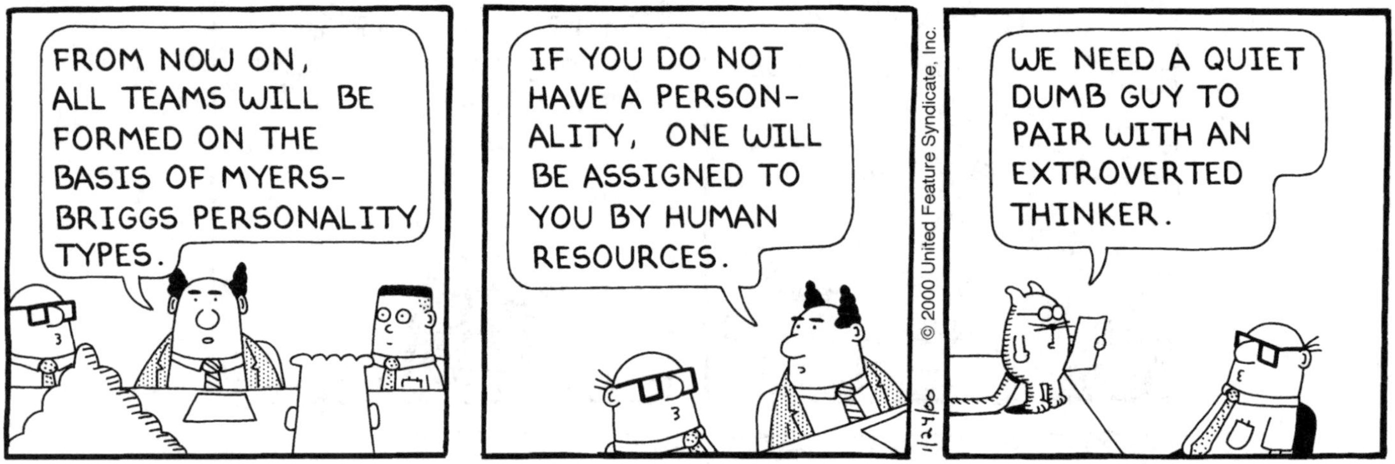
FROM NOW ON, ALL TEAMS WILL BE FORMED ON THE BASIS OF MYERS-BRIGGS PERSONALITY TYPES.
IF YOU DO NOT HAVE A PERSON-ALITY, ONE WILL BE ASSIGNED TO YOU BY HUMAN RESOURCES.
© 2000 United Feature Syndicate, Inc.
1/24/00
WE NEED A QUIET DUMB GUY TO PAIR WITH AN EXTROVERTED THINKER.

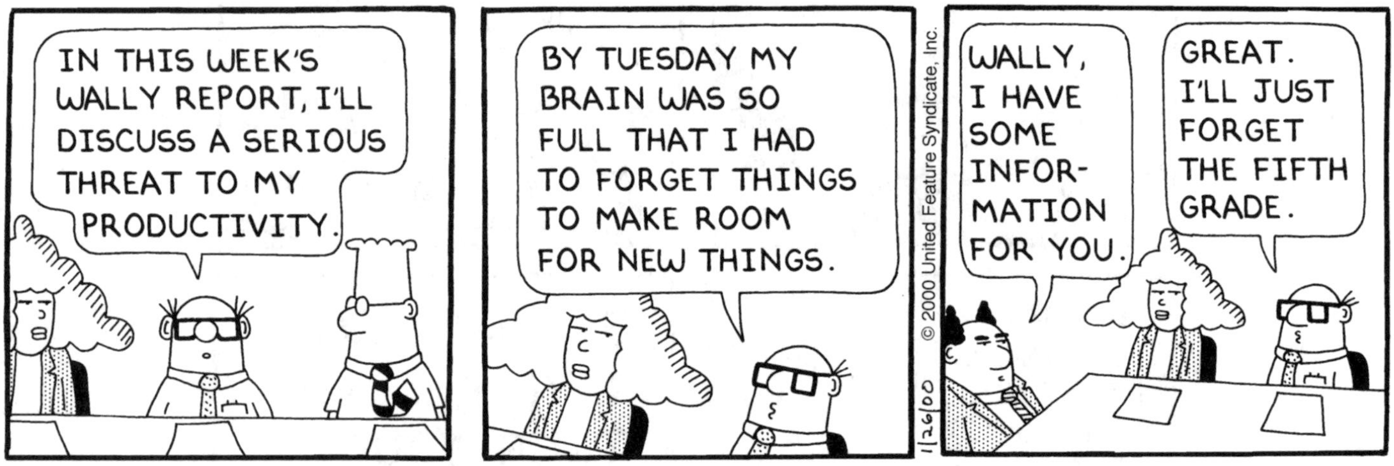
IN THIS WEEK'S WALLY REPORT, I'LL DISCUSS A SERIOUS THREAT TO MY PRODUCTIVITY.
BY TUESDAY MY BRAIN WAS SO FULL THAT I HAD TO FORGET THINGS TO MAKE ROOM FOR NEW THINGS.
© 2000 United Feature Syndicate, Inc.
1/26/00
WALLY, I HAVE SOME INFOR-MATION FOR YOU.
GREAT. I'LL JUST FORGET THE FIFTH GRADE.

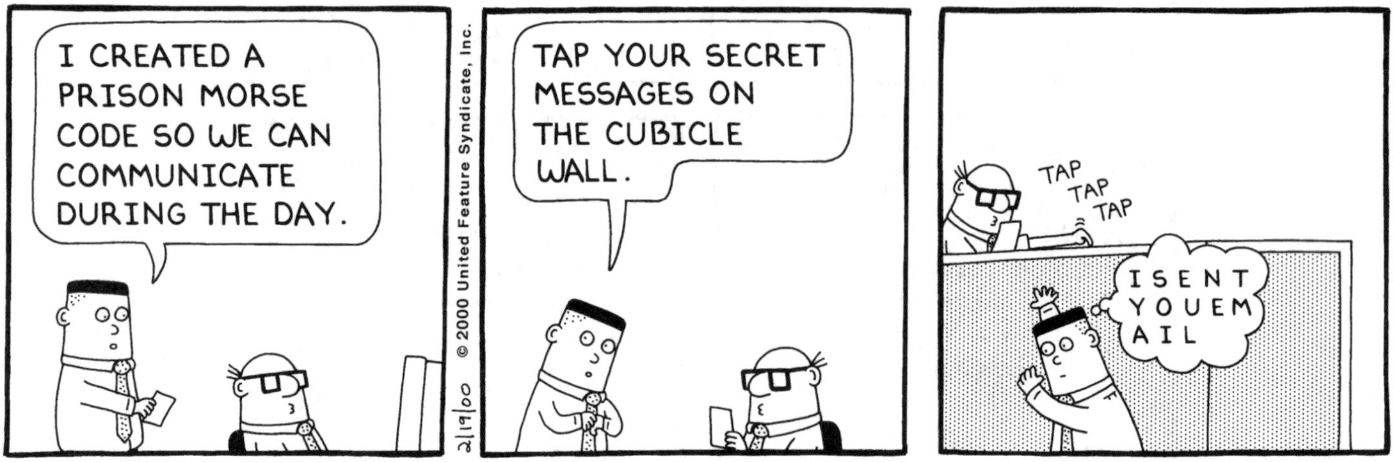
I CREATED A PRISON MORSE CODE SO WE CAN COMMUNICATE DURING THE DAY.
© 2000 United Feature Syndicate, Inc.
2/19/00
TAP YOUR SECRET MESSAGES ON THE CUBICLE WALL.
TAP
TAP
TAP
I SENT YOU EM AIL

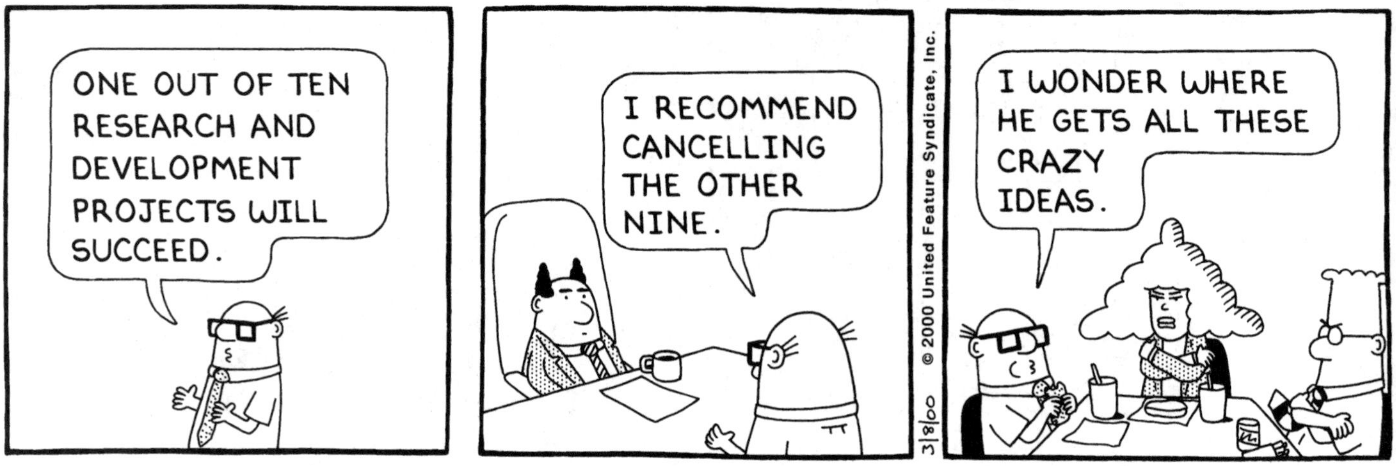
ONE OUT OF TEN RESEARCH AND DEVELOPMENT PROJECTS WILL SUCCEED.
I RECOMMEND CANCELLING THE OTHER NINE.
I WONDER WHERE HE GETS ALL THESE CRAZY IDEAS.
3/8/00 © 2000 United Feature Syndicate, Inc.

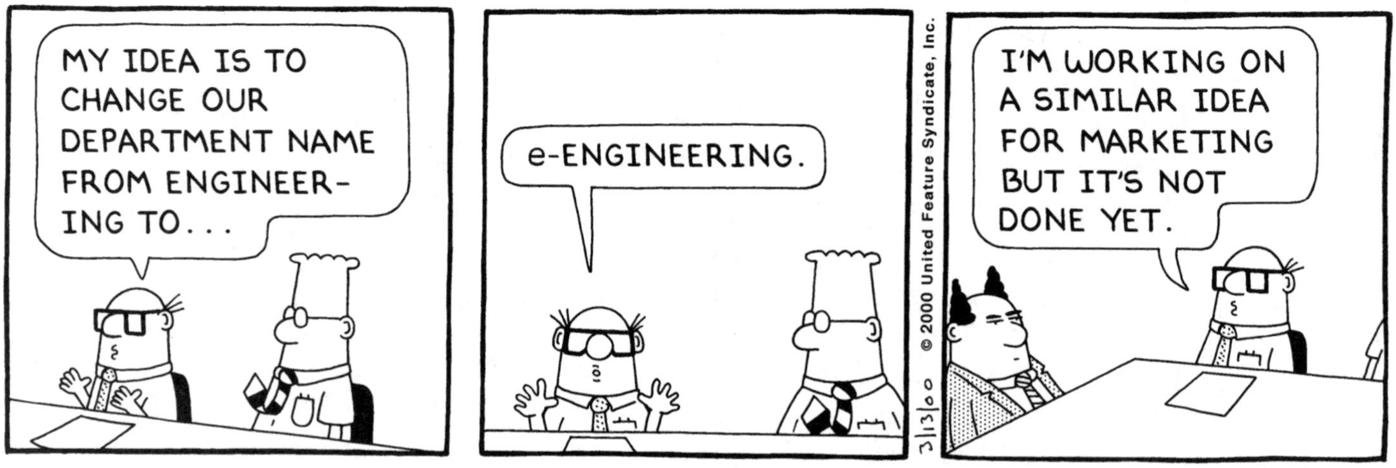
MY IDEA IS TO CHANGE OUR DEPARTMENT NAME FROM ENGINEER-ING TO . . .
e-ENGINEERING.
I'M WORKING ON A SIMILAR IDEA FOR MARKETING BUT IT'S NOT DONE YET.
3/13/00 © 2000 United Feature Syndicate, Inc.

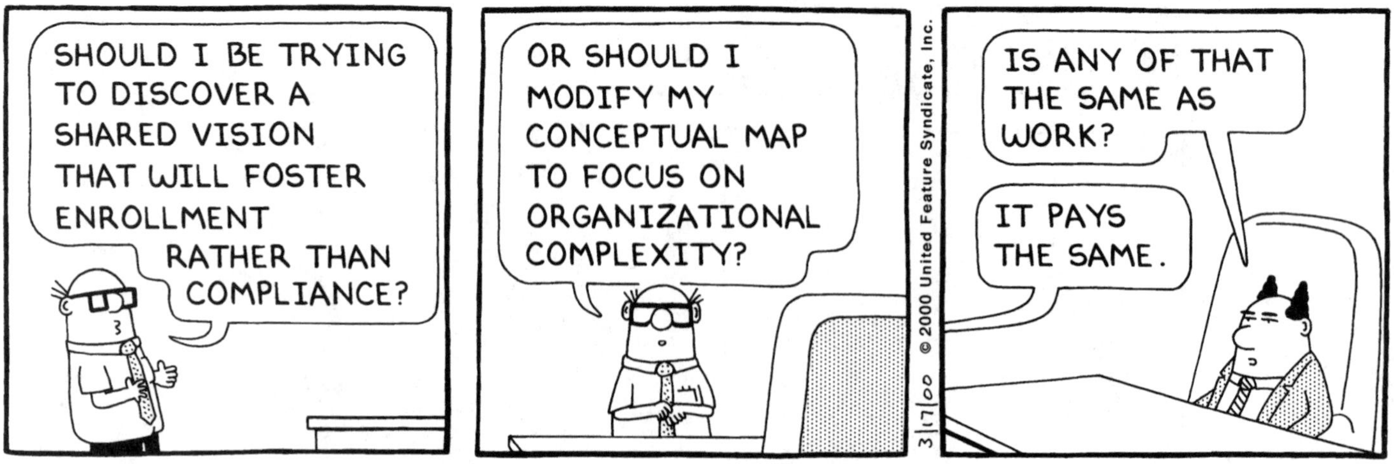
SHOULD I BE TRYING TO DISCOVER A SHARED VISION THAT WILL FOSTER ENROLLMENT RATHER THAN COMPLIANCE?
OR SHOULD I MODIFY MY CONCEPTUAL MAP TO FOCUS ON ORGANIZATIONAL COMPLEXITY?
IS ANY OF THAT THE SAME AS WORK?
IT PAYS THE SAME.
3/17/00 © 2000 United Feature Syndicate, Inc.

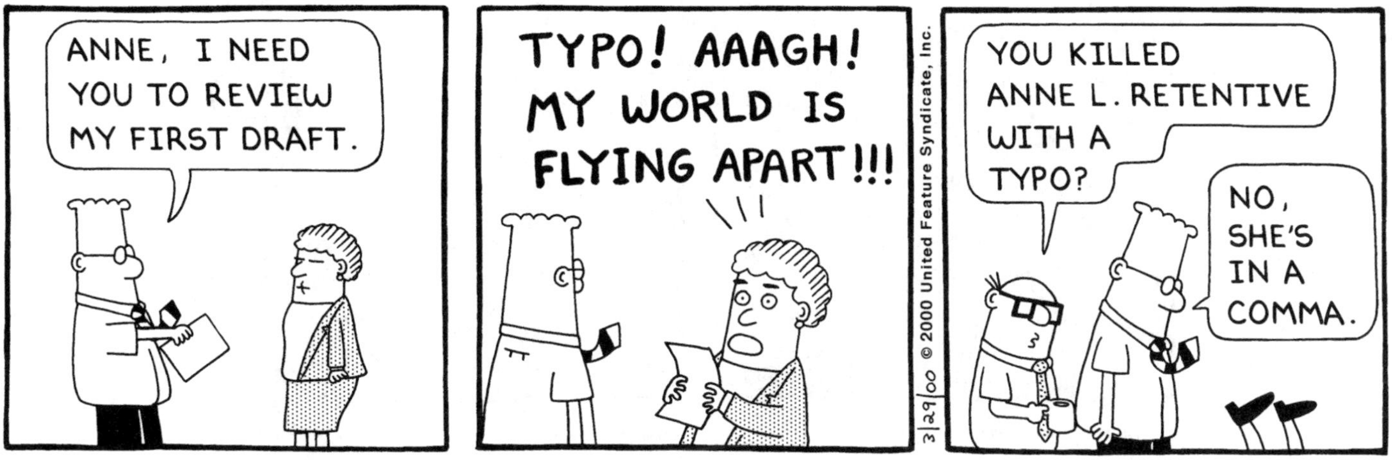
ANNE, I NEED YOU TO REVIEW MY FIRST DRAFT.
TYPO! AAAGH! MY WORLD IS FLYING APART!!!
3/29/00 © 2000 United Feature Syndicate, Inc.
YOU KILLED ANNE L. RETENTIVE WITH A TYPO?
NO, SHE'S IN A COMMA.

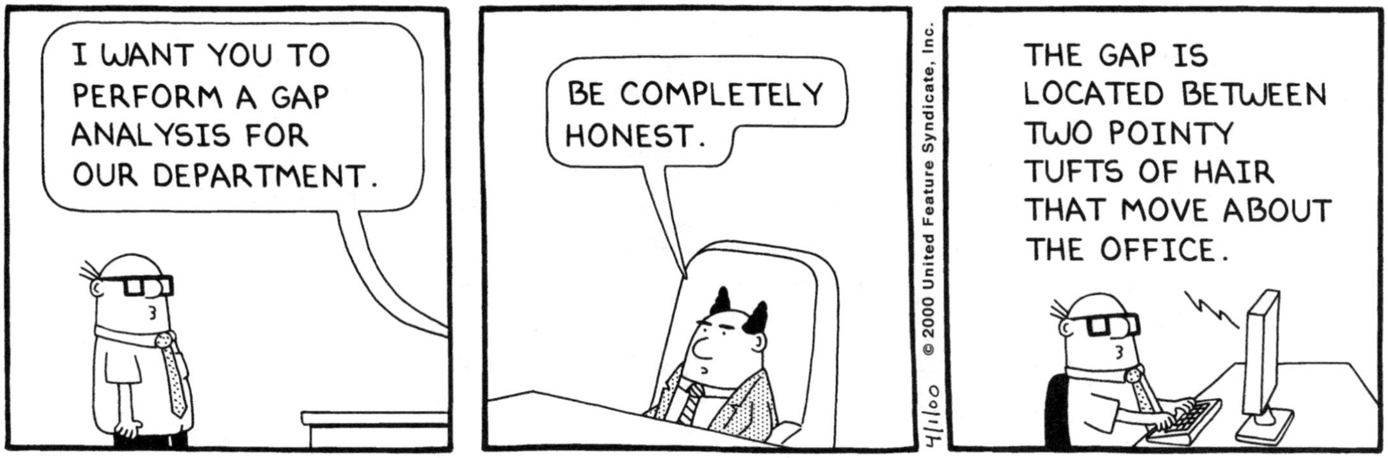
I WANT YOU TO PERFORM A GAP ANALYSIS FOR OUR DEPARTMENT.
BE COMPLETELY HONEST.
4/1/00 © 2000 United Feature Syndicate, Inc.
THE GAP IS LOCATED BETWEEN TWO POINTY TUFTS OF HAIR THAT MOVE ABOUT THE OFFICE.

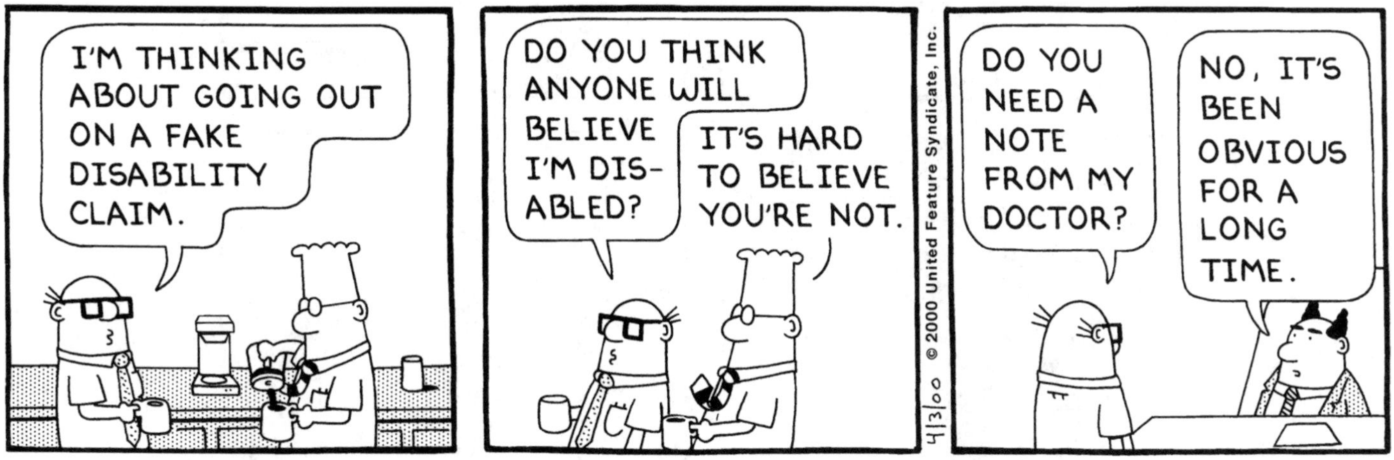
I'M THINKING ABOUT GOING OUT ON A FAKE DISABILITY CLAIM.
DO YOU THINK ANYONE WILL BELIEVE I'M DISABLED?
IT'S HARD TO BELIEVE YOU'RE NOT.
4/3/00 © 2000 United Feature Syndicate, Inc.
DO YOU NEED A NOTE FROM MY DOCTOR?
NO, IT'S BEEN OBVIOUS FOR A LONG TIME.

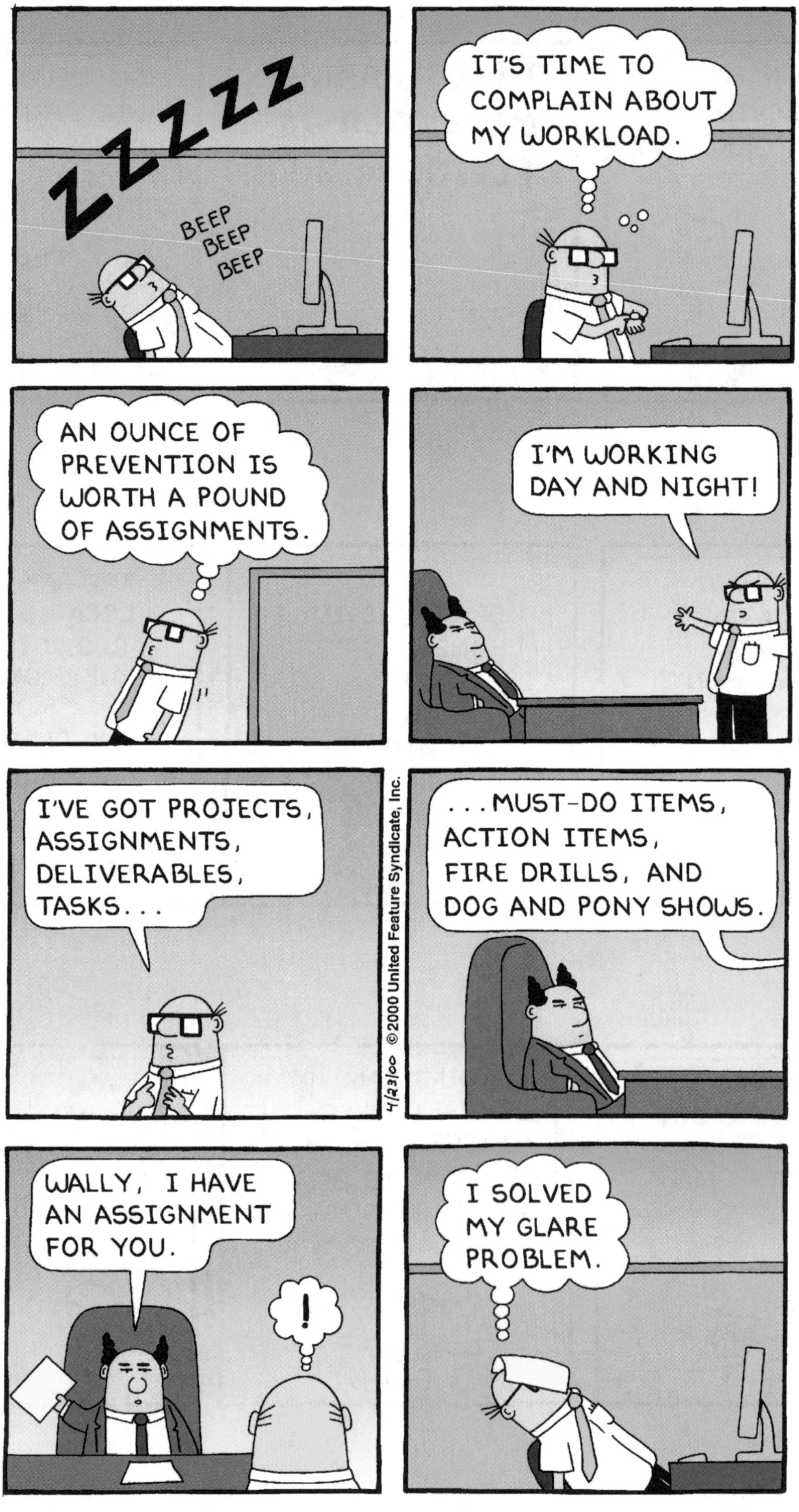
ZZZZZ
BEEP BEEP BEEP
IT'S TIME TO COMPLAIN ABOUT MY WORKLOAD.
AN OUNCE OF PREVENTION IS WORTH A POUND OF ASSIGNMENTS.
I'M WORKING DAY AND NIGHT!
I'VE GOT PROJECTS, ASSIGNMENTS, DELIVERABLES, TASKS...
...MUST-DO ITEMS, ACTION ITEMS, FIRE DRILLS, AND DOG AND PONY SHOWS.
4/23/00 ©2000 United Feature Syndicate, Inc.
WALLY, I HAVE AN ASSIGNMENT FOR YOU.
!
I SOLVED MY GLARE PROBLEM.

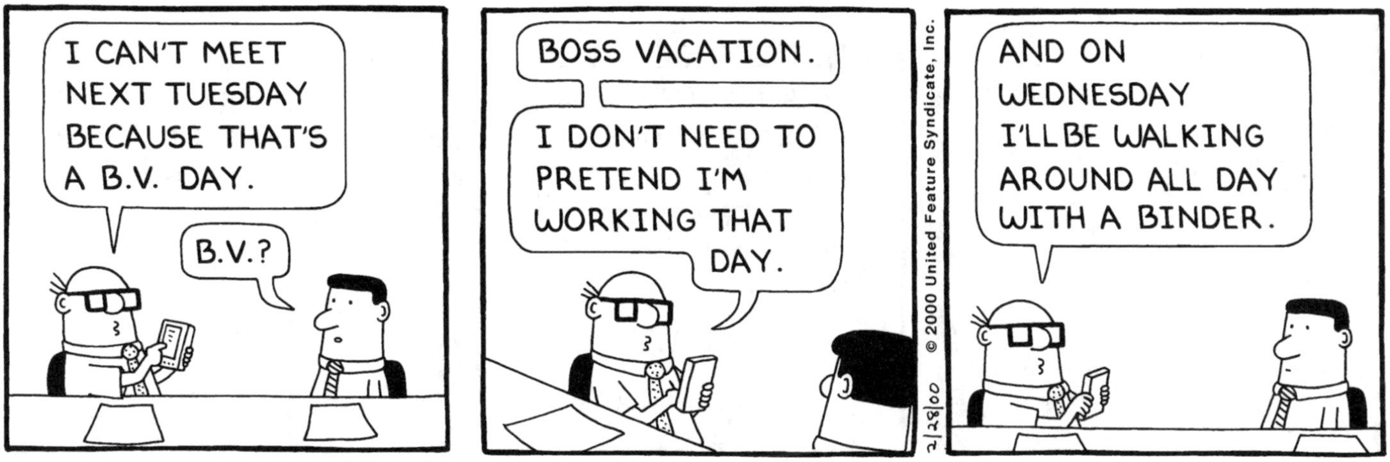
I CAN'T MEET NEXT TUESDAY BECAUSE THAT'S A B.V. DAY.
B.V.?
BOSS VACATION.
I DON'T NEED TO PRETEND I'M WORKING THAT DAY.
AND ON WEDNESDAY I'LL BE WALKING AROUND ALL DAY WITH A BINDER.
2/28/00
© 2000 United Feature Syndicate, Inc.

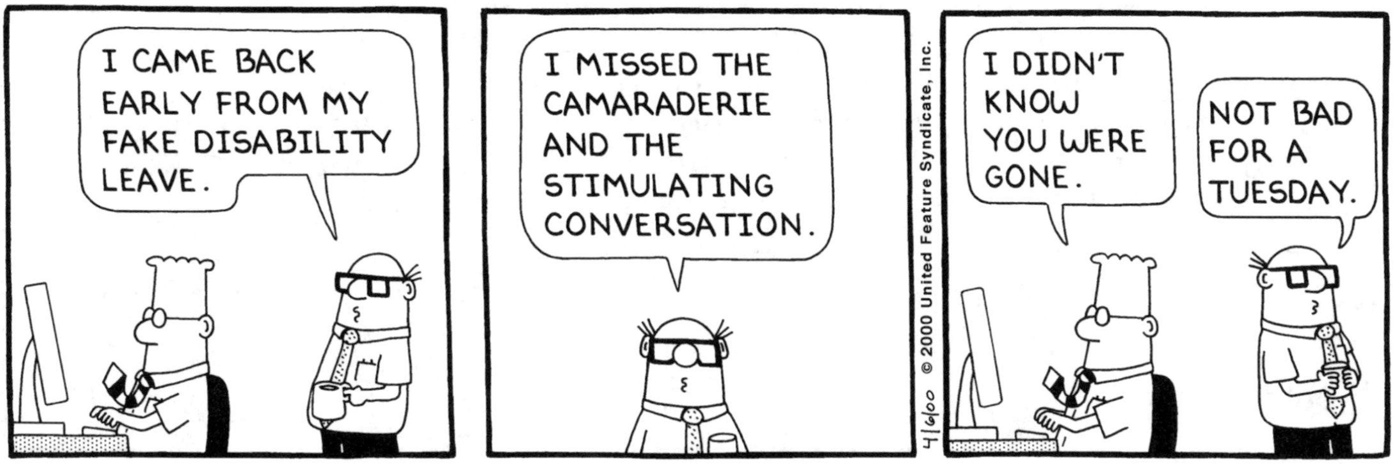
I CAME BACK EARLY FROM MY FAKE DISABILITY LEAVE.
I MISSED THE CAMARADERIE AND THE STIMULATING CONVERSATION.
I DIDN'T KNOW YOU WERE GONE.
NOT BAD FOR A TUESDAY.
4/6/00
© 2000 United Feature Syndicate, Inc.

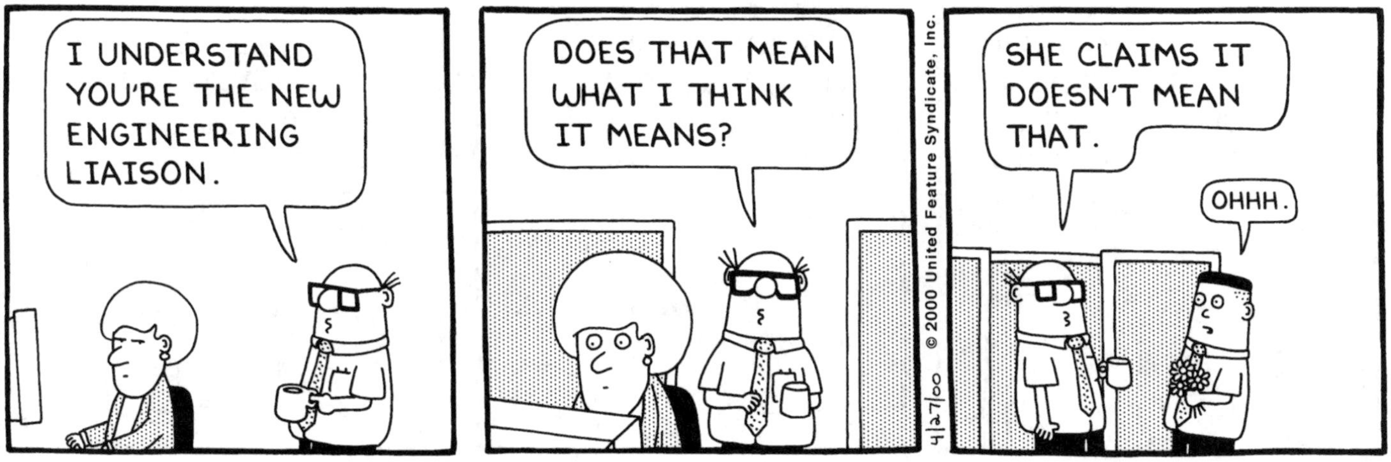
I UNDERSTAND YOU'RE THE NEW ENGINEERING LIAISON.
DOES THAT MEAN WHAT I THINK IT MEANS?
SHE CLAIMS IT DOESN'T MEAN THAT.
OHHH.
4/27/00
© 2000 United Feature Syndicate, Inc.

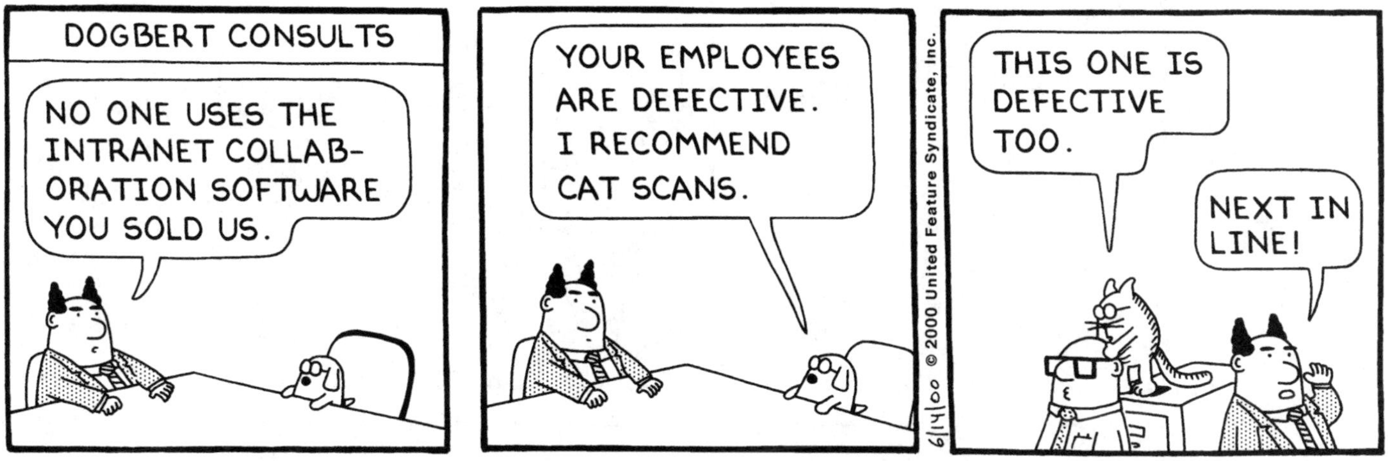
DOGBERT CONSULTS
NO ONE USES THE INTRANET COLLABORATION SOFTWARE YOU SOLD US.
YOUR EMPLOYEES ARE DEFECTIVE. I RECOMMEND CAT SCANS.
THIS ONE IS DEFECTIVE TOO.
NEXT IN LINE!
6/14/00 © 2000 United Feature Syndicate, Inc.

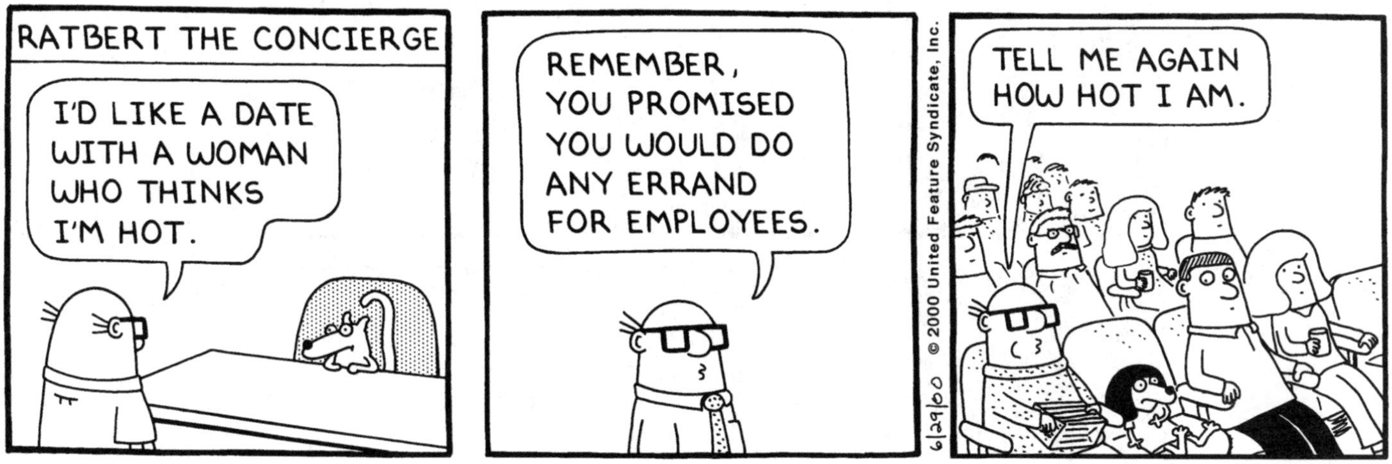
RATBERT THE CONCIERGE
I'D LIKE A DATE WITH A WOMAN WHO THINKS I'M HOT.
REMEMBER, YOU PROMISED YOU WOULD DO ANY ERRAND FOR EMPLOYEES.
TELL ME AGAIN HOW HOT I AM.
6/29/00 © 2000 United Feature Syndicate, Inc.

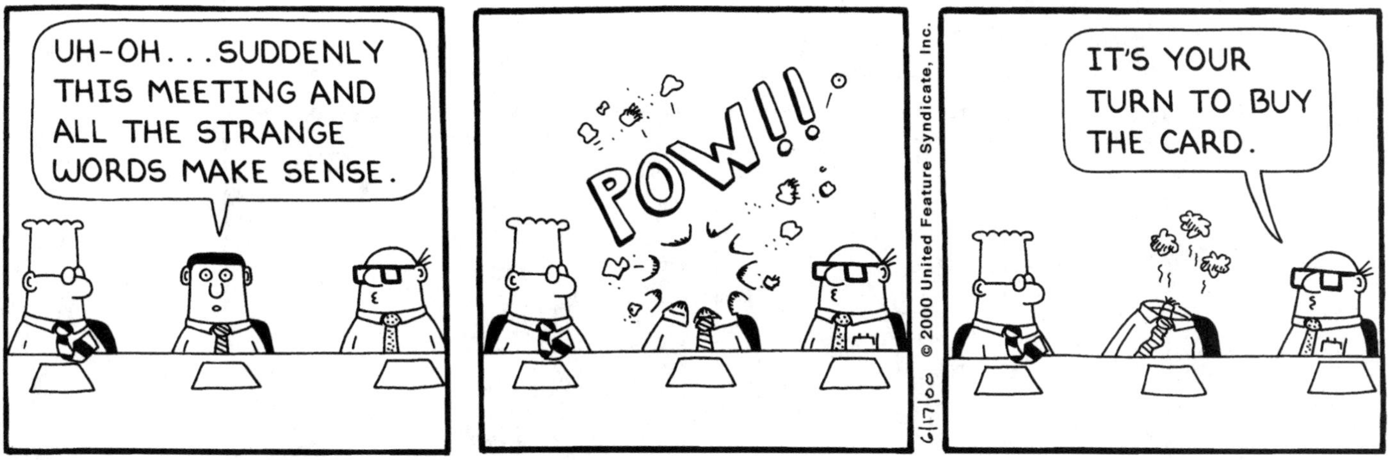
UH-OH. . . SUDDENLY THIS MEETING AND ALL THE STRANGE WORDS MAKE SENSE.
POW!!
IT'S YOUR TURN TO BUY THE CARD.
6/17/00 © 2000 United Feature Syndicate, Inc.

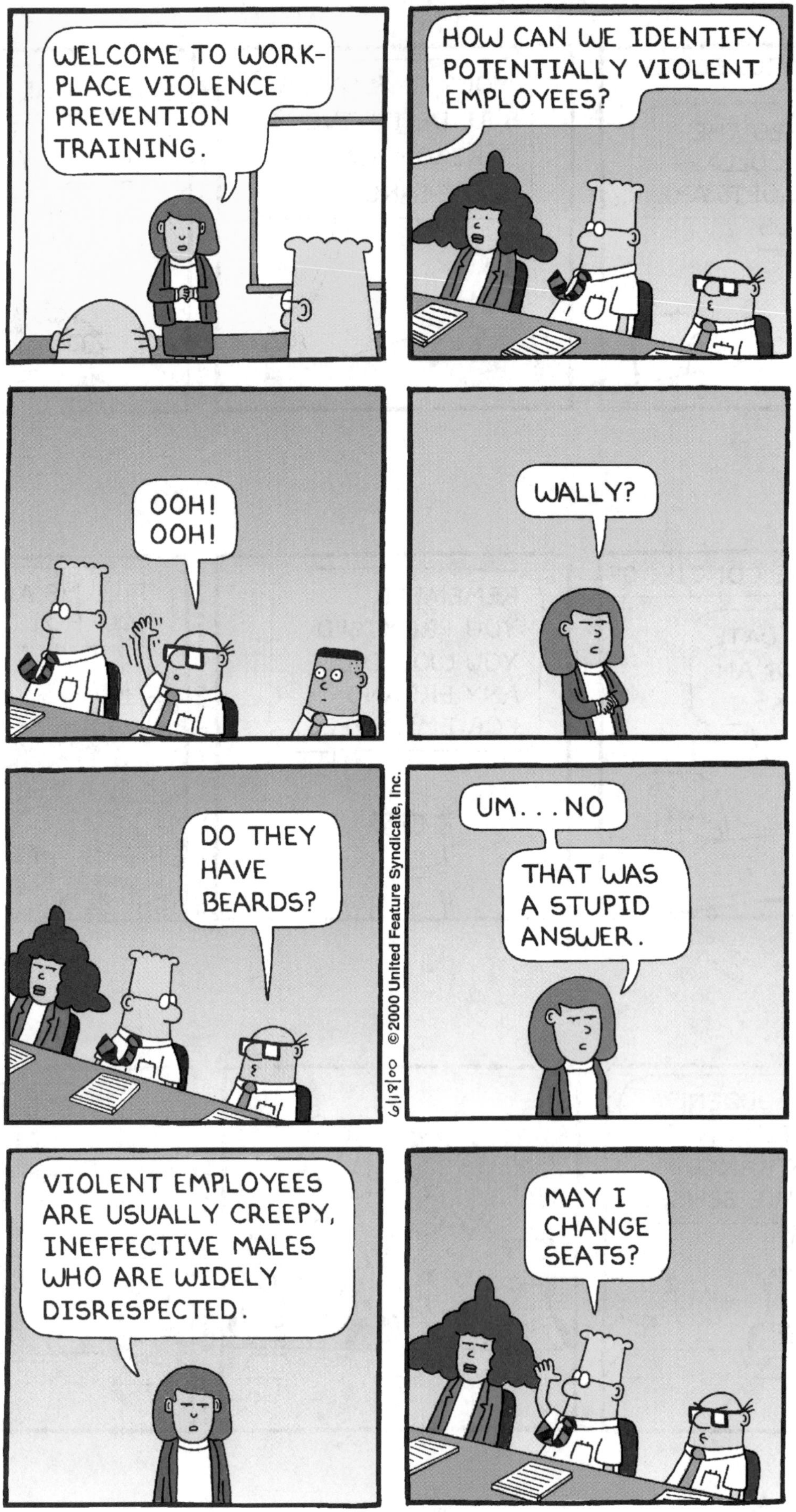

WELCOME TO WORK-PLACE VIOLENCE PREVENTION TRAINING.
HOW CAN WE IDENTIFY POTENTIALLY VIOLENT EMPLOYEES?
OOH! OOH!
WALLY?
DO THEY HAVE BEARDS?
UM...NO
THAT WAS A STUPID ANSWER.
VIOLENT EMPLOYEES ARE USUALLY CREEPY, INEFFECTIVE MALES WHO ARE WIDELY DISRESPECTED.
MAY I CHANGE SEATS?
6/18/00 © 2000 United Feature Syndicate, Inc.

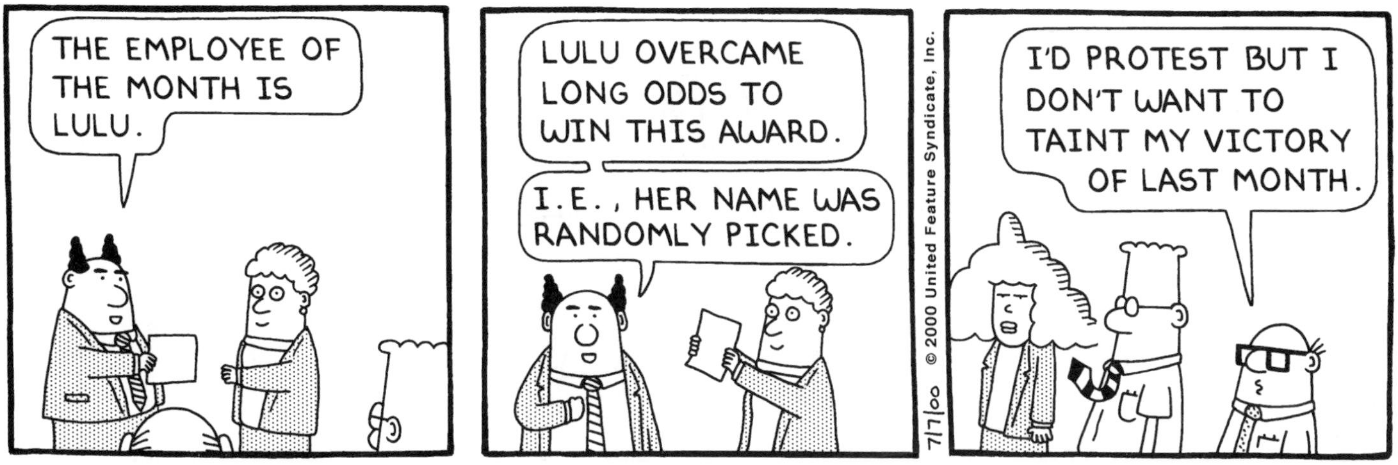
THE EMPLOYEE OF THE MONTH IS LULU.
LULU OVERCAME LONG ODDS TO WIN THIS AWARD.
I.E., HER NAME WAS RANDOMLY PICKED.
I'D PROTEST BUT I DON'T WANT TO TAINT MY VICTORY OF LAST MONTH.
© 2000 United Feature Syndicate, Inc.
7/7/00

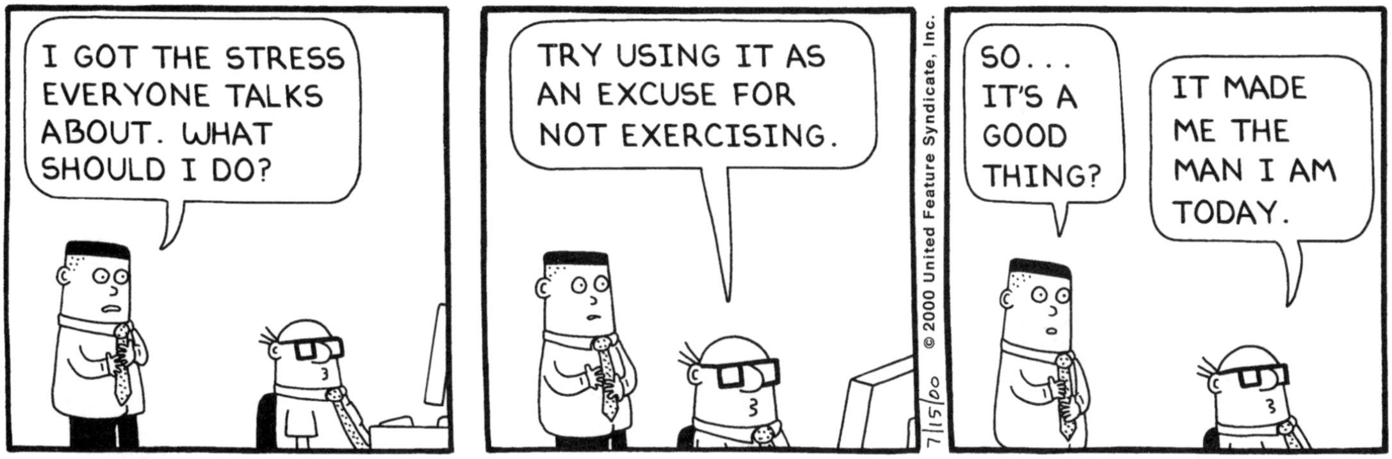
I GOT THE STRESS EVERYONE TALKS ABOUT. WHAT SHOULD I DO?
TRY USING IT AS AN EXCUSE FOR NOT EXERCISING.
SO... IT'S A GOOD THING?
IT MADE ME THE MAN I AM TODAY.
© 2000 United Feature Syndicate, Inc.
7/15/00

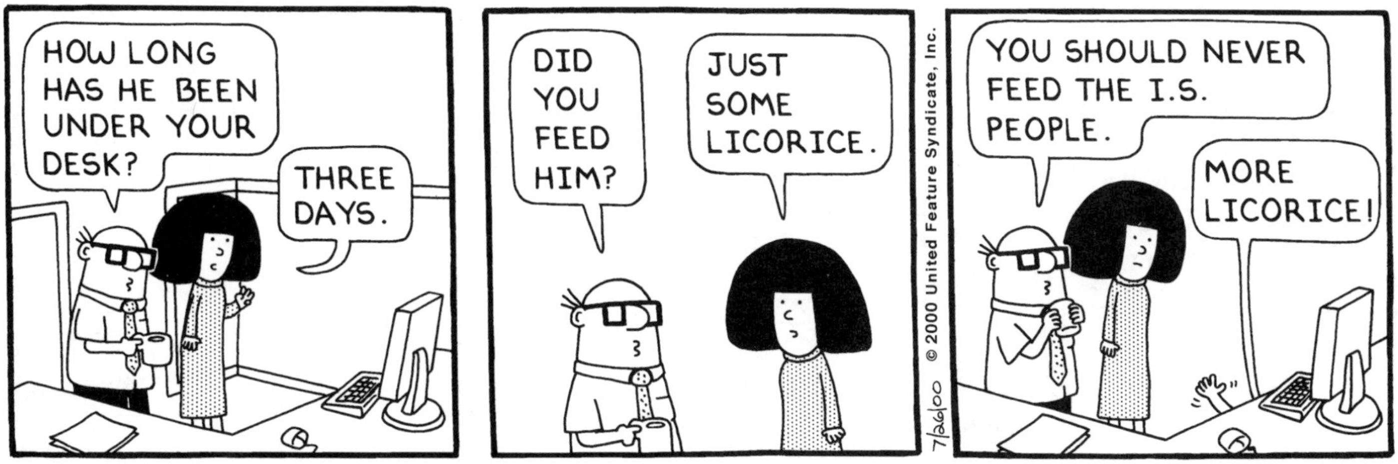
HOW LONG HAS HE BEEN UNDER YOUR DESK?
THREE DAYS.
DID YOU FEED HIM?
JUST SOME LICORICE.
YOU SHOULD NEVER FEED THE I.S. PEOPLE.
MORE LICORICE!
© 2000 United Feature Syndicate, Inc.
7/26/00

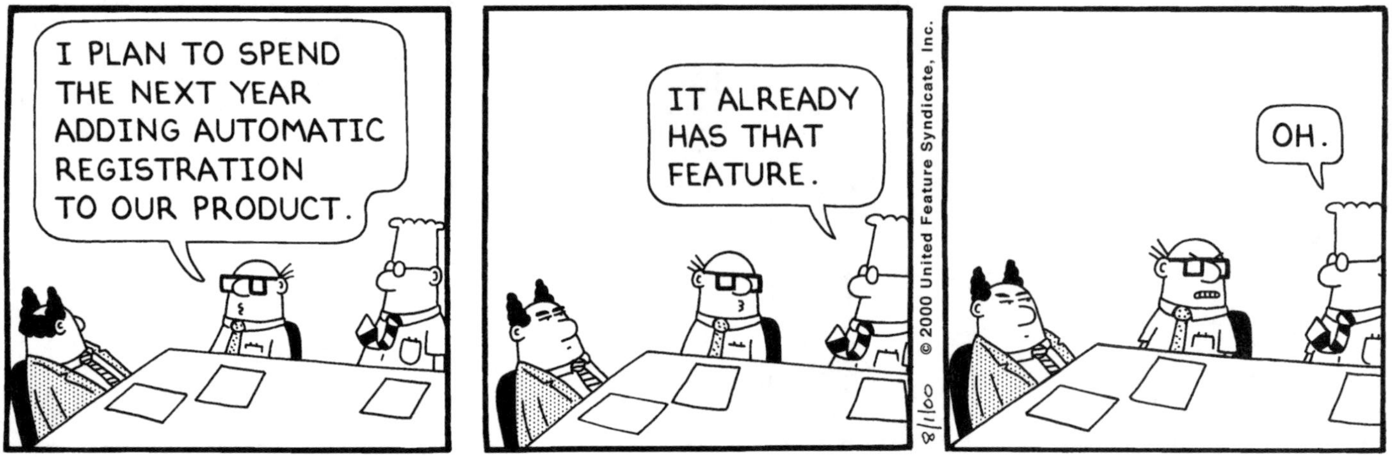
I PLAN TO SPEND THE NEXT YEAR ADDING AUTOMATIC REGISTRATION TO OUR PRODUCT.
IT ALREADY HAS THAT FEATURE.
8/1/00 © 2000 United Feature Syndicate, Inc.
OH.

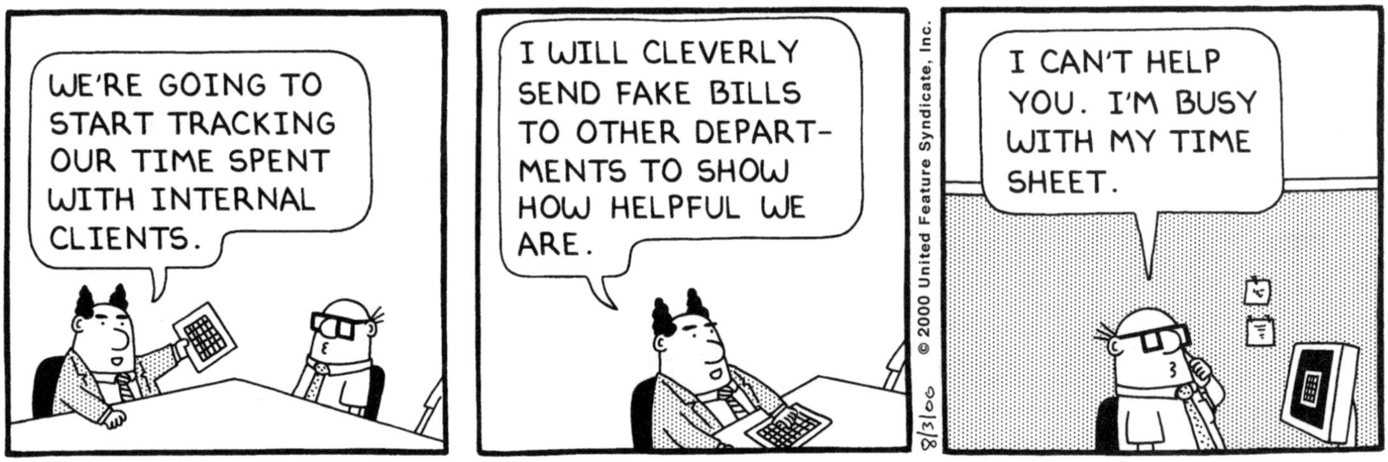
WE'RE GOING TO START TRACKING OUR TIME SPENT WITH INTERNAL CLIENTS.
I WILL CLEVERLY SEND FAKE BILLS TO OTHER DEPART-MENTS TO SHOW HOW HELPFUL WE ARE.
8/3/00 © 2000 United Feature Syndicate, Inc.
I CAN'T HELP YOU. I'M BUSY WITH MY TIME SHEET.

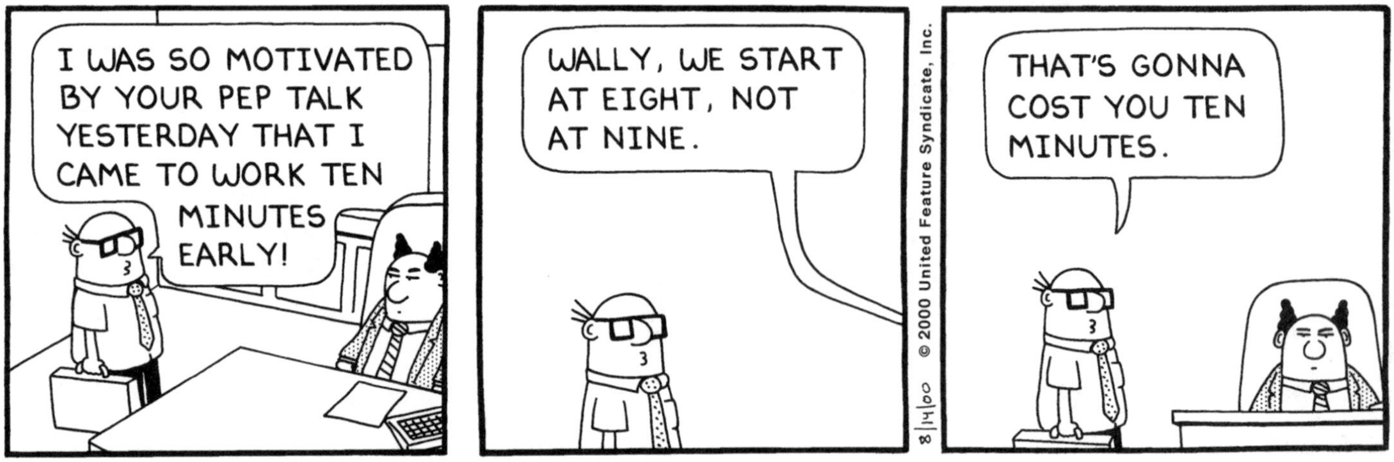
I WAS SO MOTIVATED BY YOUR PEP TALK YESTERDAY THAT I CAME TO WORK TEN MINUTES EARLY!
WALLY, WE START AT EIGHT, NOT AT NINE.
8/14/00 © 2000 United Feature Syndicate, Inc.
THAT'S GONNA COST YOU TEN MINUTES.

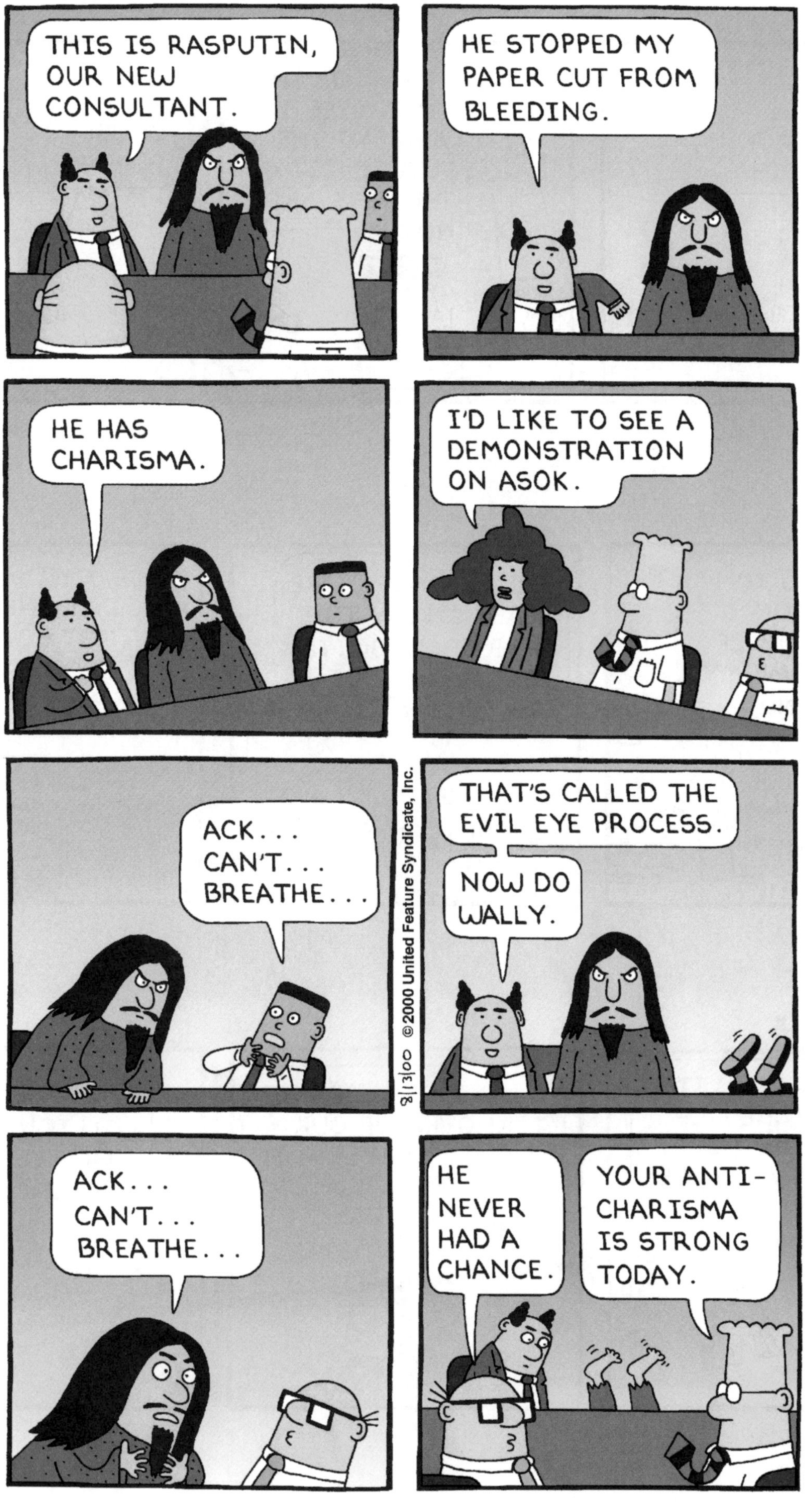
THIS IS RASPUTIN, OUR NEW CONSULTANT.
HE STOPPED MY PAPER CUT FROM BLEEDING.
HE HAS CHARISMA.
I'D LIKE TO SEE A DEMONSTRATION ON ASOK.
ACK... CAN'T... BREATHE...
©2000 United Feature Syndicate, Inc.
8/13/00
THAT'S CALLED THE EVIL EYE PROCESS.
NOW DO WALLY.
ACK... CAN'T... BREATHE...
HE NEVER HAD A CHANCE.
YOUR ANTI-CHARISMA IS STRONG TODAY.

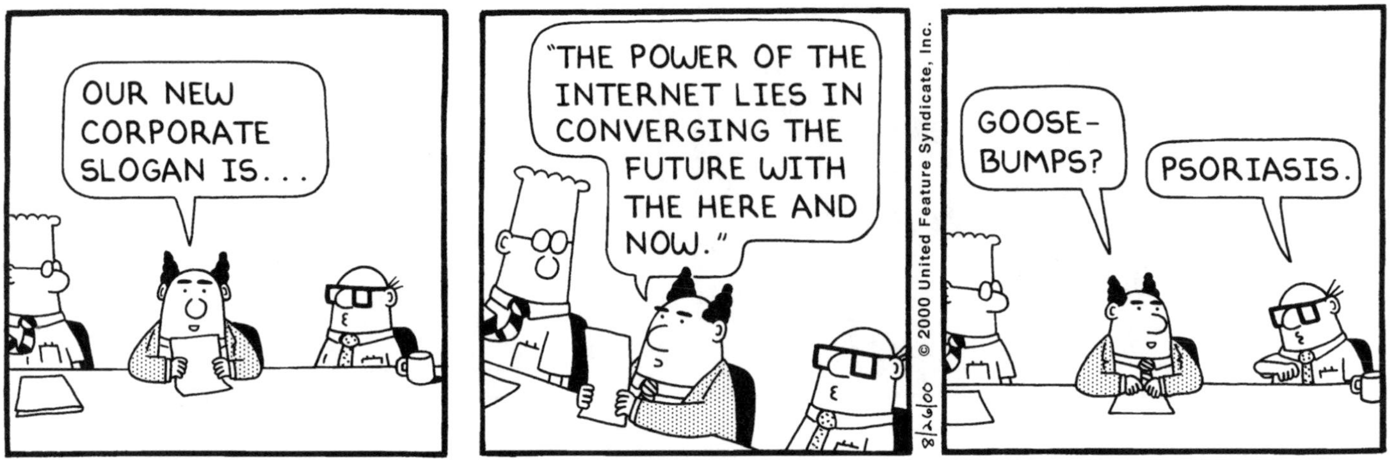
OUR NEW CORPORATE SLOGAN IS...
"THE POWER OF THE INTERNET LIES IN CONVERGING THE FUTURE WITH THE HERE AND NOW."
8/26/00 © 2000 United Feature Syndicate, Inc.
GOOSE-BUMPS?
PSORIASIS.

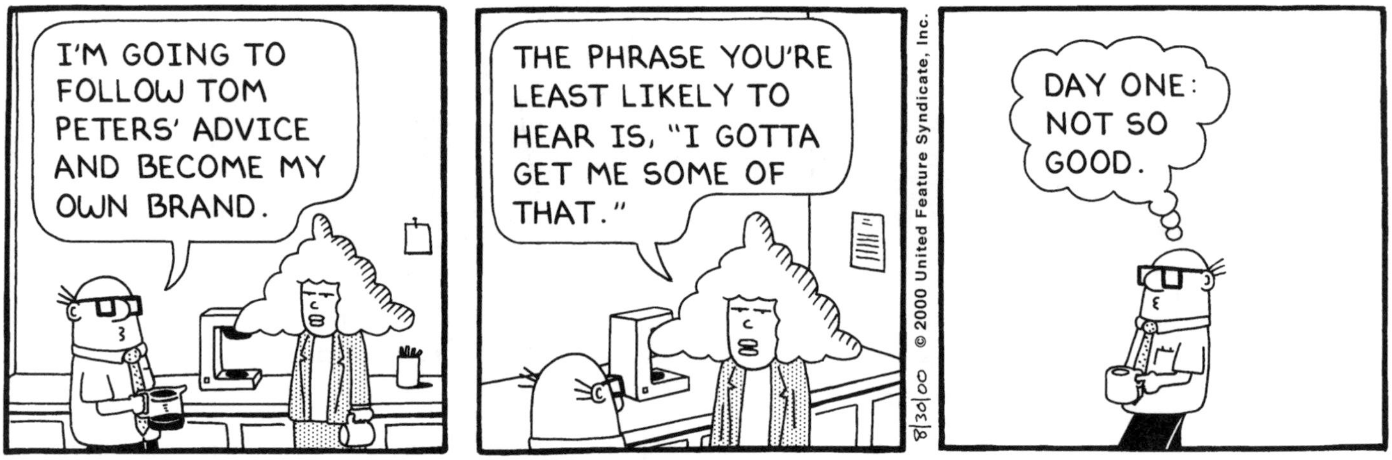
I'M GOING TO FOLLOW TOM PETERS' ADVICE AND BECOME MY OWN BRAND.
THE PHRASE YOU'RE LEAST LIKELY TO HEAR IS, "I GOTTA GET ME SOME OF THAT."
8/30/00 © 2000 United Feature Syndicate, Inc.
DAY ONE: NOT SO GOOD.

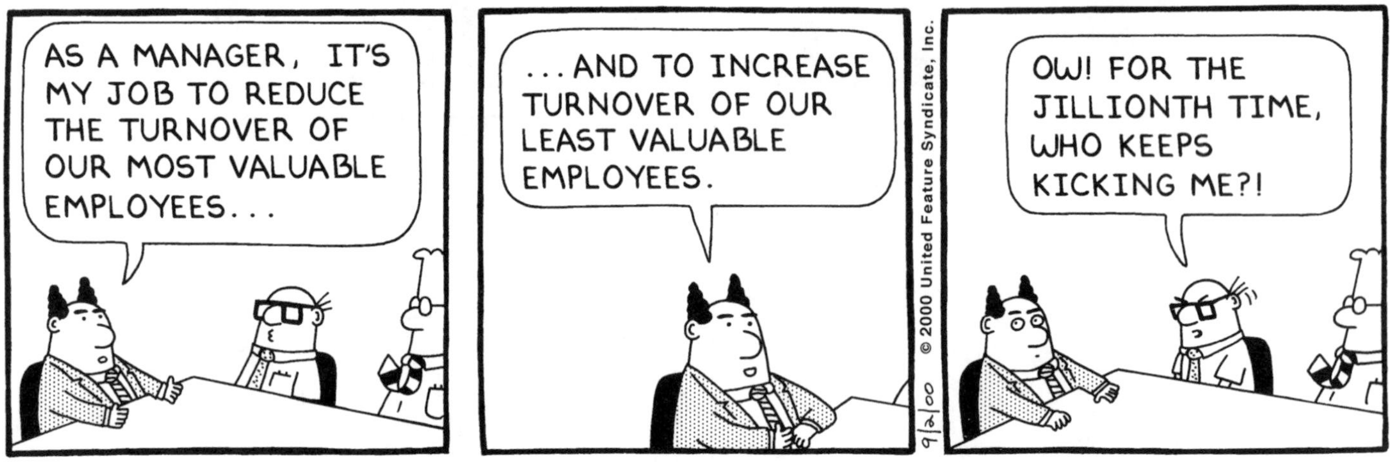
AS A MANAGER, IT'S MY JOB TO REDUCE THE TURNOVER OF OUR MOST VALUABLE EMPLOYEES...
...AND TO INCREASE TURNOVER OF OUR LEAST VALUABLE EMPLOYEES.
9/2/00 © 2000 United Feature Syndicate, Inc.
OW! FOR THE JILLIONTH TIME, WHO KEEPS KICKING ME?!

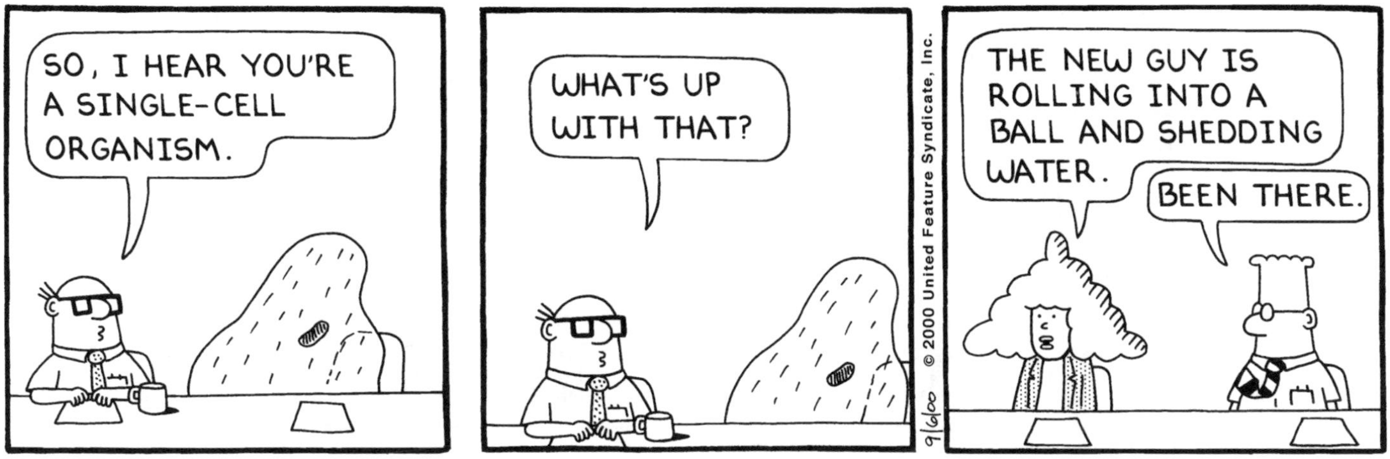
SO, I HEAR YOU'RE A SINGLE-CELL ORGANISM.
WHAT'S UP WITH THAT?
9/6/00
© 2000 United Feature Syndicate, Inc.
THE NEW GUY IS ROLLING INTO A BALL AND SHEDDING WATER.
BEEN THERE.

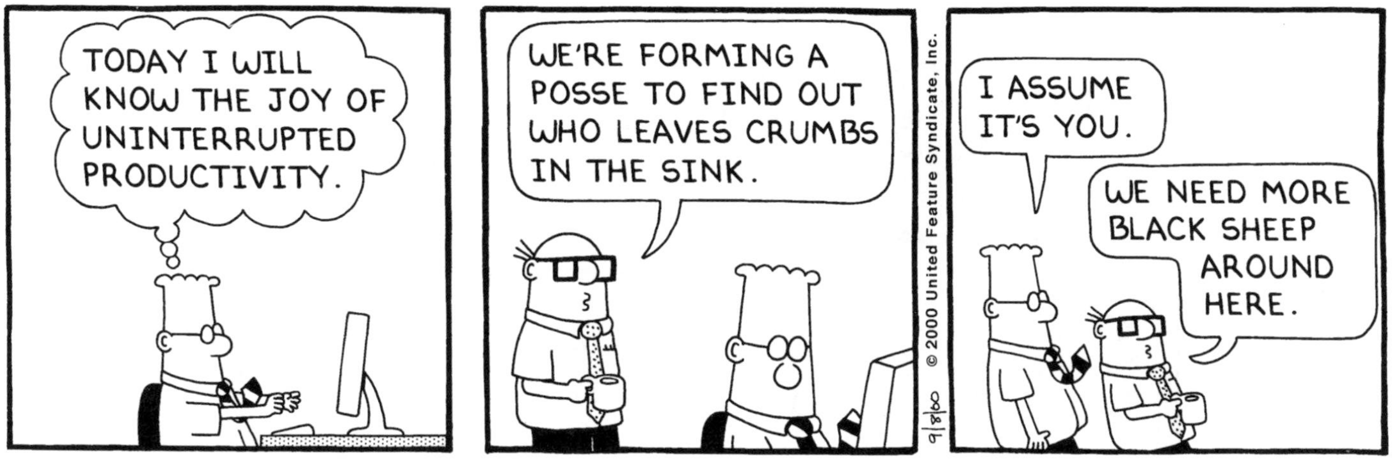
TODAY I WILL KNOW THE JOY OF UNINTERRUPTED PRODUCTIVITY.
WE'RE FORMING A POSSE TO FIND OUT WHO LEAVES CRUMBS IN THE SINK.
9/8/00
© 2000 United Feature Syndicate, Inc.
I ASSUME IT'S YOU.
WE NEED MORE BLACK SHEEP AROUND HERE.

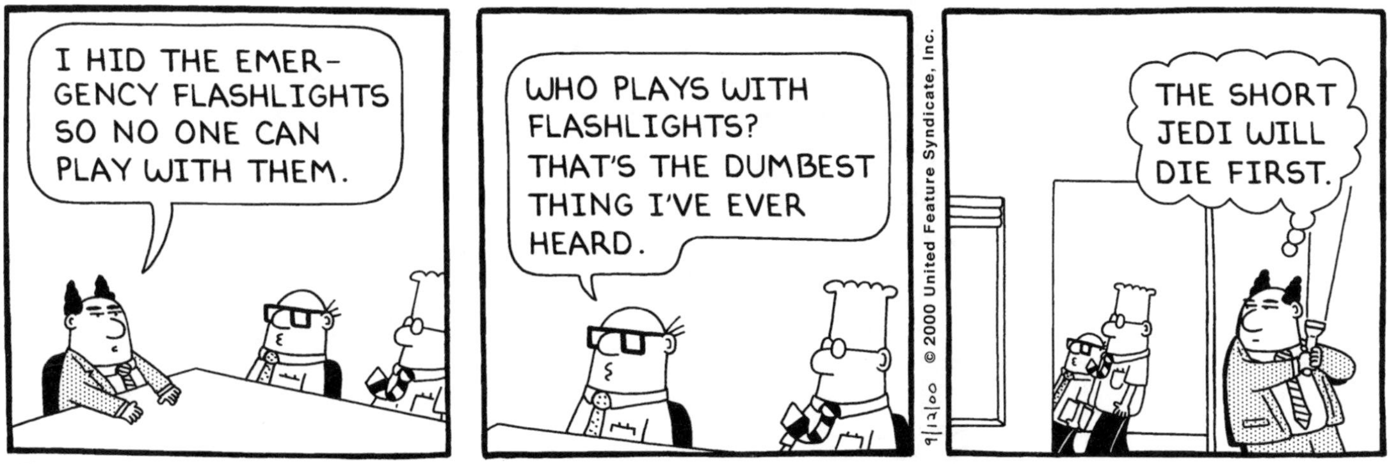
I HID THE EMER-GENCY FLASHLIGHTS SO NO ONE CAN PLAY WITH THEM.
WHO PLAYS WITH FLASHLIGHTS? THAT'S THE DUMBEST THING I'VE EVER HEARD.
9/12/00
© 2000 United Feature Syndicate, Inc.
THE SHORT JEDI WILL DIE FIRST.

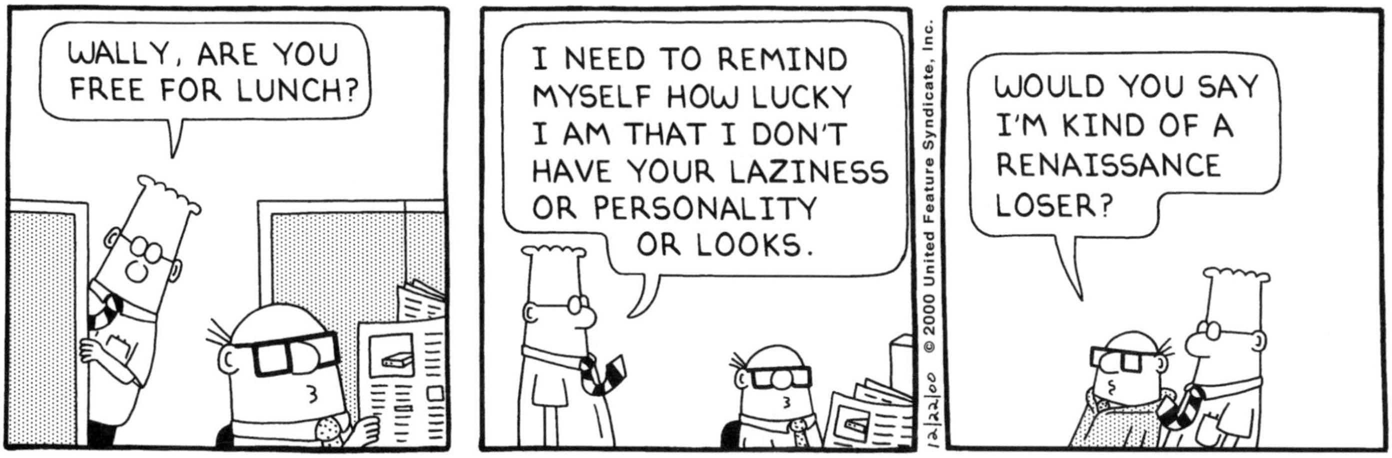
WALLY, ARE YOU FREE FOR LUNCH?
I NEED TO REMIND MYSELF HOW LUCKY I AM THAT I DON'T HAVE YOUR LAZINESS OR PERSONALITY OR LOOKS.
© 2000 United Feature Syndicate, Inc.
12/22/00
WOULD YOU SAY I'M KIND OF A RENAISSANCE LOSER?

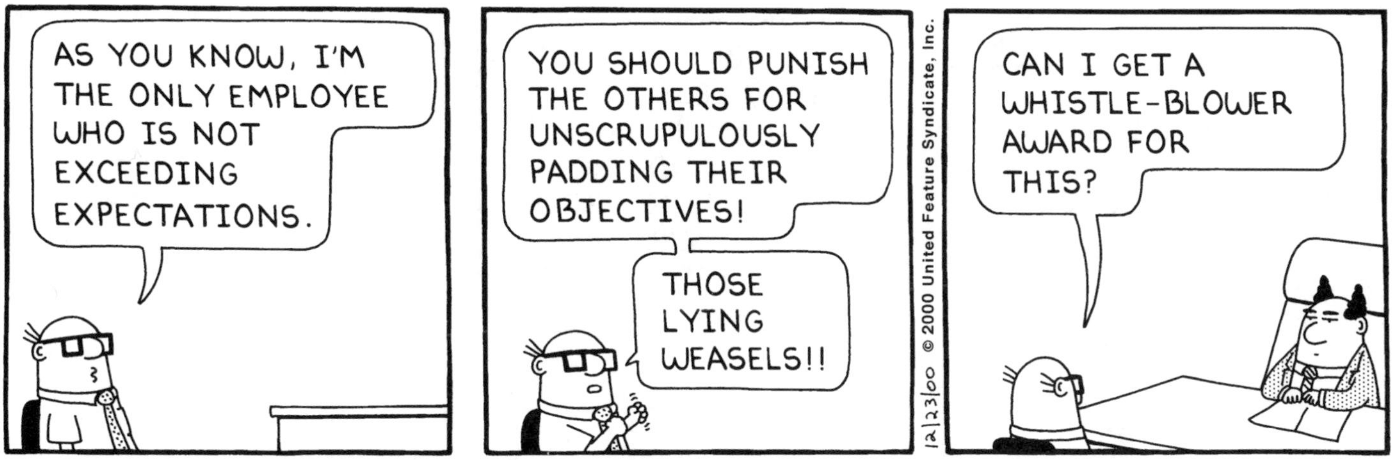
AS YOU KNOW, I'M THE ONLY EMPLOYEE WHO IS NOT EXCEEDING EXPECTATIONS.
YOU SHOULD PUNISH THE OTHERS FOR UNSCRUPULOUSLY PADDING THEIR OBJECTIVES!
THOSE LYING WEASELS!!
© 2000 United Feature Syndicate, Inc.
12/23/00
CAN I GET A WHISTLE-BLOWER AWARD FOR THIS?

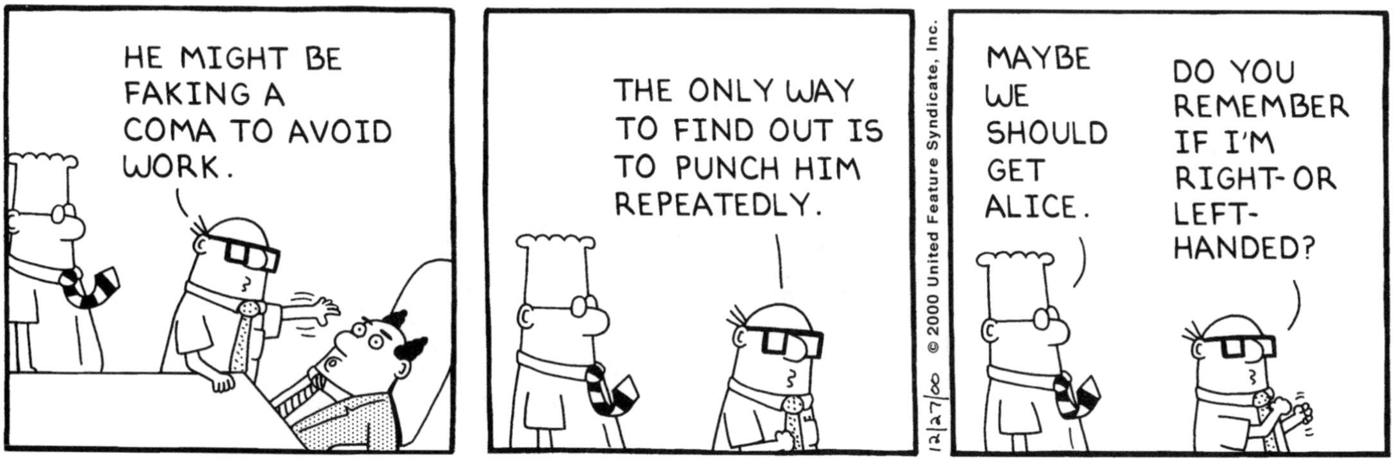
HE MIGHT BE FAKING A COMA TO AVOID WORK.
THE ONLY WAY TO FIND OUT IS TO PUNCH HIM REPEATEDLY.
© 2000 United Feature Syndicate, Inc.
12/27/00
MAYBE WE SHOULD GET ALICE.
DO YOU REMEMBER IF I'M RIGHT- OR LEFT-HANDED?

148

155

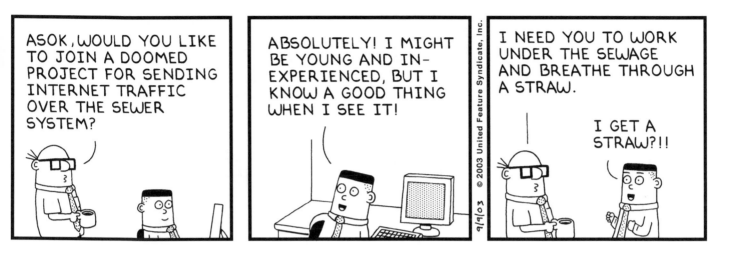

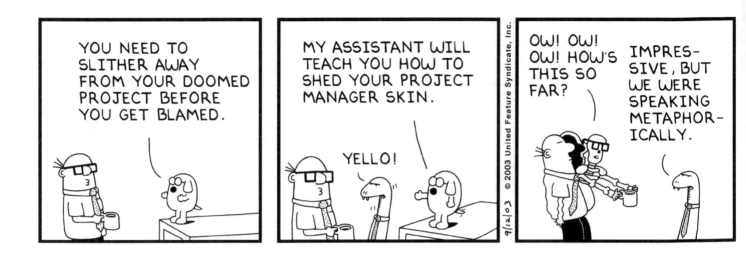

WALLY, THERE HAVE BEEN COMPLAINTS THAT YOU TAKE CONFERENCE CALLS FROM THE MEN'S ROOM.

OK, PERHAPS I HAVE A FEW IDIO-SYNCRASIES, BUT IT'S ONLY BECAUSE I CARE SO MUCH ABOUT THE WORK.

NO ONE INVITED YOU TO THOSE CONFERENCE CALLS.

WHAT IF I'VE ALREADY FINISHED THE NEWS-PAPER?

WALLY, CAN YOU SHOW ME HOW TO MAKE CHANGES TO THE SKILLS DATABASE?

I CAN'T RISK BEING KNOWN AS THE GUY WHO KNOWS HOW TO EDIT THE DATABASE.

BECAUSE?

I BARELY HAVE TIME TO AVOID THE WORK I ALREADY HAVE.

THIS MIGHT BE THE GREATEST INNOVATION IN ANNOYING CU-BICLE NOISES.

CHEWING CRUSHED ICE.

CRUNCH CRUNCH CRUNCH

MUST...DESTROY ALL REFRIGERATION FACILITIES...ON EARTH.

194

198

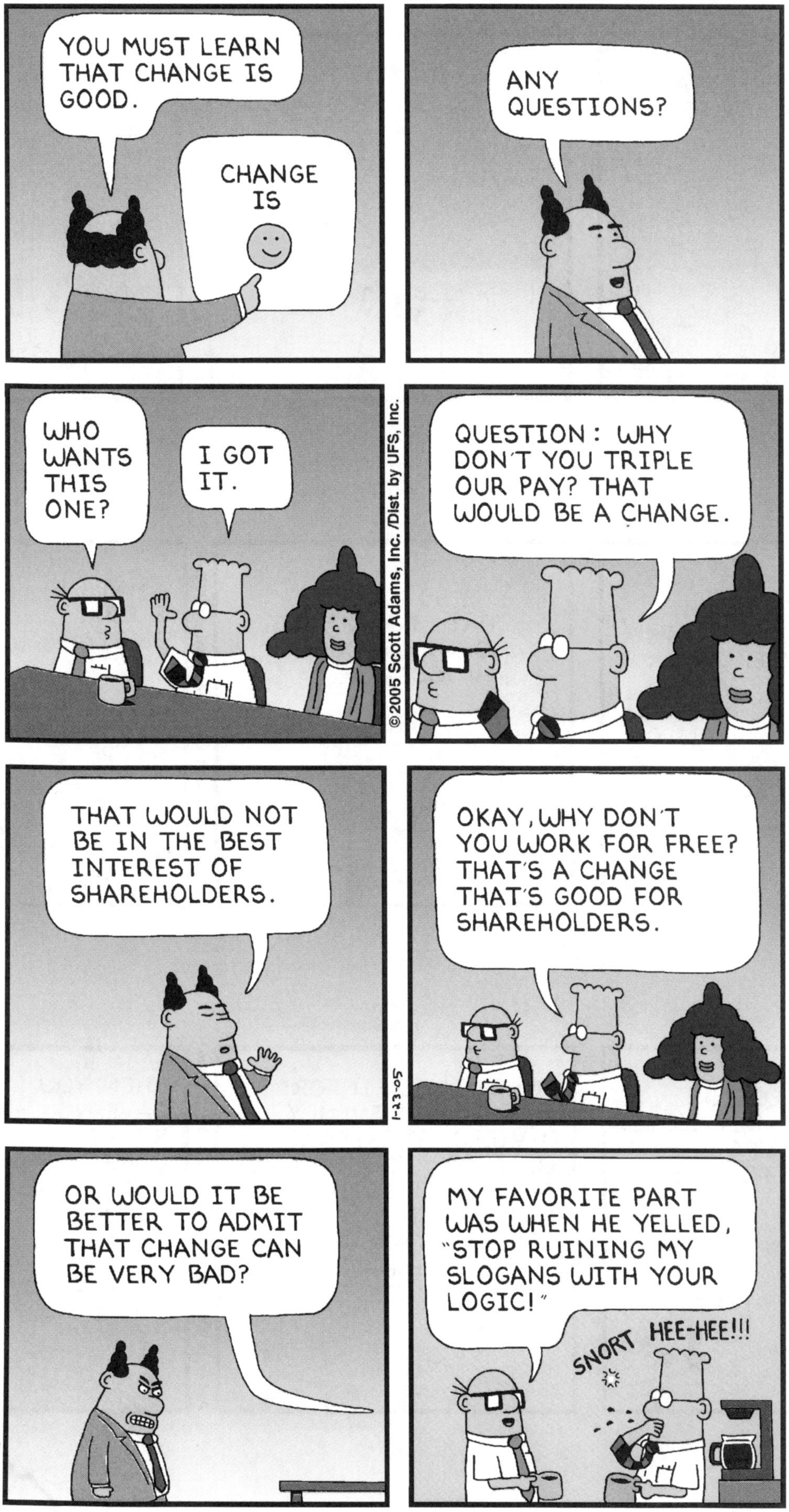
YOU MUST LEARN THAT CHANGE IS GOOD.
CHANGE IS
ANY QUESTIONS?
WHO WANTS THIS ONE?
I GOT IT.
©2005 Scott Adams, Inc. /Dist. by UFS, Inc.
QUESTION : WHY DON'T YOU TRIPLE OUR PAY? THAT WOULD BE A CHANGE.
THAT WOULD NOT BE IN THE BEST INTEREST OF SHAREHOLDERS.
1-23-05
OKAY, WHY DON'T YOU WORK FOR FREE? THAT'S A CHANGE THAT'S GOOD FOR SHAREHOLDERS.
OR WOULD IT BE BETTER TO ADMIT THAT CHANGE CAN BE VERY BAD?
MY FAVORITE PART WAS WHEN HE YELLED, "STOP RUINING MY SLOGANS WITH YOUR LOGIC!"
SNORT
HEE-HEE!!!

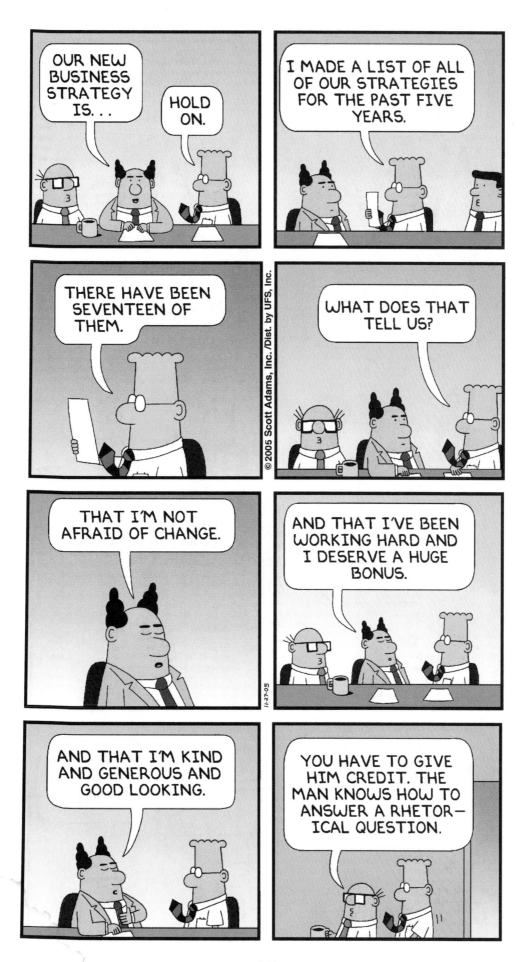

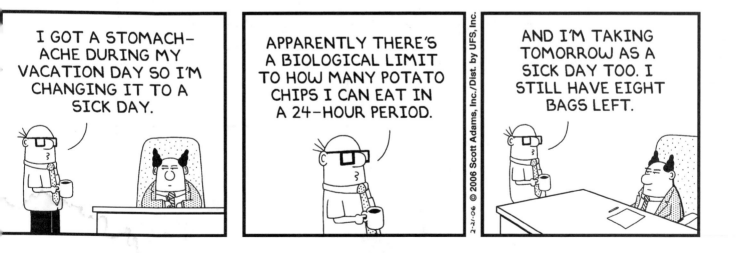